ENFORCEABILITY OF MULTI-TIERED DISPUTE RESOLUTION CLAUSES

This book analyses the contractual mechanisms requiring parties to exhaust a selected amicable dispute resolution procedure before proceedings in court or arbitration are initiated. It briefly explains the phenomenon of integrated dispute resolution, outlines ADR methods commonly used in multi-tiered clauses and presents the overview of standard clauses published by various ADR providers and professional bodies. The core of the analysis is devoted to the enforceability of multi-tiered clauses under the legal systems of England and Wales, Germany, France and Switzerland. It is essential reading for practitioners and academics working in this area.

Enforceability of Multi-tiered Dispute Resolution Clauses

Ewelina Kajkowska

• HART •
PUBLISHING
OXFORD AND PORTLAND, OREGON
2017

Hart Publishing
An imprint of Bloomsbury Publishing Plc

Hart Publishing Ltd
Kemp House
Chawley Park
Cumnor Hill
Oxford OX2 9PH
UK

Bloomsbury Publishing Plc
50 Bedford Square
London
WC1B 3DP
UK

www.hartpub.co.uk
www.bloomsbury.com

Published in North America (US and Canada) by
Hart Publishing
c/o International Specialized Book Services
920 NE 58th Avenue, Suite 300
Portland, OR 97213-3786
USA

www.isbs.com

HART PUBLISHING, the Hart/Stag logo, BLOOMSBURY and the Diana logo are trademarks of Bloomsbury Publishing Plc

First published 2017

British Library Cataloguing-in-Publication Data
A catalogue record for this book is available from the British Library.

ISBN: HB: 978-1-50991-041-0
ePDF: 978-1-50991-043-4
ePub: 978-1-50991-042-7

Library of Congress Cataloging-in-Publication Data
A catalogue record for this book is available from the Library of Congress.

Typeset by Compuscript Ltd, Shannon

To find out more about our authors and books visit www.hartpublishing.co.uk. Here you will find extracts, author information, details of forthcoming events and the option to sign up for our newsletters.

ACKNOWLEDGEMENTS

Without the many people who helped me complete this work my thoughts about multi-tiered clauses in the two main dispute resolution systems across four different jurisdictions would never have come so lucidly, if at all, to light.

I owe my greatest debt of gratitude to Professor Neil Andrews of Clare College, Cambridge, for his generous and constant teaching. His dedication to guiding his students closer to his own wisdom and his unfailing and relieving wit have been necessary, if not sufficient, for the completion this work. I would also like to thank Adam Olszewski, the Head of the Arbitration Department of the State Treasury Solicitors' Office, Warsaw, who inspired me to pursue this topic and whose thoughtful comments and stimulating discussions helped me craft the most fundamental theses of this text. I owe special thanks to Professor Karol Weitz for his tireless efforts to teach me the highest standards of continental European academic rigour, however faltering its representation in this book may be. I would also like to gratefully acknowledge those who assisted me in multiple ways at various stages of completing this project. My particular thanks go to Monika Jeziorska, Michał Drwal, Łukasz Wiśniewski, Aidan Powlesland, Ridhwaan Suliman and Tobias Raap.

Finally, I would like to thank my family: my parents, my brother, his wife and their delightful children. Their love and support made the process of completing this book all the more certain.

CONTENTS

LIST OF ABBREVIATIONS

AAA	American Arbitration Association
AC	Appeal Cases
ADR	Alternative Dispute Resolution
AI	Arbitration International
AIA	American Institute of Architects
All ER	All England Law Reports
ANWBL	Anwaltsblatt
ASA Bulletin	Bulletin of the Swiss Arbitration Association
BGB	Bürgerliches Gesetzbuch
BGBl	Bundesgesetzblatt
BGH	Bundesgerichtshof
BGHZ	Entscheidungen des Bundesgerichtshofs in Zivilsachen
BIMCO	Baltic and International Maritime Council
BLR	Building Law Reports
BOStB	Berufsordnung der Bundes-Steuerberaterkammer
CA	Court of Appeal
CC	Code civil
CEDR	Centre for Effective Dispute Resolution
CIA	Chartered Institute of Arbitrators
Civ	Civil Division
Ch	Chancery Division
CLC	Company Law Cases
Com Ct	Commercial Court
Con LR	Construction Law Reports
CPC	Code de procédure civile
CPR	Civil Procedure Rules
CPR	Institute International Institute for Conflict Prevention and Resolution

CUP	Cambridge University Press
DAB	Dispute Adjudication Board
DIS	Deutsche Institution für Schiedsgerichtsbarkeit
DIS-SchGO	DIS-Schiedsgutachtensordnung
DStRE	Deutsches Steuerrecht-Entscheidungsdienst
ECHR	European Convention on Human Rights
ECJ	European Court of Justice
EGLR	Estates Gazette Law Reports
EHRLR	European Human Rights Law Review
ENAA	Engineering Advanced Association of Japan
ENE	Early neutral evaluation
EUCON	Europäisches Institut für Conflict Management
EWCA	Court of Appeal of England and Wales
EWHC	High Court of England and Wales
FIDIC	Fédération Internationale des Ingénieurs-Conseils
Gaz Pal	Gazette du Palais
HKIAC	Hong Kong International Arbitration Centre
HL	House of Lords
ICE	Institute of Civil Engineers
ICC	International Chamber of Commerce
ICC Bulletin	International Chamber of Commerce International Court of Arbitration Bulletin
ICC DB Rules	ICC Dispute Board Rules
ICCA	International Council for Commercial Arbitration
ICLR	International Construction Law Review
IDR	International Journal of Dispute Resolution
JIA	Journal of International Arbitration
LCIA	London Court of International Arbitration
LGDJ	Librairie Générale de Droit et de Jurisprudence
Lloyd's Rep.	Lloyd's Law Reports
NJW	Neue Juristische Wohenschrift
NZM	Neue Zeitschrift für Miet- und Wohnungsrecht
OUP	Oxford University Press
QBD	Queen's Bench Division

Rec	Recueil des décisions du Conseil d'Etat
SBDW	Standard Bidding Documents—Procurement of Works
SchiedsVZ	Zeitschrift für Schiedsverfahren
TCC	Technology and Construction Court
UNCITRAL	United Nation Commission on International Trade Law
WIPO	World Intellectual Property Organization
WLR	Weekly Law Reports
ZfgG	Zeitschrift für das gesamte Genossenschaftswesen
ZPO	Zivilprozessordnung
ZZP	Zeitschrift für Zivilprozess

TABLE OF CASES

[*All references are to paragraph number*]

Australia

France

Germany

United States

Court of Justice of the European Union

ICC International Court of Arbitration

International Centre for Settlement of Investment Disputes (ICSID)

TABLE OF LEGISLATION

1

Main Features of Multi-tiered Dispute Resolution Clauses

SUMMARY

This chapter presents the issues surrounding multi-tiered dispute resolution clauses. It explains the relevance of alternative dispute resolution mechanisms and introduces the main focus of the work—the enforceability of such clauses in court and arbitral proceedings. Following the presentation the ADR methods commonly employed by multi-tiered dispute resolution clauses, the structure of the subsequent analysis is summarised. It is based on the examination of the effects of non-compliance with individual tiers of the integrated dispute resolution mechanism. Preliminary remarks describe the relevance of multi-tiered resolution clauses as a widespread phenomenon of international commerce. This is illustrated by an overview of the standard clauses contained in the internationally applied forms of contract. Finally, the absence of an international legal framework for the enforceability of multi-tiered dispute resolution clauses is recognised, and the relevance of national laws is explained.

The main points will be:

(i) In order to analyse the enforceability of an overall integrated dispute resolution mechanism, multi-tiered clauses must be broken down into distinct stages consisting of separate ADR methods and be examined in terms of each stage (1.10 and 1.11).

(ii) There are two typical types of ADR techniques involved in multi-tiered clauses. These are consensual methods (such as mediation) and quasi-adjudicative methods (such as expert determination or dispute boards). They are distinct in their nature and function, and the enforceability of both types of clauses must be analysed separately (1.12ff and 1.28ff).

(iii) Multi-tiered dispute resolution clauses have gained considerable recognition as a result of the standard forms of contracts drafted by numerous professional associations (such as architects' or engineers' bodies) as well as international organisations (1.44ff).

(iv) Unlike in the case of arbitration clauses, enforceability of ADR clauses is not regulated internationally. The guidelines to be found in the UNCITRAL Model Law on International Commercial Conciliation are insufficient in content and scope (1.84–1.86).

(v) As a result of the lack of an international framework, the enforceability of multi-tired dispute resolution clauses must be analysed from the perspective of an applicable domestic law (1.87ff).

CONTENTS

Crisis of International Commercial Arbitration. The Role of ADR[1]

1.1 International commercial arbitration is commonly considered to be a more effective dispute resolution process than court litigation. The main advantages associated with arbitration are: procedural flexibility, neutrality, finality, expertise of the

[1] Hereafter also 'alternative dispute resolution'. In the literature the term ADR is also explained variously as: 'appropriate dispute resolution' (J Sternlight, 'Is Binding Arbitration a Form of ADR?: An Argument That the Term "ADR" Has Begun to Outlive Its Usefulness' [2000] 1 *Journal of Dispute Resolution* 97, 107, fn 52); 'amicable' or 'accelerated dispute resolution' (K Mackie, D Miles, W Marsh,

arbitrators, time- and cost-effectiveness and confidentiality.[2] An important feature of arbitration in the global context is the way cross-border enforcement of arbitral awards is facilitated by the Convention on the Recognition and Enforcement of Foreign Arbitral Awards 1958.[3]

Most of the perceived advantages of arbitration, however, do not withstand scrutiny. **1.2** The purported efficiency of arbitration in terms of time and cost of the proceedings has proved illusory.[4] Procedural patterns originating in court litigation have been absorbed into arbitration, which has thus become as demanding as court litigation in terms of written submissions, documentary disclosure, witness statements and expert opinions.[5] This has seriously hindered the effectiveness of the arbitral process. The finality of arbitration has been compromised by judicial scrutiny of arbitration awards during the challenge and enforcement procedures. Even the superior cross-border enforcement of arbitration awards under the New York Convention is flawed. As observed by commentators, although some of the largest countries in the world have signed the New York Convention, they fail to demonstrate a good record of judicial compliance with its terms.[6] In addition, the facilitation of cross-border enforcement of awards under the New York Convention has ceased to be a distinguishing feature both of arbitration within the European Union[7] and of arbitration between well-established trading countries who are parties to bilateral arrangements governing transnational enforcement of court awards.[8]

T Allen, *The ADR Practice Guide* (Tottel Publishing, 2009) 5); 'additional dispute resolution' (*ibid* 9) or 'amicable dispute resolution' (The International Chamber of Commerce (ICC), see: www.iccwbo.org/products-and-services/arbitration-and-adr).

[2] See N Blackaby, C Partasides, A Redfern, M Hunter, *Redfern and Hunter on International Arbitration*, 6th edn (OUP, 2015) paras 1.129ff for an overview.

[3] Hereafter the 'New York Convention'.

[4] N Blackaby, C Partasides, A Redfern, M Hunter, *Redfern and Hunter on International Arbitration*, n 2 above, paras 1.123–1.127. See also American commentators: R Dobbins, 'The Layered Dispute Resolution Clauses: from Boilerplate to Business Opportunity' (2005) 1 *Hastings Business Law Journal* 159, 173–74; J Sternlight, 'Is Binding Arbitration a Form of ADR?' n 1 above, 99 and literature cited; J Lyons, 'Arbitration: The Slower, More Expensive Alternative?' (1985) 1–2 *American Lawyer* 107; T Stipanowich, 'Rethinking American Arbitration' (1988) 63 *Indiana Law Journal* 425, 452–76.

[5] In this context W Park emphasises the need to balance two conflicting values: on the one hand, the effectiveness of arbitration and on the other hand, the need to achieve a fair and just result (W. Park, *Arbitration of International Business*, 2nd edn (OUP, 2012) 159ff and especially 166 on the convergence between court and arbitration proceedings). On 'judicialisation' of the arbitral process see also K Lynch, *The Forces of Economic Globalization: Challenges to the Regime of International Commercial Arbitration* (Kluwer Law International, 2003) 18–21; G Philips, 'Is creeping legalism infecting arbitration?' (2003) 58 *Dispute Resolution Journal* 37.

[6] J Paulsson, *The Idea of Arbitration* (OUP, 2013) 264.

[7] Due to Regulation (EU) No 1215/2012 of the European Parliament and of the Council of 12 December 2012 on jurisdiction and the recognition and enforcement of judgments in civil and commercial matters (recast) facilitating cross-border enforcement of court awards between the EU member states.

[8] eg the Australian Foreign Judgments Act 1991 provides a framework for enforcement of foreign money judgments in Australia provided that the foreign jurisdictions to which the Acts applies will substantially reciprocate in the enforcement of judgments of the Australian Supreme and Federal Courts.

1.3 The above drawbacks of arbitration have led certain commentators to the conclusion that arbitration is undergoing a crisis not dissimilar to that affecting litigation.[9] Empirical research revealed that parties opt for arbitration because it gives solutions to specific problems of transnational court proceedings rather than because it offers a dispute resolution procedure that is fundamentally different from litigation.[10] This convergence has prompted certain authors to reformulate the definition of ADR. In an increasing number of commentaries arbitration is not considered an 'alternative' dispute resolution method at all.[11]

1.4 It is appropriate to take the binding force of a decision as a factor distinguishing arbitration from other forms of contractual dispute resolution.[12] Arbitrators exercise their jurisdictional mandate by issuing an award which, when submitted to the enforcement procedure in court, can be enforced like a court award. Other forms of contractual dispute resolution do not enjoy this feature. Consequently, 'alternative' dispute resolution methods in a narrow sense encompass those techniques which produce a result that is not enforceable on terms equal to those of a court award. They include, inter alia: mediation (conciliation), expert determination, dispute boards, mini-trial, early neutral evaluation and similar methods.[13] This narrow definition of ADR is adopted in the present study.

1.5 It has to be borne in mind that, as a substitute for litigation or arbitration, ADR is intended to be a more effective dispute resolution process, rather than to provide a more accurate result. The attraction of ADR is that it is aiming at practical solutions and so is a way of reducing and managing conflict. Contracting for ADR demonstrates the parties' intention to seek commercial compromise and preserve valuable business relationships, in which context winning in court ceases to be the ultimate goal. From this perspective devising an appropriate ADR process is an important business decision made by commercial partners.[14]

1.6 The growing popularity of multi-tiered dispute resolution clauses is a reflection of the above trends. Escalation dispute resolution mechanisms provide for distinct stages involving separate ADR procedures. Arbitration or, less commonly,

[9] C Bühring-Uhle, *Arbitration and Mediation in International Business*, 2nd edn (Kluwer Law International, 2006) 128.

[10] *ibid*, 107ff and N Blackaby, C Partasides, A Redfern, M Hunter, *Redfern and Hunter on International Arbitration*, n 2 above, paras 1.133–1.134 referring to relevant surveys.

[11] J Sternlight, 'Is Binding Arbitration a Form of ADR?', n 1 above, 97ff; D Sutton, J Gill, M Gearing, *Russell on Arbitation*, 23rd edn (Sweet & Maxwell, 2007) p 6, para 1-011, fn 58; C Bühring-Uhle, *Arbitration and Mediation in International Business*, n 9 above, 129; J Kendall, C Freedman, J Farrell, *Expert Determination*, 5th edn (Sweet & Maxwell, 2015) para 1.1.11. See also KP Berger, *Private Dispute Resolution in International Business*, 3rd edn (Wolters Kluwer, 2015) vol II, para 2-67, emphasising a different approach presented by American authors.

[12] J-F Poudret, S Besson, *Comparative Law of International Arbitration*, 2nd edn (Sweet & Maxwell, 2007) para 13; *Russell on Arbitation*, n 11 above, para 2-035.

[13] For an overview see K Mackie, D Miles, W Marsh, T Allen, *The ADR Practice Guide*, n 1 above, 8ff.

[14] On this aspect see the report published by the American Arbitration Association (AAA): *Dispute-Wise Business Management Improving Economic and Non-Economic Outcomes in Managing Business Conflicts*, available at: www.adr.org/aaa/ShowPDF?doc=ADRSTG_004326.

litigation can only be initiated if the agreed ADR steps are exhausted. Multi-tiered clauses combine adversarial proceedings with non-judicial modes of conflict management. Here arbitration or litigation serves a new function—as the ultimate level of the dispute resolution process, it is treated as the last resort for those disputes which were not resolved at the earlier stages of the escalation ladder.

Contracting for pre-arbitral ADR is considered more commercially attractive than bare arbitration. Escalation mechanisms shift the dispute resolution process toward techniques aimed at cooperation rather than confrontation, allowing the parties to better preserve business relationships and to minimise disruption to the performance of the contract. Tiered clauses are of particular significance with respect to complex contractual relationships in which various types of disputes arise.[15] They create a framework for resolving minor or financially less important issues without the formality, time, and expense of a final adjudication by a court or an arbitral tribunal. 1.7

But the role of multi-tiered clauses goes beyond providing a time- and cost-effective alternative, suitable for filtering out less significant disputes. An attempt to resolve a controversy through an ADR process helps to establish the parameters of a dispute in a structured manner, which may be of a practical benefit even if such pre-adjudication fails. A dispute that has gone through multiple stages of dispute resolution becomes more clearly defined in terms of the controversial points dividing the parties. In addition, the obligation to adhere to several ADR tiers before initiating litigation or arbitration mobilises the parties to gather evidence close to the time when the breach giving rise to the claim occurred.[16] This considerably facilitates final adjudication in court or arbitration and improves the quality of the decision.[17] 1.8

The objectives of multi-tiered dispute resolution mechanisms can only be achieved if pre-adjudicative commitments can be imposed on the parties. This issue relates to the central question of the present study: how to deal with the non-compliance with an ADR clause if a party initiates court or arbitration proceedings in breach of an agreed amicable dispute resolution process. A crucial consideration for the parties contracting for multi-step clauses is, therefore, the enforceability of particular ADR tiers of the dispute resolution mechanism under applicable law. This involves the need to identify the effects of a premature claim raised in court or arbitration in contravention of the agreed ADR procedure. 1.9

[15] On the suitability of multi-tiered clauses to particular types of disputes see T Arntz, *Eskalationklauseln. Recht und Praxis mehrstufiger Streiterledigungsklauseln* (Carl Heymanns Verlag, 2013) 72–73.

[16] This function of escalation mechanisms is amplified in clauses containing a contractual time bar (see 5.25ff).

[17] eg in construction disputes involving semi-binding expert determination where the contested Engineer's decision plays an important role in subsequent arbitration proceedings and the Engineer is one of the key witnesses (see J Jenkins, *Construction Law Arbitration*, 2nd edn (Wolters Kluwer, 2014) 57ff for details).

ADR Methods in Multi-tiered Dispute Resolution Clauses

1.10 Multi-tiered dispute resolution clauses may encompass many ADR techniques and each escalation level has its own characteristics. The distinctive features of various ADR methods involve: the decision-making powers of a neutral third party, the binding or persuasive result of the procedure, the degree to which the parties can influence the process after it has been initiated, the consensual or adversarial model of the procedure, the voluntary nature of participation in the process and the ability to unilaterally terminate it.[18]

1.11 On the basis of those factors two groups of ADR methods can be distinguished. The first group contains consensual methods based on voluntary participation of the parties. This group contains mediation (conciliation) and negotiations. The third-party engagement in the process (if any) serves a facilitative purpose—a neutral person's role being to assist the parties in reaching settlement. The second group involves quasi-adjudicative methods such as expert determination and dispute boards. Here a neutral person issues a decision which determines the outcome of the dispute between the parties. Typically the decision is not conclusive and becomes binding on the parties only if it is not contested in the later tiers of the dispute resolution process. Quasi-adjudicative ADR is of an adversarial character; the participation of both parties is not voluntary; and the party cannot terminate the process by a unilateral act. The clauses involving both types of method are distinct in their function and in the prerequisites as to their enforceability. On account of this, consensual and quasi-adjudicative clauses are examined separately in the present study.

Consensual ADR Methods

Negotiations

1.12 Negotiations involve direct discussions between the parties. This technique is commonly treated as a starting point in the escalation ladder due to the high cost-efficiency of the process.[19] This stage of dispute resolution is largely informal and

[18] KP Berger, *Private Dispute Resolution in International Business*, n 11 above, para 2-45ff. See also an illustrative description of the main ADR features in L Demeyere, 'About Dispute Resolution and Conflict Management' (2003) 3 *Arbitration International* 313, 318, table 1.

[19] J Carter, 'Issues Arising from Integrated Dispute Resolution Clauses' in AJ van den Berg (ed), *New Horizons in International Commercial Arbitration and Beyond. ICCA Congress Series 2004* (Kluwer International, 2005) 446. See also M Hunter, 'Commentary on Integrated Dispute Resolution Clauses' in AJ van den Berg (ed), *ibid*, 470; J Lew, L Mistelis, S Kröll, *Comparative International Commercial Arbitration* (Kluwer Law International, 2003) 13 ('Negotiation should normally be the first approach at resolution of any dispute'). Similarly N Andrews, *Modern Civil Process* (Mohr Siebeck, 2008) 213 considering negotiations as the most popular method for settling disputes. The use of negotiations as a

can be conducted without any assistance, and hence without the expense connected with the participation of a neutral third party.

Owing to the flexible and informal nature of negotiations, clauses providing for this dispute resolution method can pose challenges when drafted. It has been pointed out in the literature that insufficiently precise formulation of such clauses may act against the effectiveness of the entire ADR mechanism.[20] Moreover, as will be described in the following chapter of this study, the courts may refuse to enforce negotiation clauses, considering them too uncertain to have any binding force.[21] In addition, the duties of the parties are often defined in a very loose language, leaving scope for questioning the mandatory nature of this step, as illustrated below: 1.13

> If a dispute arises between the parties they shall discuss it in good faith and if the negotiations are unavailing then either party may serve notice requiring the appointment of an arbitrator.[22]

More carefully drafted clauses provide for a time-frame in which the negotiations are to be undertaken. The parties may also include an unambiguous statement as to the compulsory character of preliminary negotiations: 1.14

> Any controversy that may arise among the parties with respect to the legal relation arising out of this Agreement shall be submitted to senior management representatives of the parties who will attempt to reach an amicable settlement within fourteen (14) calendar days after submission. If an amicable solution cannot be reached by negotiation, the dispute shall be finally settled by arbitration by a panel of one (1) arbitrator, which shall be appointed by both parties.[23]

Since negotiations are commonly employed at the earliest stage of the controversy, this method usually precedes any sequence of more formalised steps leading towards binding adjudication. This is of particular importance wherever the primary concern of the parties is not the outcome, but the mere avoidance of the dispute. Contractual duty to negotiate creates the space for settlement at a time when the positions of the parties are still flexible, before they antagonise each other and escalate the conflict. Integrating negotiations into the dispute resolution framework allows the parties to resolve problems before they turn into a full-blown dispute and draws their attention to the events which are a potential source of liability at an early stage of the contract performance. In addition, direct engagement 1.15

preliminary step of the dispute resolution procedure was traditionally recommended for disputes arising from infrastructure contracts (M Latham, *Constructing the Team: Final Report of the Government/Industry Review of Procurement and Contractual Arrangements in the UK Construction Industry* (HMSO, 1994)).

[20] J Carter, 'Issues Arising from Integrated Dispute Resolution Clauses', n 19 above, 447.

[21] This view has gained a particular relevance under English law. See 2.4ff.

[22] Cited from M Pryles, 'Multi-Tiered Dispute Resolution Clauses' (2001) 18 *Journal of International Arbitration* 159, 160.

[23] Cited from (2003) 14 *ICC International Court of Arbitration Bulletin* 84.

in conflict management by the parties' representatives facilitates their taking into account the conditions relevant to a particular project or business relationship in the context of the further cooperation of the parties.

1.16 Inserting negotiations into a dispute resolution mechanism has, however, attracted a degree of criticism. Sceptical observers emphasise the problems with committing to negotiate in a contract.[24] As will be discussed below, an obligation of this kind may be considered unenforceable by courts on grounds that it is impossible to compel parties to cooperate in reaching a settlement. In addition, the parties may initiate discussions to resolve the dispute amicably at any time, even during arbitral or court proceedings, without the need to provide for this option in a contract. This type of contractual provision can also be ineffective if the parties have a statutory right to initiate formal dispute settlement procedures 'at any time'.[25]

1.17 Notwithstanding these concerns, conflict management based on preliminary discussions between the parties' representatives is commonly incorporated into contractual relationships where, due to the financial or business strategy, the parties prioritise dispute avoidance. As the least expensive and most flexible method, negotiations help to prevent full-scale dispute at the earliest possible stage. Drafting negotiation clauses, however, poses considerable difficulties in defining the nature and content of the obligations created by the relevant contractual terms.

Mediation (Conciliation)

1.18 Mediation (conciliation)[26] is another typical component of multi-stage dispute resolution mechanisms. This method, considered to be a prototype of ADR, is

[24] W Craig, W Park, J Paulsson, *International Chamber of Commerce Arbitration*, 3rd edn (Oceana Publications, 2000) 105–6 ('If one of the parties is convinced of the pointlessness of negotiation, the settlement-efforts preconditions may seem to it to be no more than a hypocritical nuisance requiring pro-forma compliance').

[25] eg statutory adjudication in accordance with Part II, Housing Grants, Construction and Regeneration Act 1996. On this institution P Coulson, *Construction Adjudication* (OUP, 2007); P Hibberd, P Newman, *ADR and Adjudication in Construction Disputes* (Blackwell, 1999) 151ff; J Jenkins, *Construction Law Arbitration*, n 17 above, 65ff.

[26] Legal scholars use these terms interchangeably: A Tweedale, K Tweedale, *Arbitration of Commercial Disputes* (OUP, 2007) para 1.17; A Redfern, M Hunter, N Blacaby, C Partasides, *Redfern and Hunter on International Arbitration*, n 2 above, para 1.138; J Jenkins, *Construction Law Arbitration*, n 17 above, 54–55, J-F Poudret, S Besson, *Comparative Law of International Arbitration*, n 12 above, para 13; G Born, *International Commercial Arbitration*, 2nd edn (Kluwer Law International, 2014) 271ff; K Mackie, D Miles, W Marsh, T Allen, *The ADR Practice Guide*, n 1 above, 11–12. cf J Lew, L Mistelis, S Kröll, *Comparative International Commercial Arbitration*, n 19 above, para 1-45, who indicate that the distinction between mediation and conciliation originates from public international law where traditionally mediators performed a more active (evaluative) function while the conciliators' role was limited to facilitative assistance. Similarly on the background of this academic discussion K Mackie, D Miles, W Marsh, T Allen, *The ADR Practice Guide*, n 1 above, 45; A Connerty, 'The Role of ADR in the Resolution International Disputes' (1996) 12 *Arbitration International* 47, 50; D Jones, 'Various Non-Binding (ADR) Processes' in AJ van den Berg (ed), *New Horizons in International Commercial Arbitration and Beyond. ICCA Congress Series 2004* (Kluwer International, 2005) 368; M Rubino-Sammartano, *International Arbitration Law and Practice*, 2nd edn (Kluwer Law International, 2001) 10–12. See also the discussion in M van Der Haegen, 'Les Procédures de Conciliation et de Médiation

associated with the involvement of a neutral person whose task is to help the parties in reaching a settlement. Mediation can take an ad hoc or institutional form. The former comprises tailor-made procedures, while the latter concerns mediation administered by professional institutions. These entail arbitration centres or dedicated ADR providers.[27]

Multi-stage dispute resolution clauses may contain specific provisions concerning mediation procedure, but often occur in a short form provided by institutions which offer mediation services. The example below shows a contractual provision providing for mediation administered by the German Institution of Arbitration (DIS) in the event of failure of preliminary negotiations: **1.19**

1. Any dispute or difference arising out of or in connection with this contract shall be settled through good faith negotiations between the parties.
2. If a dispute cannot be settled through negotiations as provided for in subsection 1 above within 14 days, or any longer period agreed upon by the parties, then either side must refer that dispute to mediation according to the Mediation/Conciliation Rules of the German Institution of Arbitration (DIS).
3. If the mediator notifies both parties in writing that the mediation initiated pursuant to subsection 2 above has failed or if one party so notifies the other party in writing, each side may—within 20 days after receipt of said written notice—refer the dispute to arbitration according to the Rules of Arbitration of the German Institution of Arbitration (DIS). The dispute shall be decided by three arbitrators.[28]

Mediation is a consensual form of ADR and its positive outcome depends on the voluntary participation of the parties. A mediator cannot impose terms of settlement on the parties and is precluded from continuing his mission if either party refuses to continue the negotiations. Commentators distinguish between facilitative and evaluative mediation. In the former the mediator only assists the parties in reaching the settlement. The latter form encompasses greater powers, with the mediator giving his recommendation as to how to solve the dispute and presenting his view as to the merits of the controversy.[29] Some authors suggest that evaluative mediation is an attractive solution for parties anticipating imminent court or arbitration proceedings.[30] It can be assumed that this variant of mediation is also of high practical utility as part of a multi-stage dispute settlement mechanism, where binding adjudication is the ultimate way of resolving the conflict. **1.20**

Organisées par les principaux instituts d'arbitrage et de médiation en Europe' (1996) 2 *Revue de Droit des Affaires Internationales* 255, 259. It has to be borne in mind that the distinction between conciliation and mediation is in certain jurisdictions made in statute, as under Swiss law, on which see 2.223ff.

[27] Such as the London-based Centre for Effective Dispute Resolution (CEDR). For standard escalation clauses promulgated by CEDR and various arbitration centres see 1.70ff.

[28] Cited after D Jiménez Figueres, 'Multi-Tiered Dispute Resolution Clauses in ICC Arbitration: Introduction and Commentary' (2003) 1 *ICC International Court of Arbitration Bulletin* 71, 87.

[29] K Mackie, D Miles, W Marsh, T Allen, *The ADR Practice Guide*, n 1 above, 11.

[30] *ibid*, 12.

1.21 As with negotiation clauses, contracting for mediation provides an institutional framework within which to attempt to resolve the dispute at an early stage before it turns into a full-scale conflict. Mediation is orientated towards the interests of the parties, rather than their rights; hence its successful conclusion tends toward a commercial compromise rather than a legally accurate outcome.[31] In the course of mediation the parties have a chance to get to know the strengths and weaknesses of their respective positions. The practitioners sometimes highlight the risks for later litigation associated with presentation of the party's argument at an early stage of the dispute.[32] In addition, the participation of a third party and a greater formalisation of procedure (not infrequently involving preparing written statements) entail a greater commitment of resources than in the case of informal discussions between the parties' representatives. As a result, mediation, as the first step in an integrated dispute resolution clause, is not as time- and cost-effective as negotiations. Despite this drawback, however, it is often considered a more attractive process than informal discussions between the parties.[33]

1.22 The critics of integrating mediation into dispute resolution mechanisms explain that a failed mediation attempt is a waste of time and resources. This inevitable risk of consensual ADR bears a particular meaning in the context of the enforceability of multi-tiered dispute resolution clauses. Anticipating further consideration, in certain jurisdictions the voluntary character of mediation renders unenforceable any contractual commitments to mediate.[34] The rationale for this position is based on the assumption that if the claimant initiated the proceedings in court or arbitration, bypassing the agreed amicable process, it means that he is not willing to negotiate settlement and any mediation attempt is bound to fail.

1.23 Despite the standpoint outlined above, mediation clauses are enforceable in most of the analysed legal systems, and premature filing of a claim gives rise to various procedural and substantive repercussions. In those jurisdictions where mediation clauses have been found to constitute a source of binding obligations, the courts emphasise that by enforcing an agreement to mediate they only create an opportunity for an amicable settlement of the dispute and they do not compel the parties to conclude a settlement.

1.24 Within the spectrum of ADR techniques utilised in multi-tiered clauses there are two offshoots of mediation: a mini-trial (executive tribunal) and early neutral evaluation (ENE).[35] Mini-trial is a method inspired by the practice of American

[31] This feature of consensual ADR is sometimes treated as a disadvantage. As opposed to binding adjudication, settlements are of no practical relevance for the resolution of future disputes of the same type. On this aspect in the context of disputes with the subcontractors J Jenkins, *Construction Law Arbitration*, n 17 above, 62.

[32] *ibid.*

[33] J Lew, L Mistelis, S Kröll, *Comparative International Commercial Arbitration*, n 19 above, para 1-46.

[34] See 2.228 on the position under Swiss law.

[35] H Brown, A Marriott, *ADR Principles and Practice*, 3rd edn (Sweet & Maxwell, 2011) paras 1.51–1.53. The suitability of mini-trial and ENE as part of a multi-stage dispute resolution mechanism is pointed out by G Born, *International Commercial Arbitration*, n 26 above, 279.

lawyers.[36] It is defined as an intermediate form between a simulated trial and mediation. Clauses entailing this technique provide that in the event of a dispute senior management personnel on behalf of both parties attend a meeting in the presence of a jointly appointed neutral expert. During mini-trial the parties, represented by lawyers, submit their positions in writing, in a way similar to litigation or arbitration, but in an abbreviated form. Subsequently, negotiations take place between the representatives of the parties, which may result in a settlement. A neutral expert may give the parties guidance as to the potential outcome of litigation or arbitration.[37]

The purpose of mini-trial is to create a framework for a rapid settlement of disputes involving complex factual and legal components. Unlike mediation, mini-trial resembles a 'day in court' and is considered to give a better opportunity to assess the strength of evidence including the performance of key witnesses.[38] Direct involvement of the senior-level representatives ensures that the controversy is tackled with the commercial context in mind. Although associated with arbitration, mini-trial may be used in conjunction with court litigation.[39] **1.25**

Early neutral evaluation (ENE, expert evaluation, non-binding appraisal) involves a neutral third party providing a non-binding opinion on the merits of the dispute. The essence of this method is to estimate the parties' chances of winning the dispute in court proceedings or arbitration. Early neutral evaluation helps the parties to make a decision whether their case should proceed to the final stage of the dispute resolution procedure, ie litigation or arbitration.[40] **1.26**

In contrast to mini-trial this method does not typically include any, even fragmentary, evidence. Early neutral evaluation engages fewer resources than is the case in quasi-adjudicative techniques.[41] By contrast with expert determination or dispute boards, the decision issued in ENE is not binding on the parties. For this reason, **1.27**

[36] Although this method is not widespread in Europe, the model solutions for mini-trial are laid down by various Europe-based ADR providers such as the Centre for Effective Dispute Resolution (CEDR), Zurich Chamber of Commerce and the Netherlands Arbitration Institute. For a commentary on mini-trial in the Zurich Chamber of Commerce Rules see M Blessing, in S Berti (ed), *International Arbitration in Switzerland. An Introduction to and a Commentary on Articles 176–194 of the Swiss Private International Law Statute* (Kluwer Law International, 2000) para 980 and M Blessing, D Hochsrasser, in H Honsell, N Vogt, A Schnyder, S Berti (eds), *Basler Kommentar. Internationales Privatrecht*, 2nd edn (Helbing Lichtenhahn Verlag, 2007) para 328 ad Einleitung zum Zwölften Kapitel.

[37] M Rubino-Sammartano, *International Arbitration Law and Practice*, n 26 above, 14ff; H Brown, A Marriott, *ADR Principles and Practice*, n 35 above, para 2-032; J Lew, L Mistelis, S Kröll, *Comparative International Commercial Arbitration*, n 19 above, paras 1-49–1-51; A Connerty, 'The Role of ADR in the Resolution of International Disputes', n 26 above, 51.

[38] N Andrews, *Arbitration and Contract Law* (Springer, 2016) para 2.41 and the literature cited.

[39] As envisaged in the CEDR Executive Tribunal Guidance Notes, available at: www.cedr.com/about_us/modeldocs/?id=10.

[40] K Mackie, D Miles, W Marsh, T Allen, *The ADR Practice Guide*, n 1 above, 12–13; J Jenkins, *Construction Law Arbitration*, n 17 above, 56 and 130–31; J Lew, L Mistelis, S Kröll, *Comparative International Commercial Arbitration*, n 19 above, paras 1-53–1-54; D Jones, 'Various Non-Binding (ADR) Processes', n 26 above, 375.

[41] See 1.28ff and 1.36ff.

the usefulness of this method is often questioned, especially for disputes of a large-scale and complex nature.[42]

Quasi-adjudicative ADR Methods

Expert Determination

1.28 Expert determination (*expertise-arbitrage, Schiedsgutachten*) involves referring a controversial issue to an impartial third party. By contracting for expert determination the parties agree that the dispute that arose between them will be referred to an expert for a binding determination. It is a common component of multi-tiered clauses in contracts involving complex legal and factual issues or requiring valuation of specified matters.[43] This method in its contemporary form is especially developed in common law countries. Alongside the expansion of ADR, expert determination has penetrated many continental legal systems.[44] The basic legal framework for this method is either regulated directly in a statute[45] or inferred from the existing rules governing similar matters.[46]

1.29 A characteristic feature of this ADR mechanism is the imperative nature of an expert's decision, which distinguishes it from early neutral evaluation or mini-trial. The decision binds the parties and can be enforced in court like a contract. Typically multi-step clauses contain provisions stating that the decision is binding until it is challenged in court or arbitration ('semi-binding', 'interim' or 'provisional' expert determination). In this form the expert's decision becomes final if it is not contested in the subsequent stages of the dispute resolution process.

1.30 Initially the expert's role typically concerned deciding narrow factual issues or technical matters and did not require him to apply law or interpret the contract. Over time expert determination developed into a fully fledged ADR technique and the restricted scope of the expert's mandate began to take on a more general power to issue decisions on disputes concerning certain types of claim.[47] In this form, where an expert makes a determination on all aspects of the claim submitted

[42] J Jenkins, *Construction Law Arbitration*, n 17 above, 130–31.

[43] Expert determination is commonly used especially in construction contracts, M&A and financial transactions, and resource industries. See J Kendall, C Freedman, J Farrell, *Expert Determination*, n 11 above, para 4.01ff; M Pryles, 'Arbitrating Disputes in the Resource Industries' (2005) 3 *Arbitration International* 405; N Horn, 'Arbitration in International Financial Transactions' (2000) 16 *Arbitration International* 279, 281; A Sessler, C Leimert, 'The Role of Expert Determination in Mergers and Acquisitions under German Law' (2004) 20 *Arbitration International* 151.

[44] Under German law: R Gerger, C Stubbe, *Schiedsgutachten: außergerichtliche Streitbeilegung durch Drittentscheidungen* (CH Beck, 2007).

[45] Art 189, Swiss Civil Procedure Code.

[46] eg determination of the price by a neutral third party under Article 1592 of the French Civil Code (*fixation du prix par un tiers*) or determination of the contract performance under §§ 317–319 of the German Civil Code (*Bestimmung der Leistung durch einen Dritten*). See further 2.207 and 2.116.

[47] J Kendall, C Freedman, J Farrell, *Expert Determination*, n 11 above, paras 1.6.7, 1.6.15. and 6.1ff; D Jones, 'Expert Determination and Arbitration' (2001) 67 *Arbitration* 17.

to him, the expert's role resembles that of an arbitrator.[48] Because of this feature, ADR techniques based on this paradigm will be referred to as quasi-adjudicative.

1.31 Despite the binding nature of expert determination, experts are not arbitrators, and the difference between the two methods is often emphasised in the literature.[49] Expert decision is not enforceable as an arbitration award is. Arbitral awards become effective as court awards after recognition and enforcement proceedings before a relevant national court. Expert determination takes place outside the legislative framework of arbitration; hence the expert's decision does not enjoy the same enforcement status. Instead, the binding force of the decision is merely of a contractual nature. Moreover, an arbitral award can be subject to challenge under the law of the arbitral seat. Expert determination, being outside that framework, can be reviewed in particular circumstances. In the absence of contractual provisions relating to this matter, the scope of the court's power to revisit the expert's findings is regulated differently in different legal systems.[50] The parties may also prescribe the criteria for review in the contract or state that the decision is fully reviewable in the later stages of the dispute resolution process (semi-binding expert determination).

1.32 Also the scope of procedural safeguards differs between arbitration and expert determination. An expert makes his determination in an informal and flexible procedure, while an arbitrator is required to reach a decision in a judicial manner based on the presentation of the parties' submissions. To protect the integrity of the process the parties can trigger judicial control of arbitral procedure and eliminate serious irregularities from the conduct of arbitration.[51] This power does not apply to expert determination, where the procedure is largely unregulated and is typically shaped by an expert himself, unless the parties include dictates relating to the expert's conduct in the contract. Moreover, arbitrators enjoy immunity which is a correlate of their adjudicative mandate. By contrast, an expert may be liable in negligence.

[48] See especially J Kendall, C Freedman, J Farrell, *Expert Determination*, n 11 above, paras 6.7.1ff; *Russell on Arbitration*, n 11 above, para 2-028.

[49] D Jones, 'Expert Determination and Arbitration', 48 above, 17ff; J Carter, 'Issues Arising from Integrated Dispute Resolution Clauses', n 19 above, 454; C Stubbe, 'Kombination des Schiedsgutachtensverfahren mit anderen Verfahrenstypen' in K-H Böckstiegel, KP Berger, J Bredow (eds), *Schiedsgutachten versus Schiedsgerichtsbarkeit* (Heymans, 2007) 75ff; G Wagner, *Prozessverträge—Privatautonomie im Verfahrensrecht* (Mohr Siebeck, 1998) 663; J Lew, L Mistelis, S Kröll, *Comparative International Commercial Arbitration*, n 19 above, para 1-34; *Russell on Arbitration*, n 11 above, paras 1-012 and 2-028–2-031; J Kendall, C Freedman, J Farrell, *Expert Determination*, n 11 above, paras 16.1ff; G Born, *International Commercial Arbitration*, n 26 above, 281–82; J-F Poudret, S Besson, *Comparative Law of International Arbitration*, n 12 above, paras 15–17. H Brown, A Marriott, *ADR Principles and Practice*, n 35 above, paras 7-057–7-064; E Gaillard, J Savage (eds), *Fouchard, Gaillard, Goldman on International Commercial Arbitration* (Kluwer Law International, 1999) paras 25–29.

[50] See 2.56–2.57 (England), 2.117 (Germany), 2.209 (France) and 2.257 (Switzerland).

[51] See eg the procedure for challenge of an arbitral award on grounds of serious irregularity under s 68, Arbitration Act 1996.

1.33 Finally, the enforceability of arbitration agreements is a widely recognised principle, unequivocally regulated by statutory provisions and unified internationally.[52] As will be shown, the enforceability of expert determination clauses is not prescribed by the legislation of the analysed legal systems. Typically the effects of non-compliance with the agreed procedure are determined by court decisions.

1.34 Expert determination is a technique utilised in a wide variety of contractual relationships.[53] It is most commonly applied in construction contracts, where the dispute resolution process typically consists of two or more ADR levels out of which at least one comprises a quasi-adjudicative method. Such techniques are adjusted to the nature of disputes arising out of construction contracts involving a complex amalgamate of factual and legal issues and where the problems must be dealt with immediately while the contract performance is carrying on. The expert's role is typically performed by a person appointed for the whole duration of the contract term (an engineer or architect) or a panel of experts (a dispute board).[54] An expert is, therefore, familiar with the circumstances of the contract and can be engaged in an issue at an initial stage of the dispute. Typically, expert determination is provisional and may be challenged in the subsequent tiers of the dispute resolution ladder. As the type of ADR best suited to the specifics of infrastructure projects, expert determination features in the standard forms of contracts promulgated by major international organisations of civil engineers and architects.[55]

1.35 Despite the wide recognition of expert determination in international commercial practice, it should be noted that, compared to mediation and arbitration, it has the least developed legal foundations. The absence of a normative framework governing expert determination can be observed especially in continental jurisdictions, where this method is derived from related institutions. Consequently, this method is particularly prone to divergences between legal systems. As will be discussed later in this study, the purely contractual character of expert determination raises questions concerning enforceability of the expert's decision and the validity of a provision giving a neutral third party a mandate to make binding determinations.

Dispute Boards

1.36 Dispute boards[56] are panels of experts appointed at the beginning of the contract whose function is to monitor the performance and decide the disputes between the parties as soon as they arise.[57] The legal nature of this ADR is similar to expert

[52] For the signatories of the New York Convention the relevant provisions are contained in Article II.

[53] See n 43.

[54] On which see 1.36ff.

[55] For particular examples see 1.45–1.65.

[56] Also referred to as 'dispute adjudication boards', 'dispute review boards', 'dispute resolution boards' or 'dispute avoidance boards'.

[57] Comprehensive on dispute boards C Chern, *Chern on Dispute Boards*, 2nd edn (Wiley-Blackwell, 2011).

determination—dispute boards issue decisions concerning controversial issues submitted to them by the parties. In the literature dispute boards are sometimes considered a specialised form of expert determination or expert determination *sui generis*.[58] Dispute boards are most commonly used in multi-tiered dispute resolution clauses in construction contracts.[59]

The decisions issued by dispute boards are usually binding on an interim basis. The determination of a controversial issue is binding and must be complied with subject to it being changed at a later stage of the dispute resolution process. A board's decision that has not been challenged becomes final. Typically, a party dissatisfied with the board's determination may refer the matter to be finally decided by a court or by arbitration. Other than by making binding determinations, dispute boards may assist the parties in the dispute resolution process by issuing non-binding recommendations. **1.37**

Similarly to expert determination, dispute boards are creations of the contract. The binding force of their determinations is derived from the parties' agreement; hence, failure to comply with the decision is considered as breach of contract.[60] Being of a contractual nature, dispute boards' decisions are not enforceable like arbitral awards. They are not subject to judicial scrutiny as arbitration would be, and an agreement compelling the parties to submit the dispute to a dispute board does not constitute an arbitration clause. The preceding remarks concerning the distinguishing features of arbitration and expert determination are thus applicable also to dispute boards.[61] **1.38**

The popularity of this ADR technique has driven various institutionalised ADR providers to promulgate standard clauses involving pre-arbitral dispute boards. Alongside model clauses those bodies commonly publish the rules governing dispute boards proceedings. One of the leading initiatives in this respect is the set of rules and clauses published by the International Chamber of Commerce. Below is an example of a clause requiring submission of the dispute to a dispute adjudication board followed by ICC arbitration:[62] **1.39**

> The Parties hereby agree to establish a Dispute Adjudication Board ('DAB') in accordance with the Dispute Board Rules of the International Chamber of Commerce (the 'Rules'), which are incorporated herein by reference. The DAB shall have [one/three] member[s] appointed in this Contract or appointed pursuant to the Rules.
>
> All disputes arising out of or in connection with the present Contract shall be submitted, in the first instance, to the DAB in accordance with the Rules. For any given dispute, the DAB shall issue a Decision in accordance with the Rules.

[58] G Born, *International Commercial Arbitration*, n 26 above, 282.

[59] See 1.45ff on ICE, NEC, FIDIC and other forms of contract for construction. Dispute Boards were used in many large infrastructure projects such as *Hong Kong Airport Project* or *Channel Tunnel Project*. Extensively on the application of Dispute Boards in particular projects, see J Jenkins, *Construction Law Arbitration*, n 17 above, 58–59 and *Chern on Dispute Boards*, n 57 above, 56ff.

[60] J Jenkins, *Construction Law Arbitration*, n 17 above, 116; *Chern on Dispute Boards*, n 57 above, 5.

[61] See 1.31–1.33.

[62] On the ICC Dispute Boards see also 1.78.

> If any Party fails to comply with a Decision when required to do so pursuant to the Rules, the other Party may refer the failure itself to arbitration under the Rules of Arbitration of the International Chamber of Commerce by one or more arbitrators appointed in accordance with the said Rules of Arbitration.
>
> If any Party sends a written notice to the other Party and the DAB expressing its dissatisfaction with a Decision, as provided in the Rules, or if the DAB does not issue the Decision within the time limit provided for in the Rules, or if the DAB is disbanded pursuant to the Rules, the dispute shall be finally settled under the Rules of Arbitration of the International Chamber of Commerce by one or more arbitrators appointed in accordance with the said Rules of Arbitration.[63]

1.40 Dispute boards as a form of ADR originate in the United States.[64] Modern dispute boards can be compared to the statutory adjudication introduced in the United Kingdom under Part II of the Housing Grants, Construction and Regeneration Act 1996. Under this regime a party to a construction contract is required to submit the dispute to an independent expert, before referring it to arbitration or, in the absence of an arbitration clause, court proceedings. Unlike in the case of dispute boards, however, an adjudicator is only appointed after the dispute has arisen and is not involved in the contract from its beginning. By contrast, dispute boards provide a regular and continuing forum for resolving contentious matters under the contract for the whole duration of the contract term.[65]

1.41 This last feature of dispute boards is commonly considered the most significant advantage of this method. By undertaking regular visits to the site, the members of dispute boards are actively involved throughout the project. Acting in an informal capacity they create a potential for better communication between the parties, which fosters dispute avoidance. As impartial members of the contract team the members of dispute boards issue decisions of a greater persuasive value than the decisions of a third party or stranger to the project. Wide knowledge of the factual background of the dispute increases the speed of the decision-making process and preserves the ongoing performance of the contract. The quality of the determination and the 'authority' of dispute boards significantly reduce the number of controversies that turn into full-scale conflict.[66] In those cases where the parties

[63] www.iccwbo.org/products-and-services/arbitration-and-adr/dispute-boards/standard-icc-dispute-boards-clauses/.

[64] The construction of the Boundary Dam on the Pend Oreille river, Washington, is considered the earliest example of a dispute board (the Joint Consulting Board) acting as a permanent panel empowered to provisionally determine disputes. See H Brown, A Marriott, *ADR Principles and Practice*, n 35 above, para 7-028. On the history of dispute boards see also *Chern on Dispute Boards*, n 57 above, 33 ff; P Chapman, *Dispute Boards in Major Infrastructure Projects*, Dispute Resolution Board Foundation Conference (Brussels 2011) 3ff, available at: www.drbfconferences.org/documents/brussels2011/1ChapmanPaper.pdf.

[65] Contractual provisions may replace statutory adjudication. It is, therefore, possible for the contracting parties to establish a dispute board to adjudicate on construction disputes within the statutory requirements of the Housing Grants, Construction and Regeneration Act 1996.

[66] R Gaitskell, J Uff, in J Murdoch, W Hughes (eds), *Construction Contracts. Law and Management*, 4th edn (Taylor & Francis Group, 2008) 354 provide statistical data according to which approximately

decide to pursue final adjudication the decision issued close to the time when the claim arose considerably simplifies subsequent arbitration and litigation.

Dispute boards are empowered to decide disputes arising out of the contract and they have authority to evaluate both facts and law. Unlike expert determination, which initially concerned narrow technical issues, dispute boards were designed as quasi-adjudicative panels deciding on certain types of claims. It is not uncommon for the board members to require additional information or evidence, inspect the site or hold meetings similar to arbitration hearings. Because the boards are of a purely contractual nature, the parties may devise the procedure by which decisions are to be made. **1.42**

The quasi-adjudicative and informal character of the board's proceedings raises questions concerning procedural safeguards that have to be observed during the decision-making process. Because there are no statutory requirements in this regard and dispute boards are merely contractual creations whose decisions can only be enforced by an action for breach of contract, it is accepted that the rules of procedural justice do not apply to the conduct of dispute board proceedings.[67] It has to be borne in mind, however, that boards' decisions are predominantly of a semi-binding nature. This means that each decision is potentially fully reviewable in court or, more commonly, arbitration. **1.43**

Multi-tiered Dispute Resolution Clauses in International Contracts

The growing popularity of ADR which results from deficiencies in arbitration and litigation has triggered various initiatives devoted to standardisation of multi-tiered dispute resolution mechanisms. These initiatives were undertaken primarily by domestic and international professional organisations of civil engineers and architects, which developed standard sets of contractual terms and included in them escalation dispute resolution mechanisms. Arbitration institutions and ADR providers also promulgate model clauses comprising various ADR methods integrated into a single system, with arbitration as the last 'rung' of a dispute resolution ladder. In addition, multi-step dispute resolution mechanisms are a part of standard contract documents issued by the World Bank and they are recognised by the United Nations Commission on International Trade Law (UNCITRAL) in the Model Law on International Commercial Conciliation.[68] **1.44**

80% of dispute boards' decisions are complied with and not questioned in subsequent arbitration proceedings.

67 J Kendall, C Freedman, J Farrell, *Expert Determination*, n 11 above, para 16.8.5; J Jenkins, *Construction Law Arbitration*, n 17 above, 101–2.

68 Hereafter: 'the Model Law'.

Standard Forms of Contract of International Professional Associations

Fédération Internationale Des Ingénieurs-Conseils *(FIDIC)*

1.45 One of the most widespread integrated dispute resolution mechanisms is contained in the forms of contract for construction published by the International Federation of Consulting Engineers (FIDIC).[69] In 1999 FIDIC published its suite of contracts consisting of four books governing different types of infrastructure contracts: (i) Conditions of Contract for Construction for Building and Engineering Works Designed by the Employer ('Red Book'), (ii) Conditions of Contract for Plant and Design-Built ('Yellow Book'), (iii) Conditions of Contract for EPC/Turnkey Projects ('Silver Book') and (iv) Short Form of Contract ('Green Book'). The dispute resolution mechanism is contained in clause 20 of the respective forms.

1.46 Model multi-tiered clauses designed by FIDIC contain several ADR tiers followed by arbitration administered by the ICC Court of Arbitration. Pre-arbitral phases of the dispute resolution mechanism are predominantly based on the expert determination paradigm. Initially FIDIC Conditions provided for the determination by the Engineer as the first and second stage of the dispute resolution process (clause 67 of the so-called 'Old Red Book').[70] In this system the Engineer was reviewing his/her own decisions. A party dissatisfied with the Engineer's decisions had effectively no other recourse than initiating arbitration. This solution was criticised on grounds of the insufficient impartiality of the Engineer who, being appointed and remunerated by one party—the Employer—could not reasonably be expected to make settlements as an independent adjudicator.[71] This imperfect system was changed in 1999 together with the introduction of the Dispute Adjudication Boards procedure in the new suite of contracts, which replaced the Engineer's second determination.[72] Following this amendment the party dissatisfied with the Engineer's determination can challenge his/her decision in a forum ensuring greater impartiality without compromising the meritorious quality of the process.

1.47 The first stage of the dispute resolution procedure in the new FIDIC Conditions remained unchanged.[73] It is based on expert determination combined with a

[69] Created in 1913 by Belgium, France, and Switzerland, FIDIC represents national associations of consulting engineers. The organisation gathers members from 68 countries across five continents, with the UK acceding in 1949 and the US in 1958. FIDIC has its secretariat in Geneva, Switzerland.

[70] 4th edition of the FIDIC Conditions published in 1987.

[71] J Jenkins, *Construction Law Arbitration*, n 17 above, 58; G Jaynes, 'Dispute Review Boards-Yes!' (1993) 10 *International Construction Law Review* 455; N Bunni, *The FIDIC Forms of Contracts* (Blackwell Publishing, 2005) 604.

[72] Dispute Boards are part of the multi-tiered dispute resolution mechanisms under the Red, Yellow and Silver Books. For the sake of clarity, the subsequent remarks will concern the Red Book only.

[73] For the analysis of the FIDC clause 20 see 5.40ff.

contractual time-bar adapted to the specific claims arising from construction contracts. In accordance with sub-clause 20.1 if the Contractor considers himself to be entitled to an extension of time for completion of the works or an additional payment, he is obliged to give notice of his claim to the Engineer for his/her determination. The notice must be given as soon as practical but not later than 28 days after the Contractor became aware, or should have become aware, of the event giving rise to the claim. Failure to give notice within the specified time extinguishes the Contractor's claim. Under sub-clause 20.1 if the Contractor fails to give notice of a claim within the 28-day period, the time for completion shall not be extended, the Contractor shall not be entitled to additional payment, and the Employer is discharged from all liability in connection with the claim.

The Engineer's determination is binding on an interim basis. Each party is obliged to comply with it, until it is changed at the later stages of the dispute resolution procedure (sub-clause 3.5). According to this rule the decision has to be implemented, despite it not being final. Such a solution preserves the contract performance from disruption, which is especially relevant for long-term projects generating a large number of disputes. An important measure aimed at increasing the accuracy of the factual basis of the determination is a duty requiring the Contractor to maintain records pursuant to any claim brought before the Engineer. This provision disciplines the parties by obliging them to gather evidence close to the time when the claim arose, which plays an important role during the subsequent stages of the dispute resolution ladder, including when the claim reaches final adjudication in arbitral proceedings. **1.48**

A party dissatisfied with the Engineer's decision may question the determination before a Dispute Board. Sub-clause 20.2 contains detailed provisions regarding the appointment of the Board members, aimed at ensuring the independence and high qualifications of the panel. The dispute must be submitted to the Dispute Board in writing. **1.49**

Sub-clause 20.4 clarifies that the Board does not act as an arbitral tribunal. The binding force of the Board's decision is purely contractual. The parties are obliged to promptly give effect to the decision unless and until it is revised in a settlement or by an arbitral award. It follows that this level of the dispute resolution procedure is also based on semi-binding expert determination. The Board's decisions are fully reviewable in arbitration proceedings. **1.50**

The procedure to challenge the decision of the Board is subject to important requirements. According to sub-clause 20.4 a party dissatisfied with the Board's decision must, within 28 days after receiving the decision, give notice to the other party of its dissatisfaction and intention to commence arbitration. Failure to give notice of dissatisfaction within the prescribed time results in the decision becoming final and binding on the parties. This provision is the second example of a time-bar provision in clause 20 of the FIDIC Conditions. Here the consequences of non-compliance with the time-limit involve losing the entitlement to review **1.51** the Board's decision, which becomes final. If the right to challenge the decision expires, and a party fails to comply with the decision, the other Party may refer the failure itself to arbitration and in this way enforce the final and binding decision.

1.52 The next tier of the dispute resolution procedure under clause 20 of the FIDIC Forms of Contract comprises informal negotiations. According to sub-clause 20.5, where the notice of dissatisfaction with the Board's decision has been properly given, both Parties shall attempt to settle the dispute amicably before the commencement of arbitration. The parties are not required to actually negotiate. The voluntary nature of this ADR method is acknowledged by setting out the time-limit within which the parties may discuss settlement, but they are not obliged to undertake this process. Under sub-clause 20.5 arbitration may only be commenced on or after the fifty-sixth day after the day on which a notice of dissatisfaction and intention to commence arbitration was given, even if no attempt at amicable settlement has been made. Sub-clause 20.5 does not oblige the parties to take real steps aimed at conciliation, but, depending on the attitude of the parties, provides an institutional framework in which such steps can take place. This 'cooling-off period' is expressed in clear terms as to its time-frame to avoid doubt as to the point at which the parties may proceed to the next level of the dispute resolution procedure.

1.53 The final stage of the dispute resolution mechanism under clause 20 of the FIDIC Conditions of Contract is final adjudication by an arbitral tribunal. Sub-clause 20.6 provides that, unless settled amicably, any dispute in respect of which the Board's decision has not become final and binding shall be finally settled by international arbitration in accordance with the Rules of Arbitration of the International Chamber of Commerce in Paris (ICC). In this system arbitration is primarily concerned with review of the Board's decisions. Otherwise, if the decision has become final and binding due to the party's failure to give a timely notice of dissatisfaction, the arbitrators can only confirm the binding decision without an authority to review it. Full review of the dispute by the arbitrators is, therefore, possible only on condition that earlier levels of the dispute resolution process have been complied with.

1.54 The FIDIC Conditions of Contract have gained widespread international application in infrastructure projects around the world. Due to the complexity of the dispute resolution mechanism, as well as the extensive case law of the ICC Court of Arbitration on clause 20, the FIDIC Conditions will frequently serve as an important point of reference in the present study. The effects of non-compliance with particular steps of clause 20 will be presented as a separate chapter, serving as a conclusion to the comparative analysis of the enforceability of multi-tiered clauses under the selected legal systems.

American Institute of Architects (AIA)

1.55 The standard forms of contracts drafted by the American Institute of Architects include A201-1997 General Conditions of the Contract for Construction, published in 1997.[74] They contain a multi-stage dispute resolution procedure consisting of expert determination, mediation and arbitration. The first level of the escalation mechanism requires the notification of a dispute to an independent architect.[75] A party dissatisfied with the decision of the architect is obliged to initiate mediation pursuant to the Industry Mediation Rules of the American Arbitration Association. In the absence of a settlement, the party may commence arbitration proceedings. The notice of intention to arbitrate must be submitted to the other party within 30 days after the receipt of the decision. Arbitration takes place pursuant to special rules of arbitration established by the American Arbitration Association, the AAA Construction Industry Arbitration Rules.

In 2007, the American Institute of Architects issued a revised version of the conditions for construction contracts. The new conditions provide for the multi-step dispute resolution mechanism in a modified form. Expert determination has been maintained as the first tier of a multi-step dispute resolution mechanism. The function of the architect was, however, now entrusted to the Initial Decision Maker and the procedure before the architect was replaced by the Construction Industry Initial Decision Maker Procedure. A party dissatisfied with the decision may challenge it in proceedings before a forum chosen by the parties. The revised conditions abandon the default competence of arbitration administered by the AAA. A mandatory mediation attempt remains a condition precedent to final adjudication whether in court or by arbitration. **1.56**

Institution of Civil Engineers (ICE)

The standard forms of contract for construction published by the Institution of Civil Engineers[76] have gained widespread recognition.[77] ICE was the first organisation to integrate arbitration with alternative dispute resolution methods into a single **1.57**

[74] The AIA is a national association of architects established in 1857. Its first uniform forms of contract were published in 1888. Its first standard general conditions for construction (the precursor of the A201-1997 General Conditions of the Contract for Construction discussed in more detail below) the AIA published in 1911. Since 1976, the AIA has revised its documents on a uniform 10-year cycle (in 1977, 1987, 1997, and 2007). Currently, the AIA Documents Committee is working to draft an updated suite of Contract Documents for release in 2017.

[75] The architect is not a party to the construction contract, but he nevertheless participates in the preparation of the contract documents and performs certain duties under the contract.

[76] The ICE was founded in 1818 in London and is the oldest professional engineering association in the world. The ICE draws its membership from over 80,000 qualified civil engineers in the United Kingdom and over 150 other countries.

[77] Over the past 20 years, the forms of contract published by the ICE have been used on a number of major infrastructure projects including the London 2012 Olympics, the development of Heathrow Airport and the construction of the Channel Tunnel. For a commentary on English construction contracts see S Furst, V Ramsey (eds), *Keating on Construction Contracts*, 10th edn (Sweet & Maxwell, 2016).

progressive system comprising a multi-level dispute resolution mechanism.[78] The organisation has published two models: the ICE Conditions of Contract and the New Engineering Contract (NEC). The Institution of Civil Engineers has also developed specialised arbitration rules adjusted to the disputes arising from construction contracts.[79]

1.58 The seventh edition of the ICE Conditions of Contract (ICE 7), published in 1997, introduces an obligation of early notification of events which can constitute a source of claims and disputes.[80] The notification duty is followed by obligatory negotiations. In the absence of settlement the parties are obliged to attempt the selected ADR process such as mediation. Issues not resolved amicably are to be submitted to an independent adjudicator whose determination is binding unless and until it is reviewed in arbitration proceedings.[81] The 2014 edition of the ICE form (the Infrastructure Conditions of Contract, ICC) provides an option to submit the dispute to the Engineer for semi-binding determination. When either party refers the dispute to the Engineer, the determination is binding, pending the decision of an adjudicator or an arbitral tribunal (clause 19.2). The new ICC conditions also provide optional conciliation or mediation procedures (clause 19.3).

1.59 The New Engineering Contract (NEC3)[82] does not contain provisions requiring the parties to attempt consensual ADR techniques. The first stage of the dispute settlement mechanism includes notification of the dispute to the Project Manager for his determination. The obligation to notify must comply with a time-limit, breach of which extinguishes the claim.[83] The determination made by the project manager is binding on an interim basis—it has to be performed until it is changed in the subsequent stages of the dispute resolution process. The next tier comprises adjudication.[84] The procedure before the adjudicator is also founded on a semi-binding expert determination framework. The adjudicator's decision is binding unless and until reviewed by the arbitral tribunal.[85] Importantly, the adjudicator's decision becomes final and binding if it is not questioned during the time period prescribed in the contract. NEC3 thus contains two types of limitation of time by contract, as is the case under clause 20 of the FIDIC Conditions.

[78] Pre-arbitral conciliation was introduced into the ICE conditions in 1988.

[79] The ICE Arbitration Procedure 2006.

[80] Clause 66(2).

[81] Clauses 66(A), 66(B) and 66(C).

[82] The first edition of the NEC was released in 1993, the second—Engineering and Construction Contract (ECC)—in 1995, and the latest—NEC3—in 2005.

[83] Clause 61.3.

[84] Under option W1. Option W2 adjusts a dispute resolution mechanism to the requirements of statutory adjudication under the Housing Grants, Construction & Regeneration Act 1996. On the two versions of a dispute resolution clause in NEC3 see N Gould, 'NEC3: construction contract of the future?' (2008) 24 *Construction Law Journal* 286, 312–13.

[85] As defined in Part 1 of the Contract Data.

Engineering Advancement Association of Japan (ENAA)

In 1986 the Engineering Advancement Association of Japan[86] published its first contract: the Model Form—International Contract for Process Plant Construction.[87] Since then ENAA has also released the Model Forms for International Contract for Power Plant Construction (Turnkey Lump-sum type)[88] and International Contract for Engineering, Procurement and Supply for Plant Construction (EPS type).[89] **1.60**

The ENAA conditions contain a multi-step dispute resolution mechanism. The first stage of the escalation ladder requires the parties to hold negotiations with a view to achieving an amicable settlement of the dispute. In the event of failing to reach an agreement, the party raising a claim is obliged to submit it to an independent expert. A party dissatisfied with the expert's decision may challenge it in arbitral proceedings according to the ICC Rules of Arbitration. **1.61**

Standard Forms of Contract of International Organisations

World Bank

In 1995 the World Bank published a revised version of its contractual terms applicable to the investment projects financed by this organisation: the Standard Bidding Documents—Procurement of Works. An extensive use of dispute boards is one of the most characteristic features of the dispute resolution mechanism included in those provisions. The World Bank incorporated into its model the 1987 FIDIC Conditions of Contract (the 'Old Red Book'). It made an important amendment to it, however, by replacing the Engineer by dispute boards as a second stage of the dispute resolution procedure.[90] **1.62**

Under the World Bank's 1995 standard forms the Dispute Review Board is a panel consisting of three members empowered to make determinations of claims exceeding US$50 million. For claims below this threshold the parties may agree to submit the dispute to the Dispute Review Expert or an independent engineer instead of referring it to the dispute board. The decision at this stage takes the form of a recommendation—it becomes final and binding if neither party gives notice of an intention to commence arbitration within 14 days after receiving the recommendation. **1.63**

[86] The ENAA is a non-profit organisation, established in 1978. It is supported by the Ministry of International Trade and Industry of Japan, as well as by various national and local government agencies, universities and research centres. The association gathers over 1,500 specialists from member companies and various experts in their respective fields.

[87] Updated in 1992 and 2010.

[88] Published in 1996, revised in 2012.

[89] Published in 2007, revised in 2013.

[90] FIDIC only adopted this solution in 1999, in its most recent suite of contracts (see 1.46).

1.64 Dispute boards as the main step preceding arbitration have been maintained in the updated version of the World Bank's Standard Bidding Documents, published in 2000. The option to refer claims below US$50 million to the independent engineer has been abolished, but the optional competence of the Dispute Review Expert has been retained. The revised conditions introduced a rule according to which the dispute board's decision is binding and must be performed unless and until it is revised in arbitration proceedings. As previously, the decision becomes final if neither party submits notice of intention to commence arbitration within 14 days from the receipt of the decision.

1.65 The latest version of the Standard Bidding Documents—Procurement of Works was published in 2005. Under these conditions the FIDIC 'Old Red Book' has been replaced by the most recent version of the FIDIC Conditions of 1999. Consequently, a Dispute Board became a single forum for all types of claims regardless of their value (the competence of a Dispute Review Expert for claims not exceeding $US50 million has been abolished).

World Intellectual Property Organization (WIPO)

1.66 The World Intellectual Property Organization drafted a number of standard multi-tiered dispute resolution clauses involving both consensual and quasi-adjudicative methods, and promulgated corresponding rules governing the respective ADR processes. Referral to WIPO dispute resolution procedures engages the WIPO Center which administers cases referred to WIPO mediation, arbitration and expert determination. In addition, the WIPO Center offers a service involving adapting the model clauses to the circumstances of a particular contractual relationship.

1.67 A clause involving mediation followed by arbitration (or expedited arbitration) provides as follows:

> Any dispute, controversy or claim arising under, out of or relating to this contract and any subsequent amendments of this contract, including, without limitation, its formation, validity, binding effect, interpretation, performance, breach or termination, as well as non-contractual claims, shall be submitted to mediation in accordance with the WIPO Mediation Rules. The place of mediation shall be [specify place]. The language to be used in the mediation shall be [specify language].
>
> If, and to the extent that, any such dispute, controversy or claim has not been settled pursuant to the mediation within [60][90] days of the commencement of the mediation, it shall, upon the filing of a Request for Arbitration by either party, be referred to and finally determined by arbitration in accordance with the WIPO [Expedited] Arbitration Rules. Alternatively, if, before the expiration of the said period of [60][90] days, either party fails to participate or to continue to participate in the mediation, the dispute, controversy or claim shall, upon the filing of a Request for Arbitration by the other party, be referred to and finally determined by arbitration in accordance with the WIPO [Expedited] Arbitration Rules. [The arbitral tribunal shall consist of [a sole arbitrator] [three arbitrators].]* The place of arbitration shall be [specify place]. The language to

be used in the arbitral proceedings shall be [specify language]. The dispute, controversy or claim referred to arbitration shall be decided in accordance with the law of [specify jurisdiction].

(* *The WIPO Expedited Arbitration Rules provide that the arbitral tribunal shall consist of a sole arbitrator.*)[91]

As mentioned, WIPO also administers an expert determination procedure. This method is combined with mediation: **1.68**

Any dispute or difference between the parties arising under, out of or relating to [describe scope of the matter referred to expert determination] under this contract and any subsequent amendments of this contract shall be submitted to mediation in accordance with the WIPO Mediation Rules. The place of mediation shall be [specify place]. The language to be used in the mediation shall be [specify language].

If, and to the extent that, any such dispute or difference has not been settled pursuant to the mediation within [60][90] days of the commencement of the mediation, it shall, upon the filing of a Request for Expert Determination by either party, be referred to expert determination in accordance with the WIPO Expert Determination Rules. Alternatively, if, before the expiration of the said period of [60][90] days, either party fails to participate or to continue to participate in the mediation, the dispute or difference shall, upon the filing of a Request for Expert Determination by the other party, be referred to expert determination in accordance with the WIPO Expert Determination Rules. The determination made by the expert shall [not] be binding upon the parties. The language to be used in the expert determination shall be [specify language].[92]

WIPO standard clauses are used in a wide variety of contracts involving intellectual property.[93] Because of the general commercial scope of the WIPO Rules, WIPO models are promoted as suitable for disputes that do not necessarily contain IP elements.[94] **1.69**

Model Clauses of International Arbitration Centres

International Chamber of Commerce (ICC)

The International Chamber of Commerce based in Paris is one of the largest organisations to develop a series of model clauses involving multi-stage dispute resolution mechanisms. Together with rules for particular ADR techniques, the standard clauses drafted by the ICC involve, inter alia, dispute boards, expert determination and mediation. **1.70**

[91] Clause: Mediation Followed, in the Absence of a Settlement, by [Expedited] Arbitration, available at: www.wipo.int/amc/en/clauses/index.html#2.

[92] Clause: Mediation Followed, in the Absence of a Settlement, by Expert Determination, available at: www.wipo.int/amc/en/clauses/index.html#2.

[93] eg patent, know-how and software licenses, trademark agreements, distribution contracts, research and development contracts, sports marketing agreements, or music and film contracts.

[94] See www.wipo.int/amc/en/clauses/index.html#13.

1.71 Under the ICC Dispute Boards Rules, there are three types of dispute board proceedings: Dispute Review Board, empowered to issue recommendations; Dispute Adjudication Board, empowered to issue binding decisions; and Combined Dispute Board, that issues recommendations with respect to any dispute referred to it but may issue a decision upon request of any party and in the absence of the other party's objection. The dispute board proceedings are administered by the ICC Dispute Board Centre.[95]

1.72 ICC offers a range of services to manage an expert determination procedure. The available options include: proposal of experts or neutral third parties, appointment of experts or neutral third parties, and administration of expert proceedings. In this last capacity ICC acts in accordance with the ICC Rules for the Administration of Expert Proceedings.

1.73 The clauses containing an obligation to submit the dispute to an expert follow two models. The first involves a non-binding expert determination and is appropriate where the parties intend to use the expert's non-binding findings as a basis for an agreed settlement:

> In the event of any dispute arising out of or in connection with [clause X of the present contract], the parties agree to submit the dispute to administered expert proceedings in accordance with the Rules for the Administration of Expert Proceedings of the International Chamber of Commerce.[96]

1.74 The second model is based on binding expert determination. As in the case of a non-binding expert determination, a standard clause contains a duty to refer the dispute to an expert. Unlike in the first model, however, the parties agree to be contractually bound by the expert's findings:

> In the event of any dispute arising out of or in connection with [clause X of the present contract], the parties agree to submit the dispute to administered expert proceedings in accordance with the Rules for the Administration of Expert Proceedings of the International Chamber of Commerce. The parties agree that the findings of the expert shall be contractually binding upon them.[97]

1.75 In addition, ICC promulgated a tiered clause containing an obligation to submit the dispute to non-binding expert determination, followed by arbitration:

> In the event of any dispute arising out of or in connection with [clause X of the present contract], the parties agree to submit the dispute, in the first instance, to administered

[95] The exemplary ICC Dispute Adjudication Board clause was quoted in 1.39.

[96] Clause B: Obligation to submit dispute to non-binding administered expert proceedings, available at: www.iccwbo.org/Products-and-Services/Arbitration-and-ADR/Experts/Administration-of-Expert-Proceedings/Suggested-clauses-referring-to-the-ICC-Rules-for-the-Administration-of-Expert-Proceedings/.

[97] Clause C: Obligation to submit dispute to contractually binding administered expert proceedings, available at: www.iccwbo.org/Products-and-Services/Arbitration-and-ADR/Experts/Administration-of-Expert-Proceedings/Suggested-clauses-referring-to-the-ICC-Rules-for-the-Administration-of-Expert-Proceedings/.

> expert proceedings in accordance with the Rules for the Administration of Expert Proceedings of the International Chamber of Commerce. After the International Centre for ADR's notification of the termination of the administered expert proceedings, the dispute, if it has not been resolved, shall be finally settled under the Rules of Arbitration of the International Chamber of Commerce by one or more arbitrators appointed in accordance with the said Rules of Arbitration.[98]

Alongside Dispute Boards and expert determination clauses, ICC developed an extensive model framework for mediation. A recommended clause introducing compulsory mediation under the ICC Mediation Rules provides: **1.76**

> In the event of any dispute arising out of or in connection with the present contract, the parties shall first refer the dispute to proceedings under the ICC Mediation Rules. If the dispute has not been settled pursuant to the said Rules within [45] days following the filing of a Request for Mediation or within such other period as the parties may agree in writing, such dispute shall thereafter be finally settled under the Rules of Arbitration of the International Chamber of Commerce by one or more arbitrators appointed in accordance with the said Rules of Arbitration.[99]

Under this clause arbitration proceedings may not be commenced until an agreed period has elapsed. In addition to this typical solution, ICC promulgated a clause providing for compulsory pre-arbitral mediation without the need to conclude the proceedings, or wait for an agreed period of time, before commencing arbitration: **1.77**

> (x) In the event of any dispute arising out of or in connection with the present contract, the parties shall first refer the dispute to proceedings under the ICC Mediation Rules. The commencement of proceedings under the ICC Mediation Rules shall not prevent any party from commencing arbitration in accordance with sub-clause y below.
>
> (y) All disputes arising out of or in connection with the present contract shall be finally settled under the Rules of Arbitration of the International Chamber of Commerce by one or more arbitrators appointed in accordance with the said Rules.[100]

Other than provisions requiring a compulsory mediation attempt, ICC published standard clauses under which mediation is expressly optional.[101] These clauses do **1.78**

[98] Clause D: Obligation to submit dispute to non-binding administered expert proceedings, followed by arbitration if required, available at: www.iccwbo.org/Products-and-Services/Arbitration-and-ADR/Experts/Administration-of-Expert-Proceedings/Suggested-clauses-referring-to-the-ICC-Rules-for-the-Administration-of-Expert-Proceedings/.

[99] Clause D: Obligation to refer dispute to the ICC Mediation Rules, followed by arbitration if required, available at: www.iccwbo.org/products-and-services/arbitration-and-adr/mediation/suggested-clauses/.

[100] Clause C: Obligation to refer dispute to the ICC Mediation Rules while permitting parallel arbitration proceedings if required, available at: www.iccwbo.org/products-and-services/arbitration-and-adr/mediation/suggested-clauses/. See a similar provision for a non-compulsory referral to an expert in Clause A: Optional administered expert proceedings, available at: www.iccwbo.org/Products-and-Services/Arbitration-and-ADR/Experts/Administration-of-Expert-Proceedings/Suggested-clauses-referring-to-the-ICC-Rules-for-the-Administration-of-Expert-Proceedings/.

[101] Clause A: Option to use the ICC Mediation Rules and Clause B: Obligation to consider the ICC Mediation Rules, available at: www.iccwbo.org/products-and-services/arbitration-and-adr/mediation/suggested-clauses/.

not impose on the parties any duty to refer the dispute to mediation. Instead, they are designed to remind the parties of the possibility to mediate and provide a basis for discussing the suitability of mediation in the event of a controversy. This type of clause is appropriate where the parties do not wish to commit to mediation at the outset, but prefer to retain flexibility on whether to use mediation to settle a dispute.

London Court of International Arbitration (LCIA)

1.79 A multi-tiered dispute resolution clause recommended by the London Court of International Arbitration provides for mediation prior to commencement of arbitral proceedings.[102] Similarly to ICC compulsory mediation, the LCIA model requires that arbitration proceedings are not commenced until an agreed period has elapsed:

> In the event of a dispute arising out of or relating to this contract, including any question regarding its existence, validity or termination, the parties shall first seek settlement of that dispute by mediation in accordance with the LCIA Mediation Rules, which Rules are deemed to be incorporated by reference into this clause. If the dispute is not settled by mediation within [...........] days of the commencement of the mediation, or such further period as the parties shall agree in writing, the dispute shall be referred to and finally resolved by arbitration under the LCIA Rules, which Rules are deemed to be incorporated by reference into this clause. The language to be used in the mediation and in the arbitration shall be [...........]. The governing law of the contract shall be the substantive law of [...........]. In any arbitration commenced pursuant to this clause, (i) the number of arbitrators shall be [one/three]; and (ii) the seat, or legal place, of arbitration shall be [City and/or Country].[103]

American Arbitration Association (AAA)

1.80 The American Arbitration Association has formulated a number of model arbitration clauses, some of which are multi-tiered and involve consensual and quasi-adjudicative methods. The sample clauses are typically accompanied by the corresponding rules suitable for a particular ADR procedure. The international ADR process is administered by the International Centre for Dispute Resolution (ICDR) which is the international division of the AAA. Among the recommended models there are two- and three-tier clauses providing for mediation or mediation preceded by negotiations. The sample three-tier clause reads:

> In the event of any controversy or claim arising out of or relating to this contract, the parties hereto shall consult and negotiate with each other and, recognizing their mutual interests, attempt to reach a solution satisfactory to both parties. If they do not reach

[102] The LCIA does not publish model clauses involving expert determination or dispute board procedures.

[103] Clause: Mediation and Arbitration, available at: www.lcia.org/Dispute_Resolution_Services/LCIA_Mediation_Clauses.aspx.

> settlement within a period of 60 days, then either party may, by notice to the other party and the International Centre for Dispute Resolution, demand mediation under the International Mediation Procedures of the International Centre for Dispute Resolution. If settlement is not reached within 60 days after service of a written demand for mediation, any unresolved controversy or claim arising out of or relating to this contract shall be settled by arbitration in accordance with the International Arbitration Rules of the International Centre for Dispute Resolution.[104]

The AAA administers construction disputes pursuant to the Industry Arbitration Rules and Mediation Procedures 2015. One of the clauses recommended for disputes arising out of construction contracts provides for compulsory mediation followed by arbitration: **1.81**

> Any controversy or claim arising out of or relating to this contract or breach thereof, shall be settled by mediation under the Construction Industry Mediation Procedures of the American Arbitration Association. If within 30 days after service of a written demand for mediation, the mediation does not result in settlement of the dispute, then any unresolved controversy or claim arising from or relating to this contract or breach thereof shall be settled by arbitration administered by the American Arbitration Association in accordance with its Construction Industry Arbitration Rules and judgment on the award rendered by the arbitrator(s) may be entered in any court having jurisdiction thereof.[105]

The AAA recognises the demand for complex dispute resolution clauses which encompass provisions as to written notification of claims within a fixed period of time, or exhaustion of other contractually established procedures, such as submission of claims to an architect or engineer.[106] Tiered clauses of this kind are labelled as 'condition precedent' clauses to emphasise the compulsory nature of the pre-arbitral steps: **1.82**

> If a dispute arises from or relates to this contract, the parties agree that upon request of either party they will seek the advice of [a mutually selected engineer] and try in good faith to settle the dispute within 30 days of that request, following which either party may submit the matter to mediation under the Commercial Mediation Procedures of the American Arbitration Association. If the matter is not resolved within 60 days after initiation of mediation, either party may demand arbitration administered by the American Arbitration Association under its [applicable] rules.[107]

Centre for Effective Dispute Resolution (CEDR)

The Centre for Effective Dispute Resolution based in London is not strictly concerned with arbitration, but is rather an institution whose activities are focused **1.83**

[104] Clause INTL5, available at: www.adr.org/aaa/ShowPDF?doc=ADRSTG_002540.

[105] Clause CONST4, available at: www.adr.org/aaa/ShowPDF?doc=ADRSTG_002540.

[106] *Drafting Dispute Resolution Clauses—A Practical Guide* (American Arbitration Association, 2013) 25, available at: www.adr.org.

[107] Clause CONPRE1, available at: www.adr.org/aaa/ShowPDF?doc=ADRSTG_002540.

on providing various ADR services.[108] The CEDR promulgates numerous model clauses involving different types of ADR administered by the centre. A multi-tiered dispute resolution clause developed by the CEDR provides for the successive steps comprising negotiation and mediation and gives the draftsmen an option whether or not to conduct court or arbitration proceedings in parallel with an ADR process:

> If any dispute arises in connection with this agreement, directors or other senior representatives of the parties with authority to settle the dispute will, within [] days of a written request from one party to the other, meet in a good faith effort to resolve the dispute.
>
> If the dispute is not resolved at that meeting, the parties will attempt to settle it by mediation in accordance with the CEDR Model Mediation Procedure. Unless otherwise agreed between the parties, the mediator will be nominated by CEDR. To initiate the mediation a party must give notice in writing ('ADR notice') to the other party(ies) to the dispute requesting a mediation. A copy of the request should be sent to CEDR Solve. The mediation will start not later than [] days after the date of the ADR notice.
>
> [The draftsperson has the choice to add Version 1, referring to court proceedings in parallel, or Version 2, no court proceeding until the mediation is completed.]
>
> Version 1: 'The commencement of mediation will not prevent the parties commencing or continuing court proceedings /arbitration.'
>
> Version 2: 'No party may commence any court proceedings/arbitration in relation to any dispute arising out of this agreement until it has attempted to settle the dispute by mediation and either the mediation has terminated or the other party has failed to participate in the mediation, provided that the right to issue proceedings is not prejudiced by a delay.'[109]

UNCITRAL Model Law on International Commercial Conciliation

1.84 The multiplicity of initiatives aimed at creating model solutions for integrated dispute resolution mechanisms illustrates the extent of this phenomenon in international trade. The increasing commercial significance of escalation clauses has also been addressed by the United Nations Commission on International Trade Law in the Model Law on International Commercial Conciliation, adopted by UNCITRAL on 24 June 2002.[110] The Model Law contains uniform rules for the conciliation process. The aim of the act was to harmonise the procedural aspects of conciliation to ensure greater predictability and certainty in its use.[111]

[108] In the domain of arbitration the CEDR performs certain supportive functions such as providing a shortlist of arbitrators for the parties to choose from, appointing an arbitrator, etc.

[109] Cited from J Carter, 'Issues Arising from Integrated Dispute Resolution Clauses', n 19 above, 451.

[110] The text of the *UNCITRAL Model Law on International Commercial Conciliation with Guide to Enactment and Use* available at: www.uncitral.org/pdf/english/texts/arbitration/ml-conc/03-90953_Ebook.pdf.

[111] The Model Law regulates numerous procedural issues including appointment of conciliators, commencement and termination of conciliation, conduct of the conciliation, communication between

1.85 The Model Law does not provide specific rules relating to the enforceability of conciliation agreements. Instead, Article 13 of the Model Law contains a general provision according to which the parties' agreement to attempt conciliation 'shall be given effect' by the court or an arbitral tribunal. Article 13 of the Model Law is the only act of an international status in which the context of multi-tiered clauses is recognised. For this reason, it should be quoted *in extenso*:

> Article 13. Resort to arbitral or judicial proceedings
>
> Where the parties have agreed to conciliate and have expressly undertaken not to initiate during a specified period of time or until a specified event has occurred arbitral or judicial proceedings with respect to an existing or future dispute, such an undertaking shall be given effect by the arbitral tribunal or the court until the terms of the undertaking have been complied with, except to the extent necessary for a party, in its opinion, to preserve its rights. Initiation of such proceedings is not of itself to be regarded as a waiver of the agreement to conciliate or as a termination of the conciliation proceedings.

1.86 Article 13 of the Model Law expressly refers to situations where the parties agreed to attempt an amicable settlement of the dispute during a fixed period of time or until a specified event has taken place. The provision is addressed to a court or arbitral tribunal before which the proceedings were initiated prematurely, in contravention of a conciliation clause. The Model Law indicates that the adjudicative body should not continue the proceedings.[112] The drafters of the Model Law did not specify, however, particular effects of non-compliance with a conciliation clause. Detailed solutions as to specific, procedural or substantive, consequences of breach of conciliation clauses are left to be determined autonomously by the national legal systems in which the Model Law has been implemented.[113]

The Relevance of National Laws

1.87 As previously indicated the Model Law on International Commercial Conciliation is the only act of international significance which touches upon the issue of the

the conciliator and the parties, confidentiality and admissibility of evidence in later proceedings, as well as post-conciliation matters, such as the conciliator acting as arbitrator and enforceability of settlement agreements. For commentary see JM Abascal Zamora, 'Some Remarks on Uncitral Model Law on International Commercial Conciliation' in AJ van den Berg (ed), *New Horizons in International Commercial Arbitration and Beyond. ICCA Congress Series 2004* (Kluwer International, 2005) 415ff. On the initiatives aimed at unification of the law of ADR, see E van Ginkel, 'The UNCITRAL Model Law on International Commercial Conciliation. A Critical Appraisal' (2004) 21 *Journal of International Arbitration* 1ff.

[112] P Binder, *International Commercial Arbitration and Conciliation in UNCITRAL Model Law Jurisdictions*, 3rd edn (Sweet & Maxwell, 2009) 501; E van Ginkel, 'The UNCITRAL Model Law on International Commercial Conciliation. A Critical Appraisal', n 112 above, 54–56.

[113] The implementation rate of this act is, however, considerably less significant than is the case for the UNCITRAL Model Law on International Commercial Arbitration, see P Binder, *International Commercial Arbitration and Conciliation in UNCITRAL Model Law Jurisdictions*, n 113 above, 458–59.

enforceability of multi-step dispute resolution clauses. The ambit of the Model Law is, however, limited, in that it covers only consensual ADR methods, and contains only a general directive as to the enforceability of conciliation clauses, leaving the detailed solutions for national legislators. In addition, it must be emphasised that ADR agreements do not equal arbitration clauses within the meaning of the New York Convention on the Recognition and Enforcement of Foreign Arbitral Awards 1958. As such, they are not covered by its Article II, which prescribes the enforceability of arbitration clauses. This lack of an international legal framework governing the effects of ADR clauses means that the issues they raise must be assessed from the perspective of each applicable domestic legal system.[114]

1.88 The absence of ADR harmonisation inevitably results in a lack of uniformity in the effects of ADR clauses.[115] As will be shown, the legal framework regulating the effects of ADR agreements is often incomplete even within domestic regulations. While the law of arbitration is well established in the modern legal systems of developed countries, the law of ADR is often only in its formative stages. An additional difficulty for lawmakers lies in the largely fluid and unspecified scope of ADR, comprising a variety of methods frequently of a diverse character. While mediation and its derivatives gradually gain recognition in the majority of modern legal systems and become increasingly reflected in their normative frameworks, the techniques based on the expert determination paradigm are generally unregulated, especially in the continental European jurisdictions. In addition, mediation as a flagship ADR technique undergoes progressive institutionalisation and harmonisation on an international level,[116] which seems a distant prospect for expert determination.

1.89 Treating the national legal systems as a point of reference in determining the effects of ADR clauses is equally valid in the context of arbitration proceedings. Although in arbitration the parties are free to determine the procedure before the arbitral tribunal, this liberty does not usually translate into defining particular remedies for failure to comply with pre-arbitral ADR commitments.[117] Moreover, the consequences of not exhausting contractual ADR procedures are not specified in the rules of the arbitration centres despite the numerous model multi-tiered

[114] H Brown, A Marriott, *ADR Principles and Practice*, n 35 above, paras 26-045–26-048.

[115] The lack of coordination between the legal systems and the scarcity of international framework for ADR is emphasised by C Bühring-Uhle, *Arbitration and Mediation in International Business*, n 9 above, 228.

[116] For the EU see Directive 2008/52/EC of the European Parliament and of the Council of 21 May 2008 on certain aspects of mediation in civil and commercial matters, [2008] OJ L136/3–8, 24/05/2008. The significance of this act is, however, questioned by the commentators, see N Andrews, 'The Duty to Consider Mediation: Salvaging Value from the European Mediation Directive' in N Trocker, A De Luca, *La Mediazione Civile all Luce della Direttiva 2008/52/CE* (Firenze University Press, 2011) 13ff.

[117] Providing for a contractual penalty for non-compliance with an ADR clause is an exception to this general tendency. On this aspect see 3.72–3.75.

clauses being formulated by those bodies.[118] The arbitral tribunal faced with a premature claim must, therefore, determine the consequences of non-compliance with a given ADR clause from the perspective of the applicable national law.[119]

The assumption that domestic legal systems should serve as a starting point for the analysis of the effects of ADR clauses has also been presented in literature.[120] The authors examine the enforceability of multi-tiered clauses trace the consequences of non-compliance with contractual ADR procedures back to national laws, and analyse how in similar circumstances the court would treat the breach of a given ADR clause.[121] This perspective will be adopted in the present study. **1.90**

[118] D Jiménez-Figueres, 'Amicable Means to Resolve Disputes: How the ICC ADR Rules Work' (2004) 21 *Journal of International Arbitration* 91, 94 points out that the ICC ADR Rules do not specify the consequences of non-compliance with pre-arbitral ADR.

[119] On the law applicable to ADR, see H Brown, A Marriott, *ADR Principles and Practice*, n 35 above, 607. See also H Eidenmüller, 'A Legal Framework for National and International Mediation Proceedings' (2002) (Beilage 7 Betriebs-Berater Heft 46/2002) *International Journal of Dispute Resolution* 14, 16 on various groups of rules applicable to distinct aspects of the mediation process.

[120] G Born, *International Commercial Arbitration*, n 26 above, 918ff; M Pryles, 'Multi-Tiered Dispute Resolution Clauses', n 22 above, 159; B Cremades, 'Multi-Tiered Dispute Resolution Clauses' (CPR Institute for Dispute Resolution, 2004) 14; F Fabian, 'The Enforceability of Mediation Clauses—the Approach of English and German Courts and ICC Arbitral Tribunals' (2005) 5 *SchiedsVZ* 250; A Jolles, 'Consequences of Multi-Tier Arbitration Clauses: Issues of Enforcement' (2006) 72 *Arbitration* 329; C Boog, 'How to Deal with Multi-Tiered Dispute Resolution Clauses-Note-June 2007-Swiss Federal Supreme Court' (2008) 26 *ASA Bulletin* 103.

[121] See especially KP Berger, 'Law and Practice of Escalation Clauses' (2006) 22 *Arbitration International* 1, 6. The author applies the provisions of the German Civil Procedure Code to the case where a claim is brought before an arbitral tribunal in contravention of the agreed ADR process.

2

Enforceability of Multi-tiered Dispute Resolution Clauses in Selected European Jurisdictions

SUMMARY

This chapter examines the enforceability of the component steps of multi-tiered dispute resolution mechanisms in the legal systems of England and Wales, Germany, France and Switzerland. It is designed as the first—descriptive—part of a comparative analysis concluded in Chapter three. In each section the discussion follows the structure set out in the introduction, and relies on the distinction between consensual and quasi-adjudicative methods of ADR. For each jurisdiction, the analysis contains a short explanation of how a particular ADR method is situated within a given legal framework. The main body of each section recounts the evolution of the judicial treatment of ADR clauses, with emphasis on the seminal cases and their subsequent reception in later judgments.

The main points will be:

(i) In England the enforceability of mediation clauses has undergone a significant evolution. The initial position leant towards unenforceability, equating mediation with negotiation clauses, the latter being treated as 'agreements to agree' and unenforceable due to the lack of valid consideration (2.4–2.11). Subsequently, this leaning was reversed and the enforceability of mediation clauses became a well-established rule in English law (2.12ff). The main remedy for non-compliance with mediation clauses is stay of the proceedings (2.20–2.23). Because mediation clauses are treated like any other provision of a contract, contractual liability arises in the event of a breach. This includes the availability of equitable remedies such as injunctions to halt prematurely initiated proceedings (2.24–2.32). English law has an established legal framework governing expert determination clauses. The enforceability of such clauses was established long before the English courts confirmed the binding nature of consensual ADR methods. The consequences of non-compliance with expert determination clauses are the same as with mediation (2.59ff). Finally, English law has developed a comprehensive conceptual framework for contractual time-bars contained in dispute resolution clauses. It distinguishes between a bar to the claim and a bar to the remedy, which is relevant to the enforceability of multi-tiered clauses containing such provisions (2.74ff).

(ii) In Germany ADR clauses are qualified as *pacta de non petendo*, agreements not to sue. German jurisprudence examines the validity of ADR clauses from the perspective of the right to fair trial, ensuring that the availability of court proceedings is not excluded unreasonably or indefinitely (2.137–2.142). A clear distinction is made between the procedural and substantive effects of ADR clauses. As far as consensual methods are concerned, failure to attempt contractually agreed mediation gives rise to mainly procedural consequences and mediation clauses are classified as procedural contracts alongside jurisdiction and arbitration agreements. Under German law mediation clauses exclude actionability (*Klagbarkeit*) of the claim. Consequently, the court treats prematurely initiated proceedings as temporarily inadmissible (*einstweilen unzulässig*), and terminates them by a procedural order without deciding on the merits of the case (2.101ff). By contrast, non-compliance with expert determination clauses gives rise to substantive consequences (2.130ff). Failure to submit a dispute to an expert results in a decision on the merits—dismissal of the claim as unfounded (*unbegründet*). Expert determination is an institution of a substantive origin. It is regulated only fragmentarily, by analogous application of the relevant provisions of the German Civil Code (2.116).

(iii) In France the enforceability of mediation clauses was examined from the perspective of the means of defence prescribed in the French Civil Procedure Code (2.170–2.179). They include: substantive defences (*défenses au fond*) objections to the procedure (*exceptions de procédure*) and objections as to admissibility (*fins de non-recevoir*). After a period of inconsistent rulings, a plea of non-compliance with a mediation clause has been conclusively qualified as the last category of defence (2.185ff). Consequently, failure to initiate the agreed mediation process renders the premature proceedings inadmissible. The same, procedural, effect is adopted for quasi-adjudicative methods, despite expert determination having a substantive origin in the Civil Code (2.212). Substantive remedies for breach of ADR clauses, such as specific performance, damages, or dismissal of the claim on its merits, are excluded in French law. The effects of such clauses were, however, analysed from the perspective of two types of obligations—an obligation of result and an obligation of conduct (2.198). The first type of obligation was rejected for mediation clauses, which are considered to compel the parties to cooperate in good faith, but not necessarily to reach a settlement.

(iv) In Switzerland a duty to undergo conciliation before submitting the claim in court is a rule to which the Civil Procedure Code prescribes only a few exceptions. Mandatory amicable discussions are treated as a condition of the court proceedings. On the other hand, in cases where conciliation is not a statutory obligation (ie where mediation is voluntarily agreed to in a contract), mediation clauses are not enforceable owing to their inherently optional character (2.228). By contrast, in cases where the provisions imposing compulsory conciliation are not applicable (eg in arbitration proceedings), mediation clauses are considered binding and capable of being enforced (2.239ff). The solution favoured by the Swiss judiciary provides that the adjudicative body lacks jurisdiction *ratione temporis* until a mediation attempt is performed. The opposite view presented by commentators suggests that compliance with contractual mediation commitments is a procedural condition of admissibility of the proceedings (*condition de recevabilité*, *Prozessvorauszetung* (2.240–2.250 and 2.251–2.255)). Less controversy surrounds expert determination, which is codified in the Civil Procedure Code. The plea of non-compliance with an expert determination clause is treated as a jurisdictional objection by the Swiss courts (2.264ff).

CONTENTS

England and Wales

2.1 Analysis of English law is crucial to understanding the mechanics of multi-tiered dispute resolution clauses. The evolution of English law in this area reflects the genesis of integrated ADR mechanisms and indicates basic directions for their enforceability. Legal concepts derived from common law operate as a model for solutions developed in international forms of contracts used globally in commerce.[1]

[1] Especially in the construction industry. See 1.45ff for details.

An impact of English law includes, inter alia, widespread application of quasi-adjudicative ADR and contractual time-bars connected with the initiation of dispute resolution procedure.

The English legal system is the only one in Europe where multi-stage dispute resolution mechanisms benefit from statutory underpinning. The English Arbitration Act 1996 refers, in two instances, to pre-arbitral ADR procedures which should be exhausted before an action is brought. The first is section 9(2) of the Arbitration Act 1996. It provides that court proceedings instituted in violation of an arbitration clause will be stayed upon an application of a party, even if the parties are supposed to exhaust a contractual ADR procedure before referring a matter to arbitration. The second provision where the legislature addresses multi-tiered arbitration clauses is section 12 of the Arbitration Act 1996. Under this section a party may apply to court for an extension of time where an arbitration clause provides that a party must adhere to a time-limit either to commence arbitration or to exhaust other dispute resolution procedures before arbitration can be begun.[2] **2.2**

Special attention should be drawn to the evolving approach to ADR in England. Three trends can be identified. The first is an increasing role for mediation under the Civil Procedure Rules. The second entails expanding the role of experts: from that of evaluators of narrow technical issues to that of quasi-arbitrators deciding on both facts and law of entire claims brought before them. Finally, a lot of the courts' attention is devoted to the enforceability of clauses where parties commit to engage in informal negotiations rather than a structured process before a neutral third party. **2.3**

Negotiations

Traditionally clauses in which parties promise to negotiate before filing a claim in court are unenforceable under English law. Under *Courtney & Fairbairn v Tolaini Brothers (Hotels)*[3] such contractual provisions were perceived as an 'agreement to agree', and so invalid. The case concerned a duty to negotiate a price under a construction contract. Lord Denning MR considered such an obligation to be too imprecise to have any binding force: **2.4**

> If the law does not recognise a contract to enter into a contract (when there is a fundamental term yet to be agreed) it seems to me it cannot recognise a contract to negotiate. The reason is because it is too uncertain to have any binding force.[4]

The clause in *Courtney* related to negotiations of a contract price, not negotiations aimed at resolving a dispute per se. Notwithstanding this difference, the reasoning presented in *Courtney* was regarded as prohibiting enforcement of the obligation to make a pre-trial settlement attempt. Such an interpretation was followed in *Paul* **2.5**

[2] On a contractual time-bar see 2.72ff.
[3] *Courtney & Fairbairn v Tolaini Brothers (Hotels)* [1975] 1 WLR 297.
[4] *ibid* at 301.

Smith LTD v H&S International Holding Inc,[5] where the court considered a clause stipulating that, before resorting to arbitration, the parties shall strive to settle the dispute amicably. Invoking *Courtney*, Steyn J concluded that clauses providing that a dispute shall, in the first place, be submitted for conciliation, do not create enforceable legal obligations. In this case an obligation to negotiate contractual terms and an obligation to attempt to resolve disputes amicably were treated equally.[6]

2.6 This reasoning was strengthened by the decision in *Walford v Miles*[7] where the House of Lords refused to uphold an agreement to negotiate in good faith for an unspecified period of time. It was held that because an agreement contained no term as to the duration of the obligation to negotiate, and made no provision for the defendant to terminate the negotiations, it was unworkable in practice and inherently inconsistent with the position of a negotiating party. The agreement lacked the necessary certainty and was not recognised as an enforceable contract.

2.7 Although not directly referring to dispute resolution clauses, the House of Lords' judgment reinforced the approach of the English courts that clauses providing for an attempt at amicable dispute resolution were unenforceable. Under this interpretation, multi-tiered clauses, which initially provided for negotiations, were not binding, and were treated as obligations to negotiate terms and conditions of a future agreement. This traditional approach has changed alongside the explicit differentiation between clauses providing for alternative dispute resolution methods and clauses expressing a mere intention of good-faith negotiations of contract terms.

2.8 In *Emirates Trading Agency LLC v Prime Mineral Exports Private Ltd*[8] Teare J distinguished the House of Lords decision in *Walfard v Miles* and rejected the approach equating 'agreements to agree' with 'agreements to negotiate'. The decision was the effect of the evolving treatment of ADR by English courts and the changing landscape for mediation in English procedural law discussed further below.[9]

Mediation

The Changing Landscape of Mediation in England

2.9 Initially, the courts extended the rule in *Courtney & Fairbairn v Tolaini Brothers (Hotels)*[10] to deny the enforceability of mediation agreements. A decision in *Halifax Financial Services Ltd v Intuitive Systems Ltd*[11] is an illustration of this reasoning. The clause in question was a tiered dispute resolution clause under which the parties,

[5] *Paul Smith Ltd v H&S International Holding Inc* [1991] 2 Lloyd's Rep 127 (Com Ct).

[6] Critically on this interpretation T Allen, *Mediation Law and Civil Practice* (Bloomsbury, 2013) 160–61.

[7] *Walford v Miles* [1992] 2 AC 128 (HL).

[8] *Emirates Trading Agency LLC v Prime Mineral Exports Private Ltd* [2014] EWHC 2104 (Comm).

[9] See 2.48.

[10] *Courtney & Fairbairn v Tolaini Brothers (Hotels)* [1975] 1 WLR 297 (CA) 301.

[11] *Halifax Financial Services Ltd v Intuitive Systems Ltd* [2000] 2 TCLR 35.

before resorting to legal action, were to attempt an amicable resolution, initially face to face, or, if that failed, with the assistance of a neutral third party. McKinnon J concluded that such a clause was not a condition precedent to initiating legal proceedings. It was held that even if the court had jurisdiction to stay the proceedings, which was doubted, it would not do so in order to enforce a consensual ADR process.

Halifax distinguished the earlier decision in *Channel Tunnel Group Ltd v Balfour Beatty Construction Ltd*[12] where the House of Lords confirmed the enforceability of expert determination clauses. McKinnon J accepted the submission that a distinction should be drawn between procedures which are determinative, such as expert determination or arbitration, and those which are not, like meditation or negotiations. According to the judge, by contracting for a determinative procedure the parties had agreed that certain issues would be finally and conclusively resolved by a third party. Non-determinative processes do not offer this level of certainty and the parties cannot be compelled to engage in an inherently co-operative mechanism. **2.10**

As it deviated from the House of Lords in *Channel Tunnel*, the *Halifax* case was subject to debate in the literature.[13] The judgment was considered to unduly equate mediation clauses with agreements to negotiate in good faith. Notwithstanding the conclusion as to the enforceability of consensual ADR, the ruling sanctioned a distinction between mediation and quasi-adjudicative ADR, and this was endorsed subsequently by the judiciary.[14] **2.11**

The increasing importance of mediation in the UK led to a significant modification in judicial treatment of mediation clauses. The direction of change was indicated in Lord Woolf's recommendation for the future reform of the civil procedure.[15] Lord Woolf's Reports shaped the Civil Procedure Rules (CPR), which took effect on 26 April 1999.[16] One of the main changes associated with the new regime is the court's role as the means of last resort and the corresponding emphasis on **2.12**

[12] *Channel Tunnel Group Ltd v Balfour Beatty Construction Ltd* [1993] AC 334 (HL). On this case 2.59–2.60.

[13] T Allen, *Mediation Law and Civil Practice*, n 6 above, 162–63; H Brown, A Marriott, *ADR Principles and Practice*, 3rd edn (Sweet & Maxwell, 2011) para 10-033; T Melnyk, 'The Enforceability of Multi-tiered Dispute Resolution Clauses: the English Law Position' (2002) 4 *International Arbitration Law Review* 113, 116–17; O Olawatura, 'Managing Multi-Layered Dispute Resolution under the Arbitration Act 1966—Smashing Bricks of Intention' (2001) 4 *International Arbitration Law Review* 70; L Mistelis, 'ADR in England and Wales: A Successful Case of Public Private Partnership' in N Alexander (ed), *Global Trends in Mediation*, 2nd edn (Kluwer Law International, 2006) 162–63.

[14] See eg *Holloway v Chancery Mead Limited* [2007] EWHC 2495 (TCC).

[15] Access to justice: interim report to the Lord Chancellor on the civil justice system in England and Wales (1995) and Access to Justice: final report (1996).

[16] See inter alia, A Zuckerman, R Cranston (eds), *The Reform of Civil Procedure: Essays on 'Access to Justice'* (OUP, 1995); R Cranston, *How Law Works: The Machinery and Impact of Civil Justice* (OUP, 2006) ch 5; N Andrews, *English Civil Procedure* (OUP, 2003) ch 2; N Andrews, 'A New Civil Procedural Code for England: Party-Control "Going, Going, Gone"' (2000) 19 *Civil Justice Quarterly* 19; J Jolowicz, 'The Woolf Report and the Adversary System' (1996) 15 *Civil Justice Quarterly* 198; M Zander, 'The Government's Plans on Civil Justice' (1998) 61 *Modern Law Review* 383; M Zander, 'The Woolf Report: Forwards or Backwards for the New Lord Chancellor?' (1997) 16 *Civil Justice Quarterly* 208; A Zuckerman, 'The Woolf Report on Access to Justice' (1997) 2 *Zeitschrift für Zivilprozess International* 31.

out-of court resolution of disputes.[17] This directive was supported with a number of instruments the purpose of which was to encourage parties to resolve their dispute amicably.[18] The duty of active case management, imposed on the judges by the CPR, includes supporting the parties' use of mechanisms such as mediation.[19] The court has the power to stay the proceedings to allow for settlement of the case either at the request of the parties or of its own initiative.[20] Furthermore, the CPR introduced costs that might be imposed on an uncooperative party.[21] The new philosophy, founded upon promoting ADR, had far-reaching repercussions in English case law which gave support to the use of mediation as the primary way of resolving disputes out of court.[22]

Enforceability of Mediation Clauses under Cable & Wireless v IBM[23]

2.13 Given the strong policy shift towards mediation, it was no longer possible to maintain the traditional approach that contractual duties to engage in pre-trial mediation are unenforceable. Although the new Civil Procedure Rules did not contain a regulation that would set out the consequences of breach of mediation agreements, it became clear that such clauses are valid contractual terms whose enforceability is not in doubt.

2.14 The turnabout took place with the Commercial Court judgment in *Cable & Wireless v IBM.*[24] The case concerned a long-term contract which contained detailed provisions for dispute resolution. At the first tier it provided for 'an attempt in good faith to resolve any dispute of claim' by negotiations between representatives of the parties within their own internal organisations. The second tier required an attempt to resolve the dispute through ADR procedure as recommended to the parties by the Centre for Dispute Resolution.[25] If the dispute was still unresolved, the claim could be brought before a court. The controversy as to the enforceability of this dispute resolution clause arose when one party bypassed the stipulated

[17] On this aspect N Andrews, *Modern Civil Process* (Mohr Siebeck, 2008) paras 11.01–11.65 and the literature cited there. English reforms inspired similar changes in Europe, see L Mistelis, 'ADR in England and Wales', n 13 above, 140.

[18] See especially CPR 1.4(2)(e) (encouraging parties to use ADR); 'Practice Direction—Pre-action Conduct' para 8.1 (litigation as a last resort).

[19] Practice Direction 29: 'The Multi-Track', para 4.10(9) supplementing CPR Pt 29.

[20] CPR 26.4.

[21] The court may impose costs on a party that rejects a settlement offer which, in the light of the outcome of the case, turned out to be rational (CPR Pt 36). Further on the influence of the new rules on the alternative methods of dispute resolution see H Brown, A Marriott, *ADR Principles and Practice*, n 13 above, para 3.001ff.

[22] Strong support for the use of mediation has been given by the courts in cases such as *R (Cowl) v Plymouth City Council (Practice Note)* [2002] 1 WLR 803 (CA); *Dunnett v Railtrack plc (Practice Note)* [2002] 1 WLR 2434 (CA) and *Hurst v Leeming* [2003] 1 Lloyd's Rep 379 (Ch).

[23] *Cable & Wireless PLC v IBM United Kingdom Ltd* [2002] EWHC 2059 (Comm); [2002] CLC 1319 (Com Ct).

[24] [2002] CLC 1319 (Com Ct).

[25] Previous name of the Centre for Effective Dispute Resolution (CEDR).

mediation procedure and, after first-level negotiations had failed, brought a claim directly before the High Court of England and Wales.

The Court decided that the mediation clause was valid and enforceable. Encouraged by the CPR, Colman J held: **2.15**

> [T]he English courts should nowadays not be astute to accentuate uncertainty (and therefore unenforceability) in the field of dispute resolution references ... Accordingly, in the present case I conclude that clause 41.2 includes a sufficiently defined mutual obligation upon the parties to go through the process of initiating a mediation, selecting a mediator and at least presenting that mediator with its case and its documents and attending upon him.[26]

Colman J seems to have distinguished three types of mediation clauses. The first appeared in the present case. Its characteristic feature was that the clause referred to an institutionalised ADR provider. Parties did not simply agree to attempt in good faith to negotiate a settlement but went further to identify a particular procedure—mediation under the auspices of the CDR. Such a clause was declared enforceable under English law. **2.16**

The second type of clause is at the other extreme and includes clauses that are unenforceable owing to uncertainty, in which parties stipulate 'a mere undertaking to negotiate a contract or settlement agreement, just as there is in an agreement to strive to settle a dispute amicably, as in *Paul Smith Ltd v H & S International Holding Inc*'.[27] Such clauses lack sufficient objective criteria to decide whether parties were in compliance or breach, and in this respect previous authority was upheld. **2.17**

Colman J went on to differentiate the third, intermediate category. Analysing the degree of certainty in the wording of the ADR clause he added that 'contractual references to ADR which did not include provision for an identifiable procedure would not necessarily fail to be enforceable by reason of uncertainty.'[28] Since it is not ultimately clear how far a procedure needs to go to be identified, this last category created some points of controversy.[29] **2.18**

Regarding available remedies, Colman J applied an analogy to an arbitration clause: **2.19**

> The reference to ADR is analogous to an agreement to arbitrate. As such, it represents a free-standing agreement ancillary to the main contract and capable of being enforced by a stay of the proceedings or by injunction absent any pending proceedings.[30]

[26] [2002] CLC 1319 at 1326.

[27] *ibid* at 1327.

[28] *ibid.*

[29] A sufficient degree of certainty was not found in *Flight Training International Inc v International Fire Training Equipment Ltd* [2004] EWHC 721 (Com Ct), where Cresswell J held that it is necessary for the clause to clearly indicate a particular technique of ADR process. On the judiciary after *Cable & Wireless* see 2.40ff. See also comments by C Debatista, 'Drafting Enforceable Arbitration Clauses' (2005) 21 *Arbitration International* 233, 236ff.

[30] [2002] CLC 1319 at 1327.

Stay of the Proceedings

2.20 The main remedy is a stay. It was held that a stay would be lifted if the party demonstrated that the mediation attempt had been made but proved unsuccessful. The remedy adopted by Colman J mirrors the court's power envisaged in section 9 of the Arbitration Act 1996 dealing with the effects of arbitration clauses. Importantly, however, stay of the proceedings brought in breach of a valid arbitration clause is obligatory. By contrast, stay of the proceedings due to the claimant's failure to exhaust contractual ADR is discretionary.[31] Colman J clarified that 'there may be cases where a reference to ADR would be obviously futile and where the likelihood of a productive mediation taking place would be so slight as not to justify enforcing the agreement.'[32]

2.21 It is not, however, possible for the parties to avoid mediation merely by claiming that it would be ineffective. Colman J went on to explain that 'Even in such circumstances ADR would have to be a completely hopeless exercise'.[33]

2.22 As emphasised in the literature a stay is merely suspension of the proceedings. It does not mean that parties are actually obliged to engage in mediation.[34] By ordering a stay the court merely creates the opportunity for the parties to explore settlement options.

2.23 Although the decision in *Cable & Wireless* concerned litigation, the same analysis is applicable if the contract provides for mediation before commencement of arbitration proceedings.[35] Non-compliance with the pre-arbitral tiers of an arbitration clause and premature commencement of arbitration may result in a stay of arbitral proceedings whenever the tribunal enforces an ADR clause under English law.

Injunction

2.24 Another remedy available for breach of mediation clauses, also mentioned by Colman J in *Cable & Wireless*, is an anti-suit injunction. This instrument is an expression of the court's general power to secure compliance with the contractual bargain.[36] A wide discretion to grant an injunction is provided under section 37 of the Senior Courts Act 1981. In the present context an injunction would be

[31] Section 49(3), Senior Courts Act 1981.

[32] [2002] CLC 1319 at 1328.

[33] *ibid.*

[34] N Andrews, *Modern Civil Process*, n 17 above, para 11.39.

[35] *ibid*, para 12.12; *Andrews on Civil Processes. vol II: Arbitration & Mediation* (Intersentia, 2013) para 2.04. The case is widely referred to by the commentators dealing with ADR clauses in arbitration (see eg C Bühring-Uhle, *Arbitration and Mediation in International Business*, 2nd edn (Kluwer Law International, 2006) 228).

[36] The classic statement of law can be found in *Donohue v Armco* [2002] 1 Lloyd's Rep 425 (HL). See R Fentiman, *International Commercial Litigation*, 2nd edn (OUP, 2015) ch 16 for a commentary.

aimed at preventing activity inconsistent with a mediation agreement. The point is, however, not developed.[37]

An application for an injunction would be aimed at restraining the offending party's continuation of premature arbitration or foreign civil proceedings brought in breach of a multi-step clause. Three situations can be distinguished: (i) the claimant commences foreign court proceedings without exhausting pre-trial ADR; (ii) the claimant commences arbitral proceedings without exhausting pre-arbitral ADR (an anti-arbitration injunction); and (iii) the claimant commences court proceedings without exhausting ADR procedures and the clause provides for arbitral proceedings as the last stage. **2.25**

In the case referred to in item (iii), an anti-suit injunction can be issued in support of an arbitration clause, rather than a mediation clause.[38] Further difficult issues arise in relation to cases (i) and (ii). **2.26**

Where the claimant commences court proceedings without exhausting contractual ADR (cases (i) and (iii)), a difficulty relates to compliance with the European jurisdiction regime prescribed in Regulation (EU) No 1215/2012 on jurisdiction and the recognition and enforcement of judgments in civil and commercial matters.[39] Under the predecessor of this act, Regulation (EU) No 44/2001,[40] the European Court of Justice ruled in *Allianz SpA v West Tankers Inc*[41] that it is incompatible with the Brussels Regulation for a Member State court to grant an anti-suit injunction to restrain a party from pursuing proceedings in the courts of another Member State in breach of an arbitration agreement. A similar conclusion was reached in relation to anti-suit injunctions in support of jurisdiction agreements in *Turner v Grovit*.[42] It can be assumed that the same reasoning would apply to enforcing mediation agreements. **2.27**

In *West Tankers* the ECJ held that, although arbitration is excluded from the European jurisdiction regime, the scope of the exception does not allow one **2.28**

[37] *Andrews on Civil Processes. vol II: Arbitration & Mediation*, n 35 above, para 1.104. An application for injunction in support of ADR was the subject of the recent case *Clyde & Co LLP, John Morris v Krista Bates van Winkelhof* [2011] EWHC 668 (QB). The injunction sought was to restrain Employment Tribunal proceedings commenced in breach of a multi-tiered dispute resolution clause. Slade J refused to grant the relief as the matter fell outside the permissible scope of contracting for ADR. It was held that the right to resort to special adjudicative bodies such as the Employment Tribunal cannot be restricted by fulfilment of contractual conditions.

[38] *Sulamerica Cia Nacional de Seguros SA v Enesa Engenharia SA* [2012] EWCA Civ 638 involved this situation. The Court of Appeal granted the insurer anti-suit relief to stop the insured from pursuing Brazilian court proceedings and instead to submit (as agreed) to arbitration proceedings pending in London. In this case the English court held that there was no mandatory mediation stage, but merely a binding arbitration agreement, which took effect so as to override the jurisdiction of the Brazilian courts in this matter.

[39] Hereafter: 'the Recast Brussels Regulation'.

[40] Hereafter: 'the Brussels Regulation'.

[41] Case C-185/07 *Allianz SpA v West Tankers Inc* [2009] ECR I-663.

[42] Case C-159/02 *Turner v Grovit* [2004] ECR I-3565.

Member State to require a party to discontinue proceedings before a court of another Member State. Instead, every Member State's court, when seised in a civil or commercial matter concerning the Regulation, must be accorded jurisdiction to determine for itself whether it does in fact have jurisdiction to hear the substantive dispute before it. The Recast Brussels Regulation strengthens the arbitration exception, clarifying its remit in recital 12. It provides that the Recast should not prevent the courts of Member States from referring parties to arbitration, from staying or dismissing proceedings in favour of arbitration, or from examining whether the arbitration agreement is null and void, inoperative or incapable of being performed, in accordance with their national law. The prohibition on anti-suit injunctions has not, however, been lifted.

2.29 The matter was addressed by the Advocate General of the Court, Melchior Wathelet in his non-binding advisory opinion issued on 4 December 2014 in relation to the *Gazprom OAO* case.[43] The case considered an anti-suit injunction issued by an arbitral tribunal (not a court) and was governed by the predecessor of the Brussels Recast Regulation—the original Brussels Regulation. Notwithstanding these differences the Advocate General not only referred to the Recast Regulation considering recital 12 as 'retroactive interpretative law', but also concluded that the decision in *West Tankers* is no longer correct in light of the reinforced arbitration exception clarified under this enactment. The Advocate General interpreted the exception as excluding from the scope of the Regulation any proceedings concerning the validity of an arbitration agreement. According to his opinion, this included anti-suit injunctions granted by national courts in support of arbitration.

2.30 The Court of Justice in *Gazprom OAO* did not go this far and refused to contradict its ruling in *West Tankers*. Instead, it confirmed that it is incompatible with the original Brussels Regulation to issue a decision preventing the party from initiating or continuing proceedings in another Member State. The prohibition on the grant of anti-suit injunctions by Member State courts still stands and it remains to be seen whether the Advocate General's broad interpretation of the arbitration exception under the Recast Regulation will be adopted.[44] In the absence of an authoritative interpretation of the Recast Brussels Regulation, it is unclear whether the prohibition continues and how it would relate to mediation agreements.

2.31 The second difficult case relates to the situation where the claimant commences arbitral proceedings without exhausting pre-arbitral ADR and the clause provides for arbitration as the final stage of the dispute resolution process (case (ii)—an anti-arbitration injunction). The availability of an injunction in such circumstances is

[43] Case C-536/13 *Gazprom OAO v Lithuania* [2015] All ER (EC) 711.

[44] J Sundaram, 'Does the Judgment of the CJEU in *Gazprom* Bring about Clarity on the Grant of Anti-Suit Injunctions under the Brussels I Regulation?' (2015) 27 *Denning Law Journal* 303. Some authors express the view that the decision in *West Tankers* remains good law under the new regime, see T Hartley, 'Antisuit Injunctions in Support of Arbitration: *West Tankers* Still Afloat' (2015) 64 *ICLQ* 965; A Leandro, 'Towards a New Interface Between Brussels I and Arbitration?' (2015) 6 *Journal of International Dispute Settlement* 188, 196–99.

considered, in the literature, to be theoretically possible.[45] Jurisdiction to grant injunctions in respect of arbitration is part of the general supervisory function exercised by the courts of the seat of the arbitration. Accordingly, where England or Wales is the seat of the arbitration, the court is empowered to grant an interim injunction in relation to arbitration proceedings.[46] However, case law indicates that the courts approach granting an injunction restraining arbitral proceedings with caution.

The main issue that arises in this context is the permissible scope of the court's interference with the *Kompetenz-Kompetenz* principle. The question is whether the matter giving rise to an application for an anti-arbitration injunction should rather be dealt with by the arbitrators themselves under their power to decide within their own jurisdiction. Notwithstanding this fundamental dilemma, English courts have occasionally granted such injunctions under their inherent jurisdiction as prescribed in section 37 of the Senior Courts Act 1981. In the present context this power is, however, untilised only in exceptional circumstances, and cannot be used as a means of overruling the tribunal's decisions on jurisdiction. In order to establish exceptional circumstances it is necessary to show that the applicant's legal or equitable rights have been infringed or threatened by a continuation of the arbitration, or that its continuation will be vexatious, oppressive or unconscionable.[47] The rationale for this approach accords with the non-interventionist model of the relationship between the courts and the arbitral process. Broad exercise of power under section 37 of the Senior Courts Act 1981 would grant the court general supervisory competence, which it does not possess under the Arbitration Act 1996. 2.32

Damages

The last remedy that should be considered is damages. In common law, a party in breach of an arbitration agreement can be ordered to pay compensation to the innocent party for any loss suffered as a result of the breach. Although they were not mentioned by Colman J in *Cable & Wireless* as a remedy for non-compliance 2.33

[45] N Andrews, *Modern Civil Process*, n 17 above, para 12.12; *Andrews on Civil Processes vol II: Arbitration & Mediation*, n 35 above, para 2.04 *in fine*. NB the grant of an anti-arbitration injunction does not entail restraining proceedings before the EU Member State court; hence, the restrictions described above do not apply.

[46] An injunction restraining the conduct of arbitration with a foreign seat will be granted only in exceptional circumstances. See eg *Claxton Engineering Services Ltd v Tam Olaj-Es Gazkutato KTF* [2011] EWHC 345 where Hamblen J held it was appropriate to grant an anti-arbitration injunction restraining arbitration in Hungary in the case where the parties entered into a binding English exclusive jurisdiction clause and there was no arbitration agreement. See also *Weissfisch v Julius* [2006] EWCA Civ 218; *A v B* [2007] 1 Lloyd's Rep 237; *A v B (No 2)* [2007] 1 Lloyd's Rep 358; *C v D* [2007] EWHC 1541 (Comm); *AmTrust Europe Ltd v Trust Risk Group SpA* [2015] EWHC 1927 (Comm).

[47] *Elektrim SA v Vivendi Universal SA (No 2)* [2007] EWHC 571 (Comm). See also *Intermet FZCO v Ansol Ltd* [2007] EWHC 226 (Comm); *Albon (t/a NA Carriage Co) v Naza Motor Trading Sdn Bhd* [2007] EWCA Civ 1124 (CA) and the note above. On anti-arbitration injunctions exhaustively H Seriki, *Injunctive Relief and International Arbitration* (Informa Law, 2015) ch 7.

with ADR clauses, damages must be considered by virtue of an analogy to the violation of an arbitration or jurisdiction clause.[48]

2.34 English courts treat damages for breach of arbitration or jurisdiction agreements with caution. An injunction is deemed the preferred remedy with which to enforce contractual obligations under such clauses.[49] However, claims for compensation may be awarded as a secondary enforcement provided that a party is able to show that the violation of the clause caused a quantifiable loss.[50] A claim for damages is available despite the fact that the party may also seek to stay proceedings commenced in breach of a valid arbitration clause.[51]

2.35 The most complex aspect of damages for breach of an arbitration or jurisdiction clause is the quantum. The amount of compensation may be composed of costs incurred by one party in connection with proceedings instituted by the other in violation of the relevant agreement between the parties.[52] It is not, however, limited to the sum of costs arising from appearance before a forum not competent to hear the case. In *Donohue v Armco Inc.*[53] it was confirmed that compensation for violation of a jurisdiction agreement may, apart from costs of proceedings, also include the equivalent of an amount awarded by a forum not competent to hear the case.[54]

2.36 A similar rule has been applied to breach of an arbitration agreement. In *CMA CGM SA v Hyundai MIPO Dockyard Co Ltd*[55] the court considered breach of an arbitration clause committed when a party commenced proceedings in France. Burton J held that the damages to be awarded for breach of the arbitration agreement comprised the amount paid by the innocent party in response to the French judgment, the costs of opposing the French proceedings, and management time wasted during the proceedings before a *forum* not competent to hear the case.[56]

[48] In the decision in *Sunrock Aircraft Corp Ltd v Scandinavian Airlines System Denmark-Norway-Sweden* [2007] Lloyd's Rep 612 concerning expert determination clauses Thomas LJ confirmed that it is an established rule of English law that damages can be awarded for a loss incurred by the failure to comply with the terms of an alternative dispute resolution clause (at [37]). On this case see 2.68–2.70.

[49] *OT Africa Line Ltd v Magic Sportwear Corp (The Kribi)* [2005] 2 Lloyd's Rep 170; *Anggeliki Charis Compania Maritima SA v Pangan SpA (The Angelic Grace)* [1995] 1 Lloyd's Rep 87 (CA); *Donohue v Armco Inc* [2002] 1 Lloyd's Rep 425 (HL); *Royal Bank of Canada v Centrale Raiffeisen* [2004] 1 Lloyd's Rep 471 (CA); *Toepfer International GmbH v Société Cargill France* [1998] 1 Lloyd's Rep 379, 384 (CA). See also D Joseph, *Jurisdiction and Arbitration Agreements*, 3rd edn (Sweet & Maxwell, 2015) para 12.30ff; R Fentiman, *International Commercial Litigation*, n 36 above, para 16.42.

[50] *Randell, Saunders & Co Ltd v Thompson* (1876) 1 QBD 748, 752.

[51] *Mantovani v Carapelli SpA* [1980] 1 Lloyd's Rep 375 (CA).

[52] *Union Discount Co Ltd v Zoller (Union Cal Ltd, Pt 20 defendant)* [2001] EWCA Civ 1755. See also the discussion in D Joseph, *Jurisdiction and Arbitration Agreements*, n 49 above, paras 14.05–14.12.

[53] *Donohue v Armco Inc* [2002] 1 Lloyd's Rep 425 (HL).

[54] See also *Ellerman Lines Ltd v Read* [1928] 2 KB 144 (CA). On this aspect R Fentiman, *International Commercial Litigation*, n 36 above, para 2.250.

[55] *CMA CGM SA v Hyundai MIPO Dockyard Co Ltd* [2009] 1 Lloyd's Rep 213 (Com Ct).

[56] On this case *Andrews on Civil Processes. vol II: Arbitration & Mediation*, n 35 above, para 10.65 and R Fentiman, *International Commercial Litigation*, 1st edn (OUP, 2010) para 2.93ff.

It has been pointed out in the literature that the compensation for breach of an arbitration clause may also include the financial consequences of defending an action before a public court whose proceedings are non-confidential. This entails damages arising from disclosure of trade secrets and loss of reputation.[57]

It is unclear how the above considerations will apply where compensation is sought for breach of a mediation clause. In England mediation clauses, like arbitration or jurisdiction agreements, are regarded as a species of contract whose breach can expose the offending party to the usual array of remedies for breach of contract, including compensatory damages. An additional difficulty arises, however, with regard to the unascertainable amount of loss resulting from failure to mediate. Applying a general rule for quantifying damages, a party in breach of a mediation agreement should place the other party in the same position as if the mediation process had been carried out. The difficulty lies in uncertainty both as to whether a settlement would have been achieved, had the party pursued the agreed mediation attempt, as well as with regard to the sum of such settlement.[58] 2.37

A solution to the difficulties in establishing the quantum of damages for breach of an ADR clause is contracting for liquidated damages.[59] This is, however, subject to an important caveat. English law does not allow punitive damages to be awarded for breach of contract. In consequence, a provision in the contract which constitutes a penalty is unenforceable.[60] Considering the nature of the duty under an agreement to mediate, a proportionate amount of compensation may be difficult to pre-estimate. 2.38

In summary, the decision in *Cable & Wireless* establishes the scope of available remedies for breach of mediation clauses, and is one of the key precedents relating to the enforceability of multi-step dispute resolution mechanisms. The case extended the earlier rule established by *Channel Tunnel Group Ltd v Balfour Beatty Construction Ltd*[61] with regard to the enforceability of expert determination, and confirmed that clauses providing for consensual ADR are also enforceable. For the first time, it was clearly stated that the consequences of non-compliance with all ADR clauses should be assessed similarly to the consequences of violating arbitration clauses. Although the main remedy is a stay of prematurely initiated 2.39

[57] D Joseph, *Jurisdiction and Arbitration Agreements*, n 49 above, para 14.16 and the authorities cited.

[58] See also the remarks on this issue in *Courtney & Fairbairn v Tolaini Brothers (Hotels)* [1975] 1 WLR 297, Lord Denning LJ at 301.

[59] *Thackwray v Winter* (1880) 6 VLR (L) 128 (liquidated damages of £50 were provided for breach of an arbitration agreement). See also J Bailey, *Construction Law* (Informa Law, 2011) para 25.92, fn 302 and A Jolles, 'Consequences of Multi-Tiered Arbitration Clauses: Issues of Enforcement' (2006) 72 *Arbitration* 329, 337 in relation to ADR clauses.

[60] See the recent exposition of this rule in *Cavendish Square Holding BV v El Makdessi* and *ParkingEye Ltd v Beavis* [2015] UKSC 67. The Supreme Court regarded as a penalty a contractual provision which imposes a detriment on the party in breach of a primary obligation, which is out of all proportion to any legitimate interest of the innocent party in the performance of that obligation.

[61] *Channel Tunnel Group Ltd v Balfour Beatty Construction Ltd* [1993] 2 WLR 262.

proceedings, English law does not exclude injunctive relief or damages for non-compliance with dispute resolution clauses.

*Enforceability of Consensual ADR Methods Post-*Cable & Wireless

2.40 The decision in the *Cable & Wireless* case was welcomed as 'a step in the right direction … vital in ensuring the efficacy of ADR processes as well as preserving the contractual bargains made between business people'.[62] As noted, in *Cable & Wireless* Colman J distinguished three types of clauses: clauses providing for mediation under the auspices of an institutionalised ADR provider (enforceable); clauses expressing the mere intention to strive to settle a dispute (unenforceable); and an intermediate category of clauses which do not include a reference to an identifiable procedure but are sufficiently certain to be enforced. Colman J did not clarify to what extent an ADR procedure must be defined in a clause. This was explored in subsequent case law.

2.41 The standard for preciseness of ADR clauses has been clarified in *Holloway v Chancery Mead*[63] where Ramsey J identified three necessary requirements for enforceable clauses:

> [T]he ADR clause must meet at least the following three requirements: first, that the process must be sufficiently certain in that there should not be the need for an agreement at any stage before matters can proceed. Secondly, the administrative processes for selecting a party to resolve the dispute and to pay that person should also be defined. Thirdly, the process or at least a model of the process should be set out so that the detail of the process is sufficiently certain.[64]

2.42 Under this authority the standard for enforceable ADR clauses is high. It requires (i) no further agreement before the matter may proceed to mediation; (ii) a defined procedure for appointment of a mediator; and (iii) a defined procedure for the mediation process itself (whether set out in a clause or by reference to institutional rules).

2.43 An example of an unenforceable clause was considered in *Balfour Beatty Construction Northern Ltd v Modus Corovest (Blackpool) Ltd.*[65] The clause in question provided that: '[if] any dispute or difference arises under or in connection with this Contract, where the parties have agreed to do so, the dispute or difference may be submitted to mediation in accordance with the provisions of clause 39B'. Clause

[62] J Lee, 'ADR Clauses and Enforcement' (2003) *Lloyd's Maritime & Commercial Law Quarterly* 164, 167–68. For further comments, see A Colman, 'ADR: An Irreversible Tide' (2003) 19 *Arbitration International* 303; K Mackie, 'The Future of ADR Clauses after Cable & Wireless v. IBM' (2003) 19 *Arbitration International* 345.

[63] *Holloway v Chancery Mead Ltd* [2007] EWHC 2495 (TCC).

[64] *ibid* at [81].

[65] *Balfour Beatty Construction Northern Ltd v Modus Corovest (Blackpool) Ltd* [2008] EWHC 3029 (TCC).

39B stated: 'The objective of mediation under clause 39 shall be to reach a binding agreement in resolution of the dispute or difference.' Coulson J classified this provision as falling into the second category of clauses distinguished by Colman J in *Cable & Wireless*. In consequence, the judge refused to enforce such a provision, as it was too uncertain to have any binding force. The clause also failed to fulfil the first requirement identified in *Holloway v Chancery Mead*, as it only provided for mediation subject to the later agreement of the parties.

Similarly, in *Sulamerica Cia Nacional De Seguros SA and others v Enesa Engenharia SA and others*[66] the Court of Appeal considered the mediation clause in question to be void due to its uncertainty. The clause provided that in case of a dispute the parties 'will seek to have the dispute amicably resolved by mediation'. The clause further specified that each party would be entitled to terminate mediation by notice served to the other party not earlier than after the first mediation meeting or discussion. The clause also contained a time-frame for mediation providing that if the controversy had not been resolved within 90 days from the commencement of mediation, each party might refer the dispute to arbitration. In addition, the parties introduced a provision relating to confidential information exchanged during the process and agreed on how costs of mediation would be borne. Notwithstanding these detailed contractual arrangements, the court found the clause in question impossible to enforce, as the clause failed to stipulate the means by which a mediator would be appointed. Furthermore, it neither referred to nor expressly fashioned any mediation process. The rights and obligations under the clause were, therefore, considered insufficiently certain to be binding.[67] 2.44

The same reasoning prevailed in *Wah (Aka Alan Tang) & Another v Grant Thornton International Ltd & Others*.[68] The multi-tiered procedure provided for a two-stage settlement negotiation followed by arbitration.[69] The claimant initiated 2.45

[66] *Sulamerica Cia Nacional De Seguros SA and others v Enesa Engenharia SA and others* [2012] EWCA Civ 638 (CA).

[67] With reference to the mediation clause in question Moore-Bick LJ observed (*ibid* at [36]): 'The most that might be said is that it imposes on any party who is contemplating referring a dispute to arbitration an obligation to invite the other to join in an ad hoc mediation, but the content of even such a limited obligation is so uncertain as to render it impossible of enforcement in the absence of some defined mediation process.'

[68] *Wah (Aka Alan Tang) & Another v Grant Thornton International Ltd & Others* [2012] EWHC 3198 (Ch).

[69] '(a) Any dispute or difference as described in Section 14.2 shall in the first instance be referred to the Chief Executive in an attempt to settle such dispute or difference by amicable conciliation of an informal nature. The conciliation provided for in this Section 14.3 shall be applicable notwithstanding that GTIL may be a party to the dispute or difference in question.

(b) The Chief Executive shall attempt to resolve the dispute or difference in an amicable fashion. Any party may submit a request for such conciliation regarding any such dispute or difference, and the Chief Executive shall have up to one (1) month after receipt of such request to attempt to resolve it.

(c) If the dispute or difference shall not have been resolved within one (1) month following submissions to the Chief Executive, it shall be referred to a Panel of three (3) members of the Board to be selected by the Board, none of whom shall be associated with or in any other way related to the Member Firm or Member Firms who are parties to the dispute or difference. The Panel shall have up to one (1) month to attempt to resolve the dispute or difference.

arbitration, bypassing the conciliation steps. The tribunal rejected the defendant's jurisdictional objections and proceeded to give an award, which was subsequently challenged by the defendant under section 67 of the Arbitration Act 1996. The court decided on the enforceability of pre-arbitral ADR as part of its supervisory power over the tribunal's jurisdiction. Although the clause at issue contained very detailed provisions regarding the conciliation process, the court refused to consider that it created an enforceable precedent sufficient to justify the commencement of arbitration. Relying on *Cable & Wireless v IBM*, *Holloway v Chancery Mead* and *Sulamérica CIA Nacional de Seguros SA and others v Enesa Engenharia SA*, Hildyard J concluded that the clause failed to meet the threshold for sufficient definition and certainty of commitments to pursue the agreed ADR process.

2.46 This rigorous approach of English law was criticised in the literature. It has been suggested that certainty as to the enforceability of a mediation clause can be achieved in practice only by contracting for mediation administered by one of the recognised ADR providers.[70] If parties decide against involving an institutional mediator and tailor-make their dispute resolution clause, then it is likely to be found by English courts to be ineffective if it does not meet the three-part test for certainty under *Holloway v Chancery Mead*.[71]

2.47 A more liberal stand on the enforceability of the parties' pre-action negotiation commitments was taken obiter in *Petromec Inc v Petroleo Brasiliero SA*.[72] The case concerned a commitment to negotiate in good faith to establish a price under the contract. Although answering the question as to the enforceability of such a provision was not essential to the disposition of the appeal, Longmore LJ observed that in the particular circumstances there were no good reasons for saying that the obligation to negotiate was unenforceable.[73] It must be noted, however, that the case concerned negotiation of a contractual term (rather than negotiations in relation to a dispute under the contract), and hence is of limited assistance in the present context.[74]

(d) Until the earlier of (i) such date as the Panel shall determine that it cannot resolve the dispute or difference, or (ii) the date one (1) month after the request for conciliation of the dispute or difference has been referred to it, no party may commence any arbitration procedures in accordance with this Agreement.'

[70] *Andrews on Civil Processes. Vol II: Arbitration & Mediation*, n 35 above, para 1.52.

[71] *ibid*, paras 1.46 and 1.54. The author suggests that even the most general contractual terms providing for mediation should be considered effective, as is the case with arbitration clauses. In the opinion of the author, the interpretation of mediation clauses should cover the reconstruction of implied terms thereof.

[72] *Petromec Inc v Petroleo Brasiliero SA* [2005] EWCA Civ 891 (CA).

[73] Longmore LJ (*ibid* at [73]) observed that to consider the provision in question as devoid of legal content would 'defeat the reasonable expectations of honest men'.

[74] The point made by Hildyard J in *Wah (Aka Alan Tang) & Another v Grant Thornton International Ltd & Others* [2012] EWHC 3198 (Ch) (at [55]).

A significant departure from the English court's traditional approach towards the enforceability of ADR clauses can be observed in *Emirates Trading Agency LLC v Prime Mineral Exports Private Ltd.*[75] In this case Teare J held that the requirement to seek to resolve the claim by friendly discussions before resorting to arbitration was mandatory.[76] The case arose under section 67 of the Arbitration Act and involved a challenge to an arbitral award. The grounds for challenge involved the tribunal's lack of substantive jurisdiction due to the claimant's failure to comply with the condition requiring friendly pre-arbitral discussions. **2.48**

Considering the enforceability of the clause in question Teare J distinguished the decision in *Walford v Miles.*[77] It was held that *Walford*, unlike the present case, was not a case of a dispute resolution clause within a binding contract, obliging the parties to seek to settle a dispute under that contract within a limited period. Teare J also distinguished *Sulamerica Cia Nacional De Seguros SA and others v Enesa Engenharia SA and others*[78] by observing that the clause in *Sulamerica* was incomplete due to the absence of a named mediator or an agreed process whereby a mediator could be appointed. The judge concluded that an agreement to seek to resolve a dispute by friendly discussions in good faith was not incomplete. **2.49**

Finally, it has been considered that public interest militates in favour of giving effect to an obligation to negotiate to resolve disputes amicably. Teare J referred to the Australian and Singaporean authority, as well as to the decisions of the International Centre for the Settlement of Investment Disputes (ICSID) tribunals supporting the position that contractual discussion obligations are enforceable. The Australian decision in *United Group Rail Services v Rail Corporation New South Wales*[79] was of particular relevance. Teare J relied on the analysis of **2.50**

[75] [2014] EWHC 2104 (Comm).

[76] The relevant clause read: '11. Dispute Resolution and Arbitration

11.1 In case of any dispute or claim arising out of or in connection with or under this LTC including on account of breaches/defaults mentioned in 9.2, 9.3, Clauses 10.1(d) and/or 10.1(e) above, the Parties shall first seek to resolve the dispute or claim by friendly discussion. Any party may notify the other Party of its desire to enter into consultation to resolve a dispute or claim. If no solution can be arrived at between the Parties for a continuous period of 4 (four) weeks then the non-defaulting party can invoke the arbitration clause and refer the disputes to arbitration.

11.2 All disputes arsing out of or in connection with this LTC shall be finally resolved by arbitration in accordance with the Rules of Arbitration of the International Chamber of Commerce ("ICC"). The place of arbitration shall be in London ("UK"). The arbitration shall be conducted in the English language.

11.3 The arbitration shall be referred to a tribunal of three (3) arbitrators, each Party shall appoint one arbitrator and the third shall be appointed by the ICC. Any award of a majority of the arbitrators shall be final and binding upon the parties thereto, and may be entered for enforcement in any court having jurisdiction.'

[77] *Walford v Miles* [1992] 2 AC 128 (HL) on which 2.6.

[78] *Sulamerica Cia Nacional De Seguros SA and others v Enesa Engenharia SA and others* [2012] EWCA Civ 638 (CA).

[79] *United Group Rail Services v Rail Corporation New South Wales* (2009) 127 Con LR 202, Alssop J. The clause in question provided that the parties should 'meet and undertake genuine and good faith negotiation with a view to resolving the dispute'.

English authorities conducted in this case by an Australian judge, Alssop JA in the New South Wales Court of Appeal:

> In relation to the Courtney & Fairbairn case [1975] 1 All ER 716, [1975] 1 WLR 297, the reasoning of Lord Denning MR equated an agreement to negotiate with an agreement to agree. The latter is, of course, not enforceable … It does not follow, however, that an agreement to undertake negotiations in good faith fails for the same reason.[80]

2.51 Alssop JA further observed:

> Nor, with respect, do I find the views of Lord Ackner in Walford v Miles [1992] 1 All ER 453, [1992] 2 AC 128 persuasive. An obligation to undertake discussions about a subject in an honest and genuine attempt to reach an identified result is not incomplete.[81]

2.52 The judge also emphasised the public policy considerations in favour of amicable resolution of disputes without recourse to court or arbitration:

> The public policy in promoting efficient dispute resolution, especially commercial dispute resolution, requires that, where possible, real and enforceable content be given to clauses as cll 35.11 and 35.12 to encourage approaches by, and attitudes of, parties conducive to the resolution of disputes without expensive litigation, arbitral or curial.[82]

2.53 Applying this reasoning to the case before him, Teare J concluded that an obligation to negotiate was sufficiently constrained and the court should seek to give effect to the parties' bargain. On the facts of the case, however, the obligation to have friendly discussions had been satisfied and the claimant had been entitled to commence arbitration. The challenge to an arbitral award was, therefore, dismissed.

Expert Determination

The Meaning and Function of Expert Determination

2.54 Expert determination is an institution of very long tradition in common law. Alongside mediation, it is one of the most popular ADR techniques. Expert determination based on an English law model was the prototype for contemporary solutions applied internationally in standard forms of contract.[83] Traditionally the main area of expert determination activity is construction contracts. Currently all disputes arising from construction contracts performed in the UK are subject to compulsory adjudication.[84] The uses of expert determination further include

[80] At [64].
[81] At [65].
[82] At [80].
[83] See 1.45ff.
[84] Under the Housing Grants, Construction and Regeneration Act 1996. On the development of expert determination in construction contracts see also M McGaw, 'Adjudicators, Experts and Keeping out of Court' (1992) 4 *Construction Law Journal* 332.

commodities contracts, mergers and acquisitions (M&A), financial transactions, and resource industry contracts.[85]

Initially, the expert's role was confined to valuation or determination of narrow technical issues under the contract.[86] The limited remit of the expert's activity did not require him to apply law or interpret the contract. Subsequently the scope of the experts' mandate was considerably expanded. Apart from issues that were traditionally subject to binding evaluation, more general clauses became commonplace. Such clauses provided for expert determination in relation to entire claims under a contract, rather than only specific technical matters. As a result, the role of the expert became a quasi-adjudicative one. In this model an expert applies law and interprets the contract like an adjudicator. As such expert determination resembles arbitration, although without procedural safeguards and the court's supervision.[87] Expert determination in multi-tiered dispute resolution mechanisms is a predominant feature of this modern formula, wherein an expert is appointed to adjudicate on entire claims between parties. **2.55**

As far as the binding force of an expert's decision is concerned, two models can be distinguished. In the first model expert determination is final and binding on the parties and the court adjudicating on a legal relationship between them. In this formula the parties agree that by contracting for expert determination they will be bound by the expert's decision and the court will not reanalyse the matter that was subject to the determination. This model of expert determination is usually utilised by parties requiring determination of a narrow technical issue. **2.56**

The second model was developed alongside the evolution of expert determination towards a fully fledged form of ADR. In this formula the expert's findings may be reviewed by a court or arbitral tribunal subsequently judging the dispute. Here the expert's decision is binding only temporarily, until it is verified by a court or in arbitration. Due to this feature, this model is commonly referred to as 'interim' or 'semi-binding' expert determination. If neither party questions the decision, it becomes final and binding.[88] If, however, the decision is challenged in a way prescribed in the contract, it is subject to review at subsequent stages of the dispute resolution process. The second model is inherently compatible with multi-tiered dispute resolution mechanisms. It is often connected with a time-bar for **2.57**

[85] Exhaustively on this issue J Kendall, C Freedman, J Farrell, *Expert Determination*, 5th edn (Sweet & Maxwell, 2015) para 4.1ff.

[86] The term 'expert determination' was used for the first time in *Bottomley v Ambler* (1876) 38 LT 545. On the development of expert determination in England: J Kendall, C Freedman, J Farrell, *Expert Determination*, n 85 above, para 1.1.5ff.

[87] The two methods are clearly distinguished. Expert determination is not governed by the Arbitration Act 1996. On this aspect see J Kendall, C Freedman, J Farrell, *Expert Determination*, n 85 above, ch 16; *Russell on Arbitation*, 23rd edn (Sweet & Maxwell, 2007) para 2-028; A Redfern, 'Experts and Arbitrators—an International Perspective' (2001) 4 *International Arbitration Law Review* 105, 106–7.

[88] As such it can be enforced by way of summary judgment under Pt 24 CPR.

questioning the expert's findings.[89] It is frequently used in construction contracts where an engineer's decision is reviewable in arbitral or court proceedings.[90]

2.58 For the sake of completeness it must be noted that English law developed a narrow catalogue of grounds for questioning final and binding determinations.[91] They are interpreted strictly and involve qualified violation of the procedure before an expert or abuse of power under the agreement.[92] In particular, the court may not deny the binding force of the decision if a party proves that the determination was erroneous or based on wrong premises.[93] An expert is not required to apply rules of procedural justice; hence the decision cannot be challenged on this ground.[94]

Enforceability of Expert Determination Clauses

Stay of the Proceedings

2.59 Under the House of Lords authority in *Channel Tunnel Group Ltd v Balfour Beatty Construction Ltd*,[95] the court will impose a stay on the proceedings brought in breach of an expert determination clause. In *Channel Tunnel* the Court analysed a two-tier dispute resolution procedure. It required an initial reference of the dispute to the 'Panel of Experts'. Either party dissatisfied with the decision of the Panel was then under a duty to notify the other party that the dispute would be referred to arbitration. All disputes in respect of which proper notice had been given were to be resolved under the ICC Rules of Arbitration.[96] The case came before the House of Lords concerning the award of an injunction. The plaintiffs commenced the proceedings when the defendants threatened to stop work over a controversy as to sums payable. An injunction was sought to stop the threat being carried out. The application was made straight to the Court, in breach of the stipulated procedure.

2.60 The House of Lords held that the English court had the power to stay the proceedings since the disputes between the parties were to be decided by a method

[89] See 2.72ff for details.

[90] See eg clause 19.2 of the Infrastructure Conditions of Contract (2014 Edition), on which S Furst, V Ramsey (eds), *Keating on Construction Contracts*, 10th edn (Sweet & Maxwell, 2016) para 21-212.

[91] See J Kendall, C Freedman, J Farrell, *Expert Determination*, n 85 above, ch 14 for a commentary.

[92] Potential grounds cover fraud, collusion or manifest lack of impartiality (*Campbell v Edwards* [1976] 1 WLR 403).

[93] *Campbell v Edwards* [1976] 1 WLR 403; *Toepfer v Continental Grain Co* [1974] 1 Lloyd's Rep 1; *Jones v Sherwood Computer Services* [1992] 1 WLR 277; *Nikko Hotels v MEPC Ltd* [1991] 2 EGLR 103; *Owen Pell Ltd v Bindi (London) Ltd* [2008] EWHC 1420 (TCC).

[94] On this aspect see J Kendall, C Freedman, J Farrell, *Expert Determination*, n 85 above, para 16.8.5. S Furst, V Ramsey, *Keating on Construction Contracts*, n 90 above, para 21-210 with reference to the Infrastructure Conditions of Contract (2014 edition).

[95] *Channel Tunnel Group Ltd v Balfour Beatty Construction Ltd* [1993] AC 334 (HL).

[96] 'If any dispute or difference shall arise between the employer and the contractor during the progress of the works … [it] shall at the instance of either the employer or the contractor in the first place be referred … to be settled by a panel of three persons (acting as independent experts but not as arbitrators) … [If] either the employer or the contractor be dissatisfied with any unanimous decision of the [expert] panel … [that party] may … notify the other party … that the dispute or difference is to be referred to arbitration.'

other than litigation. The stay was available both under the court's inherent jurisdiction,[97] and under a statutory power.[98] This was so notwithstanding the fact that the first tier of the alternative method did not constitute arbitration.[99] Lord Mustill clearly stated that irrespective of whether a dispute resolution clause amounted to an 'arbitration agreement' for the purposes of, at that time, section 1 of the 1975 English Arbitration Act, the Court could stay the plaintiffs' attempt to litigate under its inherent power. Lord Mustill referred to the interests of the orderly regulation of commerce and said: 'those who make agreements for the resolution of disputes must show good reasons for departing from them.'[100] It was held that, having promised to take the controversies to the experts and, if necessary, to the arbitrators, the appellants should refer the dispute to the agreed bodies, instead of bypassing the stipulated procedure.

Undoubtedly, at the time when *Channel Tunnel* was decided, ADR did not benefit from so strong a statutory underpinning as arbitration did. Nevertheless, it became clear that an ADR clause is something more than an agreement to negotiate, something unknown to English law on the authority of the Court of Appeal in *Courtney*.[101] The effect of *Channel Tunnel* could be observed in *Cott UK v FE Barber*[102] where Judge Hegarty QC dealt with a breach of the clause providing for expert determination. Although he refused to grant a stay of the proceedings, he held that: **2.61**

> [I]n the light of the observations of Lord Mustill in the Channel Tunnel Group case, and in the light of the changing attitudes of our legal system, the court plainly has a jurisdiction to stay under its inherent jurisdiction, where the parties have chosen some alternative means of dispute resolution.[103]

By contrast to *Channel Tunnel*, the decision in *Amoco (UK) Exploration Co v Amerada Hess Ltd*[104] related to the traditional expert determination where an expert is appointed to determine a narrow issue under the contract. On the facts of the case the parties agreed to jointly develop an oil field. The agreement provided for a procedure for the appointment of committees to quantify their respective interests in this undertaking. Under the clause, 'unagreed elements' were to be referred to an expert whose decision would be binding. The parties stipulated that no legal proceedings would be brought 'in respect of any matters in dispute' which were referred to the expert. The controversy arose whether a technical issue in dispute fell within the expert determination clause and whether the court should stay the **2.62**

97 Section 49(3), Senior Courts Act 1981.

98 Under the currently applicable s 9(2), Arbitration Act 1996, it is unambiguously the case that the courts have statutory power to grant a stay of proceedings brought in breach of an arbitration clause if a party failed to fulfil its pre-arbitral ADR commitments.

99 Note the distinction between arbitration and expert determination, mentioned at 1.31–1.33.

100 [1993] AC 334 at 353.

101 *Courtney & Fairbairn v Tolaini Brothers (Hotels)* [1975] 1 WLR 297. On this case see 2.4.

102 *Cott UK Ltd v FE Barber Ltd* [1997] 3 All ER 540 (QB). On this case see also at 2.64–2.65.

103 Judge Hegarty QC, *ibid*, at 548.

104 *Amoco (UK) Exploration Co v Amerada Hess Ltd* [1994] 1 Lloyd's Rep 33.

proceedings to allow an expert to determine the technical question. Notwithstanding the narrower mandate of an expert, Morritt J followed the decision in *Channel Tunnel* and stayed the proceedings for the agreed process to be exhausted.

2.63 The court's discretionary power to stay proceedings brought in breach of an ADR clause is derived from section 49(3) of the Senior Courts Act 1981. It follows that the court does not stay the proceedings automatically, and can take into consideration the reasons why the proceedings should be continued despite violation of an expert determination clause. The reasons for refusal of the stay constitute the circumstances in which an expert determination clause may be ineffective under English law. As the decision on the stay of the proceedings is made at the court's discretion, the court will determine this issue on a case-by-case basis.

2.64 In *Cott v Barber*[105] Judge Hegarty QC refused to stay the proceedings, concluding that the clause in question was badly drafted and the agreed procedure too imprecise to be binding. The case arose over the parties' obligations under a contract concerning the packaging of soft drinks. The dispute resolution clause provided that all disputes arising from the construction or performance of the agreement were to be referred for a decision by a person appointed by the Director General of the British Soft Drinks Association who 'shall be an independent consultant and shall act as an expert and not as an arbiter and his decision shall be final and binding on the parties'. The party bringing the claim referred the matter to the Director General, who appointed a particular person to act as an expert. The person appointed had experience of the soft drinks industry, but not of dispute resolution.

2.65 Refusing to grant a stay, Judge Hegarty QC confirmed that the court had inherent jurisdiction to stay the proceedings brought in breach of a binding expert determination clause. According to the judge the burden is on the person opposing the clause to show grounds for refusal. As grounds for refusal in this particular case Judge Hegarty QC considered the lack of experience of dispute resolution of the person appointed to act as an expert. The judge also took into account that the clause in question provided no rules or principles to guide an expert through the dispute resolution process. It was held that enforcing the clause would delay the resolution of the dispute rather than provide a fast and cheap method of conflict avoidance.

2.66 Similar policy considerations were examined in *Thames Valley Power Ltd v Total Gas & Power Ltd*,[106] where Clarke J refused to stay the proceedings brought in breach of an expert determination clause. On the facts of the case the parties were fully prepared to have the case heard in court in terms of evidence and submissions. A plea of non-compliance with an expert determination clause was raised only 'out of caution'. In these circumstances staying the proceedings and referring

[105] [1997] 3 All ER 540 (QB).

[106] *Thames Valley Power Ltd v Total Gas & Power Ltd* [2005] EWHC 2208 (Comm).

the parties to expert determination seemed an unnecessary duplication of costs and time, considering that the case would need to be prepared anew.

Other grounds on which the proceedings will not be stayed notwithstanding the breach of an expert determination clause include reasons affecting the validity of the clause under contract law rules. In particular, an expert determination clause may be considered invalid under the consumer protection laws if the clause incorporated into an agreement was imposed on a consumer, is onerous, or detrimentally affects the balance of a consumer's interest.[107] **2.67**

Damages

As an expert determination clause is equivalent to all other terms of a contract, the violation of such clauses may result in liability for damages. This remedy was considered by the Court of Appeal in *Sunrock Aircraft Corp Ltd v Scandinavian Airlines System Denmark–Norway–Sweden.*[108] Thomas LJ began with restating that it is an established rule of English law that damages can be awarded for a loss incurred due to the failure to comply with the terms of an alternative dispute resolution clause.[109] Notwithstanding this statement of principle, the judge refused to award damages on the facts in question. The damages sought comprised costs to repair an aircraft. On the evidence, however, it was clear that it would have been unreasonable to effect the repairs and that the alleged damage had no effect on the value of the aircraft. It followed that, on the evidence before the court, the damages, to which the claimant was entitled, were nominal damages as no loss was suffered. **2.68**

The claimant argued that it was nonetheless entitled to damages for breach of the agreement to refer the matter for expert determination. The amount of the damages claimed was the cost of the repairs as that was the amount the expert would have awarded had the claim been presented to him. The judge refused to award such damages. It was assumed that the expert would have approached the issue of damages for breach of the repair obligation in the same way as the court, applying the established principles of law.[110] Furthermore, there was no suggestion that the evidence available to the expert would be any different to that adduced before the court. The claimant's argument that the decision reached by an expert would have been more favourable to him was, therefore, rejected. **2.69**

The decision in *Sunrock* confirms that damages for breach of expert determination clauses are theoretically available under English law. It illustrates, however, the **2.70**

[107] *Picardi (t/a Picardi Architects) v Cuniberti* [2002] EWHC 2923 (TCC) under then applicable Reg 5(1) and Sch 2, Unfair Terms in Consumer Contract Regulations 1999 and Art 3(1), Unfair Contract Terms Directive 93/12.

[108] *Sunrock Aircraft Corp Ltd v Scandinavian Airlines System Denmark–Norway–Sweden* [2007] Lloyd's Rep 612.

[109] *ibid* at [37].

[110] The judge observed that the outcome could be different if an expert was empowered to make the determination *ex aequo et bono*, rather than on a basis of applicable law (cf s 46(1)(b), Arbitration Act 1996 providing for this power in arbitration).

difficulty in quantifying the amount of compensation. It appears that the special nature of expert determination, resulting from the fact that an expert resolves a dispute pursuant to a simplified and confidential procedure, is irrelevant for contractual liability. In *Sunrock* the argument that an expert would resolve the matter otherwise than the court did not establish any basis for claiming compensation due to the omission of the agreed procedure.[111]

Dismissal of a Claim

2.71 The parties can contractually modify the consequences of non-compliance with expert determination clauses. In practice, the stipulations of this kind are commonly contained in construction contracts, where submission of a dispute to an engineer or an architect is treated as a condition precedent.[112] Frequently such clauses contain a time-bar for notification of a dispute to an expert. This aspect will be analysed further below.

Contractual Time-bar in Multi-tiered Dispute Resolution Clauses

2.72 Provisions to the effect that certain steps must be performed in the specified time, or otherwise the claim will be time-barred are common in multi-tiered dispute resolution mechanisms. Integrating a time-bar into a dispute resolution clause is valid under English law.[113] The prototype of such contractual arrangements is the following 'Centrocon' arbitration clause:[114] 'Any claim must be made in writing and claimant's arbitrator appointed within three months of final discharge, and where this provision is not complied with the claim shall be deemed to be waived and absolutely barred.'

[111] See the comments in D Joseph, *Jurisdiction and Arbitration Agreements and their Enforcement*, n 49 above, para 14.15; J Bailey, *Construction Law*, n 59 above, para 23.39.

[112] See eg clause 66(A) ICE (7th edn 1999). See also *Lubenham Fidelities and Investment Co Ltd v South Pembrokeshire District Council* (1986) 33 BLR 39, 55 (May LJ); *Bernhard's Rugby Landscapes Ltd v Stockley Park Consortium* (1998) 14 *Construction Law Journal* 329, 349; *Gillatt v Sky Television Ltd* 2000 WL 453 and a commentary by J Kendall, C Freedman, J Farrell, Expert Determination, n 85 above, para 7.2.9; S Furst, V Ramsey, *Keating on Construction Contracts* paras 5-023–25; J Bailey, Construction Law, n 59 above, 6.252–6.254.

[113] Note that J Lew, L Mistelis, S Kröll, *Comparative International Commercial Arbitration* (Kluwer Law International, 2003) paras 20-10ff refer solely to English law when examining time-bar in arbitration clauses.

[114] *Williams and Mordey v WH Muller & Co (London) Ltd* (1924) 18 Lloyd's Rep 50 (KB). On Centrocon clauses see further M Mustill and S Boyd, *Commercial Arbitration*, 2nd edn (Butterworths, 1989) 201–2. Clauses based on the Centrocon framework are applied in time charter contracts, consecutive voyage charter contracts or bills of lading. Contractual time-bars connected with the institution of arbitral proceedings are also provided for by arbitration rules of certain institutions dealing with sea arbitration or commodity arbitration, such as GAFTA and FOSFA. See further J Lew, L Mistelis, S Kröll, *Comparative International Commercial Arbitration*, n 113 above, para 20–13.

The contractual time-bar within arbitration clauses has been subject to statutory regulation in English arbitration law since 1934.[115] Since then, consecutive arbitration acts have contained a regulation enabling the court to extend a contractual time-limit upon an application of a party.[116] At present, time-bar provisions are commonly used in multi-tiered dispute resolution clauses providing for mandatory ADR steps before bringing an action in arbitration. Clauses of this type can be formulated in various ways regarding both the step to be completed and the effect of the stipulated time-limit lapsing. They are most frequently utilised in construction contracts.[117] **2.73**

Bar to the Right and Bar to the Remedy

English courts distinguish between two types of contractual time-bar.[118] The first operates in the same way as a statutory time-bar. Failure to perform a stipulated step within the agreed time-scale extinguishes the claim. It does not affect the right to have the case heard in arbitration. When a claimant raises an extinguished claim in arbitration the tribunal must dismiss it as time-barred.[119] This type of time-bar provision is contained in construction contracts in which a dispute resolution clause requires a party to notify an engineer or an architect of a claim within a specified time. Failure to perform this step results in losing the claim entirely.[120] **2.74**

The second type of contractual time-bar defeats the right to have the claims heard in arbitration. This category of clauses requires a party to perform certain steps in a timely manner in order to enforce its claims in arbitration. By contrast to the first type of a time-bar, this provision does not extinguish the claim itself but rather the right to obtain a remedy in arbitration. Lapse of a contractual time-limit removes jurisdiction of the tribunal to hear a claim. In consequence, the party may raise the claim in court.[121] Conversely, if the tribunal proceeds to hear the case notwithstanding that the parties' right to have the claim heard in arbitration is time-barred, an arbitral award given in such circumstances can be challenged, or its enforcement refused, on jurisdictional grounds.[122] In construction contracts the second type of contractual time-bar commonly relates to taking the step of challenging a decision obtained at an earlier stage of the dispute resolution process.[123] **2.75**

[115] The Arbitration Act 1930 was the first statutory act in which the court's power to extend contractual time limits was provided for.

[116] The current regulation is contained in s 12, Arbitration Act 1996 on which 2.79ff.

[117] J Bailey, *Construction Law*, n 59 above, paras 6.286ff; J Jenkins, *Construction Law Arbitration*, 2nd edn (Wolters Kluwer, 2014) 87–88; A Tweeddale, K Tweeddale, 'Commencement of Arbitration and Time-Bar Clauses' (2009) 75 *Arbitration* 480. See also 1.45 and 1.51 (FIDIC) and 1.59 (NEC3).

[118] M Mustill and S Boyd, *Commercial Arbitration*, n 114 above, 202–4.

[119] *Smeaton Hanscomb & Co v Sassoon I Setty Son & Co (No 1)* [1953] 2 Lloyd's Rep 580.

[120] See eg clauses 61.3 NEC3; 20.1 FIDIC ('New Book')); 67.1 FIDIC ('Old Book').

[121] *Pinnock Bros v Lewis & Peat Ltd* [1923] 1 KB 690; *Indian Oil Corporation v Vanol Inc* [1992] 2 Lloyd's Rep 563. See also R Merkin, L Flannery, *Arbitration Law* (LLP, 2004) para 13.23.

[122] *Ayscough v Sheed, Thomson & Co Ltd* (1924) 19 Lloyd's Rep 104.

[123] See eg clauses 20.4 FIDIC ('New Book'); 66.9(b) ICE Conditions of Contract (7th edn); 93.1 ECC (Engineering and Construction Contract, 2nd edn).

In particular, it may relate to notifying the other party of dissatisfaction with the decision of a dispute board.

2.76 It must be noted that a time-limit whose expiry results in the loss of a right to have claims heard in arbitration typically carries further consequences when contained in multi-tiered clauses. A bar to challenging an expert's decision issued at an earlier stage of the dispute resolution process is usually connected with the decision becoming final and binding. In such cases the right to have claims heard in arbitration is related to the ability to obtain a full review of the expert's findings.[124] It follows that if the second type of time-bar is not observed, a party can only bring a claim in court, rather than arbitration, but the expert's decision will not be reviewed as it became final and binding with the expiry of the contractual period.

2.77 Determining what type of contractual time-bar the parties incorporated into their dispute resolution clause is a matter of construction. If the clause does not provide a clear indication regarding this matter, the courts would lean towards interpreting it as barring the entire claim rather than only extinguishing a right to pursue the claim in arbitration.[125] The rationale for this approach is that, in the absence of clear wording, it is more likely that the parties intended to bar the entire claim rather than merely barring the right to have it heard by an arbitral tribunal, while leaving the litigation option open.

2.78 A forum competent to adjudicate on the effects of both types of time-bar provision is the arbitral tribunal.[126] In the first type of contractual time-bar, arbitrators are empowered to adjudicate on the merits of the case and decide whether to dismiss the claim as time-barred.[127] In the second category of time-bar the arbitrators adjudicate on their own jurisdiction in accordance with the *Kompetenz-Kompetenz* principle.[128]

Extension of Time

2.79 The consequences of failing to observe a contractual time-bar may be severe for the party in default. In the first type of a time-bar, it is the complete loss of the claim. In the second type of a time-bar access to arbitration is precluded, often with the consequence that the determination obtained at an earlier stage of the dispute resolution procedure becomes final. A relief from these consequences of a

[124] See eg Clause 20.4 FIDIC on which 1.51 and 5.46–5.49.

[125] *Metalimex Foreign Trade Corporation v Eugenie Maritime Co Ltd* [1962] 1 Lloyd's Rep 378; *Intermare Transport GmbH v Naves Transoceanicas Armadora SA, The Aristokratis* [1976] 1 Lloyd's Rep 552; *Evgeros Naftiki Eteria v Cargill plc, The Voltaz* [1997] 1 Lloyd's Rep 35; *Metalfer Corporation v Pan Ocean Shipping Co Ltd* [1998] 2 Lloyd's Rep 632.

[126] *Legis AB v Berg & Sons* [1964] 1 Lloyd's Rep 203.

[127] *Smeaton Hanscomb & Co Ltd v Sassoon I Setty Son & Co (No 1)* [1953] 2 Lloyd's Rep 580.

[128] Section 30, Arbitration Act 1996. See also R Merkin, L Flannery, *Arbitration Law*, n 121 above, para 13.19.

time-bar is provided under section 12 of the Arbitration Act 1996 which prescribes the power of the court to extend a contractually agreed time-limit.[129]

Section 12(1) of the Arbitration Act 1996 sets forth that **2.80**

> Where an arbitration agreement ... provides that a claim shall be barred, or the claimant's right extinguished, unless the claimant takes, within a time fixed by the agreement, some step
>
> (a) to begin arbitral proceedings, or
> (b) to begin other dispute resolution procedures which must be exhausted before arbitral proceedings can be begun,
>
> the court may by order extend the time for taking that step.

The court may extend the time for such a period and on such terms as it thinks fit, but will only do so **2.81**

> 'if satisfied that:
>
> (a) the circumstances are such as were outside the reasonable contemplation of the parties when they agreed the provision in question, and that it would be just to extend the time, or
> (b) that [sic] the conduct of one party makes it unjust to hold the other party to the strict terms of the provision in question'.

The instrument set out by section 12 of the Arbitration Act 1996 may be used by parties to an arbitration clause only after a claim has arisen, whether or not the contractual time has expired. The court's decision under section 12 can be appealed with the leave of the court in accordance with general rules.[130] **2.82**

It must be noted that section 12 of the Arbitration Act 1996 provides a relief from both types of contractual time-bar provisions. The regulation states that the time-limit can be extended in case of both a time-bar extinguishing an entire claim and a time-bar merely restricting the claimant's right to arbitrate. Furthermore, section 12(1)(b) of the Act expressly acknowledges that a time-bar, and the court's power to extend the agreed time-limit, may relate to an ADR procedure other than arbitration. This aspect is of particular importance to parties of multi-tiered dispute resolution clauses. **2.83**

It is suggested in the literature that an extension of time to commence arbitration under section 12(1)(a) of the Arbitration Act 1996 has no impact on the substantive rights and obligations of the parties which have been transformed as a result of **2.84**

[129] See M Mustill and S Boyd, *Commercial Arbitration*, n 114 above, 207ff for comments on other instances of relief from contractual time-bar.

[130] See R Merkin, L Flannery, *Arbitration Law*, n 121 above, paras 13.35–13.57; R Merkin, L Flannery, *Arbitration Act 1996* (Informa, 2008) 44–48; M Mustill and S Boyd, *Commercial Arbitration. 2001 Companion Volume to the Second Edition* (Butterworths, 2001) 407–9; A McGee, *Limitation Periods*, 7th edn (Sweet & Maxwell, 2014) paras 16.022ff for commentary.

expiry of the agreed time-limit.[131] Thus, if a multi-tiered clause provides that with the expiry of a relevant time the party is no longer allowed to commence arbitration *and* an earlier expert's decision becomes final and binding, the extension of time by the court affects only the permissibility of beginning arbitral proceedings. According to this view, section 12(1)(a) of the Arbitration Act 1996 empowers the court to extend the time to commence arbitration but it does not grant the power to review the decision that became final and binding. If follows that in such a case an extension of time will only affect the forum which would confirm the binding force of an expert's decision. If the extension is granted, it is an arbitral tribunal which will be competent to adjudicate on this matter. If the extension is refused, the competence will remain with the court.

Summary

2.85 The consequences of non-compliance with multi-step dispute resolution clauses are precisely defined under English law. The courts enforce clauses providing for both mediation and quasi-adjudicative ADR methods such as expert determination or dispute boards. The latter were found enforceable earlier than mediation. Currently both types of clauses are recognised by English courts as giving rise to enforceable obligations.

2.86 The main remedy for breach of both types of clauses is stay of the proceedings. The basis of the stay is discretionary. As far as other remedies are concerned, the courts mention injunction to restrain proceedings brought in breach of an ADR clause and damages. The latter remedy poses significant difficulties in quantifying the extent of the loss resulting from breach of a particular ADR commitment.

2.87 The English judiciary traditionally puts a particular emphasis on the preciseness of the agreed dispute resolution procedure. In the most recent case law, however, the judges depart from the very high standard of preciseness developed in relation to mediation clauses by the English courts after the ruling in *Cable & Wireless v IBM*.[132] The enforceability of ADR clauses that have provided a sufficiently detailed ADR procedure may be refused only in exceptional cases.

Germany

2.88 In Germany mediation and expert determination developed within significantly different normative backgrounds. Influenced by the global trend to institutionalise

[131] R Merkin, L Flannery, *Arbitration Law*, n 121 above, para 13.46 and the authority cited. The author observes that this position is not adopted uniformly by the English courts and cites *McLaughlin & Harvey v P&O Developments* (1992) 55 BLR 101 where the court extended the time limit for commencing arbitration to challenge the final certificate issued by an architect under the JCT Forms of Contract. The extension of time in this case opened the way to review the architect's findings.

[132] *Cable & Wireless v IBM* [2002] CLC 1319 (Com Ct).

consensual ADR, mediation enjoyed increasing attention from the legislature and became the most codified of all methods in the German ADR landscape. By contrast, expert determination is not expressly regulated by statute and is construed under the provisions of the German Civil Code (BGB).[133] Importantly, the enforceability of both types of ADR clauses has been the subject of judicial interpretation, not statutory regulation. The jurisprudence of the *Bundesgerichtshof* and lower courts brought about an exhaustive framework for the enforceability of ADR clauses notwithstanding a lack of codified remedies.

Mediation

Mediation in German Procedural Law

Mediation in Germany[134] is codified in a separate statute (*Mediationgesetz*, 2012).[135] The act regulates fundamental matters regarding the mediation process, including: the mediator's duties and the conduct of mediation proceedings (§ 2); impartiality of the mediator (§ 3); confidentiality (§ 4) and the necessary qualifications of the mediator (§§ 5 and 6). Furthermore, the act modifies provisions of the German Civil Procedure Code[136] relating to mediation in the course of court proceedings. In particular, *Mediationgesetz* introduces § 278a ZPO prescribing the inherent jurisdiction of the court to refer the parties to mediation or other forms of alternative dispute resolution. Under this provision the court may stay proceedings for the duration of the referral. **2.89**

The framework within which mediation takes place is supplemented by the rules of various ADR and arbitration centres whose seats are in Germany. The leading institutions include DIS (*Deutsche Institution für Schiedsgerichtsbarkeit eV*) and EUCON (*Europäisches Institut für Conflict Management eV*).[137] The rules of institutionalised ADR providers are of a contractual nature—they apply if the parties opt for mediation administered by such a centre. They contain detailed provisions governing mediation procedure, the duties of a mediator, and duties of the parties in the course of mediation. They are typically silent on the interplay between mediation and litigation or arbitration. **2.90**

Commentators observe that contracting for mediation in advance of a dispute is not very common in Germany, notwithstanding ADR being recognised as **2.91**

[133] *Bürgerliches Gesetzbuch*, hereafter also 'BGB'.

[134] For the definition of mediation see J Risse, *Wirtschaftsmediation* (CH Beck, 2003) 5.

[135] *Gesetz zur Förderung der Mediation und anderer Verfahren der außergerichtlichen Konfliktbeilegung* vom 21.07.2012, BGBl. I S. 1577. The act implements Directive 2008/52/EC of the European Parliament and of the Council of 21 May 2008 on certain aspects of mediation in civil and commercial matters, [2008] OJ L136/3–8, 24/05/2008.

[136] *Zivilprozessordnung*, hereafter also 'ZPO'.

[137] *DIS-Mediationsordnung* and *EUCON Verfahrensordnung* respectively.

potentially useful in commerce.[138] Despite the advancing institutionalisation of mediation, the status of mediation clauses is not clearly defined in statutes.[139] In the absence of statutory sources, many aspects of mediation agreements have been clarified by jurisprudence. It is now a commonplace that the core element of contracts for consensual ADR is the parties' duty to appoint an impartial mediator. It must also be possible to infer that the parties agree to a voluntary process in which the mediator is not empowered to issue binding decisions.[140] Mediation clauses can be concluded by reference to the standard forms of contract if incorporated in accordance with § 305ff BGB.[141]

2.92 Importantly, neither *Mediationgesetz*, nor ZPO regulates the consequences of non-compliance with mediation clauses. Equally, the rules of the institutionalised ADR centres are silent in this matter. In consequence, the enforceability of mediation clauses under German law remains a domain of jurisprudence. The sanctions for premature filing of claims in breach of an agreed ADR process have been devised exclusively by the German courts.

Non-compliance with Mediation Clauses: Procedural Consequences

2.93 German jurisprudence treats the nature of a mediation clause as a starting point in determining the consequences of failure to adhere to an agreed ADR process. The sanction for a breach depends on whether a mediation clause is treated as a procedural or substantive contract. This distinction is well established for arbitration and jurisdiction agreements. Since this is relevant in the present context, it is worth reporting the main views expressed on this matter.

2.94 According to the first standpoint arbitration clauses are of a substantive nature and should be subjected to the rules of contract law.[142] This view was initially supported by a number of judicial decisions, according to which arbitration agreements should be governed by the provisions of BGB.[143] Identification of substantive

[138] P Tochtermann, in K Hopt, F Steffek (eds), *Mediation. Principles and Regulation in Comparative Perspective* (OUP, 2013) 538.

[139] Both *ZPO* and *Mediationgesetz* are silent as to the form or the minimum content of valid mediation clauses; cf § 1031, ZPO concerning arbitration clauses.

[140] Exhaustively on the form of content of mediation clauses see P Tochtermann, *Die Unabhängigkeit und Unparteilichkeit des Mediators* (Mohr Siebeck, 2008) 126ff; F Friedrich, 'Schlichtungs- und Mediationsklauseln in Allgemeinen Geschäftsbedingungen' (2007) 1 *SchiedsVZ* 31, 32–33.

[141] On this aspect H Eidenmüller, 'Vertrags- und verfahrensrechtliche Grundfragen der Mediation: Möglichkeiten und Grenzen privatautonomen Konfliktmanagements' in Breidenbach et al (eds), *Konsensuale Streitbeilegung: akademisches Symposion zu Ehren von Peter F. Schlosser aus Anlass seines 65. Geburtstages* (Gieseking, 2001) 58ff. See also F Friedrich, 'Schlichtungs- und Mediationsklauseln in Allgemeinen Geschäftsbedingungen', n 140 above, 31ff; P Tochtermann, 'Mediationklauseln Teil I. Mediationklauseln in Allgemeinen Geschäftsbedingungen' (2008) 2 *Zeitschrift für Konfliktmanagement* 57ff.

[142] P Hartmann, in A Baumbach, W Lauterbach, J Albers, P Hartmann (eds), *Zivilprozessordnung mit FamFG, GVG und anderen Nebengesetzen*, 74th edn (CH Beck, 2016) p 2737, para 16 ad Grundz § 1025 ZPO.

[143] BGH NJW 1957, 589; BGH NJW 1964, 591.

elements in contracts for dispute resolution was particularly relevant for a second point of view. According to this view arbitration clauses are of a mixed nature, displaying both contractual (ie substantive) and procedural features.[144] The third view focuses on the purely procedural aspects of dispute resolution clauses.[145]

The debate as to the nature of dispute resolution clauses extends to mediation agreements. Some commentators support a stance that such contractual stipulations are of an exclusively procedural nature.[146] An alternative view suggests that mediation clauses are substantive contracts akin to partnership agreements. Under this interpretation the duty to attempt amicable settlement cognates with the parties' obligation to promote a common purpose (§ 705 BGB).[147] It has also been claimed that mediation clauses are agreements *sui generis*, involving a continuous and atypical performance.[148] **2.95**

The German judiciary rarely undertakes theoretical analysis of the substantive components of mediation agreements.[149] Judgments dealing with the enforceability of mediation clauses are focused on the purely procedural consequences of non-compliance with the agreed pre-action procedure.[150] Contractual liability and substantive remedies for breach of mediation clauses, if identified at all, are considered peripheral.[151] **2.96**

The leading judgment dealing with the consequences of non-compliance with conciliation clauses is the *Bundesgerichtshof* decision of 23 November 1983.[152] The clause in question was contained in a contract concerning the take-over of a veterinary practice. It provided that in the event of a dispute the parties would first exhaust a conciliation procedure to be held before the competent veterinary chamber.[153] The claimant bypassed the agreed procedure and filed the claim in court. In response, the defendant argued that the claim was inadmissible until the **2.97**

144 W Voit, in H-J Musielak, W Voit (eds), *Zivilprozessordnung mit Gerichtsverfassungsgesetz*, 13th edn (Vahlen, 2016) p 2603, para 3 ad § 1029 ZPO; K Lionnet, *Handbuch der internationalen und nationalen Schiedsgerichtsbarkeit*, 3rd edn (Boorberg, 2005) 180. J-P Lachmann, *Handbuch für die Schiedsgerichtspraxis*, 3rd edn (Schmidt, 2008) 74.

145 G Wagner, *Prozessverträge—Privatautonomie im Verfahrensrecht* (Mohr Siebeck, 1998) 578–82; KH Schwab, G Walter, *Schiedsgerichtsbarkeit*, 7th edn (CH Beck, 2005) 65–66.

146 B Hess, 'Rechtsgrundlagen Mediation' in F Haft, K von Schlieffen (eds), *Handbuch Mediation. Verhandlungstechnik, Strategien, Einsatzgebiete*, 2nd edn (CH Beck, 2010) 1062ff.

147 A Hunter, *Das Internationale Privat- und Verfahrensrecht der Wirtschaftsmediation* (Mohr Siebeck, 2005) 38ff and the literature cited; A Hunter, 'Die Mediationsvereinbarung—Regelungsgegenstände und vertragrechtliche Qualifizierung' (2003) 5 *SchiedsVZ* 226, 229ff.

148 H Eidenmüller, *Vertrags- und Verfahrensrecht der Wirtschaftsmediation* (Schmidt, 2001) 23.

149 See eg BGH, NJW 1999, 647.

150 See 2.97ff below.

151 On this aspect 2.111–2.115.

152 BGH NJW 1984, 669. Although the case concerned conciliation, it was consistently followed by courts and is relevant for the enforceability of modern mediation clauses, see J Risse, *Wirtschaftsmediation*, n 134 above, 98ff and 2.105ff.

153 'Bei Unstimmigkeiten zwischen den Vertragspartnern oder bei Auseinandersetzungen über die Auslegung der Vertragsvorschriften soll in jedem Fall zunächst die für den Sitz der Praxis zuständige Landestierärztekammer Niedersachsen Hannover als Schlichtungsinstanz angerufen werden.'

agreed conciliation procedure had been attempted before the competent veterinary chamber in Hannover. The claimant did not contest the fact that no such an attempt had been made.

2.98 The defence was rejected at first instance. The court regarded the claim as admissible and proceeded to judgment on the merits. The court declared that the clause requiring the parties to undergo pre-action conciliation was merely an expression of intention by the parties, devoid of any binding force. The defendant repeated his plea of inadmissibility in the appeal. The appeal succeeded in the *Bundesgerichtshof*, which overturned the decision of the lower court and enforced the conciliation clause.

2.99 The *Bundesgerichtshof* begun by explaining that the clause in question was not an arbitration clause as defined in § 1025 ZPO. According to the contract the regional veterinary chamber was not acting as an adjudicator but rather as a mediator assisting the parties toward an amicable resolution of the dispute. The court pointed out that the chamber had no decision-making powers and its function was solely facilitative.

2.100 On this basis the court analysed the enforceability of the conciliation agreement and concluded that the conciliation clause was imperative (*Mußbestimmung*). This was despite the permissive language of the provision, which stipulated that the dispute *should* be submitted to the competent chamber for conciliation. The court construed that the parties' intention was to be bound by the ADR procedure, from the wording of the clause, which stipulated that the conciliation should take place 'in every event' (*in jedem Fall*). According to the court the mandatory character of the clause was supported by its purpose. The ADR procedure was part of the standard conditions of contract issued by the veterinary chamber with a view to keeping the disputes between its members out of court. It was also in the interest of the members to have an opportunity to resolve their disputes within the framework of the relevant chamber, ie cheaply and confidentially. Having regard to those reasons, the court concluded that exhausting the agreed procedure was a necessary condition of bringing the claim in court.

2.101 Having confirmed the binding force of the conciliation clause, the *Bundesgerichtshof* continued to analyse the consequences of non-compliance with the agreed ADR procedure. The court referred to the judgment of *Oberlandesgericht (OLG) Celle* of 31 July 1970,[154] where the sanctions for breach of conciliation clauses were ascertained. This case established that failure to attempt conciliation before filing the claim in court, excluded actionability of a claim (*Klagbarkeit*), understood as the ability to raise the claim in court. Actionability is excluded until conciliation is attempted in accordance with the contract. The court observed that under German law the parties can contractually agree that the ability to bring a claim in court will be conditional or temporarily excluded. In particular, raising the claim

[154] OLG Celle NJW 1971, 288.

in court can be conditional upon fulfilling certain steps prior to the commencement of litigation. Lack of actionability results in the claim being inadmissible (*unzulässig*).

The *Bundesgerichtshof* followed the reasoning presented in the judgment of *OLG Celle* and applied the doctrine of actionability to conciliation clauses. It was held that until amicable settlement is attempted the claim has to be dismissed as inadmissible. The court clarified that lack of actionability excludes the public right to enforce the claim; it does not, however, affect the merits of the claim. For this reason, the claim in repect of which actionability is excluded has to be dismissed as inadmissible (*unzulässig*) and not as unfounded (*unbegründet*). The court held that exclusion of actionability through ADR agreements is permitted, and does not unduly restrict access to court.[155] **2.102**

Although the court underlined the difference between the conciliation clause in question on the one hand, and an arbitration clause governed by the provisions of ZPO on the other, it acknowledged that both types of clauses are enforced by the same procedural order. § 1032(1) ZPO provides that a claim filed in court in contravention of a valid arbitration agreement must be dismissed as inadmissible. The same sanction has been adopted for conciliation clauses albeit with a different reasoning.[156] **2.103**

The court's conclusion has been supported in the literature. Commentators agreed that parties may exclude actionability by contract and provide for a private dispute resolution mechanism that would precede court litigation.[157] An agreement resulting in exclusion of actionability is a procedural contract referred to as *pactum de non petendo* (also called *Stillhalteabkommen*). By concluding such an agreement the parties promise not to initiate court proceedings until they exhaust a prescribed out-of-court dispute resolution process.[158] Actionability of the claim is treated as a condition of admissibility of the proceedings (*Prozeßvoraussetzung*).[159] Failure to satisfy the condition results in the claim being dismissed as inadmissible **2.104**

155 Establishing the permissibility of such a stipulation the *Bundesgerichtshof* followed its earlier decision of 4 July 1977 (BGH, NJW 1977, 2263) and the above-mentioned decision of OLG Celle of 31 July 1970 (OLG Celle NJW 1971, 288). On this aspect also 2.137–2.142.

156 Subsequent judicial decisions adopted this analogy with arbitral proceedings, see eg BGH NJW 1999, 647.

157 A Hacke, *Der ADR-Vertrag. Vertragsrecht und verträgliche Gestaltung der Mediation und anderer alternativer Konfliktlösungsverfahren* (Recht und Wirtschaft, 2011) 116ff; G Wagner, Prozessverträge—Privatautonomie im Verfahrensrecht, n 145 above, 425ff; J Risse, Wirtschaftsmediation, n 134 above, 98ff; H Eidenmüller, 'Vertrags- und verfahrensrechtliche Grundfragen der Mediation', n 141 above, 12ff; A Loos, M Brewitz, 'Hindert eine Mediationsvereinbarung an der Klage?—Wie lange?' (2012) 6 *Schieds VZ* 305.

158 P Hartmann, in A Baumbach, W Lauterbach, J Albers, P Hartmann (eds), *Zivilprozessordnung mit FamFG, GVG und anderen Nebengesetzen*, 74th edn (CH Beck, 2016) p 2745, para 20 ad § 1029 ZPO; L Rosenberg, KH Schwab, P Gottwald, *Zivilprozeßrecht*, 17th edn (CH Beck, 2010) 1024. The term *pactum de non petendo* has also been adopted by the judiciary, see eg LG Münster DStRE 2001, 614.

159 Or *Verfahrensvoraussetzung* as in BayObLG NJW-RR 1996, 910 and LG Stralsund NZM 2003, 327.

via a procedural order (*Prozeßurteil*) which must be contrasted with *Sachurteil* relating to the merits of the claim.[160]

2.105 Subsequent cases supported the classification of ADR clauses as *pacta de non petendo* and confirmed the theoretical framework for the enforceability of conciliation clauses based on exclusion of actionability. In the decision of 18 November 1998[161] the *Bundesgerichtshof* analysed the consequences of the claimant's failure to adhere to the dispute resolution procedure requiring conciliation before the relevant body of the tax advisors' chamber. The court considered itself to be in the position to adjudicate upon factual and legal issues arising under the contract (including its validity) only after the conciliation attempt has been made and proved unsuccessful. The court compared the effects of conciliation clauses with those of arbitration agreements under § 1032(1) ZPO and concluded that in both cases bringing the proceedings in breach of a relevant clause results in dismissal of the claim as inadmissible.

2.106 The interpretation adopted by the *Bundesgerichtshof* has been followed by the lower courts and applied to dispute resolution mechanisms in their modern contractual form. In the decision of *Brandenburgisches OLG* of 18 September 1996[162] the court considered a multi-level ADR clause contained in a partnership agreement concluded between solicitors and tax advisors. The clause provided for negotiations, followed by conciliation before the relevant professional chamber.[163] The court considered the claim brought in breach of the contractual ADR mechanism to be temporarily inadmissible (*einstweilen unzulässig*). A similar conclusion was reached in a decision of 7 November 1997 by *OLG Frankfurt am Main*,[164] where the court analysed a conciliation clause contained in an agreement for sale of a tax advisor's practice.

2.107 Particular attention should be drawn to the decision of *LG Münster* of 21 December 2000.[165] Like the *Bundesgerichtshof* judgment of 18 November 1998, and the aforementioned decisions of *Brandenburgisches OLG*[166] and *OLG Frankfurt am Main*,[167] the case concerned conciliation duties before the tax advisors' chamber. The relevant clause, however, was contained in the tax advisors' rules regulating the conduct of the profession.[168] The court held that the status of the provision

[160] P Hartmann, in A Baumbach, W Lauterbach, J Albers, P Hartmann (eds), *Zivilprozessordnung mit FamFG, GVG und anderen Nebengesetzen*, 74th edn (CH Beck, 2016) p 2745, para 20 ad § 1029 ZPO; L Rosenberg, KH Schwab, P Gottwald, *Zivilprozeßrecht*, 17th edn (CH Beck, 2010) 1024.

[161] BGH NJW 1999, 647.

[162] Brandenburgisches OLG ANWBL 1998, 281.

[163] 'Bei allen Streitigkeiten aus diesem Vertrag soll eine gütliche Beilegung unter den Gesellschaftern angestrebt werden. Ist dies nicht erreichbar, wird der Präsident der Rechtsanwaltskammer bzw. der Steuerberaterkammer, um Vermittlung angegangen. Falls auch insoweit keine Einigung erzielbar ist, bleibt der ordentliche Rechtsweg bestehen.'

[164] OLG Frankfurt a.M. NJW-RR 1998, 778.

[165] LG Münster DStRE 2001, 614.

[166] Brandenburgisches OLG ANWBL 1998, 281.

[167] OLG Frankfurt a.M. NJW-RR 1998, 778.

[168] § 31(4) *Berufsordnung der Bundes-Steuerberaterkammer* (BOStB).

requiring the parties to exhaust certain ADR steps before filing a claim in court is of no relevance for the enforceability of the parties' commitment to attempt amicable settlement. The court equated ADR clauses provided for in the rules of professional organisations with conciliation clauses of a purely contractual nature. The clause in question was treated as an agreement suspending the ability to bring claims in court (*pactum de non petendo*), and the proceedings that had been initiated prematurely were ruled temporarily inadmissible (*derzeit nicht zulässig*).

A noteworthy terminology relating to the enforceability of ADR clauses was adopted in the judgment of the Bavarian Supreme Regional Court (*BayObLG*) of 16 November 1995.[169] On the facts of the case the court considered a conciliation clause contained in the constitution of a housing cooperative. The clause provided that disputes between the members of the cooperative in relation to their property rights would first be submitted to the board of the cooperative whose duty was to facilitate an amicable settlement.[170] The court held that such a provision constituted a valid condition of proceedings (*Verfahrensvoraussetzung*), requiring the parties to exhaust the ADR process as a first step. The court observed that by undertaking conciliation commitments the parties created a temporal constraint on the proceedings (*Verfahrenshindernis*).[171] Fulfilment of a conciliation attempt has been described as a pre-process (*Vorschaltverfahren*) and been treated as a necessary condition for the adjudication of claim on the merits. Consequently, premature claims have been declared inadmissible until the relevant attempt has been made. **2.108**

A similar clause in the constitution of a housing cooperative was considered in the decision of *LG Stralsund* of 6 December 2001.[172] The court confirmed that enforceable conciliation commitments may stem from sources other than a contract. The court clarified that this not strictly contractual source of ADR duties does not affect the enforceability of ADR commitments. The court also clarified that ZPO's requirements as to the form of arbitration clauses do not apply to conciliation clauses. **2.109**

The discussion reported so far has concerned the enforceability of conciliation clauses in litigation. According to scholarly opinion the same reasoning should be applied in the context of arbitration under German law.[173] Consequently, any premature action brought in contravention to pre-arbitral ADR procedure should **2.110**

[169] BayObLG NJW-RR 1996, 910.

[170] 'Streitigkeiten zwischen den Wohnungseigentümern, das Wohnungseigentum betreffend, sind vor der Einleitung gerichtlicher Schritte dem Verwaltungsbeirat vorzutragen. Dieser ist verpflichtet, auf eine gütliche Einigung hinzuwirken.'

[171] cf the term 'an obstacle to action' (*Anfechtungshindernis*) used by LG Stralsund NZM 2003, 327.

[172] LG Stralsund NZM 2003, 327.

[173] P Tochtermann, in K Hopt, F Steffek (eds), *Mediation. Principles and Regulation in Comparative Perspectives*, n 138 above, 541; K Böckstiegel, S Kröll, P Nacimiento, *Arbitration in Germany*, n 194 above, 59. See also: KP Berger, 'Law and Practice of Escalation Clauses' (2006) 1 *Arbitration International* 1, 6; A Jolles, 'Consequences of Multi-Tier Arbitration Clauses: Issues of Enforcement' (2006) 72 *Arbitration* 329, 332.

be declared as inadmissible by an arbitration tribunal. This was confirmed in a decisionof *OLG Frankfurt am Main*,[174] where the court held that if conciliation is an element of a dispute resolution mechanism containing an arbitration clause, a conciliation attempt should precede arbitration in the same way as would be the case in litigation.

Non-compliance with Mediation Clauses: Substantive Consequences

2.111 Contractual remedies for non-compliance with mediation clauses are only available if one assumes that such clauses are contracts governed by substantive law. This assumption has been adopted by those authors who accept that ADR clauses are of a substantive or mixed (procedural and substantive) nature. Discussion in this area largely reflects the spectrum of views expressed in relation to the character of arbitration and jurisdiction clauses.[175]

2.112 It has been suggested that a party pleading non-compliance with a conciliation clause may request specific performance of the contractual duty.[176] An order of specific performance should require the other party to take part in the agreed procedure. The difficulty with this interpretation lies in the precise delineation of the scope of the duty to undergo the agreed ADR process. Participation in mediation is an inherently voluntary exercise requiring cooperation between the parties. As it is impossible to force the party to negotiate, this view was never widely taken up in the literature. Similarly, the judiciary rejected orders for specific performance as a remedy for breach of mediation clauses. To an extent, the decision of *OLG Frankfurt am Main* of 7 November 1997[177] was an exception to this standpoint. In this case the court held that specific performance relates to the implied duty of the parties to support the agreed dispute resolution process (*Verfahrensförderungspflicht*).[178] This perspective never gained wider recognition, however.

2.113 A further contractual remedy that has to be considered is compensation (damages). As with an order for specific performance, award of damages entails delineation of the duties of the parties to undergo voluntary mediation. Further difficulty surrounds the precise quantification of loss resulting from breach of the duty to mediate. For this reason, claims for damages have only been considered in theory, rather than in judicial practice.[179]

[174] OLG Frankfurt aM NJW-RR 1998, 778.

[175] See 2.93–2.96.

[176] H Eidenmüller, 'Vertrags- und verfahrensrechtliche Grundfragen der Mediation', n 141 above, 23.

[177] OLG Frankfurt aM (Senat Darmstadt) NJW-RR 1998, 778.

[178] In the context of arbitral proceedigns see BGH NJW 1988, 1215.

[179] F Fabian, 'The Enforceability of Mediation Clauses—the Approach of English and German Courts and ICC Arbitral Tribunals' (2005) 5 *SchiedsVZ* 250, 253; C Bühring-Uhle, *Arbitration and Mediation in International Business*, n 35 above, 231.

Finally, an interesting, but isolated, view was taken in the decision of *OLG Düsseldorf* of 30 November 1973.[180] In this judgment the court considered the consequences of non-compliance with a conciliation clause included in the constitution of an agricultural cooperative. The clause set out a detailed procedure before a conciliation body which was to be exhausted before the claim could reach final adjudication in litigation. In the first instance the claim was dismissed as inadmissible under the provisions regulating the effects of arbitration clauses. This decision was overturned by *OLG Düsseldorf* which ruled that the claim should be dismissed as unfounded (*unbegründet*). The court assumed that conciliation clauses are different in nature to arbitration clauses, which excludes analogous application of the provisions governing the effects of the latter. Finding no grounds for a procedural order as to inadmissibility, the court enforced the conciliation clause by an award *in meriti* dismissing the claim as unfounded. **2.114**

This view, as well as other interpretations identifying substantive remedies for breach of mediation clauses, has never been widely taken up by the German judiciary. The majority of cases focus on what consequences contractual dispute resolution mechanisms have for the proceedings initiated prematurely. The dominant view accepts inadmissibility of claims as the main consequence of bypassing agreed dispute resolution processes. Consequently, conciliation clauses are enforced by way of procedural orders instead of awards relating to the merits of the case. **2.115**

Expert Determination (*Schiedsgutachten*)

Expert Determination in the German Civil Code

Unlike mediation, expert determination is not expressly provided for in the statute. Traditionally expert determination has been derived from the provisions of BGB regulating the determination of the performance by the third person (*Bestimmung der Leistung durch einen Dritten*). Under §§ 317–319 BGB the parties may leave performance under contract to be determined by a neutral person. These provisions were applied, by analogy, to expert determination understood as a means to resolve contractual disputes. This thinking determined the nature, effects, and grounds for challenging expert decisions where experts were empowered to decide on factual or legal controversies between the parties.[181] **2.116**

[180] OLG Düsseldorf ZfgG 1975, 228.

[181] M Würdinger, in W Krüger (ed), *Münchener Kommentar zum Bürgerliches Gesetzbuch*, 7th edn (CH Beck, 2016) p 2024, para 6 ad § 317 and pp 2029ff, paras 28–54 ad § 317; V Rieble, in *J. von Staudingers Kommentar zum Bürgerlichen Gesetzbuch mit Einführungsgesetz und Nebengesetzen* (Sellier–de Gruyter 2015) pp 149ff, para 18ff ad § 317 BGB; M Gehrlein, in H Bamberger, H Roth (eds), *Kommentar zur Bürgerlichen Gesetzbuch*, 3rd edn (CH Beck, 2012) pp 1648ff, paras 5ff ad § 319 BGB; C Stubbe, 'Kombination des Schiedsgutachtensverfahren mit anderen Verfahrenstypen' in K-H Böckstiegel, KP Berger, J Bredow (eds), *Schiedsgutachten versus Schiedsgerichtsbarkeit* (Heymans, 2007) 75ff; G Wagner, *Prozessverträge—Privatautonomie im Verfahrensrecht*, n 145 above, 663.

2.117 According to the provisions of BGB governing expert determination, the expert's decision is binding on the parties as well as the court if one party initiates litigation. Under § 318(2) BGB the parties may challenge the determination on limited grounds involving duress, misrepresentation or fraud. Other than on the above basis the court may refuse to take into account the expert's decision only if it is manifestly inequitable (*offenbar unbillig*).[182] If so the determination maybe substituted by a court award (*Ersetzung durch Urteil* or *Leistungsbestimmung durch Urteil*). § 319(1) BGB provides that the court may review the expert decision if the third party was empowered to make the determination at their reasonable discretion.

2.118 Parties may relax or tighten the grounds for challenge of the neutral person's decision.[183] § 319(2) reinforces the flexible character of this provision by stating that parties may agree that determination is to be made at the discretion of the third party. Opting for this alternative the parties depart from the requirement of reasonableness prescribed under § 319(1) BGB. In such a case the court cannot review the decision even if it is manifestly inequitable. The court cannot substitute the decision with its own award and the determination can only be challenged on limited grounds relating to the underlying contract, such as illegality or public policy.[184]

2.119 Equally, § 319(1) BGB allows the parties to agree that the expert's findings will be fully reviewable by a court or by arbitration. In such a case the binding force of the decision is likely to be provisional (*vorläufiger Bindungswirkung*), which means that it has to be complied with until reviewed in the further stages of the dispute resolution process. Expert determination in this form reflects the modern approach to expert determination as a fully fledged dispute resolution method. This variant of expert determination features in international standard rules and forms of contracts[185] and is likely to be combined with arbitral proceedings where the tribunal will be empowered to fully review the expert's findings.[186] It is also provided for

[182] On this aspect see 2.121 below.

[183] § 319(1) is considered as *ius dispositivum*. See M Würdinger, in W Krüger (ed), *Münchener Kommentar zum Bürgerliches Gesetzbuch*, 7th edn (CH Beck, 2016) p 2038, para 3 ad § 319; C Grüneberg, in *Otto Palandt Bürgerliches Gesetzbuch*, 75th edn (CH Beck, 2016) p 547, para 10 ad § 319 BGB; V Rieble, in *J. von Staudingers Kommentar zum Bürgerlichen Gesetzbuch mit Einführungsgesetz und Nebengesetzen* (Sellier–de Gruyter 2015) p 180, paras 4 and 22 ad § 319.

[184] M Gehrlein, in H Bamberger, H Roth (eds), *Kommentar zur Bürgerlichen Gesetzbuch*, 3rd edn (CH Beck, 2012) p 1649, para 7 ad §319 BGB.

[185] See eg ICC Dispute Board Rules and clause 20 FIDIC, on which 1.39 and 1.45ff.

[186] M Gehrlein, in H Bamberger, H Roth (eds), *Kommentar zur Bürgerlichen Gesetzbuch*, 3rd edn (CH Beck, 2012) p 1648, para 6 ad § 319 BGB. The leading German arbitration provider, *Deutsche Institution für Schiedsgerichtsbarkeit eV* (*DIS*), published a standard two-tiered dispute resolution clause comprising provisionally binding expert determination and arbitration ('Hinsichtlich aller Streitigkeiten, die sich aus oder in Zusammenhang mit dem Vertrag (... Bezeichnung des Vertrags ...) ergeben, wird ein Schiedsgutachtensverfahren gemäß der Schiedsgutachtensordnung der Deutschen Institution für Schiedsgerichtsbarkeit e.V. (DIS) (DIS-SchGO) durchgeführt.

under the model rules for expert determination (*DIS-Schiedsgutachtensordnung*) published by the leading German arbitration centre—*Deutsche Institution für Schiedsgerichtsbarkeit eV* (DIS). Finally, the parties may agree that the expert's decision will only act as a recommendation without any binding force.[187]

In the absence of contractual provisions modifying § 319(1) BGB, the general rule will apply under which an expert's decision is final and binding and can only be challenged if the decision is manifestly inequitable. The interpretation of this ground is restrictive. The challenge will only be successful if the flaws in the decision are evident and unambiguous.[188] It has been established that the test under § 319(1) BGB must take into account the perspective of a person qualified to make the determination in question. The court is empowered to conduct a reasonably detailed investigation of the defects of a decision which need not be immediately apparent.[189] **2.120**

It is worth noting that, in order to challenge the binding force of a decision, the third party determination needs to be proved manifestly inequitable (*offenbar unbillig*), rather than manifestly incorrect (*offenbar unrichtig*).[190] The latter criterion is especially relevant in the context of expert determination traditionally associated with valuation of technical issues, where the result is more easily ascertained as incorrect than inequitable.[191] Despite this feature of expert determination, judicial decisions have confirmed that the accuracy of a determination is not decisive for challenging its binding force under German law.[192] It must be noted that § 319 BGB only allows the court to review the *effect* of expert determination, **2.121**

Nach Beendigung des Schiedsgutachtensverfahrens werden alle Streitigkeiten nach der Schiedsgerichtsordnung der Deutschen Institution für Schiedsgerichtsbarkeit e.V. (DIS) unter Ausschluss des ordentlichen Rechtsweges endgültig entschieden; im Fall der Nichtbeachtung der Bindungswirkung einer Entscheidung nach der DIS-SchGO unter Einbeziehung der Ergänzenden Regeln für beschleunigte Verfahren der DIS, wobei in diesem Fall der berechtigten Partei auch der ordentliche Rechtsweg offensteht.'). See C Stubbe, 'DIS-Schiedsgutachtensordnung (DIS-SchGO) und DIS-Gutachtensordnung (DIS-GO)' (2010) 3 *SchiedsVZ* 130 for a commentary.

[187] BGH NJW 1977, 2263. On various forms of expert determination under German law, see W Acker, S Konopka, 'Schiedsgutachten im Bau- und Anlagenbauvertrag: Grenzen und Möglichkeiten' (2003) 6 *SchiedsVZ* 256; C Stubbe, 'Schiedsgutachten als modernes ADR-Instrument' (2006) 3 *SchiedsVZ* 150.

[188] BGH NJW 1996, 452; BGH ZIP 1988, 162; M Gehrlein, in H Bamberger, H Roth (eds), *Kommentar zum Bürgerlichen Gesetzbuch*, 3rd edn (CH Beck, 2012) p 1647, para 2 ad §319 BGB.

[189] The scope of such investigation depends on the circumstances of each individual case: see BGH, NJW 2001, 3775; NJW-RR 1993 1034; NJW-RR 1988, 506 and BGHZ 43, 374.

[190] On this aspect BGH, NJW 1977, 801.

[191] BGH, NJW 1983, 1854; M Würdinger, in W Krüger (ed), *Münchener Kommentar zum Bürgerlichen Gesetzbuch*, 7th edn (CH Beck, 2016) pp 2040ff, paras 14ff ad § 319 BGB; V Rieble, in *J. von Staudingers Kommentar zum Bürgerlichen Gesetzbuch mit Einführungsgesetz und Nebengesetzen* (Sellier–de Gruyter, 2015) p 178, paras 10 ad § 319 BGB; M Gehrlein, in H Bamberger, H Roth (eds), *Kommentar zum Bürgerlichen Gesetzbuch*, 3rd edn (CH Beck, 2012) p 1647, para 3 ad §319 BGB.

[192] For instance, departing from the correct result by 16.79% has not been considered as justifying the court's review of the decision (BGH, NJW 1991, 2761).

not the *process* of reaching the decision.[193] The statute is silent on *Schiedsgutachten* procedure and an expert is not required to produce the reasoning of his decision.

2.122 Despite the lack of statutory regulation relating to expert determination *sensu stricto*, the clauses providing for *Schiedsgutachten* are increasingly used in German commercial practice.[194] The main advantage of this ADR method is its flexibility and the cost-effectiveness of taking the determination of complex technical issues out of court. The areas in which *Schiedsgutachten* has gained particular importance in German legal practice coincide with traditionally recognised fields of expert activity, which notably include the construction industry.[195] In addition, *Schiedsgutachten* begins to play a vital role in legal relationships where valuation of certain assets is important, such as in M&A transactions.[196] Other areas in which *Schiedsgutachten* is common include insurance and the evaluation of the quality of performance and warranty claims brought under sale of goods contracts.[197]

2.123 As a method based on the paradigm of expert determination, dispute boards have become increasingly popular in Germany. This ADR method is referred to as 'adjudication' (*Adjudikation*) and, in line with the international trend, it is used predominantly in construction contracts.[198] As a relatively new phenomenon, this ADR technique relies heavily on the anglo-saxon model.[199] Dispute board procedure is offered as one of the ADR services administered by the DIS, according to the standard rules *DIS-Verfahrensordnung für Adjudikation* (2010). As was the case with expert determination, the rules contain a provision under which a board's decision is fully reviewable in arbitration.[200]

[193] BGH WM 1977, 413. See also V Rieble, in *J. von Staudingers Kommentar zum Bürgerlichen Gesetzbuch mit Einführungsgesetz und Nebengesetzen* (Sellierde Gruyter 2015) p 179, para 15 ad § 319 BGB; M Gehrlein, in H Bamberger, H Roth (eds), *Kommentar zum Bürgerlichen Gesetzbuch*, 3rd edn (CH Beck, 2012) p 1647, para 2 ad § 319 BGB. cf the judgments reviewing experts' decisions due to errors in the adopted valuation method: BGH, WM 1988, 628; BGH, NJW 1991, 2698; BGH, NJW-RR 1988, 506.

[194] G Wagner, in K-H Böckstiegel, SM Kröll, P Nacimiento, *Arbitration in Germany*, 2nd edn (Kluwer Law International, 2015) 59.

[195] A Boldt, in B Messerschmidt, W Voit (eds), *Privates Baurecht*, 2nd edn (CH Beck, 2012) pp 678 ff, paras 54ff ad I. Teil Systematische Darstellungen, T Außergerichtliche Streitbeilegung; W Acker, S Konopka, 'Schiedsgutachten im Bau- und Anlagenbauvertrag: Grenzen und Möglichkeiten', n 187 above, 256ff.

[196] A Sessler, C Leimert, 'The Role of Expert Determination in Mergers and Acquisitions under German Law' (2004) 20 *Arbitration International* 151, 151ff.

[197] M Würdinger, in W Krüger (ed), *Münchener Kommentar zum Bürgerlichen Gesetzbuch*, 7th edn (CH Beck, 2016) p 2029, para 28 ad § 317; P Schlosser, in *Stein/Jonas Kommentar zur Zivilprozessordnung*, 23rd edn (Mohr Siebeck, 2014) pp 26–28, paras 43–44 ad vor § 1025 ZPO.

[198] A Aldinger, V Mahnken, in A Roquette, A Otto (eds), *Vertragsbuch Privates Baurecht*, 2nd edn (CH Beck, 2011) paras 1ff ad D. 'Alternative Konfliktlösungsverfahren', IV. 'Adjudikation'; R Harbst, 'Adjudication on the Rise in Germany?' (2010) 26 *Construction Law Journal* 698ff.

[199] *ibid.*

[200] § 22(1).

German jurisprudence focuses particular attention on distinguishing *Schiedsgutachten* and dispute board procedures from arbitration.[201] The main difficulty lies in the fact that an expert may be empowered to decide not only factual, but also legal issues, which likens his mandate to an arbitrator's.[202] The relevance of the distinction between the two methods concerns the question whether an expert is under a duty to apply standards of due process in a manner akin to arbitral proceedings. Such standards include impartiality of the decision-maker, the parties' right to be heard and submit evidence, and other procedural safeguards.[203] **2.124**

The majority view emphasises the differences between expert determination and arbitration and accepting weaker standards of procedural fairness in expert determination proceedings.[204] This view is based on the assumption that the statute does not regulate the procedure before an expert and is silent on minimum procedural standards to be observed in the course of *Schiedsgutachten*. Moreover, the grounds for challenge of an expert's decision are different to those relating to arbitral awards, permitting a far narrower judicial scrutiny of expert determination than is the case with arbitration. In addition, the statute does not prescribe any requirements as to the form of an expert determination clause, which further distinguishes this ADR method from arbitration.[205] The opposite view, not widely held in German jurisprudence, suggests applying the rules governing arbitral procedure to expert determination.[206] **2.125**

Although the majority view rejects analogous application of the procedural standards governing arbitration to *Schiedsgutachten*, the independence of the **2.126**

[201] BGH, BGHZ 17, 366; BGH, BGHZ 48, 26; BGH, NJW 1984, 669; M Würdinger, in W Krüger (ed), *Münchener Kommentar zum Bürgerlichen Gesetzbuch*, 7th edn, (CH Beck, 2016) pp 2025–26, paras 8–13 ad § 317 BGB; J Münch, in *Münchener Kommentar zur Zivilprozessordnung*, 4th edn (Beck, 2013) pp 29–30, paras 55–57 ad vor §§ 1025 ff. ZPO; P Hartmann, in A Baumbach, W Lauterbach, J Albers, P Hartmann, *Zivilprozessordnung mit FamFG, GVG und anderen Nebengesetzen*, 74th edn (CH Beck 2016) pp 2737ff, paras 15ff ad Grundz § 1025 ZPO; R Greger, C Stubbe, *Schiedsgutachten: aussergerichtliche Streitbeilegung durch Drittentscheidungen* (CH Beck, 2007) paras 11–15; C Stubbe, 'Kombination des Schiedsgutachtensverfahren mit anderen Verfahrenstypen' in *Schiedsgutachten versus Schiedsgerichtsbarkeit*, n 181 above, 75ff; G Wagner, *Prozessverträge—Privatautonomie im Verfahrensrecht*, n 145 above, 663. Generally on the difference between expert determination and arbitration see 1.31–1.33.

[202] BGH BGHZ 48, 25; BGH BB 1967, 694; BGH NJW 1982, 1878; BGH NJW 1991, 2698; J Münch, in *Münchener Kommentar zur Zivilprozessordnung*, 4th edn (Beck, 2013) p 29, para 55 ad vor §§ 1025 ff ZPO; P Schlosser, in *Stein/Jonas Kommentar zur Zivilprozessordnung*, 23rd edn (Mohr Siebeck 2014) p 26, para 42 ad vor § 1025 ZPO.

[203] See § 1036ff ZPO in relation to procedural standards in arbitration.

[204] BGH, NJW 1952, 1296; OLG München 7.08.2006 SchiedsVZ 2006, 286, 288; J Münch, in *Münchener Kommentar zur Zivilprozessordnung*, 4th edn (Beck, 2013) p 29, para 55 ad vor §§ 1025 ff ZPO; G Wagner, *Prozessverträge—Privatautonomie im Verfahrensrecht*, n 145 above, 663 and literature cited.

[205] P Hartmann, in A Baumbach, W Lauterbach, J Albers, P Hartmann, *Zivilprozessordnung mit FamFG, GVG und anderen Nebengesetzen*, 74th edn (CH Beck, 2016) p 2737, para 16 ad Grundz § 1025 ZPO.

[206] P Schlosser, in *Stein/Jonas Kommentar zur Zivilprozessordnung*, 23rd edn (Mohr Siebeck, 2014) pp 38ff, paras 64ff ad vor § 1025 ZPO.

decision-maker is considered inherent to expert determination. It has been suggested in the literature that expert bias may satisfy the ground for challenging the decision as manifestly inequitable under § 319(1) BGB.[207] Some authors submit that the impartiality of an expert is an implied term of an expert determination agreement.[208]

2.127 Finally, it has to be noted that the parties may contractually agree the procedural standards to govern the expert determination process. Provisions to this effect are contained in the standard rules for expert determination administered by DIS: *DIS-Schiedsgutachtensordnung* (2010). The rules include, among other grounds for challenge of an expert's decision, lack of impartiality (§ 7), and violation of the right to be heard or unequal treatment of the parties (§ 16). The rules also lay down the right of either party to request a hearing (§ 14).

2.128 The legal nature of expert determination is contentious in German jurisprudence.[209] According to the majority view, *Schiedsgutachten* is an institution of substantive law due to a normative framework derived from the provisions of the German Civil Code.[210] This view assumes that expert determination is governed entirely by the provisions of substantive law. A concurrent interpretation suggests that *Schiedsgutachten* is of a procedural character.[211] This view is based on the assumption that the nature of the expert's mandate is multifaceted. First, an expert may be empowered to determine a contentious factual issue. Secondly, the parties may submit to an expert any contentious issues relating to interpretation of the contract or the scope of the duties arising under the agreement. Thirdly, an expert may be appointed to supplement the legal relationship between the parties by specifying what constitutes contractual performance. Only in this third variant under § 317 BGB is the nature of the expert's function purely substantive. In the first and second areas expert mandate is of a quasi-judicial nature, which equates expert determination clauses with procedural contracts such as arbitration agreements.

2.129 German law does not specify the consequences of non-compliance with expert determination clauses. As with consensual ADR, the jurisprudence of the

[207] M Würdinger, in W Krüger (ed), *Münchener Kommentar zum Bürgerlichen Gesetzbuch*, 7th edn (CH Beck, 2016) p 2032, para 41 ad § 317 BGB.

[208] G. Wagner, *Prozessverträge—Privatautonomie im Verfahrensrecht*, n 145 above, 676–77.

[209] Exhaustively on this aspect KH Schwab, G Walter, *Schiedsgerichtsbarkeit*, n 145 above, 7ff.

[210] BGH, NJW 1952, 1296; BGH, NJW 1953, 825; BGH, NJW 1955,1473; BGH, NJW 1955, 665; BGH, NJW 1991, 2761; M Würdinger, in W Krüger (ed), *Münchener Kommentar zum Bürgerlichen Gesetzbuch*, 7th edn (CH Beck, 2016) p 2032, para 40 ad § 317 BGB; P Hartmann, in A Baumbach, W Lauterbach, J Albers, P Hartmann, *Zivilprozessordnung mit FamFG, GVG und anderen Nebengesetzen*, 74th edn (CH Beck, 2016), p 2737 para 16 ad Grundz §1025 ZPO; J Münch, in *Münchener Kommentar zur Zivilprozessordnung*, 4th edn (Beck, 2013) p 29, para 58 ad vor §§ 1025 ff ZPO; V Rieble, in *J. von Staudingers Kommentar zum Bürgerlichen Gesetzbuch mit Einführungsgesetz und Nebengesetzen* (Sellierde Gruyter, 2015) pp 149ff, para 18ff ad § 317.

[211] W Habscheid, 'L'Expertise-arbitrage' in P Sanders (ed), *International Arbitration. Liber Amicorum for Martin Domke* (Martinus Nijhoff, 1967) 108, adopted by P Schlosser, in *Stein/Jonas Kommentar zur Zivilprozessordnung*, 23rd edn (Mohr Siebeck, 2014) pp 35ff, paras 56ff ad vor § 1025 ZPO.

Bundesgerichtshof has developed a coherent framework that regulates remedies for breach of clauses providing for *Schiedsgutachten*. The solutions adopted are the subject of a separate analysis below.

Consequences of Breach of an Expert Determination Clause

The framework governing expert determination under German law is of a substantive origin, which distinguishes this ADR method from mediation. In consequence, the German judiciary has approached breach of expert determination clauses from a different perspective to the one adopted for consensual ADR. In the leading case of 8 June 1988[212] the *Bundesgerichtshof* adopted autonomous sanctions for non-compliance with expert determination clauses, departing from the reasoning devised for procedural contracts. **2.130**

The clause in question concerned claims arising under an agreement for lease of land. The contract contained a provision that the cost of construction works on the property had to be evaluated by the panel appointed in accordance with the contract. The claimant who undertook the construction works initiated the court proceedings without first submitting his claim to the panel. In the first instance the court disregarded the defendant's objection as to non-compliance with an expert determination clause contained in the contract and proceeded to adjudicate the merits of the case. The *Bundesgerichtshof* reversed this judgment and referred the case to review in the lower court. In the reasons for its decision the *Bundesgerichtshof* held that non-compliance with an expert determination clause should result in dismissal of an action as temporarily unfounded (*zur Zeit unbegründet*) until the relevant procedure is exhausted in accordance with the contract. The court clarified that until such a determination is obtained by the party bringing a claim, the court cannot adjudicate on the merits of the case. **2.131**

The *Bundesgerichtshof* confirmed that the court may set a time-limit for submission of an expert determination. This power was derived from §§ 356 and 431 ZPO prescribing the competence of the court to set a time-limit for submission of evidence.[213] It was held that the court cannot proceed with adjudication until such a time-limit expires. Failure by the claimant to observe the time-frame for submission of an expert's decision opens up ground for the court to dismiss the claim as unfounded. **2.132**

The decision of the *Bundesgerichtshof* has been followed in subsequent cases dealing with the enforceability of modern expert determination clauses[214] and has **2.133**

[212] BGH NJW-RR 1988, 1405.

[213] On the application of §§ 356 and 431 to *Schiedsgutachten* see P Schlosser, in *Stein/Jonas Kommentar zur Zivilprozessordnung*, 23rd edn (Mohr Siebeck, 2014) p 29, para 49 ad vor 1025 ZPO.

[214] See eg the *Bundesgerichtshof* judgment of 24.11.2005 BGH (2006) 4 *SchiedsVZ* 217. See also the earlier judgments BGH NJW 1979, 1543 and BGH NJW 82, 1878.

been generally endorsed by commentators.[215] It is emphasised in the literature that the plea of non-compliance with an expert determination clause does not relate to the lack of the court's inherent jurisdiction to hear the case.[216]

2.134 It must be observed that the court's sanction for breach of expert determination clauses is different to the one devised for mediation clauses. In the former case the court dismisses an action as unfounded (*unbegründet*) by making a substantive award. In the latter case, the court dismisses an action as inadmissible (*unzulässig*) via a procedural order. Furthermore, in cases of expert determination the court has expressly provided for the possibility to set time-limits for submission of an expert decision.

2.135 Dismissal of an action as unfounded is the consequence of breach of expert determination clauses providing for the binding force of an expert's decision. For non-binding expert determination the court adopted a similar approach to that governing conciliation clauses. In its judgment of 4 July 1977[217] the *Bundesgerichtshof* considered a clause requiring the parties to obtain an expert's opinion (*gutachtliche Stellungnahme*) as to any controversial issue before filing the claim in court. The court considered the function of an expert to be that of a facilitator who helps the parties to reach settlement. In consequence, the court held that so long as the parties obtain a recommendation as to the dispute from an expert, actionability of the claim is excluded and the claim must be dismissed as inadmissible. In consequence, the effects of non-compliance with non-binding expert determination clauses have been equated with those relating to consensual ADR.

Limitations on Enforceability of ADR Clauses

2.136 Whilst giving effect to ADR clauses, German courts have analysed the limits to their enforceability. A fundamental issue decided by the German judiciary focuses on the boundaries within which the parties are allowed to enter into a *pactum de non petendo* and exclude actionability of the claim. As far as clauses providing for consensual ADR are concerned, the main problem surrounds the voluntary and cooperative nature of the process. A further issue determined by the judiciary has concerned the question of whether non-compliance with an ADR clause is an

[215] J Münch, in *Münchener Kommentar zur Zivilprozessordnung*, 4th edn (Beck, 2013) p 31, para 60 ad vor §§ 1025ff ZPO; P Hartmann, in A Baumbach, W Lauterbach, J Albers, P Hartmann (eds), *Zivilprozessordnung*, 74th edn (CH Beck, 2016), p 2737, para 17 ad Grundz § 1025; V Rieble, in *J. von Staudingers Kommentar zum Bürgerlichen Gesetzbuch mit Einführungsgesetz und Nebengesetzen* (Sellier–de Gruyter 2015) pp 184, para 42 ad 317 BGB; G Wagner, *Prozessverträge—Privatautonomie im Verfahrensrecht*, n 145 above, 655ff; G Wagner, 'Alternative Streitbeilegung und Verjährung' (2001) 3 NJW 182, 183;

[216] J Münch, in *Münchener Kommentar zur Zivilprozessordnung*, 4th edn (Beck, 2013) p 31, para 60 ad vor §§ 1025ff. ZPO; P Hartmann in A Baumbach, W Lauterbach, J Albers, P Hartmann (eds), *Zivilprozessordnung*, 74th edn (CH Beck, 2016) p 2737, para 17 ad Grundz § 1025.

[217] BGH, NJW 1977, 2263.

obstacle to hearing the merits of a case which the court is empowered to take into account at its own discretion, or only an obstacle upon a plea by a defendant.

Pactum de non petendo *and Freedom of Contract*

Delineating the scope of the parties' freedom to enter into an agreement not to sue is a starting point for ascertaining the limits to enforceability of ADR clauses under German law. Because failure to exhaust the agreed ADR procedure may create a bar to litigating the dispute, the main question that has to be answered is whether entering into ADR agreements unduly restricts access to court. **2.137**

An important exposition of the German courts' approach is contained in the decision of *OLG Celle* of 31 July 1970,[218] approved by the *Bundesgerichtshof* in its seminal case of 23 November 1983.[219] In this judgment the court held that exclusion of actionability, understood as an ability to enforce the claim in court, is permitted so long as the relevant right to which actionability relates is at the party's free disposal. The court confirmed that access to court is a fundamental public right. This right is not, however, unlimited and may be subject to constraints. The court applied *argumentum a maiore ad minus* and concluded that if the parties are permitted to mutually modify and even terminate their obligations, there is no reason why they would not be permitted to limit the enforceability of their rights in court. Such exclusion can be achieved by entering into a conciliation clause. Contractual exclusion of actionability has been, thus, regarded as within the scope of freedom of contract. **2.138**

The court further observed that conciliation clauses do not fall short of the standards of public policy (*guten Sitten*), as prescribed under § 138(1) BGB. It was held that such contractual stipulations do not contain any inequitable limitation of rights. It follows that so long as an ADR clause equally binds both parties, it is valid. The court further remarked that the permissibility of such contractual arrangements is also justified under purposive interpretation, as the function of ADR clauses is to keep the parties' disputes out of court. **2.139**

A more rigorous approach was taken by the *Bundesgerichtshof* in a decisionof 4 July 1977.[220] In this case the court refused to enforce an ADR clause, considering that it created too far-reaching obstacles to access to court. The *Bundesgerichtshof* confirmed the general rule that exclusion of actionability is permissible under German law. It, however, qualified this principle by stating that conciliation clauses can be valid so long as they do not result in excessive difficulties in resorting to court for a final resolution of the dispute. **2.140**

The controversial clause was contained in a partnership agreement. The dispute concerned withdrawal of one member from the partnership. The court began by **2.141**

[218] OLG Celle NJW 1971, 288.
[219] BGH NJW 1984, 669.
[220] BGH NJW 1977, 2263.

confirming that the subject matter of the dispute did not hinder the enforceability of a conciliation clause. The court agreed with the first instance court's decision that the clause was separable from the main agreement, and that the termination of the relationship with the partner did not automatically remove the duties arising under an ADR clause. The court proceeded to establish that entering into contracts for dispute resolution (other than arbitration clauses expressly permitted under the statute) was generally permissible as falling within the freedom of contract.

2.142 Turning to the analysis of the clause in question, the court held that it contained too far-reaching obstacles to court access as the clause lacked sufficient certainty. On the facts of the case the conciliation procedure had been made conditional on the payment of a deposit fee toward the cost of conciliation. The partnership agreement did not, however, contain a clear basis upon which such fee was to be calculated. Notwithstanding the contract's silence on this matter, the conciliation body charged the claimant a certain amount in respect of this fee. The claimant refused to pay the amount and filed the claim straight in court. The *Bundesgerichtshof* held that on the facts of the case initiation of conciliation was excessively burdensome, considering the lack of clear grounds for calculating the conciliation fee. The court concluded that enforcing an ADR procedure in such circumstances would unduly restrict the claimant's access to court.[221]

Non-enforceability Resulting from the Wording of a Clause

2.143 The requirement that the clause be sufficiently clear is an important consideration for the drafters of multi-tiered clauses. Insufficiently clear clauses may be considered to hinder the parties' access to court and therefore be invalid under German law. In the judgment of 4 July 1977[222] the *Bundesgerichtshof* observed that precise wording of a clause is critical for accepting the enforceable nature of the duties it creates. The court also found that the parties should prescribe a time-frame within which the conciliation is to take place, so that access to court is not restricted indefinitely.

2.144 This view was reinforced in the *Bundesgerichtshof* judgment of 23 November 1983.[223] The court confirmed that exclusion of actionability in favour of out-of-court dispute resolution should be clearly defined. The court emphasised the importance of prescribing the time-frame in which actionability is restricted. To achieve clarity the parties may also prescribe conditions which have to be fulfilled to commence litigation. The court held that ambiguity may cause excessive difficulties

[221] The subsequent case law clarified that the duty to pay a deposit fee upon the commencement of an ADR procedure does not automatically render the relevant clause unenforceable as long as the grounds for such fees are mutually agreed (OLG Frankfurt NJW-RR 1998, 778). See also BGH NJW 1999, 647.

[222] BGH NJW 1977, 2263.

[223] BGH, NJW 1984, 669.

in enforcing duties under ADR clauses and may, thereby, unduly restrict access to court. In such a case the clause would be considered invalid.

In practice precise formulation of conciliation clauses can be achieved by providing a time-frame for negotiations. Lapse of the prescribed period means that the ADR phase is fulfilled. Lack of clear provisions in this respect may hinder the enforceability of the entire dispute resolution mechanism. Similarly, the courts may refuse enforcement if clauses do not give clear guidance as to which steps should be fulfilled to discharge a contractual bargain. Clarity in this respect is particularly important if the parties provided for more than one dispute resolution method. **2.145**

The court may refuse to enforce a clause containing too burdensome terms. This issue was discussed by *LG Stralsund* in the decision of 6 December 2001[224] where the court analysed a clause in a housing cooperative agreement. It was held that in order to be enforceable clauses must not impose excessive duties on parties bringing claims. On the facts of the case, however, the court considered that the contested clause did not unduly restrict actionability of the claim. **2.146**

Clear wording of clauses should also cover the extent to which the character of the agreed dispute resolution procedure is obligatory. In ascertaining this German courts interpret ADR clauses in terms of the entire context of the agreement rather than by purely focusing on the language of a particular clause. In the precedent-setting case of 23 November 1983[225] the *Bundesgerichtshof* held that despite the apparently permissive stipulation regarding conciliation attempts, the term was binding (*Mußbestimmung*).[226] Similarly, in the judgment of *LG Münster* of 21 December 2000[227] it was held that, although the relevant clause stated that conciliation *should* be attempted by the parties before resort to court proceedings, the clause was of an imperative nature. In both cases the courts referred to the purpose in opting for out-of-court dispute resolution. The enforceability of arguably loose stipulations has been regarded as a step to promote ADR. **2.147**

Finally, the requirement for impartiality of a neutral person has a bearing on the enforceability of mediation and expert determination clauses. In the award of 4 July 1977[228] the *Bundesgerichtshof* held that evidence of biased behaviour by the conciliator might entitle the party to bypass contractual steps and bring a claim straight to the court. The court clarified, however, that the stipulation, under which an organ of a legal entity is empowered to act as conciliator in disputes between the entity and its members, does not automatically violate the requirement for impartiality. **2.148**

[224] LG Stralsund NZM 2003, 327.
[225] BGH, NJW 1984, 669.
[226] BGH, NJW 1984, 669. The clause is reported *in extenso* in n 153 above.
[227] LG Münster DStRE 2001, 614.
[228] BGH NJW 1977, 2263.

Lack of Cooperation in a Consensual ADR Process

2.149 Consensual ADR methods are founded on the assumption that the parties will cooperate towards reaching amicable settlement. Contracting for mediation in advance of dispute allows for the risk that the parties' attitude to settlement may fluctuate according to circumstances. A party bringing a claim might not be interested in undertaking settlement negotiations, but rather may want to have its claim adjudicated in court as quickly as possible.

2.150 Under German law the voluntary nature of mediation is not an obstacle to the enforceability of contracts in which parties agreed in advance to exhaust a mediation process before resorting to court. This has been confirmed in the seminal case of the *Bundesgerichtshof* of 23 November 1983[229] and followed by lower courts. In this judgment the court held that the reluctance of one party to mediate is not an obstacle to the enforceability of a contractual commitment to negotiate. The court clarified that even if the claimant maintains that any mediation attempt will be futile, the chances for a settlement may increase if the contractual ADR procedure is launched before the competent body.

2.151 A similar approach was taken in the judgment of *LG Münster* of 21 December 2000[230] where the court adjudicated on the enforceability of a mediation clause before the relevant body of the tax advisors' chamber. It was held that, on the one hand, mediation before the chamber is voluntary. On the other hand, the clause did not require anything more than presenting the case before the relevant mediation body. The court emphasised that notwithstanding the parties' reluctance to settle, the parties should at least launch the agreed ADR process in accordance with the contract.

2.152 Despite a rigorous position as to enforceability of contractual ADR commitments, German courts do not impose on parties the duty to actually participate in negotiations. By refusing to hear the case until mediation is attempted, the courts create a framework for amicable discussions without adopting unrealistic assumptions that the parties will in fact negotiate. By enforcing mediation clauses the courts give effect to the parties' contractual promises in accordance with the *pacta sunt servanda* principle.

2.153 This understanding was confirmed by *LG Straslund* in a judgment of 6 December 2001.[231] The court emphasised that the *rationale* for the enforceability of ADR clauses is not directed at creating formalistic difficulties for the parties or delaying the final adjudication by a court. The standard for compliance with clauses providing for consensual ADR requires mere instigation of the agreed process to discharge the contractual bargain.

[229] BGH, NJW 1984, 669.
[230] LG Münster DStRE 2001, 614.
[231] LG Stralsund NZM 2003, 327.

Lack of cooperation between the parties is more problematic in cases where initiation of the agreed ADR procedure is dependent on certain acts performed by both parties. An example of such difficulty was analysed by the *Bundesgerichtshof* in relation to a provision requiring both parties to pay a proportion of the conciliation fee before commencement of the conciliation process.[232] Such an arrangement may lead to a deadlock where conciliation cannot take off due to the other party's refusal to pay its share of the fee. It was held that in such cases the court can depart from the requirement of strict compliance with an ADR clause and proceed to hear the case without enforcing the contractual ADR procedure. **2.154**

Lack of a Requisite Plea

A further limitation concerning the enforceability of ADR clauses is the way in which the court takes into account non-compliance with the agreed procedure. The German judiciary unanimously accepts that the court is not empowered to take into account breaches of ADR clauses at its own volition. Instead, the party wishing to enforce the agreed ADR process should bring the breach to the attention of the court by raising the requisite plea.[233] Lack of a plea implies waiver of the rights arising under ADR clauses and empowers the court to adjudicate on the merits of the case. This solution mirrors the one adopted for arbitration agreements under ZPO.[234] **2.155**

It must be noted that the plea of non-compliance with an ADR clause will not be accepted if failure to comply with an agreed procedure was caused by unfair behaviour of the defendant prior to litigation. This problem was discussed in the judgments of the *Bundesgerichtshof* of 18 November 1998[235] and *OLG Frankfurt am Main* of 7 November 1997.[236] On the facts of both cases the defendant first boycotted the claimant's attempts to initiate conciliation by refusing to pay its share of the initial fee for conciliation. Subsequently, when the claimant brought the claim in court, the defendant raised the plea of non-compliance with an ADR clause. **2.156**

In the first case the *Bundesgerichtshof* refused to accept the plea, reasoning that in the circumstances of the case it would amount to impermissible (abusive) exercise of rights (*unzulässige Rechtsausübung*). Rejecting the plea, the court relied on the implication of dispute resolution clauses under which the parties are obliged to cooperate to support the dispute resolution process (*Verfahrensförderungspflicht*). It was held that invoking non-compliance with an ADR process which was first boycotted by the party raising the plea was contrary to the principle of **2.157**

[232] BGH NJW 1999, 647.
[233] BGH NJW 1984, 669, BGH NJW 1999, 647.
[234] §1032(1) ZPO.
[235] BGH NJW 1999, 647.
[236] OLG Frankfurt aM (Senat Darmstadt) NJW-RR 1998, 778.

loyalty and trust (*Treuwidrigkeitseinwand*).[237] The court concluded that the duty to support the agreed dispute resolution process prevents a party from invoking non-compliance with an ADR clause if such a plea contradicts the earlier actions of the party raising it.

2.158 A different reasoning has been presented by *OLG Frankfurt am Main* the court clarified that the duty to support a dispute resolution process is confined to cooperative participation in the process. Such duty should not be extended to include financial contributions towards meeting the cost of conciliation. In the court's view, the party against whom the claim is brought should not be expected to financially support the proceedings brought against it. In reaching this conclusion the court showed sympathy with the 'natural reflex' of the 'attacked party' to ignore the financial consequences of such an attack. The court held that the contradictory behaviour of a defendant who first boycotted the ADR by not paying the requisite deposit and then invoked an ADR clause as a defence in court proceedings is of no relevance to blocking the enforceability of a disputed clause.

2.159 The court did not clarify what steps should be taken by the claimant who, due to lack of cooperation by the other party, could not initiate the contractual procedure to which the parties were subsequently referred. The *Bundesgerichtshof* treats participation in the costs of the proceedings as included in the duty to support the agreed dispute resolution process. Notwithstanding diverging views on this mater, these cases show that unconscionable conduct of the defendant may render the plea of non-compliance with an ADR clause ineffective due to an abuse of right.

Summary

2.160 An important characteristic of German ADR law was early crystallisation of sanctions for non-compliance with mediation and expert determination clauses. A majority of cases concerned consensual ADR. Expert determination, although recognised by German law, is less popular than mediation and does not benefit from a comprehensive statutory framework. German courts have enforced ADR clauses in various contexts where they have found them; most prominently, in institutional rules governing members of certain professions.

2.161 The consequences of non-compliance with conciliation clauses are not prescribed in statute but have been devised by the courts. The courts focus on procedural effects of bypassing agreed dispute resolution steps. The sanctions are analogous to those for breach of an arbitration clause (dismissal of an action as inadmissible). In the case of mediation clauses inadmissibility results from temporal exclusion of actionability. The court dismisses the action as premature by a procedural order without adjudicating the merits of the case.

[237] The principle is contained in § 242 BGB and applies to both ADR and arbitration clauses.

The German judiciary treats differently the consequences of non-compliance with expert determination clauses. Failure to submit a dispute to an expert in accordance with a contract results in dismissal of an action as unfounded with anjudgment on the merits. However, if an expert's mandate involves merely a non-binding recommendation, rather than a final decision, the effects of non-compliance with such a clause are equated to those under clauses providing for consensual ADR. 2.162

France

In France the leading ADR[238] techniques involve consensual methods such as mediation and conciliation.[239] French law recognises expert determination (*expertise arbitrage*) as a means of out-of-court dispute resolution.[240] The most important features of mediation and expert determination in French jurisprudence will be presented below together with the French courts' position as to the enforceability of clauses in both types of ADR. 2.163

Mediation

Mediation in French Law

Consensual ADR became popular in France at the same time as the use of mediation, imported from America, increased. French mediation practice has been particularly shaped by mediators from Quebec, who obtained their education on dispute management in the United States during the 'ADR boom'.[241] Under this 2.164

[238] The French acronym for alternative dispute resolution is 'RAD' (*règlement alternatif des différends, résolution amiable des différends)* or 'MARC' (*modes alternatifs de règlement des conflits*). The latter term is used, inter alia, by C Jarrosson, 'Les modes alternatifs de règlement des conflits' (1997) 49 *Revue Internationale de droit comparé* 325, 328 and L Cadiet, J Normand, S Mekki, *Théorie générale du procès* (Presses Universitaires de France, 2010) 197ff. In the present chapter the term ADR will be used, as an acronym of international application.

[239] Mediation and conciliation were traditionally considered as distinct methods of dispute resolution in France. Under this approach conciliation does not require the participation of a neutral third party and may be conducted between the parties themselves, while mediation involves the role of a mediator (M Guillaume-Hofnund, *La Médiation* (Presses Universitaires de France, 2005) 76ff). The distinction between mediation and conciliation is not free of controversy and some authors reject the traditional approach using both terms interchangeably, see C Jarrosson, 'Note—Cour de cassation (Ch. commerciale) 28 novembre 1995: Peyrin et autres v. société Polyclinique des Fleurs' (1996) 4 *Revue de l'arbitrage* 614, fn 1. The author points out that there is no difference in the normative regime governing mediation and conciliation under French law. Also in the present work the terms 'mediation' and 'conciliation' are used interchangeably (see also 1.18 on this aspect).

[240] On the spectrum of ADR methods available in France, see L Cadiet, 'Panorama des modes alternatifs de règlement des conflits en droit français' (2011) 28 *Ritsumeikan Law Review* 147.

[241] See, especially in relation to family mediation, the report of M Sassier, Arguments et propositions pour un statut de la Médiation Familiale en France: Rapport remis à Madame la Ministre déléguée à la famille, à l'enfance et aux personnes handicapées (Ministère délégué à la famille, à l'enfance et aux personnes handicapées, 2001) 9, available at: www.ladocumentationfrancaise.fr/var/storage/rapports-publics/014000484.pdf.

influence French jurisprudence assimilated mediation patterns originating in the common law tradition.

2.165 The first initiatives to institutionalise mediation in France were undertaken in the 1990s.[242] Legislative attention focused on mediation in criminal litigation.[243] Mediation in civil cases developed largely without any statutory framework. The first act codifying mediation in civil and commercial matters was passed in 1995[244] and a year later mediation was introduced to the French Civil Procedure Code[245] (*Code de procédure civile*).[246] Under these regulations mediation can be ordered by consent of both parties at any stage of the proceedings.[247]

2.166 France implemented the European Mediation Directive into its domestic legal order.[248] One significant change resulting from this was a statutory definition of mediation. In accordance with the Directive 'mediation' means a structured process, however named or referred to, whereby two or more parties to a dispute attempt by themselves, on a voluntary basis, to reach an agreement on the settlement of their dispute with the assistance of a mediator.[249]

2.167 The most significant development in French mediation law is the introduction of the duty to consider ADR. Under the decree of 15 March 2015,[250] which entered into force on 1 April 2015, in all civil and commercial matters it is mandatory to demonstrate that the claimant attempted to find an amicable resolution of

[242] See the report of J-M Coulon, *Réflexions et propositions sur la procédure civile, Rapport au garde des Sceaux* (Ministre de la Justice, 1997) Chapter 3, and the author's remarks on the development of the movement which he describes as *justice de compromis* (available at: www.ladocumentationfrancaise.fr/var/storage/rapports-publics/974024100.pdf).

[243] Loi n° 93-2 du 4 janvier 1993 portant réforme de la procédue pénale, JORF n° 0003 du 4 janvier 1993, p 215.

[244] Loi n° 95-125 du 8 février 1995 relative à l'organisation des juridictions et à la procédure civile, pénale et administrative, JORF n° 0034 du 9 février 1995, p 2175.

[245] Hereafter 'CPC'.

[246] Décret n° 96-652 du 22 juillet 1996 relatif à la conciliation et à la mediation judiciaires, JORF n° 0170 du 23 juillet 1996, p 11125.

[247] Art 21 Loi n° 95-125 du 8 février 1995 relative à l'organisation des juridictions et à la procédure civile, pénale et administrative and Art 131(1), Décret n° 96-652 du 22 juillet 1996 relatif à la conciliation et à la mediation judiciaires.

[248] Directive 2008/52/EC of the European Parliament and of the Council of 21 May 2008 on certain aspects of mediation in civil and commercial matters, [2008] OJ L136/3–8, 24/05/2008, implemented into French law by Ordonnance n° 2011-1540 du 16 novembre 2011 portant transposition de la directive 2008/52/CE du Parlement européen et du Conseil du 21 mai 2008 sur certains aspects de la médiation en matière civile et commerciale, JORF n° 0266 du 16 novembre 2011, p 19286. For a critical evaluation of the Directive from the perspective of French law see B Gorchs-Gelzer, 'Regard critique sur l'ordonnance n° 2011-1540 transposant la directive médiation' (2012) 117 *Droit et procédures* 2. See also J-P Tricot, 'Chronique de droit des modes amiables de règlement des conflits' (2011) 1 *Revue de l'arbitrage* 207, 208. Generally on the European Mediation Directive see 1.88.

[249] Art 21 Loi n° 95-125 du 8 février 1995 relative à l'organisation des juridictions et à la procédure civile, pénale et administrative. It must be noted that, before the statutory definition was introduced, mediation was similarly defined by jurisprudence, see Cour de cassation, Cass Civ 2e, 16 June 1993, *Bulletin Civil* II, no 211, 114; M Guillaume-Hofnund, *La Médiation*, n 239 above, 76ff.

[250] Décret n° 2015-282 du 11 mars 2015 relatif à la simplification de la procédure civile à la communication électronique et à la résolution amiable des différends, JORF n° 0062 du 14 mars 2015, p 4851.

the dispute.[251] Parties are exempt from the duty to attempt ADR only in cases of urgency. Including compulsory ADR in the parties' pre-action conduct is an important manifestation of the mediation-oriented approach, strengthened by the recent legislative changes in France.[252]

With the consent of both parties the court may refer the parties to mediation during the conduct of proceedings (*médiation judiciaire*).[253] In such a case mediation is carried out by a neutral third party appointed by the judge. The court also determines the time period for which the referral to mediation is granted, and may resume the proceedings at any time if satisfied that mediation is ineffective. Equally, a party or the mediator can apply to the court to terminate mediation and resume the proceedings at any time. **2.168**

Mediation can also occur as a result of a contract (*médiation conventionnelle*).[254] The parties can contract for mediation in advance by way of a dispute resolution clause, or conclude a mediation agreement after the dispute has arisen. Contractual mediation is governed by Articles 1528–1567 CPC. The statute does not, however, contain provisions regulating the consequences of non-compliance with mediation clauses. The changing attitude to out-of-court dispute resolution in France prompted the courts to devise solutions for this matter. **2.169**

Enforceability of Mediation Clauses

Means of Defence

The lack of any statutory sanction for breach of mediation clauses required judges to rely on general rules of civil procedure. Discussion of the enforceability of ADR concentrates on the means of defence that may be employed under French procedural law. The means of defence (*les moyens de défense*) are codified in Title V of the French Civil Procedure Code. Under this enactment the defendant may raise three types of pleading: defences on the merits (*les défenses au fond*), procedural pleas (*les exceptions de procédure*) and pleas as to inadmissibility (*fins de non-recevoir*).[255] **2.170**

[251] Art 58, CPC, as modified by Décret n° 2015-282 du 11 mars 2015.

[252] This development must be contrasted with the position during early 2000s when mediation was considered to be far less prevalent in France than was the case in common law jurisdictions. On this aspect see M Lindeperg, *Médiation et conciliation de proximité* (Rapport presenté au nom de la section du cadre de vie, Conseil économique et social, 2001) II-29. The author submits that jurisdictions derived from Roman law are characterised by the culture of conflict, rather than compromise. See also B Lasserre, 'Optimising the Management of your International Disputes. Thanks for Mediation: The French Experience' (2003) 25 *Betriebs-Berater* 22, 24. cf L Cadiet, 'Conciliation in France: a Cross between Tradition and Modernity' in *The Recent Tendencies of Development in Civil Procedure Law—between East and West* (Justitia, 2007) 58, who emphasised a clear tendency of French judiciary in favour of ADR.

[253] Arts 131-1 to 131-15, CPC.

[254] Arts 1528–1564, CPC, as added by Décret n° 2012-66 du 20 janvier 2012 relatif à la résolution amiable des différends, JORF n° 0019 du 22 janvier 2012, p 1280.

[255] S Guinchard, C Chainais, F Ferrand, *Procédure civile. Droit interne et droit de l'Union européenne*, 30th edn (Dalloz, 2010) para 316.

The first type is classified as defence *in meriti*. The second and third are classified as procedural.[256]

Defence on the Merits

2.171 The first type of pleading codified in CPC is a defence on the merits.[257] The definition of this defence is contained in Article 71 CPC, according to which it involves any means directed at attacking the merits of the claim.[258] A substantive defence may apply to both the legal and factual grounds of a claim. By way of substantive defence the defendant can raise issues such as objections as to the title, invalidity of the contract or other matters relating to the merits of the claim. Article 72 CPC clarifies that a substantive defence can be pleaded at any stage of proceedings. The successful pleading of a substantive defence results in dismissal of the claim by way of an award on the merits.

2.172 The French courts never considered that this type of defence could arise from breach of mediation clauses. Instead, debate as to the enforceability of contractual commitments to mediate focused on procedural types of pleading: *fins de non-recevoir* and *exceptions de procédure*. These two types of procedural defence are discussed further below.

Procedural Defence

2.173 A statutory definition of *exceptions de procédure* is contained in Article 73 CPC, which provides that a procedural plea means one on any grounds that lead to the procedure being declared irregular or being extinguished or stayed.[259] The types of procedural pleas are expressly enumerated in the Code. They comprise: pleas of lack of jurisdiction (*les exceptions d'incompétence*—Articles 75–99 CPC), pleas of *lis pendens* and related cases (*les exceptions de litispendance et de connexité*—Articles 100–107 CPC), dilatory pleas (*les exceptions dilatoires*—Articles 108–111 CPC) and pleas of nullity (*les exceptions de nullité*) relating to nullity of pleadings (Articles 112–116 CPC) and nullity resulting from lack of capacity to be a party to the proceedings (Articles 117–121 CPC). The consequences of successfully entering procedural pleas can be two-fold. Dilatory pleas may result in stay of the

[256] J Héron, *Droit judiciaire privé* (Montchrestien, 1991) paras 111ff; S Guinchard, *Droit et practique de la procédure civile* (Dalloz, 2004) para 190.08.

[257] Also referred to as 'substantive defence'. For a commentary see J Héron, *Droit judiciaire privé*, n 256 above, para 103 (definition of substantive defence) and paras 108–10 (procedural regime); S Guinchard, *Droit et practique de la procédure civile*, n 256 above, paras 191.11–191.21; S Guinchard, C Chainais, F Ferrand, *Procédure civile*, n 255 above, paras 317–18.

[258] Art 71, CPC: 'Constitue une défense au fond tout moyen qui tend à faire rejeter comme non justifiée, après examen au fond du droit, la prétention de l'adversaire.'

[259] Art 73, CPC: 'Constitue une exception de procédure tout moyen qui tend soit à faire déclarer la procédure irrégulière ou éteinte, soit à en suspendre le cours.'

proceedings.[260] Other types of pleas may lead to conclusion of the proceedings without adjudicating the merits of the case.[261]

The procedural regime is not as flexible as the one governing defence on the merits. Unlike substantive defences, which can be raised at any stage of the proceedings, procedural pleas must be raised within a restricted time-frame. Under Article 74 CPC, procedural pleas, in order to be admissible, must be raised simultaneously and prior to any defence on the merits or *fins de non-recevoir.* It follows that procedural pleas must precede any other pleading of the defendant. Failure to raise a procedural plea in a timely manner results in the court disregarding the plea.[262] **2.174**

The catalogue of *exceptions de procédure* is not exhaustive. It is submitted that the general definition of procedural pleas was included in the Code to provide for the new types of *exceptions* to be included in this category.[263] The open-ended scope of procedural pleas gave rise to interpretations to the effect that breach of ADR clauses may be subjected to the statutory regime of *exceptions de procédure.* **2.175**

The second type of procedural defence in the CPC is a plea as to inadmissibility—*fin de non-recevoir.* Article 122 CPC defines this type of defence as any ground whose purpose is to get the opponent's claim declared inadmissible, without entering into the merits of the case.[264] The provision clarifies the circumstances which may give rise to a plea of inadmissibility. They include lack of a right of action, such as not being the proper party to initiate the proceedings, lack of interest in bringing the claim, lapse of the limitation period for action and res judicata. Article 122 CPC governs the conditions for admissibility of the claim (*recevabilité de la demande*). Defendant objections as to admissibility can be pleaded by way of *fins de non-recevoir.* **2.176**

In scholarly opinion, pleas as to inadmissibility are of mixed character as they comprise elements of the defence on the merits and of procedural pleas.[265] The substantive character of pleas of inadmissibility is signified by conclusion of the **2.177**

[260] See S Guinchard, C Chainais, F Ferrand, *Procédure civile*, n 255 above, paras 988–991 for particular examples of dilatory pleas.

[261] See J Héron, *Droit judiciaire privé*, n 256 above, paras 118–126; S Guinchard, *Droit et practique de la procédure civile*, n 256 above, paras 192.11–192.91; S Guinchard, C Chainais, F Ferrand, *Procédure civile*, n 255 above, paras 319–324 for details.

[262] On preclusion of procedural pleas see S Guinchard, *Droit et practique de la procédure*, n 256 above, para 192.72 and the case law cited.

[263] *ibid*, para 192.13; S Guinchard, C Chainais, F Ferrand, *Procédure civile*, n 255 above, para 320. The same view was present under the predecessor to the CPC which codified *exceptions de procédure* in Art 166ff.

[264] Art 122, CPC: 'Constitue une fin de non-recevoir tout moyen qui tend à faire déclarer l'adversaire irrecevable en sa demande, sans examen au fond, pour défaut de droit d'agir, tel le défaut de qualité, le défaut d'intérêt, la prescription, le délai préfix, la chose jugée.'

[265] S Guinchard, C Chainais, F Ferrand, *Procédure civile*, n 255 above, para 326 and the literature cited. Historically *fins de non-recevoir* were regarded as defence on the merits as they constituted a bar to hearing the claim in its entirety, H Solus, R Perrot, *Droit judiciaire privé* (Sirey, 1969) para 316. See also A Joly, *Procédure civile et voies d'exécution* (Sirey, 1969) para 113.

proceedings as a result of successful raising of a plea, and the fact that the grounds of *fin de non-recevoir* may arise from substantive law (eg a statute of limitations or other substantive norms determining the right of action). The procedural character of *fins de non-recevoir* is manifested by the fact that successfully raising a plea bars hearing the claim on the merits and results in the court declaring the proceedings inadmissible. Due to this diverse nature, *fins de non-recevoir* are traditionally considered the most problematic type of defence.[266]

2.178 Successfully pleading inadmissibility results in the court concluding the proceedings without adjudicating the merits of the case. A declaration of inadmissibility is an order confirming a state of affairs (*jugement en l'etat*) without a res judicata effect.[267] If an obstacle to admissibility comes to an end, a party may submit the claim in court again. Because a declaration as to inadmissibility is not equivalent to judgment on the merits, the party is free to recommence litigation.

2.179 The procedural regime governing *fins de non-recevoir* is more relaxed than the one concerning procedural pleas.[268] Under Article 123 CPC a plea as to inadmissibility can be raised at any time. The court, however, has discretion to impose costs against parties whose pleas are raised late.[269] Pleas as to inadmissibility can arise from statute, a court order or a contract.[270] Article 122 CPC expressly provides that the list of *fins de non-recevoir* contained in this provision is merely an illustrative one. Contractual *fins de non-recevoir* are the most important in the context of the enforceability of multi-tiered clauses.

Evolving Jurisprudence of the *Cour de Cassation*

2.180 Judicial responses to the enforceability of mediation clauses were initially very diverse. The controversy concerned issues as fundamental as the mere existence of any enforceable duties arising from mediation clauses. In certain cases the *Cour de cassation* denied the binding force of mediation clauses, treating the voluntary nature of mediation as a bar to any remedy for breach of a contractual commitment to mediate.[271] An additional argument against the enforceability of

[266] H Solus, R Perrot, *Droit judiciaire privé*, n 265 above, paras 317–319. See also S Guinchard, *Droit et practique de la procédure civile*, n 256 above, paras 193.21–193.23 on the distinction between *fin de non-recevoir* and *exceptions de procédure*.

[267] Cour de cassation 2e civ 20 juin 1985, *Bull civ* II, n° 125; Cour de cassation 3e civ, 4 oct 1995, *Procédures* novembre 1995, n° 293, obs Perrot; 2e Civ—3 juillet 2008, BICC n° 692 du 1er décembre 2008; R Perrot, 'Note sous 2e Civ.—3 juillet 2008 (Jugement d'irrecevabilité rendu en l'état)', *Procédures*, n° 10, octobre 2008, n° 259, p 11.

[268] *Fins de non-recevoir* were not included in the initial text of the procedural code and were subsequently created to avoid a rigid procedural regime of *exceptions* (see *Répertoire de procédure civile et commerciale. Exceptionis et Fins de Non-Recevoir*, Dalloz, Paris 1955, no 8 for details).

[269] Cour de cassation (2e civ), 1 juillet 1981, Gaz Pal 1981, 750; Cour de cassation (2e civ), 27 février 2003. *Procédures* 5/2003, n° 111.

[270] S Guinchard, C Chainais, F Ferrand, *Procédure civile*, n 255 above, para 330 and cases cited.

[271] Cour de cassation (1re Ch civ) 23 janvier 2001, RTD *civ* 2001, 359, (2001) 4 *Revue de l'arbitrage* 751; Cour de cassation (Ch soc) 26 janvier 1994, *Bulletin*, V, no 32.

mediation clauses arose under Article 1174 of the French Civil Code.[272] Under this provision an obligation is void if it is subject to a condition entirely dependent on the will of the party which binds itself (*condition potestative*).[273]

Treating mediation clauses as purely voluntary arrangements attracted scholarly criticism.[274] It was submitted that meditation clauses should be governed by Article 1134(1) CC, which provides that agreements lawfully entered into constitute the law between the parties and must be performed in good faith. Treating ADR clauses as enforceable contracts opened discussion as to what remedy should be awarded for breach of the parties' commitment to mediate before commencing litigation. As indicated, the discussion as to how to enforce mediation clauses focused on whether failure to undergo the agreed process gives rise to a procedural plea or a plea as to inadmissibility. **2.181**

Initially, French courts supported the stand that failure to exhaust pre-action mediation gives rise to a procedural plea—*exception de procédure*.[275] This interpretation relied on an assumption that the *exceptions* enumerated in CPC do not constitute a complete list and that the courts can identify new procedural pleas not included in statutory regulation. According to this view, breach of ADR clauses was classified as giving rise to a similar type of defence as breach of an arbitration clause or a jurisdiction agreement. **2.182**

Some authors distinguished this view, suggesting that breach of an ADR clause gives rise to a dilatory plea (Article 108 CPC), rather than a plea based on the lack of jurisdiction (Articles 75ff CPC).[276] Under this interpretation a successful plea based on non-compliance with a mediation clause leads to a stay of the proceedings. The court orders a stay upon an application of the parties but without receiving any submissions to this effect other than the plea of non-compliance with a mediation clause. This approach has never been adopted by French judiciary, and was criticised in the literature as lacking statutory grounds.[277] **2.183**

[272] *Code Civil*, hereafter also 'CC'.

[273] See C Jarrosson, 'La sanction du non- respect d'une clause instituant un préliminaire obligatoire de conciliation ou de mediation: 'Note—Cour de cassation (2e Ch. civ.) 6 juillet 2000; Cour de cassation (1re civ.) 23 janvier et 6 février 2001' (2001) 4 *Revue de l'arbitrage* 752, 757 for an analysis. *Condition potestative* is defined in Article 1170 CC as 'one which makes the fulfillment of the agreement contingent on an event which one or the other of the contracting parties has the power to make happen or to prevent'.

[274] L Cadiet, J Normand, S Mekki, *Théorie générale du process*, n 238 above, 469; C Jarrosson, 'La sanction', n 273 above, 756–59 and the literature cited.

[275] Cour de cassation (2e civ), 15 janvier 1992, (1992) 4 *Revue de l'arbitrage* 646, obs Cohen; Cour d'Appel Fort-de-France, 20 décembre 1996, RGDP 1998, 174, obs C Jarrosson.

[276] X Lagarde, 'L'efficacité des clauses de conciliation ou de mediation' (2000) 3 *Revue de l'arbitrage* 377, 377ff.

[277] S Guinchard, C Chainais, F Ferrand, *Procédure civile*, n 255 above, para 330; S Guinchard, *Droit et practique de la procédure civile*, n 256 above, para 193.15; C Jarrosson, 'Observations on Poiré v Tripier' (2003) 3 *Arbitration International* 363, 364. See also C Jarrosson, 'La sanction', n 273 above, 762–36, who submits that this solution unjustifiably expands the discretionary powers of the judge but, in principle, is an attractive proposition *de lege ferenda*.

2.184 An alternative standpoint assumed that a claim in court bypassing the agreed mediation procedure enables the defendant to plead inadmissibility of the proceedings. Under this interpretation breach of mediation clauses gives rise to a *fin de non-recevoir* type of defence. This approach gained recognition in the jurisprudence of the *Cour de cassation*[278] and was advocated in the literature.[279] It provided an alternative to the approach under which the effects of ADR clauses are equated with breach of arbitration or jurisdiction agreements.

2.185 The *Cour de cassation* put an end to the uncertainty connected with a number of possible interpretations[280] and clarified the consequences of non-compliance with mediation clauses in the joint chambers decision in *Poiré v Tripier*.[281] In this seminal case breach of mediation clauses was classified as giving rise to a plea of inadmissibility (*fin de non-recevoir*). The controversial clause was contained in a contract for the sale of shares in a company. The clause provided that in case of a dispute, the parties must resort to mediation before bringing an action in court. The claimant commenced litigation without first attempting to mediate.

2.186 In the first instance the court gave an award on the merits, thereby disregarding breach of the mediation clause. The appellate court overturned this decision and declared the proceedings temporarily inadmissible (*irrecevable en l'état*).[282] The defendant's plea of non-compliance with a mediation clause was considered a plea of inadmissibility—*fin de non-recevoir*. This interpretation was subsequently followed by the joint chambers of the *Cour de cassation*.

2.187 The *Cour de cassation* took the opportunity to conclusively clarify the status of mediation clauses under French law.[283] The court began by confirming that Article 122 CPC does not contain an exhaustive list of possible *fins de non-recevoir*. It was held that pleas as to inadmissibility can be of both contractual and statutory sources. The court departed from its earlier line of reasoning according to which a bar to admissibility cannot result from a contractual provision.[284] Looking at the clause in question, the court held that it contained a binding obligation to attempt mediation before resorting to court proceedings. The court rejected the argument that the voluntary nature of mediation renders mediation clauses

278 Cour de cassation (2e civ), 6 juillet 2000, (2001) 4 *Revue de l'arbitrage* 749; Cour de cassation (3e civ), 5 juillet 1989, *Bulletin*, no 18, p 87.

279 C Jarrosson, 'Note—Cour de cassation (Ch. commerciale) 28 novembre 1995: Peyrin et autres v. société Polyclinique des Fleurs', n 239 above, 616.

280 C Jarrosson (*ibid*, 753) points out the characteristic discrepancy of interpretations adopted by the first and second chamber of the *Cour de cassation*.

281 Cour de cassation (ch mixte), 14 février 2003, pourvoi n°00-19423; 00-19424, Bulletin civ 2003 MIXTE N° 1 p 1.

282 Cour d'appel de Paris (14e Ch A) 23 mai 2001, (2003) 2 *Revue de l'arbitrage* 405.

283 The adjudicating panel consisted of the judges of the five chambers of Cour de cassation (Première chambre civile, Deuxième chambre civile, Troisième chambre civile, Chambre sociale, Chambre commerciale) chaired by the President of the Court.

284 This approach was historically adopted in eg Cour de cassation (2e civ), 10 février 1988, Bulletin, II, no 41, p 22.

unenforceable.[285] Valid mediation clauses were considered to prevent admission of a claim until the prescribed steps were complied with. The court conclusively stated that breach of a mediation clause gives rise to the procedural defence of *fin de non-recevoir*.

The court further clarified that initiation of ADR in compliance with a contractual clause suspends the running of a limitation period. Before the ruling in *Poiré v Tripier* there was some uncertainty in this area. It was submitted that the principle *contra non valentem agere non currit praescriptio* ('a prescription does not run against one who is unable to act') protects the claimant from suffering adverse consequences of limitation during the ADR process.[286] The joint chambers of *Cour de cassation* endorsed this conclusion. The court also confirmed that taking into account the claimant's failure to exhaust ADR is appropriate upon the plea of a defendant, and not ex officio. **2.188**

The ruling in *Poiré v Tripier* has been well received by commentators.[287] By stating that a limitation period is not initiated during mediation the court addressed the main concern expressed by opponents of the enforceability of contractual ADR. Commentators also analysed whether the court's declaration of inadmissibility was conclusive and could be re-litigated.[288] It was put forward that the court's decision as to inadmissibility is final and conclusive only in the particular set of circumstances at hand. Nothing bars the party from submitting the claim anew once those circumstances change ie after the parties have attempted the mediation required by contract. In this way inadmissibility due to non-compliance with ADR is of a temporary nature (*irrecevabilité en l'état*). The solution adopted by the *Cour de cassation* was also considered optimal in terms of its procedural ramifications. Although Article 123 CPC gives the parties flexibility as to the timing of the plea, delay in entering a *fin de non-recevoir* defence could be regarded as a waiver of the rights under a conciliation clause.[289] **2.189**

In the wake of *Poiré v Tripier* the judiciary followed the interpretation of the joint chambers of the *Cour de cassation*.[290] The courts, however, tend to apply a restrictive threshold as to the validity of clauses at issue. In *Clinique du Golfe v Le Gall*[291] the court refused to enforce a conciliation clause which had not been expressly incorporated into the agreement. The case concerned a dispute between a doctor and a private hospital and the clause in question derived from standard terms **2.190**

[285] See cases cited above (2.180).

[286] C Jarrosson, 'La sanction', n 273 above, 763.

[287] L Cadiet, J Normand, S Mekki, *Théorie générale du process*, n 238 above, 469–71 and the literature cited.

[288] C Jarrosson, 'Note—Cour de cassation (Chambre Mixte), 14 février 2003 et Cour d'appel de Paris (14e Ch. A), 23 mai 2001' (2002) 2 *Revue de l'arbitrage* 406, 408–9.

[289] Unlike exceptions, which have to be invoked *in limine litis*, pleas as to admissibility can be raised at any stage of proceedings (*en tout état de cause*).

[290] See eg Cour de cassation (Ch comm), 17 Juin 2003, N° de pourvoi: 99-16001, Bulletin 2003 IV, N° 101, p 112.

[291] Cour de cassation (1re civ), 6 mai 2003, N° de pourvoi: 01-01291; Bulletin 2003 I N° 108 p 85.

of contracts. The standard terms, however, had not been incorporated into the contract even by reference and the court held that they did not form a part of the agreement. It was clarified that conciliation clauses must be agreed in writing and cannot be incorporated into the legal relationship as customary terms under Articles 1135 and 1160 CC.[292]

2.191 In *Placoplâtre v SA Eiffage TP*[293] the court applied a high threshold for determining the mandatory character of mediation clauses. The disputed clause required the parties to engage in 'consultations' prior to resorting to arbitration. The court held that the parties' failure to reference the process properly as 'conciliation' rendered the clause unenforceable. The court interpreted the contractual stipulation as an expression of the parties' intention to hold informal discussions whether or not to commence arbitration, which could not be equated with an ADR clause.[294]

2.192 By contrast, apparently permissive language in an escalation clause providing for negotiations prior to CIETAC arbitration was upheld in *Séribo v Hainan Yangpu Xindadao Industrial Co Ltd*.[295] The clause provided that disputes arising out of the performance of the agreement between the parties should be settled by amicable consultation. Disputes that could not be so settled should be submitted to the China International Economic and Trade Arbitration Commission (CIETAC) for mediation or arbitration.[296] The court was confronted with an alternative translation of the clause in question, which provided that in case of a dispute, the parties shall 'endeavour to reach an amicable solution'. Notwithstanding the lack of precise language the court enforced the clause.

2.193 Finally, the scope of conciliation clauses has been limited strictly to claims arising under contract. In *SAS Eurauchan v Sté Moyrand Bally*[297] the court held that a mandatory conciliation provision in a distribution agreement did not extend to claims based in tort. The action was founded on the French Commercial Code providing for liability in tort for an abrupt termination of an established commercial relationship.[298] It was held that such a claim falls outside the scope of an escalation clause. The court reached this conclusion notwithstanding the express wording of the clause that it applied to all disputes relating to the termination or expiration of the contract 'for any cause whatsoever'.

[292] Art 1135, CC 'Les conventions obligent non seulement à ce qui y est exprimé, mais encore à toutes les suites que l'équité, l'usage ou la loi donnent à l'obligation d'après sa nature'; Art 1160, CC: 'On doit suppléer dans le contrat les clauses qui y sont d'usage, quoiqu'elles n'y soient pas exprimées'.

[293] Cour de cassation (1re civ), 6 fevrier 2007, N° de pourvoi: 05-17573; Bulletin 2007 I N° 55 p 50.

[294] The same conclusion was reached on similar facts in *Knappe Composites v Art Métal* (Cour de cassation (3e civ) N° de pourvoi: 13-10833, available at: www.legifrance.gouv.fr).

[295] *Séribo v Hainan Yangpu Xindadao Industrial Co Ltd*, Cour de cassation (1ere civ), N° de pourvoi: 11-10347, available at: www.legifrance.gouv.fr.

[296] The clause stated that 'disputes arising out of the performance of the agreement between the parties shall be settled by amicable consultation' and 'disputes that could not be so settled shall be submitted to the China International Economic and Trade Arbitration Commission (CIETAC) for mediation or arbitration'.

[297] Cour de cassation (Ch comm), N° de pourvoi: 11-18852, available at: www.legifrance.gouv.fr.

[298] Art L 442-6(I)(5), Commercial Code (*Code de Commerce*).

The above exemplary cases demonstrate that recent French law has crystallised the consequences of non-compliance with mediation clauses. The decision in *Poiré v Tripier* conclusively classified breach of mediation clauses as giving rise to the procedural defence of inadmissibility, and this interpretation was followed by the judiciary. An important feature of the French solution is that the court declares prematurely initiated proceedings as inadmissible without adjudicating on the merits of the case. A declaration of inadmissibility is temporary (*irrecevabilité en l'état*) and does not create a bar to a subsequent claim, which can be raised once contractual ADR is complied with.[299] This removes uncertainty regarding the limitations imposed on access to court. A declaration of inadmissibility does not amount to a denial of justice,[300] and it is accepted that the parties may temporarily 'neutralise' actionability of the claim (*neutraliser l'action en justice*).[301] So long as the parties to ADR clauses do not purport to exclude access to court completely, such a stipulation is valid under French law. Importantly, French courts emphasise the availability of interim measures, whether or not the parties underwent the agreed dispute resolution procedure.[302] **2.194**

Finally, the ruling in *Poiré v Tripier* equated the consequences of non-compliance with contractual dispute resolution procedures with those arising under statute. For instance, failure to undergo a procedure before the Agricultural Land Tribunal (*tribunal paritaire des baux ruraux*) in accordance with Article 880 CPC gives rise to a *fin de non-recevoir* defence, as established in a long-standing interpretation of the *Cour de cassation*.[303] The same sanction has been adopted for those who bypass out-of-court dispute resolution procedures prescribed by administrative law.[304] It can be anticipated that inadmissibility of the claim will also be a consequence of failure to exhaust the compulsory ADR process prescribed by the decree of 15 March 2015.[305] **2.195**

[299] C Jarrosson, 'Note—Cour de cassation (Chambre Mixte), 14 février 2003 et Cour d'appel de Paris (14e Ch. A), 23 mai 2001' (2002) 2 *Revue de l'Arbitrage* 406, 408–9.

[300] L Cadiet, J Normand, S Mekki, *Théorie générale du procès*, n 238 above, 467; C. Jarrosson, 'Note—Cour de cassation (Chambre Mixte), 14 février 2003', n 288 above, 409–10; C Jarrosson, 'La sanction', n 273 above, 760.

[301] See especially C Jarrosson, 'La sanction', n 273 above, 760.

[302] *Poiré v Tripier*, Cour de cassation (ch mixte), 14 février 2003, pourvoi n°00-19423; 00-19424, Bulletin civil 2003 MIXTE N° 1 p 1 ('L'existence d'un préliminaire obligatoire de conciliation n'exclut pas que la partie intéressée puisse, en cas d'urgence, saisir le juge des référés d'une demande tendant au prononcé d'une mesure relevant de ses attributions').

[303] Cour de cassation (3e civ), 15 février 1978, *Bulletin*, III, no 83, p 64.

[304] Conseil d'Etat, 9 decembre 1991, N° 84308, Snoy, (1991) *Recueil Lebon* 423. In this case the *Conseil d'Etat* upheld the decision declaring inadmissibility of the procedure before an administrative court where a party failed to exhaust a compulsory 'arbitration' procedure, understood as mandatory conciliation.

[305] Décret n° 2015-282 du 11 mars 2015 relatif à la simplification de la procédure civile à la communication électronique et à la résolution amiable des différends, JORF n°0062 du 14 mars 2015, p 4851. The decree lays down that the claimant is obliged to demonstrate that, before resorting to court, an amicable resolution of the dispute was attempted, but proved unsuccessful.

Substantive Effects of Mediation Clauses

2.196 The substantive consequences of mediation clauses have been the subject of scholarly debate in France. It is accepted that mediation clauses are contractual terms which must be performed in accordance with the above-mentioned provisions of the Civil Code, notwithstanding their procedural consequences.[306] Application of contract law provisions is relevant to ascertain the validity of and scope of the duty created by mediation clauses.[307] The main provisions of the Civil Code invoked in this context are Articles 1134 and 1135. The former states that agreements lawfully entered into take the place of the law for those who have made them and must be performed in good faith. The latter provides that a contract binds parties not only according to its wording, but also as to the consequences resulting from equity, custom and the law.

2.197 Contract law was also applied to ascertain the waiver of rights arising under mediation clauses by not invoking the claimant's failure to adhere to the agreed procedure before the relevant body.[308] Finally, Article 1134 CC allowed the binding force of any obligation, once concluded, to remain valid regardless of the subsequent wishes of the parties.[309] This feature of contract was particularly relevant for the enforceability of clauses providing for consensual ADR. As previously indicated, one of the problematic issues surrounding this type of clauses is the requirement for voluntary participation in the agreed process.

2.198 French jurisprudence identifies two types of obligations in mediation clauses. The first type is an obligation of the result (*obligation de résultat*).[310] It entails initiating mediation, selecting the neutral person and presenting him with the case, as well as participating in the first mediation session. Failure by the claimant to initiate mediation constitutes breach of the duty to mediate. Equally, refusal by the other party to cooperate in initiating mediation amounts to breach of a contractual commitment. The second type of duty distinguished in French doctrine is an

[306] L Cadiet, J Normand, S Mekki, *Théorie générale du process*, n 238 above, 469; C Jarrosson, 'Les clauses de renégociation, de conciliation et de mediation' in *Les principales clauses de contrats conclus entre professionnels* (Presses Universitaires d'Aix-Marseille, 1990) 141; C Jarrosson, 'Les modes alternatifs de règlement des conflicts', n 238 above, 337; C Jarrosson, 'Note—Cour de cassation (Ch. commerciale) 28 novembre 1995', n 239 above, 618; X Lagarde, 'L'efficacité des clauses de conciliation ou de mediation', n 276 above, 398–99 and the literature cited.

[307] L Cadiet, J Normand, S Mekki, *Théorie générale du procès*, n 238 above, 469.

[308] See eg Cour de cassation (Ch comm), 28 novembre 1995, (1996) 4 *Revue de l'Arbitrage* 613. See also L Cadiet, J Normand, S Mekki, *Théorie générale du procès*, n 238 above, 467 on *mutuus dissensus* as a bar to the effectiveness of mediation clauses.

[309] G Rouhette, 'La force obligatoire du contrat, observations critiques' in D Tallon, D Harris (eds), *Le contrat aujourd'hui, comparaisons franco-anglaises* (LGDJ, 1987) 35–38.

[310] L Cadiet, J Normand, S Mekki, *Théorie générale du process*, n 238 above, 467; C Jarrosson, 'Les clauses de renégociation', n 306 above, 141; C Jarrosson, 'Note—Cour de cassation (Ch. commerciale) 28 novembre 1995', n 239 above, 618–19; C Jarrosson, 'Les modes alternatifs de règlement des conflicts', n 238 above, 337; X Lagarde, 'L'efficacité des clauses de conciliation ou de mediation', n 276 above, 386–90.

obligation of means (*obligation de moyens*). In the context of mediation clauses it implies participation in mediation in good faith with an intention of amicable resolution of the dispute. The parties are required to display a constructive attitude to the selected dispute resolution procedure. They are free to unilaterally terminate mediation so long as they acted in good faith, genuinely attempting to resolve the dispute amicably.[311] The dual nature of the obligation to mediate is sometimes compared to an analogous set of duties arising under renegotiation, *force majeure* or hardship clauses.[312] In addition to these obligations, some authors point out that mediation clauses give rise to negative duties not to initiate litigation until the agreed procedure is exhausted or the clause mutually terminated.[313]

Certain commentators question the appropriateness of distinguishing obligations of means in mediation clauses.[314] It is submitted that legal obligations cannot be inferred from the internal attitude of the parties towards achieving an amicable resolution of the dispute. Furthermore, a duty to perform contracts in good faith should not be equated with a duty of loyalty during negotiations. Due to the immeasurable nature of the duties involved, it is considered impractical to enforce any obligations of means arising under mediation clauses. On this view, the court is unable to verify the parties' good faith during settlement negotiations. This is notwithstanding the fact that some of the parties' uncooperative behaviours may appear abusive.[315] **2.199**

Confidentiality of mediation is a further argument against enforcing substantive rights under mediation clauses.[316] The paramount purpose of confidentiality is to encourage open discussions by the parties, secure in the knowledge that nothing disclosed during the mediation process will be used against them in court. Accepting contractual liability on the basis of conduct during mediation would compromise this objective. **2.200**

[311] C Jarrosson, 'Note—Cour de cassation (Ch. commerciale) 28 novembre 1995', n 239 above, 618. The author submits that the parties to mediation clauses are under a duty to 'participate in the game and show a constructive attitude' ('jouer le jeu et d'adopter une attitude constructive'). See also L Cadiet, J Normand, S Mekki, *Théorie générale du procès*, n 238 above, 467. The authors identify an obligation of means in mediation clauses by pointing to the duty of the parties to seek an amicable settlement of the dispute in good faith ('rechercher de bonne fois les termes d'une solution conventionnelle du différend'). Failure to discharge this duty is sometimes compared to the liability arising from *culpa in contrahendo*. C Jarrosson, 'Les modes alternatifs de règlement des conflicts', n 238 above, 337.

[312] R Ibara, L'aménagement de la force majeure dans le contrat: essai de théorie générale sur les clauses de force majeure dans les contrats internes et internationaux de longue durée (Université de Poitiers, 2012) 188; C Jarrosson, 'Les clauses de renégociation, de conciliation et de mediation', n 306 above, 141.

[313] L Cadiet, J Normand, S Mekki, *Théorie générale du procès*, n 238 above, 467.

[314] X Lagarde, 'L'efficacité des clauses de conciliation ou de mediation', n 276 above, 390–92.

[315] Notably, in his later works C Jarrosson limited the analysis of substantive components of mediation clauses by confining obligations of result to initiating mediation in accordance with the contract ('Note—Cour de cassation (Chambre Mixte), 14 février 2003', n 288 above, 410 and 'La sanction', n 273 above, 754).

[316] X Lagarde, 'L'efficacité des clauses de conciliation ou de mediation', n 276 above, 392–94.

2.201 The analysis of substantive rights involves ascertaining whether a defendant can claim any contractual remedies while pleading non-compliance with a mediation clause. The possible options include: specific performance, damages, or liquidated damages. Specific performance is the primary contractual remedy under French law.

2.202 The availability of specific performance for breach of mediation clauses was analysed with reference to arbitration.[317] Specific performance as a means of enforcement of arbitration clauses is understood as a right to apply to the court to nominate an arbitrator in cases where another party refuses to cooperate in the appointment.[318] Due to the lack of statutory foundation, this remedy cannot be applied to mediation. The court is not empowered to interfere in a mediation process and so cannot nominate a mediator over the heads of the parties. Furthermore, due to the voluntary nature of the process, an order for specific performance of a mediation clause cannot require the parties to engage in settlement negotiations.[319] It has been observed that breach of mediation clauses may instead give rise to *astreinte* means of enforcement where the claimant faces a financial penalty for failure to perform an order requiring it to attempt mediation.[320] This view has not been, however, shared by the judiciary.

2.203 The secondary remedy for breach of contract entails damages for pecuniary loss. Under 1142 CC a claim in damages arises for breach of either a positive or negative obligation under the contract. In the present context the availability of this remedy is considerably reduced (if not excluded) due to the difficulties connected with quantification of loss resulting from the party's failure to attempt mediation.[321] Since mediation is a purely voluntary process which does not have to conclude in the parties reaching a settlement, it is impossible to attach a monetary value to a mediation attempt. For these reasons the availability of damages under Article 1142 CC is considered by legal scholars as either purely theoretical,[322] or entirely inoperative.[323] However, in order to avoid the difficulty of quantifying the amount of compensation, the parties may provide for liquidated damages in their mediation clause.[324]

[317] *ibid*, 396–97.

[318] P Fouchard, E Gaillard, B Goldman, *Traité de l'arbitrage commercial international* (Litec, 1996) 398–401.

[319] C Jarrosson, 'Observations on *Poiré v Tripier*', n 277 above, 364.

[320] C Jarrosson, 'La sanction', n 273 above, 754. *Astreinte* is a sanction envisaged in, inter alia, Arts 11, 134, 137, 139, 491, 501, CPC.

[321] X Lagarde, 'L'efficacité des clauses de conciliation ou de mediation', n 276 above, 397; C Jarrosson, 'La sanction' 754; C Jarrosson, 'Observations on *Poiré v Tripier*', n 277 above, 364.

[322] C Jarrosson, 'La sanction', n 273 above, 755.

[323] X Lagarde, 'L'efficacité des clauses de conciliation ou de mediation', n 276 above, 398. A similar conclusion has been reached in relation to the availability of damages for breach of arbitration agreements. Here the loss arising from the breach has been regarded as loss of the chance to arbitrate, and so as impossible to quantify in monetary terms. P Fouchard, E Gaillard, B Goldman, *Traité de l'arbitrage commercial international*, n 318 above, 398.

[324] See eg C Jarrosson, 'La sanction', n 273 above, 754.

2.204 In summary, mediation clauses contain substantive elements and are analysed with regard to the provisions of contract law. The difficulty arises, however, in relation to the availability of substantive (contractual) remedies for breach of clauses providing for consensual ADR. Both specific performance and damages are considered as inadequate remedies for breach of mediation clauses. This is due to the voluntary nature of the process and the difficulty in ascertaining whether it would have resulted in a settlement (and on what terms) had mediation been pursued in accordance with the contract. For the above reasons the French judiciary has focused solely on the procedural consequences of premature claims in breach of parties' mediation commitments.

Expert Determination (*Expertise-arbitrage*)

Expert Determination in the French Civil Code

2.205 Expert determination (*expertise-arbitrage*) is considered as one of the most important ADR methods in France, alongside mediation and conciliation.[325] *Expertise-arbitrage* is utilised predominantly in contracts requiring determination of a technical issue by a neutral third party. Traditionally, the main field of expert determination was in construction disputes. Expert determination has also been used for neutral valuation of loss in insurance contracts, an estimate of the quality of goods in sale of goods contracts or pricing of property in real estate contracts.[326] The main advantage of this method is that it allows early resolution of a dispute without causing major disruption to the performance of the contract.[327]

2.206 The normative framework governing expert determination in France is not as complete as the one governing consensual ADR. *Expertise-arbitrage* is not expressly provided for in the statute, and the functioning of expert determination relies predominantly on rules derived from French jurisprudence. Two forms of expert determination have been distinguished. The first one, *expertise amiable*, is a non-binding expert determination whereby the expert gives the parties a recommendation as to how to resolve the dispute. The second type is a binding expert determination where the expert is empowered to make final determination of the dispute binding on the parties and binding on the court enforcing the decision.[328]

[325] J-L Delvolvé, J Rouche, G Pointon, *French arbitration law and practice*, 2nd edn (Wolters Kluwer, 2009) 22; C Jarrosson, 'Les modes alternatifs de règlement des conflicts', n 238 above, 331. The authors refer to the extensive application of dispute resolution clauses contained in the FIDIC forms of contract, on which 1.45ff and 5.40ff.

[326] J-L Delvolvé, J Rouche, G Pointon, *French arbitration law and practice*, n 325 above, 22; C Jarrosson, *La notion d'arbitrage* (LGDJ, Bibliothequè de droit privé, Thome CXCVIII, 1987) p 137ff.

[327] L Cadiet, J Normand, S Mekki, *Théorie générale du procès*, n 238 above, 465; Y Derains, 'Expertise technique et référé arbitral' (1982) 3 *Revue de l'Arbitrage* 239.

[328] W Habscheid, 'L'Expertise-arbitrage', n 211 above, 104.

In addition, French law permits a semi-binding expert determination. In this formula, an expert's decision is biding on an interim basis subject to arbitration.[329]

2.207 The legal framework for binding expert determination is inferred from Article 1592 CC. This provision enables parties to empower a neutral third party to determine the price in a contract between them (*fixation* or *determination du prix par un tiers*). A neutral person supplements the terms of the legal relationship. The determination is binding and cannot be challenged by the parties in court.[330] If a neutral person refuses or is unable to determine the price, the contract is invalid.

2.208 Article 1592 CC has been applied to regulate the emerging phenomenon of expert determination as a means of dispute resolution.[331] The legal framework governing *expertise-arbitrage* is, therefore, of a substantive nature. The binding force of an expert's decision is the creation of a contract and on this basis the parties can enforce it in court or arbitration.[332] Some authors submit that, although substantive provisions apply to expert determination, it has a special status under French law.[333]

2.209 By contracting for expert determination the parties agree to be bound by the expert's decision. The grounds for challenging a final determination are interpreted narrowly. In principle, the parties may only disregard the decision if it was obtained by way of evident fraud (*dol manifeste*) or when it is affected by an obvious error (*erreur évidente*). The French judiciary clarified that, since it is in the nature of expert determination for the third party to act impartially, the decision can be disregarded on grounds of bias.[334]

2.210 Apart from impartiality of the neutral person, procedural safeguards applicable to expert determination include the requirement to treat both parties equally, the right to present a claim and the right to present a defence.[335] These values are treated as core requirements resulting from the principle of loyalty.[336] It is, however, accepted that, due to its informal nature, expert determination procedure is not a fully adversarial process.

[329] Semi-binding expert determination is used in clause 20 FIDIC. On this aspect J-L Delvolvé, J Rouche, G Pointon, *French arbitration law and practice*, n 325 above, 22.

[330] Cour de cassation (Ch comm), 12 novembre 1962, *Bulletin*, III, no 444.

[331] M de Boisséson, M de Juglart, P Bellet, *Le droit Français de l'arbitrage* (Gide, Loyrette, Nouel, 1983) 191; C Jarrosson, 'Les modes alternatifs de règlement des conflicts', n 238 above, 339.

[332] C Jarrosson, *La notion d'arbitrage*, n 236 above, 134 and 137; W Habscheid, 'L'Expertise-arbitrage', n 211 above, 104; J-L Delvolvé, J Rouche, G Pointon, *French arbitration law and practice* 22. See also Cour d'appel de Paris (1re civ), 29 avril 2003 (2003) 4 *Revue de l'arbitrage* 1296 and Cour d'appel de Paris (1re civ), 30 juin 1995 (1996) 3 *Revue de l'arbitrage* 500.

[333] C Jarrosson, *La notion d'arbitrage*, n 236 above, 134 citing W Habscheid, 'L'Expertise-arbitrage', n 211 above, 115.

[334] Cour d'appel de Paris (1re civ), 30 juin 1995 (1996) 3 *Revue de l'arbitrage* 500.

[335] C Jarrosson, 'Les modes alternatifs de règlement des conflicts', n 238 above, 339ff and the literature cited.

[336] *ibid*, 340–42. See also with reference to consensual ADR, X Lagarde, 'Droit processuel et modes alternatifs de règlement des litiges' (2001) 3 *Revue de l'Arbitrage* 423, 436ff.

The question of which safeguards should be maintained in expert determination procedure is commonly assessed by distinguishing this ADR method from arbitration. Arbitration procedure is statutorily regulated and supervised by the courts. By contrast, expert determination procedure, if set out at all, is of a purely contractual nature. While higher procedural standards apply to arbitral proceedings, expert determination is not a dispute resolution process *stricto sensu* and enjoys greater flexibility in this respect.[337] The distinction between the two methods is frequently examined by French jurisprudence, which focuses on construction of the parties' intention.[338] Amongst the main differences pointed out by commentators is the way in which parties may challenge the result of expert determination and arbitration. While an arbitration award can be annulled on defined statutory grounds, an expert's decision is binding on the parties in the same way as a contract and cannot be questioned on the grounds applicable to arbitral awards.[339] Equally, if the procedure for appointing an expert fails as a result of an uncooperative approach by one of the parties, the court is not empowered to nominate a substitute.[340] **2.211**

Consequences of Breach of an Expert Determination Clause

In France expert determination as a means of out-of-court dispute resolution is not as popular as mediation. Consequently, judicial decisions dealing with the enforceability of ADR clauses focus predominantly on the effects of non-compliance with consensual ADR. Importantly, however, the sanctions for non-compliance with expert determination clauses mirror those devised for mediation. In the jurisprudence of the *Cour de cassation* proceedings initiated in breach of an expert determination clause are considered inadmissible (*irrecevable*).[341] A plea of non-compliance with an expert determination clause gives rise to the *fin de non-recevoir* type of defence under Articles 122 and 123 CPC. As with mediation clauses, bringing a claim prematurely is a breach of contract, interpreted in accordance with **2.212**

[337] This is notwithstanding the fact that an expert can be empowered to adjudicate on not only factual, but also legal matters.

[338] P Mayer, 'Note Cour de cassation (3e civ.), 9 Octobre 1984, Cour de cassasion (1re civ.), 1 décembre 1984, Cour de cassation (Ch. comm.), 3 janvier 1985' (1986) 2 *Revue de l'arbitrage* 263, 268ff. If the contract does not specify whether a dispute resolution clause provides for arbitration or expert determination, the court will analyse the intention of the parties: Cour de cassation (2e civ), 7 novembre 1974 (1975) 4 *Revue de l'arbitrage* 302; Cour de cassation (1re civ), 26 octobre 1976 (1977) 4 *Revue de l'arbitrage* 306; Cour d'appel de Paris (1re civ), 14 mars 2002 (2002) 3 *Revue de l'arbitrage* 772; Cour d'appel de Paris (1re civ), 7 février 2002 (2005) 4 *Revue de l'arbitrage* 1056.

[339] See especially Cour d'appel de Paris (1re civ), 30 juin 1995, (1996) 3 *Revue de l'arbitrage* 500; Cour d'appel de Paris (1re civ), 29 avril 2003 (2003) 4 *Revue de l'arbitrage* 1297. See also C Jarrosson, 'Note—Cour d'appel de Paris (1re Chambre civile) 29 avril 2003' (2003) 4 *Revue de l'arbitrage* 1299.

[340] Under Art 1592, CC the sale does not take effect if a third party fails or is unable to fix the price. On this aspect in the context of *expertise-arbitrge* Cour de cassation (1re civ.), 25 avril 1952, JCP 1952, II, 7181 with critical comments by J Huet, in Jacques Ghestin (ed), *Traité de droit civil* (Librairie Générale de Droit et de Jurisprudence, 1996) para 11190, fn 309.

[341] Cour de cassation (3e civ), 5 juillet 1989, *Bulletin*, no 18, p 87.

1134 CC. The consequences of bypassing an expert determination procedure are, therefore, similar to those attached to bypassing a compulsory mediation attempt.

2.213 This approach follows scholarly opinion. According to a traditional view, failure to exhaust the expert determination procedure before bringing a claim in court results in such premature proceedings being inadmissible.[342] More recently, this interpretation has been applied to the enforceability of clauses providing for semi-binding expert determination under the FIDIC Forms of Contract for Construction.[343] It follows that *fin de non-recevoir* is a broad category of defence under which parties may bring actions for non-compliance with various types of ADR clauses. This coherence in the treatment of different ADR commitments is a characteristic feature of French law.

Fin de Non-recevoir in Arbitration

2.214 Classification of ADR clauses as affecting admissibility of the proceedings has been applied to arbitration.[344] In this context the distinction between procedural objections (*exceptions*) and pleas as to inadmissibility (*fins de non-recevoir*) is particularly acute.[345] As explained above, by pleading inadmissibility a party does not address jurisdictional issues. Equally, by declaring inadmissibility of the proceedings the court or arbitral tribunal does not deny jurisdiction but instead confirms that the claim lacks sufficient properties for hearing the merits of the case. By contrast, *exceptions* are the type of defence by which parties may raise jurisdictional objections. Since the French judiciary has rejected the latter interpretation, it is clear that failure to exhaust pre-arbitral ADR is not a matter affecting the jurisdiction of a tribunal.[346] Instead, a premature claim results in the tribunal declaring the proceedings inadmissable. As a result, an arbitral award which was issued despite the claimant's non-compliance with pre-arbitral ADR procedures cannot be challenged, or its enforcement refused, on jurisdictional grounds.

2.215 Such an interpretation was adopted by the *Cour d'appel de Paris* in a decision of 4 March 2004.[347] In this case the court refused to annul an arbitral award on jurisdictional grounds. The applicant claimed the arbitral body lacked jurisdiction owing to non-compliance with pre-arbitral ADR. The court held that failure to follow the contractual ADR procedure does not affect a tribunal's competence to hear a case but is a matter relating to admissibility of the claim. As such, it

[342] W Habscheid, 'L'Expertise-arbitrage', n 211 above, 116.

[343] C Jarrosson, 'Observations on *Poiré v Tripier*', n 277 above, 367.

[344] Cour d'appel de Paris (1re civ), 4 mars 2004, (2005) 1 *Revue de l'arbitrage* 143; F-X Train, 'Note—Cour d'appel de Paris (1re Ch C), 4 mars 2004' (2005) 1 *Revue de l'arbitrage* 151, 156ff.

[345] Generally on the types of procedural defences see 2.173–2.179.

[346] J-F Poudret, S Besson, *Comparative Law of International Arbitration*, 2nd edn (Sweet & Maxwell, 2007) para 13, fn 59(b).

[347] Cour d'appel de Paris (1re civ), 4 mars 2004, (2005) 1 *Revue de l'arbitrage* 143.

cannot be reviewed by the court under its supervisory powers (Article 1502 CPC). The court clarified that failure to attempt conciliation was of no relevance for the validity of an arbitration clause and did not affect its effectiveness. Similarly, non-compliance with pre-arbitral ADR commitments does not justify challenge of the award on public policy grounds.[348]

Classification of pre-arbitral commitments as necessary conditions for proceedings to be admissible has been endorsed in the literature.[349] It has been pointed out, however, that declaration of inadmissibility as a sanction for non-compliance with pre-arbitral ADR has certain drawbacks in the arbitration context. A declaration of inadmissibility is typically an order concluding the proceedings. Although no res iudicata is attached to such an order, it is unclear whether the arbitrators' mandate continues if the claim is filed anew, after fulfilment of contractual ADR. It has been suggested that, in order to remove uncertainty regarding the duration of the tribunal's mandate, the arbitrators should specify that their mission is suspended pending fulfilment of contractual ADR steps.[350] This solution is based on the assumption that the tribunal's mission expires only after issuing an award on the merits. Since declaring a claim inadmissible is not an award on the merits, the originally composed tribunal remains competent to hear the case. **2.216**

Rather than concluding the proceedings the tribunal can order a stay. This alternative is regarded as more appropriate in arbitration for its flexibility and cost-effectiveness owing to the fact that a stay may be lifted without the need to re-file the claim. It also provides more certainty for the parties, as the arbitrators' mandate remains intact. In addition, this solution removes complications connected with the limited time-frame of the arbitrators' mission under Article 1463 CPC which, in the absence of the parties' agreement to the contrary, lasts for six months.[351] **2.217**

Summary

The enforceability of ADR clauses is determined in French jurisprudence by reference to the fundamental concepts of procedural law. The debate has concerned how non-compliance with ADR clauses gives rise to appropriate types of defence. **2.218**

[348] Cour d'appel de Paris, 19 octobre 2010, unreported. The judgment was subsequently reversed by the Cour de cassation on different grounds.

[349] F-X Train, 'Note—Cour d'appel de Paris (1re Ch. C), 4 mars 2004' (2005) 1 *Revue de l'Arbitrage* 151; J-F Poudret, S Besson, *Comparative Law of International Arbitration*, n 346 above, para 13; C Jarrosson, 'Note—Cour de cassation (Chambre Mixte), 14 février 2003', n 288 above, 409; C Jarrosson, 'La sanction', n 273 above, 763.

[350] C Jarrosson, 'Note—Cour de cassation (Chambre Mixte), 14 février 2003', n 288 above, 409.

[351] C Jarrosson, 'La sanction', n 273 above, 763 *de lege ferenda*. cf X Lagarde, 'L'efficacité', n 276 above, 377ff on stay of the proceedings as a preferred sanction for breach of ADR clauses in litigation and G Virassamy, 'Les collèges et les comissions dans le règlement des litiges contractuels' in *Etudes offertes à Jacques Ghestin: Le contrat au début du XXIe siècle* (LGDJ, 2001) 959 on stay of the proceedings in cases where the duty to conciliate arises under a statute.

Amongst the available ADR methods mediation dominates the French ADR landscape. Expert determination is a recognised form of ADR; however, it is less popular than consensual ADR. The consequences of non-compliance with both types of clauses are the same under French law.

2.219 Initially, consensual ADR was treated as creating non-binding obligations. This view was rejected by the *Cour de cassation* and currently both consensual and quasi-adjudicative ADR clauses are enforceable under French law. The court classified breach of ADR clauses as giving rise to the *fin de non-recevoir* type of defence. In consequence, proceedings initiated in breach of an existing ADR commitment are considered inadmissible (*irrecevable*). The court takes into account non-compliance with ADR clauses if this objection is raised by a party at an early stage of the dispute.

2.220 French jurisprudence focuses on procedural sanctions for non-compliance with ADR clauses. Although commentators identify substantive duties in ADR clauses, contractual remedies are unlikely to be awarded by French courts. The provisions of the Civil Court are, however, relevant to assessing issues such as the validity of ADR clauses and the conditions for waiver of the rights arising under them.

2.221 The solutions devised for the enforceability of ADR clauses in litigation have been adopted in arbitration. Non-compliance with escalation mechanisms preceding arbitration is treated as a matter affecting admissibility of the claim rather than the jurisdiction of the tribunal. In consequence, French courts refuse to annul arbitral awards on jurisdictional grounds even when the tribunal failed to take into account breach of pre-arbitral ADR commitments and proceeded to give an award.

Switzerland

2.222 Swiss law recognises both consensual and quasi-adjudicative ADR.[352] Swiss law's position in relation to the enforceability of multi-tiered clauses is, however, unsettled. There is no decisive jurisprudence regarding the effects of ADR clauses, and the case law of the Swiss *Bundesgericht* cannot be considered uniform in this matter.[353] Characteristically, the enforceability of both types of clauses has drawn the attention of the courts and commentators more in the context of arbitral

[352] On the spectrum of ADR methods available under Swiss law, see M Blessing, in S Berti (ed), *International Arbitration in Switzerland. An Introduction and a Commentary on Articles 176–194 of the Swiss Private International Law Statute* (Kluwer Law International, 2000) para 962ff and M Blessing, *Introduction to Arbitration—Swiss and International Perspectives* (Helbing & Lichtenhahn, 1999) paras 962ff.

[353] M Scherer, M Dawidowicz, *Arbitration Guide IBA Arbitration. Switzerland* (Lalive, 2012) 5; U Feller, M Frey, in *Multi-Tiered Dispute Resolution Clauses* (IBA Litigation Committee, 1 October 2015) 202.

proceedings, than in litigation. As will be shown below, the treatment of ADR in those two environments can be contrasted.

Mediation and Conciliation

Mediation and Conciliation in Swiss Law

The tradition of consensual ADR in Switzerland is rich and diversified.[354] Swiss law distinguishes between mediation and conciliation,[355] giving primacy to the latter.[356] Conciliation is regulated in Title I of the Swiss Civil Procedure Code (*Zivilprozessordnung*), Articles 197–212.[357] Undertaking pre-action conciliation (*Schlichtungsversuch*) is a duty of the claimant in a majority of cases. By contrast, mediation is an institution based entirely on voluntary agreement of the parties. It has been introduced to ZPO as a new form of out-of-court dispute resolution of American provenance.[358] **2.223**

A duty to undertake a conciliation attempt before bringing a claim in litigation is prescribed in Article 197 ZPO. Obligatory pre-action conciliation is a rule to which Swiss law provides only few exceptions, provided for under Article 198 ZPO.[359] In cases where conciliation is required, it is treated as a necessary condition of the proceedings. Failure to satisfy this requirement is taken into account by the court ex officio.[360] Conciliation can also take place in the course of proceedings. A settlement resulting from conciliation can be enforced like a court award.[361] **2.224**

An institution akin to conciliation is 'proposal for the judgment' (*Urteilsvorschlag*), contained in the same Title of the ZPO (Articles 210–212). It envisages that a neutral person, acting as conciliator, presents the parties with a proposal to resolve the dispute. If neither party challenges the proposal within the prescribed **2.225**

354 See P Gelzer, P Ruggle, in K Spühler, L Tenchio, D Infanger (eds), *Basler Kommentar. Schweizerische Zivilprozessordnung*, 2nd edn (Helbing Lichtenhahn Verlag, 2013) p 1074, para 5 ad Vorbemerkungen zu Arts 213–218 ZPO; P Bösch, 'Der Nachbarstreit und dessen Beilegung, Mediation—ein neuer Weg' (1998) 94 *Schweizerische Juristen-Zeitung* 77, 10 for details.

355 On the differences between the two methods see E Habscheid, 'Die aussergerichtliche Vermittlung (Mediation) als Rechtsverhältnis' (2001) 8 *Aktuelle Juristische Praxis* 938, 941. In an arbitration context some Swiss commentators use those terms interchangeably see, inter alia, J-F Poudret, S Besson, *Comparative Law of International Arbitration* n 346 above, p 11, A Jolles, 'Consequences of Multi-Tier Arbitration Clauses', n 173 above, 329, fn 1.

356 I Meier, in N Alexander (ed), *Global Trends in Mediation*, n 13 above, 372–73.

357 Hereafter also ZPO.

358 P Gelzer, P Ruggle, in K Spühler, L Tenchio, D Infanger (eds), *Basler Kommentar. Schweizerische Zivilprozessordnung*, 2nd edn (Helbing Lichtenhahn Verlag, 2013) pp 1072–74, paras 1–4 ad Vorbemerkungen zu Arts 213–218 ZPO.

359 This includes cases relating to registration, divorce or family law; see D Infanger, in K Spühler, L Tenchio, D Infanger (eds), *Basler Kommentar. Schweizerische Zivilprozessordnung*, 2nd edn (Helbing Lichtenhahn Verlag, 2013) pp 1019 ff, para 1ff ad Arts 197–198 ZPO for details.

360 Art 59, ZPO; *ibid*.

361 Art 208(2), ZPO.

time-frame, the proposal becomes binding and is enforceable like a court award. This technique is available only in selected categories of cases.[362]

2.226 Mediation is prescribed by Articles 213–218 ZPO. By contrast to conciliation, mediation is not compulsory and can be undertaken only if both parties agree. Under Article 213 ZPO mediation can replace the conciliation required by law. Undertaking a mediation attempt substitutes the *Schlichtungsversuch* requirement in those cases where conciliation is compulsory.

2.227 ZPO does not contain detailed provisions to regulate mediation procedure. The burden of providing a procedural framework for mediation rests on the parties who should include appropriate provisions in their mediation clauses.[363] Commentators present diverging views as to the status of mediation agreements. According to one view, mediation clauses are akin to partnership agreements by which the parties undertake to cooperate with a view to achieving a common purpose.[364] An alternative view assumes that mediation clauses are contracts *sui generis*.[365]

2.228 ZPO does not prescribe any sanctions for non-compliance with mediation clauses.[366] In cases where conciliation is not compulsory filing a claim in court in breach of a mediation clause is not penalised. Swiss law assumes that mediation is entirely voluntary, which renders mediation clauses unenforceable in litigation.[367] Commencing litigation in breach of a mediation clause means that the claimant is not willing to attempt amicable dispute resolution. Unlike in conciliation, fulfilling the terms of a mediation attempt is not a necessary condition of litigation.[368]

2.229 The unenforceability of mediation clauses is not without controversy in Swiss jurisprudence. It has been suggested that breach of mediation clauses gives rise to contractual liability.[369] An alternative interpretation assumes that compliance with the agreed mediation procedure is a necessary condition of the proceedings

[362] eg in cases concerning recovery of outstanding rent under landlord and tennant law or claims for debt not exceeding 5000 CHF. See also D Infanger, in K Spühler, L Tenchio, D Infanger (eds), *Basler Kommentar. Schweizerische Zivilprozessordnung*, 2nd edn (Helbing Lichtenhahn Verlag, 2013) pp 1062ff, paras 1ff ad Art 210 ZPO.

[363] In practice this is done by institutionalised ADR providers. For a comprehensive list see M Blessing, *Introduction to Arbitration—Swiss and International Perspectives* (Helbing & Lichtenhahn, 1999) para 953; M Blessing, in *International Arbitration in Switzerland* para 953.

[364] E Habscheid, 'Die aussergerichtliche Vermittlung (Mediation) als Rechtsverhältnis', n 355 above, 939 and literature cited there.

[365] H Einholzer, Die Streitbeilegungsabrede. Ein Beitrag zu alternativen Formen der Streitbeilegung, namentlich zur Mediation (Universitätsverlag Freiburg, 1998) para 350.

[366] By contrast to arbitration agreements, the statute does not provide that non-fulfilment of ADR clauses bars the court from hearing the case on the merits.

[367] C Kupman, C Bauer, in K Hopt, F Steffek (eds), *Mediation: Rechtstatsachen, Rechtsvergleich, Regelungen* (Mohr Siebeck, 2008) 866. See also I Meier, in N Alexander (ed), *Global Trends in Mediation*, n 13 above, 385.

[368] P Ruggle, in Spühler, L Tenchio, D Infanger (eds), *Basler Kommentar. Schweizerische Zivilprozessordnung*, 2nd edn (Helbing Lichtenhahn Verlag, 2013) p 1080, para 8 ad Art 213 ZPO.

[369] On this aspect see 2.230ff.

which the court could enforce at its own discretion.[370] The enforceability of mediation clauses has been advocated obiter in the judgment of *Obergericht Thurgau* of 23 April 2001.[371] The court held that a claim bypassing conciliation before the parties' professional organisation (*Gastrosuisse*) should be inadmissible until the relevant procedure was complied with. Similarly, in the judgment of 6 June 2007[372] the *Bundesgericht* rejected the assumption that mediation clauses are unenforceable. The case concerned mediation integrated into arbitration proceedings and will be analysed separately in this study.[373]

Non-compliance with Mediation Clauses: Substantive Consequences

Enforcement of mediation clauses by way of substantive remedies was accepted in the decision of 15 March 1999 of the *Kassationsgericht Zürich*.[374] The judgment is one of few Swiss cases dealing with the enforceability of mediation clauses in litigation. Although the Swiss judiciary has not given a conclusive answer as to the consequences of non-compliance with consensual ADR, this judgment is commonly referred to as one of the most important rulings in relation to this matter.[375] **2.230**

The case concerned a construction contract containing a multi-tiered dispute resolution mechanism. The clause provided that, before the parties could engage in litigation, all contractual disputes must be submitted to the panel of conciliators empowered to issue non-binding recommendations. The clause prescribed a 30-day time-frame for settlement negotiations after the recommendation of the panel had been given. The parties were permitted to commence litigation after the lapse of this 30-day period from when the panel gave its recommendation. **2.231**

After the completion of the works the Employer raised two claims and subjected them to the conciliation procedure in accordance with the contract. After the panel gave its recommendation the parties started negotiations and entered into a settlement. The terms of the settlement obliged the Contractor to remedy defects in performance. The Contractor failed to adhere to the settlement, which prompted the Employer to commence litigation. The Employer's action contained not only two initial claims, but also additional demands which had not been subjected to the dispute resolution procedure prescribed by the contract. In his defence the **2.232**

370 J Schütz, *Mediation und Schiedsgerichtsbarkeit in der Schweizerischen Zivilprozessordnung: eine Untersuchung zur Streitbehandlungslehre: Verfahrensvergleich und -auswahl anhand gesetzlich geregelter Alternativen zum staatlichen Zivilprozess—Mediation, Schiedsgerichtsbarkeit und deren Hybridisierung* (Stämpfli, 2009) 184ff.

371 (2003) 21 *ASA Bulletin* 418.

372 BGer 4A_18/2007, (2008) 26 *ASA Bulletin* 87.

373 See 2.236–2.237.

374 15 März 1999—Kassationsgericht Zürich (2002) 20 *ASA Bulletin* 373.

375 C Boog, 'How to Deal with Multi-Tiered Dispute Resolution Clauses—Note—June 2007—Swiss Federal Supreme Court' (2008) 26 *ASA Bulletin* 103, 107, fn 10; J-F Poudret, S Besson, *Comparative Law of International Arbitration*, n 346 above, para 13; A Jolles, 'Consequences of Multi-Tier Arbitration Clauses', n 173 above, 329.

Contractor pleaded that the court should consider itself as temporarily incompetent to hear the merits of the case to the extent that it related to claims not subjected to the contractual ADR procedure. Alternatively, the Contractor argued that the claim should be temporarily inadmissible due to non-fulfilment of the necessary condition of the proceedings.

2.233 The Contractor's arguments were rejected in all instances. Dismissing the defence, *Kassationsgericht* held that a clause prescribing a contractual conciliation process creates duties of a substantive, rather than procedural nature. As such it does not have any procedural implications. The court took the view that concluding an ADR agreement neither affects the court's competence to hear the case, nor creates a necessary condition of court proceedings. The court considered both limbs of the Contractor's defence as having no grounds in the provisions of Swiss procedural law. The court contrasted conciliation clauses with arbitration and jurisdiction agreements. The effects of the latter are statutorily prescribed, while the statute is silent about the former. For this reason, the court refused to treat compliance with conciliation clauses as a necessary condition of court proceedings (*Prozessvoraussetzung*).

2.234 The court further explained that, although conciliation clauses have no effect on prematurely initiated litigation, they are valid contracts in the eyes of substantive law. The duties under such contracts involve refraining from exercising certain rights relating to the claim. These rights may include commencing the proceedings in court.[376] According to the court, an agreement of this kind can only have substantive consequences. In order for such a clause to affect court procedure, a specific sanction would have to be provided in the code. In the absence of such regulation the parties may only raise substantive remedies for breach of the agreed procedure.

2.235 Among potential remedies the court enumerated damages, dismissal of the claim, and other remedies resulting from non-performance of the obligation by the other party. In addition to this list, the commentators pointed out that repudiation of the contract,[377] and liquidated damages would be appropriate.[378] On the facts of the case, however, the *Kassationsgericht Zürich* did not find grounds to award any of the remedies from the theoretically available spectrum.

2.236 Substantive remedies for breach of mediation clauses have also been considered in the arbitration context. In the *Bundesgericht* judgment of 6 June 2007[379] the court

[376] An ADR clause was labelled as a 'non-aggression pact' (*Nichtangriffspakt*).

[377] C Boog, 'How to Deal with Multi-Tiered Dispute Resolution Clauses', n 375 above, 108.

[378] D Brown-Berset, 'La médiation commerciale: le géant s'éveille' (2002) 2 *Revue de Droit Suisse* 319, 369; M Liatowitsch, J Menz, in E Geisinger, N Voser (eds), *International Arbitration in Switzerland. A Handbook for Practitioners*, 2nd edn (Wolters Kluwer, 2013) 327, fn 83. The authors observe, however, that there are no examples of such remedies being awarded by Swiss courts in relation to breach of ADR clauses.

[379] BGer 4A_18/2007, (2008) 26 *ASA Bulletin* 87.

enumerated damages as one of the possible sanctions for non-compliance with the agreed ADR procedure. The case concerned a challenge of an arbitral award on the basis that the tribunal lacked jurisdiction. According to the applicant, the tribunal had no competence to hear the case because the claimant in the arbitral proceedings had failed to exhaust pre-arbitral dispute resolution steps prescribed in a contract.[380]

The court refused to annul the award, finding that the clause in question was too uncertain to have any binding force.[381] Importantly, however, the court confirmed the theoretical possibility of conciliation clauses being enforceable. Apart from substantive remedies, the court pointed to possible procedural sanctions such as inadmissibility of the claim or denial of jurisdiction by the adjudicative body.[382] Although the challenge was dismissed without the court having to state conclusively whether non-compliance with ADR clauses is of purely substantive, or also procedural consequences, the case is an important statement in favour of the enforceability of ADR clauses in arbitration. **2.237**

Non-compliance with Mediation Clauses: Procedural Consequences

Purely substantive consequences for breach of mediation clauses have been rejected in jurisprudence.[383] Criticism focuses on the difficulties in quantifying loss arising from breaches. Inability to ascertain the sum of compensation leads to damages becoming an illusory remedy. As an alternative it has been suggested that non-compliance with pre-action ADR should give rise to procedural consequences. On this view, failure to exhaust pre-action ADR constitutes a bar to prematurely initiated proceedings. In support of this, some authors point out that the enforceability of conciliation clauses has been well established in arbitration.[384] **2.238**

As far as specific procedural solutions are concerned, two main propositions can be distinguished. The first assumes that the adjudicating body is not competent to **2.239**

[380] The controversial clause provided: 'Toute controverse et tout différend en rapport avec le présent contrat et qui ne pourront être résolus à l'amiable (y compris la conciliation selon les règles de l'OMPI) devront être soumis au tribunal arbitral'.

[381] The court applied contract law rules to determine the content and scope of the clause.

[382] The court referred to views expressed in the literature: H Einholzer, *Die Streitbeilegungsabrede* n 365 above, paras 643ff; D Brown-Berset, 'La médiation commerciale: le géant s'éveille', n 378 above, 372; N Voser, 'Sanktion bei Nichterfüllung einer Schlichtungsklausel. Note—Kassationsgericht Zürich, 15 März 1999' (2002) 20 *ASA Bulletin* 376; C Jarrosson, 'La sanction du non-respect d'une clause instituant un préliminaire obligatoire de conciliation ou de mediation', n 273 above, 752. On inadmissibility of the claim and lack of competence of the tribunal see 2.251ff and 4.15ff.

[383] N Voser, 'Sanktion bei Nichterfüllung einer Schlichtungsklausel', n 382 above, 376ff; D Brown-Berset, 'La médiation commerciale: le géant s'éveille', n 378 above, 364, 368 and 372; C Boog, 'How to Deal with Multi-Tiered Dispute Resolution Clauses', n 375 above, 108, A Jolles, 'Consequences of Multi-Tier Arbitration Clauses', n 173 above, 336; J-F Poudret, S Besson, *Comparative Law of International Arbitration*, n 346 above, para 13.

[384] M Liatowitsch, J Menz, in *International Arbitration in Switzerland. A Handbook for Practitioners*, n 378 above, 327 and the literature cited.

hear the dispute until the prescribed ADR procedures are complied with. Under the second interpretation non-compliance with pre-action ADR renders the claim premature and therefore inadmissible. Because mediation clauses are unenforceable in litigation, the judiciary has analysed these sanctions almost exclusively in relation to arbitral proceedings. For this reason, subsequent remarks will focus on multi-tiered dispute resolution mechanisms integrated into an arbitration framework.

Lack of Jurisdiction of the Adjudicating Body

2.240 Lack of jurisdiction in arbitral proceedings as a consequence of breach of conciliation clauses is the leading position adopted by the *Bundesgericht*.[385] Under this interpretation unless and until the prescribed ADR procedure is exhausted in accordance with the contract, the tribunal cannot accept competence to hear the case. Disregarding the claimant's failure to comply with pre-arbitral ADR by the tribunal implies that the tribunal is hearing the case without requisite jurisdiction. An award made in such circumstances can be challenged on jurisdictional grounds and annulled as given by a tribunal lacking competence to do so.[386]

2.241 This interpretation has been applied by the *Bundesgericht* in a seminal case of 17 August 1995.[387] The case concerned a contract for delivery of coal concluded between a Dutch company, Transporten Handelsmaatschappij 'Vekoma' BV (the claimant), and a US company, Maran Coal Corporation (the defendant). The contract contained a dispute resolution clause providing, as the last tier of an escalation mechanism, for arbitration in Geneva pursuant to the ICC Rules of Arbitration. Under the clause the dispute could be submitted to arbitration within 30 days after it was established that an amicable settlement through negotiations was not possible.[388] An important feature of the clause in question was a time-bar limiting the availability of arbitration to 30 days after the failure of the negotiation phase.

2.242 Before filing the claim in arbitration Vekoma sent the settlement proposal to Maran, specifying that if the proposal were not accepted within seven days, Vekoma would commence arbitral proceedings. Maran did not respond to Vekoma's proposal. After two months from the proposal Vekoma renewed its settlement offer.

[385] This interpretation has been rejected for court litigation by Kassationsgericht Zürich in the award of 15 March 1999 (15 März 1999—Kassationsgericht Zürich, (2002) 20 *ASA Bulletin* 373).

[386] Under Article 190(2) of the Swiss Private International Law Act (*Bundesgesetz über das Internationale Privatrecht*, hereafter also 'IPRG') with regards to international arbitral awards and Article 393(b) ZPO with regards to domestic arbitral awards.

[387] Bundesgericht, I. Zivilabteilung, 17 August 1995, (1996) 14 *ASA Bulletin* 673. Hereafter also '*Vekoma v Maran*'.

[388] 'Jede Streitigkeit irgendwelcher Art, die aus dem Vertrag entsteht oder damit zusammenhängt oder sich aus dessen Auslegung oder Erfüllung ergibt, kann einem Schiedsgericht unterbreitet werden, welches seinen Sitz in Genf (Schweiz) haben muss und nach den Regeln der Internationalen Handelskammer zu entscheiden hat. Die Streitigkeit oder Meinungsverschiedenheit ist dem Schiedsgericht von der einen oder anderen Partei innert dreissig Tagen zu unterbreiten, nachdem übereinstimmend festgestellt wurde, dass eine gütliche Beilegung auf dem Verhandlungsweg nicht möglich ist.'

This time Maran expressly rejected it and Vekoma immediately commenced arbitral proceedings.

The dispute arose as to the date from which the 30-day period for commencing arbitration should be calculated. The fundamental question concerned establishing the moment at which it could be considered that the negotiation phase failed and it became clear that an amicable settlement was not possible. Under the clause in question, from this moment the 30-day period for commencement of arbitration started running. **2.243**

Maran, acting as the defendant, raised objections as to tribunal's jurisdiction, reasoning that the proceedings were commenced after the expiry of the contractual time-frame and were time-barred. It was argued that Maran's lack of response to the first settlement proposal sent by Vekoma was equivalent to definitive failure of the negotiation phase. The proceedings should have been commenced within 30 days from the expiry of the time-frame given by Vekoma for Maran's response in its first letter containing the settlement offer. **2.244**

The tribunal, chaired by J-L Devolvé, did not uphold this argument. The arbitrators took the stance that the moment at which negotiations can be considered definitively unsuccessful should be established by reference to clear and unambiguous statements of the parties. The tribunal held that the time-limit for commencing arbitration should therefore be calculated from the Maran's response to the second settlement offer. In such a case the proceedings were commenced within the 30-day period and were not time-barred. The tribunal clarified that the defendant should have responded in good faith to the first settlement proposal sent by Vekoma. Until Maran clearly communicated its position to Vekoma, it was not possible to establish whether the parties had definitely ruled out amicable resolution of the dispute. Following this reasoning the tribunal assumed jurisdiction and in the final award found in favour of the claimant awarding the sum of US$650,000 to be paid by Maran. This judgment was subsequently challenged by the defendant in the Swiss court. The challenge was based on the tribunal's lack of jurisdiction to make an award. **2.245**

The *Bundesgericht* hearing the challenge reached the opposite conclusion to the tribunal's. The court held that the 30-day time limit for negotiations had not been observed. The court assessed differently the moment from which the negotiation phase should have been considered to have failed. According to the *Bundesgericht* the time-period for bringing an action in arbitration had started running when Maran did not respond to the first settlement letter within the time prescribed by Vekoma. The court held that at this stage it was apparent to both parties that the dispute could not be resolved by amicable negotiations. In the court's view it was not necessary to make an express statement in this matter and the 30-day period for commencement of arbitration had started running earlier than argued by the claimant. The court held that arbitral proceedings were time-barred and the tribunal wrongfully assumed jurisdiction to hear the case. Consequently, it was decided that the award merited annulment under Article 190(2) IPRG. **2.246**

2.247 The case is an example of the difficulties connected with an interpretation of an insufficiently precise ADR clause. The clause in dispute provided scope for controversy, as it did not precisely state when the negotiation phase could be considered completed. The court and the tribunal reached different conclusions as to from which moment the time-limit for commencement of arbitration should be calculated, which proved fatal for the arbitral award. Importantly, however, regardless of the diverging views on when arbitration should have been commenced to comply with the time-limit under the clause, both the *Bundesgericht* and arbitral tribunal adopted the same fundamental assumption. It was agreed that non-compliance with multi-tiered clauses in question was a matter affecting tribunal's jurisdiction. The consequences of non-compliance with pre-arbitral ADR were first assessed by the arbitral tribunal as part of the *Kompetenz-Kompetenz* enquiry,[389] and subsequently by the court as part of judicial scrutiny of an arbitral award.[390]

2.248 A similar approach has been adopted by the *Obergericht Zürich* in a decision of 11 September 2001.[391] On the facts of the case the party refused to nominate an arbitrator, arguing that the commencement of arbitral proceedings was premature due to the other party's non-compliance with pre-arbitral conciliation procedure. The court held that observance of the parties' contractual ADR commitments was for the arbitrators to decide within their power to assess their own jurisdiction. Pre-arbitral ADR as prescribed in the contract was treated as one of the necessary conditions of arbitral proceedings (*Prozessvoraussetzungen des Schiedsverfahrens*) and, as such, was left for the arbitrators to examine as part of their *Kompetenz-Kompetenz* exercise.[392]

2.249 This line of reasoning has become a source of controversy in literature. The approach taken by the *Bundesgericht* in *Vekoma v Maran* was critically assessed by a number of commentators.[393] It has been posited that, by reaching a different conclusion as to whether the contractual ADR procedure was observed in accordance with the contract, the court annihilated the effects of over two-years of arbitral proceedings. The approach taken by the *Bundesgericht* unduly expanded the scope of judicial supervision of arbitration. It has been mooted that even an erroneous conclusion regarding compliance with contractual ADR is not a flaw

[389] Art 186(1), IPRG.
[390] Art 190(2)(b), IPRG.
[391] Obergericht Zürich, 11 September 2001, ZR 2002 (101) No 21, 77–81.
[392] On this case see A Jolles, 'Consequences of Multi-Tier Arbitration Clauses', n 173 above, 331–32.
[393] P Friedland, 'The Swiss Supreme Court Sets Aside an ICC Award' (1996) 13(1) *Journal of International Arbitration* 111; T Varady, 'The Courtesy Trap Arbitration "if no amicable settlement can be reached"' (1997) 14(4) *Journal of International Arbitration* 5, 8ff; W Park, 'Determining Arbitral Jurisdiction: Allocation of Tasks between Courts and Arbitrators' (1997) 8 *American Review of International Arbitration* 133; P Karrer, C Kälin-Nauer, 'Is there a Favor Iurisdictionis Arbitri?' (1996) 13(3) *Journal of International Arbitration* 31; J Paulsson, 'Jurisdiction and Admissibility' in Gerald Aksen (ed), *Global Reflections on International Law, Commerce and Dispute Resolution, Liber Amicorum in honour of Robert Briner* (ICC Publishing, 2005) 601.

in an award which would merit its annulment. It was observed that the potential for post-award litigation would compromise the efficiency of the arbitral process.

Some authors supported the stand adopted by the *Bundesgericht*.[394] B Berger and F Kellerhals submit that contractual stipulation providing for pre-arbitral ADR affects the tribunal's jurisdiction *ratione temporis*.[395] Under this approach assessing whether a dispute is within the temporal scope of arbitral jurisdiction is a procedural question referred to as a condition of admissibility of the proceedings (*condition de recevabilité, Prozessvoraussetzung*).[396] It is also treated as a condition of giving an award on the merits (*Sachurteilvoraussetzung*), as non-fulfilment of pre-arbitral ADR restricts the tribunal's competence to hear the case *in meriti*. Lack of jurisdiction *ratione temporis* can be invoked as a ground for annulment of the award under Article 190(2) IPRG. In consequence, proceeding to hear the merits of the case, notwithstanding the defendant's plea of non-compliance with pre-arbitral ADR, may affect validity of an arbitral award. The authors emphasise that, as with any type of jurisdictional objection, non-compliance with ADR commitments must be considered before submitting the defence on the merits.[397] **2.250**

Inadmissibility of the Proceedings

An alternative view rejects classification of ADR clauses as conditions of arbitral jurisdiction. Under this interpretation non-compliance with pre-arbitral ADR does not affect a tribunal's competence to hear a case but rather is a matter affecting conduct of the proceedings.[398] Arbitrators faced with a premature claim cannot hear the merits of the case. This, however, does not imply denial of jurisdiction over the dispute. The tribunal faced with a premature action should declare the claim temporarily inadmissible (*die Klage als zurzeit unzulässig abzuweisen*) or stay the proceedings (*das Verfahren vorläufig sistieren*). **2.251**

[394] B Berger, F Kellerhals, *International and Domestic Arbitration in Switzerland*, 3rd edn (Stämpfli Publishers/Hart Publishing/ C.H. Beck/ Manz, 2015) para 583. See also B Cremades, 'Multi-tiered Dispute Resolution Clauses' (CPR Institute for Dispute Resolution, 2004) 7. The author supports the similar interpretation adopted by the ICC Court of International Arbitration and his view is cited in the context of the Swiss courts' jurisprudence (C Boog, 'How to Deal with Multi-Tiered Dispute Resolution Clauses', n 375 above, 109, fn 23 with reference to the judgment of Bundesgericht of 6 June 2007, BGer 4A_18/2007, (2008) 26 *ASA Bulletin* 87).

[395] B Berger, F Kellerhals, *International and Domestic Arbitration in Switzerland*, n 394 above, paras 582–84.

[396] *ibid.* The authors adopt the term *admissibility* to explain the meaning of *jurisdiction ratione temporis* without distinguishing the two spheres. The need for distinction between jurisdiction and admissibility is analysed further in this work (4.15ff).

[397] Art 186(2), IPRG.

[398] M Schott, M Courvoisier, in H Honsell, N Vogt, A Schnyder, S Berti (eds), *Basler Kommentar Internationales Privatrecht*, 3rd edn (Helbing Lichtenhahn Verlag, 2013) p 1919, para 60 ad Art 186 IPRG. See also A Jolles, 'Consequences of Multi-Tier Arbitration Clauses', n 173 above, 335; C Boog, 'How to Deal with Multi-Tiered Dispute Resolution Clauses', n 375 above, 109.

2.252 The proponents of this stand emphasise the distinction between jurisdiction of an arbitral tribunal and admissibility of the claim.[399] Failure to adhere to a contractually prescribed sequence of steps preceding arbitration is a matter affecting admissibility (*recevabilité*, *Zulässigkeit*) of the claim, rather than the tribunal's competence to hear the case. In this interpretation fulfilment of pre-arbitral ADR commitments is not a condition of an arbitration clause.

2.253 It has been submitted that treating ADR as a condition of an arbitration clause leads to poor results.[400] Jurisdictional classification of ADR clauses implies that the party bringing the claim may unilaterally deprive an arbitration clause of its binding force by refusing to submit the dispute to the contractually agreed procedure. It has been observed that by contracting for ADR the parties did not make their agreement to exclude litigation in favour of arbitration contingent on compliance with pre-arbitral negotiation or conciliation.[401] Jurisdictional classification of pre-arbitral ADR is criticised, in addition, for creating uncertainty regarding *lis pendens*, the interruption of limitation periods, as well as the availability of preliminary measures.[402] It has also been put forward that denial of jurisdiction as a consequence of breach of an ADR clause contravenes Article 13 of the UNCITRAL Model Law on International Commercial Conciliation.[403] The act provides that where the parties have agreed to conciliate and have expressly undertaken not to initiate arbitral or judicial proceedings during a specific period of time or until a specified event has occurred, such an undertaking shall be given effect by the arbitral tribunal or the court.[404] It was observed that in order to 'give effect' to the parties' undertaking the tribunal must first accept jurisdiction to do so.

2.254 Alternative sanctions for non-compliance with ADR clauses, not involving jurisdictional determination include dismissal of the claim as inadmissible or stay of the proceedings. Commentators widely advocate the practical advantages of the latter solution.[405] First, stay of the proceedings removes uncertainty as to the duration of the arbitrators' mandate. In cases where the tribunal concludes the proceedings by declaring the claim inadmissible, it may be unclear whether the previously

[399] M Schott, M Courvoisier, in H Honsell, N Vogt, A Schnyder, S Berti (eds), *Basler Kommentar Internationales Privatrecht*, 3rd edn (Helbing Lichtenhahn Verlag Basel, 2013) p 1919, para 60 ad Art 186 IPRG, with reference to J Paulsson, 'Jurisdiction and Admissibility', n 393 above, 601ff.

[400] A Jolles, 'Consequences of Multi-Tier Arbitration Clauses', n 173 above, 335.

[401] *ibid.* The author observes that it hardly corresponds with the parties intention for a multi-tier arbitration clause to be conditional 'in the sense that, if one party had known that the other would not engage in the agreed pre-arbitral steps, it would have preferred to submit the dispute to litigation rather than to arbitration.'

[402] *ibid.*; C Boog, 'How to Deal with Multi-Tiered Dispute Resolution Clauses', n 375 above, 109.

[403] A Jolles, 'Consequences of Multi-Tier Arbitration Clauses', n 173 above, 335.

[404] On this provision also 1.84–1.86.

[405] M Liatowitsch, J Menz, in *International Arbitration in Switzerland. A Handbook for Practitioners*, n 378 above, 327; D Brown-Berset, 'La médiation commerciale: le géant s'éveille', n 378 above, 373; N Voser, 'Sanktion bei Nichterfüllung einer Schlichtungsklausel', n 382 above, 378ff; A Jolles, 'Consequences of Multi-Tier Arbitration Clauses', n 173 above, 336–37; C Boog, 'How to Deal with Multi-Tiered Dispute Resolution Clauses', n 375 above, 109; J-F Poudret, S Besson, *Comparative Law of International Arbitration*, n 346 above, para 13.

nominated tribunal retains the mandate to hear the case, should an ADR attempt prove unsuccessful and the parties return to arbitration. Secondly, stay of the proceedings is considered a more cost- and time-effective solution. A stay assumes that the arbitrators' mission continues during the referral of the parties to the contractual ADR procedure. The parties may apply to the tribunal to resume the adjourned proceedings after they fail to reach an amicable solution, which is quicker and cheaper than commencing the proceedings anew. Thirdly, stay of the proceedings removes uncertainty regarding limitation periods in those legal systems where initiating arbitration suspends the limitation period but a mere mediation attempt does not. In such cases the limitation period could lapse in the course of ADR proceedings. In addition, concluding that the proceedings are inadmissible, ie without making an award *in meriti*, could be interpreted as reversing the suspending effect of submitting the claim in arbitration.[406]

It is suggested that, when referring the parties to ADR, the tribunal should prescribe a time-frame within which the agreed procedure is to be conducted.[407] **2.255** Uncertainty in this matter may create a barrier to having the claims adjudicated by the competent forum. It is also emphasised that, because there is no appeal with which to challenge stay of the proceedings, a too long suspension of arbitral proceedings may constitute denial of justice (*Rechtsverweigerung, déni de justice*).

Expert Determination

Expert Determination in Switzerland

Expert determination (*Schiedsgutachten, expertise-arbitrage, arbitrato irrituale*) is **2.256** present in Swiss commercial practice.[408] Swiss law expressly provides for expert determination in the procedural code, Article 189 ZPO. Under this provision the

406 Some authors suggest that in order to avoid this consequence the clause should contain stipulations under which the parties waive any plea of limitation for the duration of the ADR procedure (M Liatowitsch, J Menz, in *International Arbitration in Switzerland. A Handbook for Practitioners*, n 378 above, 328). It is observed that even if the parties do not include such a provision in their contract, relying on limitation may in such circumstances be regarded as an abuse of right (*offenbarer Missbrauch eines Rechtes, abus manifeste d'un droit*) and so be disregarded under Article 2(2) of the Swiss Civil Code (*Zivilgesetzbuch*, ZGB).

407 S Berti, AK Schnyder, in S Berti (ed), *International Arbitration in Switzerland. An Introduction and a Commentary on Articles 176–194 of the Swiss Private International Law Statute* (Kluwer Law International, 2000) 578, para 45 ad Art 190. In such cases the authors suggest the possibility of recourse to the ordinary courts under Art 185, IPRG which establishes the competence of the court of the seat of arbitration in all matters in which the support of a national court is required.

408 The areas in which Schiedsgutachten is utilised include: construction contracts, M&A transactions, (determination of the value of shares, party contributions, intellectual property rights), insurance contracts (determination of the amount of damage) and adaptation clauses (determination of the revised performance), see D Hochstrasser, S Fuchs, in H Honsell, N Vogt, A Schnyder, S Berti (eds), *Basler Kommentar. Internationales Privatrecht*, 3rd edn (Helbing Lichtenhahn Verlag, 2013) pp 1689–90, para 296 ad Einleitung zum Zwölften Kapitel.

parties may empower a neutral third party to make a binding determination on a given factual issue.[409]

2.257 Article 189 ZPO prescribes the conditions which the decision must satisfy, in order to be binding. First, the legal relationship to which the determination relates must be at the parties' free disposal (Article 189(3)(a) ZPO). Secondly, there must be no ground for disqualification of the expert from deciding the issue (Article 189(3)(b) ZPO). Thirdly, the decision must be made in an impartial manner and it must not be manifestly erroneous[410] (Article 189(3)(c) ZPO). The parties may challenge the decision using two alternative routes. If the decision has been given, but no court proceedings have yet been commenced, the party may apply to the court for a declaration that the expert's decision is not binding. The party may make an application so long as it has a legal interest in obtaining such a declaration.[411] If court proceedings are already pending, the party may challenge the result of expert determination by way of a plea relating to the merits of the case. Other than by these two means, the parties cannot question the binding force of an expert's decision.[412]

2.258 Article 189 ZPO prescribes the binding force of expert determination in litigation. The provision is not directly applicable in arbitral proceedings.[413] Some authors suggest that Article 189 should *mutadis mutandis* apply to arbitral proceedings and govern the binding force of *Schiedsgutachten* in cases where the seat of arbitration is in Switzerland.[414] In this interpretation the permissibility of expert determination in arbitration relates to the arbitrability of the main dispute.[415]

2.259 The legal nature of expert determination is a subject of controversy under Swiss law.[416] The jurisprudence of the *Bundesgericht*, as well as the conclusions of

[409] Although Art 189, ZPO expressly refers to factual issues as matters for expert determination, it is widely accepted that also legal issues can be submitted to an expert for a binding decision. See A Dolge, in K Spühler, L Tenchio, D Infanger (eds), *Basler Kommentar. Schweizerische Zivilprozessordnung*, 2nd edn (Helbing Lichtenhahn Verlag, 2013) p 982, para 12 ad Art 189 ZPO; B Berger, F Kellerhals, *International and Domestic Arbitration in Switzerland*, n 394 above, para 153. See also M Schöll, 'Reflexions sur l'expertise-arbitrage en droit Suisse' (2006) 24 *ASA Bulletin* 621.

[410] *Offensichtlich unrichtig, entaché d'erreur mainfeste.* Exhaustively on the criteria for challenging binding expert determination A Dolge, in K Spühler, L Tenchio, D Infanger (eds), *Basler Kommentar. Schweizerische Zivilprozessordnung*, 2nd edn (Helbing Lichtenhahn Verlag, 2013) pp 988ff, paras 46ff ad Art 189 ZPO.

[411] Art 59(2)(a), ZPO.

[412] B Berger, F Kellerhals, *International and Domestic Arbitration in Switzerland*, n 394 above, para 160.

[413] Art 189 ZPO is located outside Part Three, ZPO governing domestic arbitration and Chapter 12, IPRG concerning international arbitration.

[414] B Berger, F Kellerhals, *International and Domestic Arbitration in Switzerland*, n 394 above, para 152; M Liatowitsch, J Menz, in *International Arbitration in Switzerland. A Handbook for Practitioners*, n 378 above, 322, fn 60. Cf a critical approach taken by M Schöll, 'Reflexions sur l'expertise-arbitrage en droit Suisse', n 409 above, 641, fn 77.

[415] As per Art 177, IPRG. See B Berger, F Kellerhals, *International and Domestic Arbitration in Switzerland*, n 394 above, para 156.

[416] A Dolge, in K Spühler, L Tenchio, D Infanger (eds), *Basler Kommentar. Schweizerische Zivilprozessordnung*, 2nd edn (Helbing Lichtenhahn Verlag, 2013) pp 980–81, paras 5–9 ad Art 189 ZPO; M Schöll, *Das Schiedsgutachten im Schwietzer Recht—Grundriss und Praxisfrage* (Heymanns, 2007) 27ff.

commentators, tend to perceive *Schiedsgutachten* as substantive, notwithstanding its statutory source in ZPO.[417] Some authors emphasise the procedural character of expert determination, and compare *Schiedsgutachten* to contracts governing admissibility of evidence.[418] From a compromising standpoint expert determination contains elements of substantive contract but is, in principle, an institution of procedural law.[419] Under this interpretation two variants of expert determination are distinguished. In the first, an expert's decision contains a factual determination and is of a procedural nature. In the second, the decision supplements the legal relationship between the parties and should be equated with the parties' own statements.

Notwithstanding diverging views about the legal nature of *Schiedsgutachten*, there is a consensus as to the fundamental procedural safeguards that have to be observed in expert determination procedure.[420] These involve the impartiality and independence of the expert and the requirement for equal treatment of the parties. The need to observe the fundamental rules of fair process are derived from Article 189(3)(b) and (c) ZPO directly, and are not construed by analogy with arbitral proceedings. As mentioned, this provision prescribes when the decision is not binding on the parties or the court. **2.260**

The provisions governing arbitral proceedings, contained in Part Three, ZPO and Chapter 12, IPRG, do not apply to *Schiedsgutachten*.[421] It follows that the only grounds for challenging an expert's decisions are prescribed in Article 189 ZPO. Equally, the court's supervisory powers do not extend beyond this provision. A clear distinction between arbitration and expert determination also means that the parties to expert determination clauses cannot rely on the courts' support of arbitral proceedings.[422] The two methods are clearly demarcated and the **2.261**

[417] See literature and cases cited in A Dolge, in K Spühler, L Tenchio, D Infanger (eds), *Basler Kommentar. Schweizerische Zivilprozessordnung*, 2nd edn (Helbing Lichtenhahn Verlag, 2013) pp 980–81, para 6 ad Art 189 ZPO. See also J-F Poudret, S Besson, *Comparative Law of International Arbitration*, n 346 above, paras 15–16.

[418] M Guldener, *Schweizerisches Zivilprozessrecht der Schweiz*, 3rd edn (Schulthess, 1979) para 16a.

[419] W Habscheid, *Droit Judiciaire Privé Suisse*, 1st edn (Libraire de l'Université Georg et Cie SA, 1981) 551–52; W Habscheid, 'Das Scheidsgutachten. Ein Grnezgebiet zwischen materiallen Recht und Prozessrecht' in H Nipperdey (ed), *Das deutsche Privatrecht in der Mitte des 20. Jahrhunderts: Festschrift für Heinrich Lehmann zum 80. Geburtstag* (Tom II, W de Gruyte, 1956) 809ff.

[420] A Dolge, in K Spühler, L Tenchio, D Infanger (eds), *Basler Kommentar. Schweizerische Zivilprozessordnung*, 2nd edn (Helbing Lichtenhahn Verlag, 2013) p 988, para 41 ad Art 189 ZPO; M Liatowitsch, J Menz, in *International Arbitration in Switzerland. A Handbook for Practitioners*, n 378 above, 323; M Schöll, *Das Schiedsgutachten im Schwietzer Recht*, n 416 above, 46.

[421] A Dolge, in K Spühler, L Tenchio, D Infanger (eds), *Basler Kommentar. Schweizerische Zivilprozessordnung*, 2nd edn (Helbing Lichtenhahn Verlag, 2013) p 981, para 9 ad Art 189 ZPO; D Hochstrasser, S Fuchs, in H Honsell, N Vogt, A Schnyder, S Berti (eds), *Basler Kommentar. Internationales Privatrecht*, 3rd edn (Helbing Lichtenhahn Verlag, 2013) p 1688, para 294 ad Einleitung zum Zwölftes Kapitel.

[422] eg in situations where there is lack of cooperation between the parties as to the nomination of an expert, see Jugement du Tribunal de Première Instance de Gèneve, 12ème Chambre, JTPI/9028/2004, 5 juillet 2004, (2006) 24 *ASA Bulletin* 779 with a commentary by M Schöll, 'Reflexions sur l'expertise-arbitrage en droit Suisse', n 409 above, 621.

distinction between legal frameworks of *Schiedsgutachten* and arbitration is widely accepted.[423]

2.262 Notwithstanding the separation of the two regimes, the mission of an expert is sometimes described as quasi-arbitral.[424] The difficulty in distinguishing between an expert's and an arbitrator's mandate lies in the fact that the parties may empower an expert to make binding decisions not only on factual questions, but also on legal issues in dispute. The latter likens the function of an expert to that of an adjudicator.[425] A quasi-arbitral mandate bestowed on an expert implies a fiduciary relationship between the parties and the expert. It is comparable to an agency agreement, sometimes referred to as a contract *sui generis.*[426]

Enforceability of an Expert Determination Clause

2.263 Despite providing for *Schiedsgutachten* in ZPO, the statute does not contain express provisions governing sanctions for non-compliance with expert determination clauses. It has also been observed in the literature that ZPO is silent on whether the court can adjudicate on matters reserved for an expert in situations where a party has successfully challenged an expert's decision on one of the grounds prescribed by Article 189 ZPO. Deficient regulation gives rise to the variety of solutions enacted by Swiss jurisprudence.

2.264 It has been suggested that the binding force of expert determination implies that a matter for expert determination is excluded from the scope of court adjudication (*Kognitionsbefugnis*).[427] A similar view advocates that contracting for expert determination excludes the court from competence (*schliesst die Zuständigkeit des Gerichts aus*) to decide any matter submitted to an expert.[428] This is consonant with the jurisdictional classification of non-compliance with expert determination clauses adopted by the *Bundesgericht* in arbitration.

[423] D Hochstrasser, S Fuchs, in H Honsell, N Vogt, A Schnyder, S Berti (eds), *Basler Kommentar. Internationales Privatrecht*, 3rd edn (Helbing Lichtenhahn Verlag, 2013) p 1690, para 297 ad Einleitung zum Zwölftes Kapitel; M Liatowitsch, J Menz, in *International Arbitration in Switzerland. A Handbook for Practitioners* 322; B Berger, F Kellerhals, *International and Domestic Arbitration in Switzerland*, n 394 above, para 161; J-F Poudret, S Besson, *Comparative Law of International Arbitration*, n 346 above, para 15.

[424] D Hochstrasser, S Fuchs, in H Honsell, N Vogt, A Schnyder, S Berti (eds), *Basler Kommentar. Internationales Privatrecht*, 3rd edn (Helbing Lichtenhahn Verlag, 2013) p 1690; para 297 ad Einleitung zum Zwölftes Kapitel; M Blessing, in *International Arbitration in Switzerland* para 974.

[425] See also a classic statement of W Habscheid, *Droit Judiciaire Privé*, n 419 above, 551–52, who distinguishes two variants of expert determination described in 1.31 and 2.206.

[426] Exhaustively on this aspect A Dolge, in K Spühler, L Tenchio, D Infanger (eds), *Basler Kommentar. Schweizerische Zivilprozessordnung*, 2nd edn (Helbing Lichtenhahn Verlag, 2013) pp 985–86, paras 28–33 ad Art 189 ZPO.

[427] D Hochstrasser, S Fuchs, in H Honsell, N Vogt, A Schnyder, S Berti (eds), *Basler Kommentar. Internationales Privatrecht*, 3rd edn (Helbing Lichtenhahn Verlag, 2013) p 1690, para 298 ad Einleitung zum Zwölften Kapitel.

[428] A Dolge, in K Spühler, L Tenchio, D Infanger (eds), *Basler Kommentar. Schweizerische Zivilprozessordnung*, 2nd edn (Helbing Lichtenhahn Verlag, 2013) p 988, para 39 ad Art 189 ZPO.

Breach of a *Schiedsgutachten* clause as a matter affecting jurisdiction has been accepted in a judgment of 16 May 2011.[429] The contract containing a multi-tiered clause concerned with delivery and installation of industrial plant. The clause in dispute contained a provision under which the parties were obliged to submit disputes relating to the quality of the delivered items to an expert.[430] The clause also provided that the parties would attempt amicable resolution of the controversy before the dispute could be finally adjudicated by the panel of three arbitrators.[431] **2.265**

The dispute arose as to whether the delivered items conformed with the agreement. The party questioning the performance commenced arbitral proceedings without first submitting the dispute to an expert and without attempting conciliation. The defendant raised objections as to arbitral jurisdiction due to non-compliance by the claimant with the agreed ADR procedure. Alternatively, the defendant applied for stay of the proceedings. The tribunal dismissed the defence and proceeded to adjudicate on the merits of the case. The arbitrators concluded that referral to an expert was not necessary on the facts of the case because an expert was empowered to decide the questions of a largely technical character and the dispute at hand concerned legal matters. An expert's decision, if obtained, would be therefore irrelevant to the case. As for the conciliation requirement, the tribunal regarded the wording of the clause as too uncertain to have any binding force. Given the antagonistic positions of the parties, the tribunal concluded that conciliation was unlikely and refused to stay the proceedings for settlement negotiations. In consequence, the arbitrators proceeded to hear the case on the merits. The defendant challenged the final award on jurisdictional grounds. **2.266**

The *Bundesgericht* accepted in principle the defendant's reasoning according to which failure to submit the dispute to an expert affected the tribunal's jurisdiction to hear the case. It was confirmed that non-compliance with pre-arbitral ADR commitments might serve as grounds for challenge of an award under Article 190(2)(b) IPRG. The court, however, agreed with the arbitrators that submission of the dispute to an expert would be largely pointless on the facts of the case. As for the conciliation requirement, the court did not find precisely formulated duties in the disputed clause. In consequence, the challenge was dismissed in so far as it was founded on jurisdictional objections.[432] **2.267**

[429] Tribunal fédéral, Ière Cour de droit civil, 4A_46/2011, Arrêt du 16 mai 2011, (2011) 29 *ASA Bulletin* 643.

[430] 'En cas de contestations concernant la conformité ou la non-conformité des fournitures et prestations, l'acheteur et le fournisseur doivent avoir recours à un expert neutre avant de soumettre le litige à un tribunal arbitral.'

[431] '(1) En cas de litige à l'occasion de l'interprétation ou de l'exécution des présents, un accord à l'amiable sera d'abord recherché par les parties. (2) Les litiges éventuels qui viendraient à naître du fait de l'interprétation ou de l'exécution des dispositions du présent MARCHE seront soumis, après échec d'une tentative de conciliation, à un tribunal arbitral, sans aucun recours aux tribunaux judiciaires. Le tribunal arbitral sera composé de 3 arbitres. Chacune des parties désigne un arbitre.'

[432] The defendant, however, sucessfully challenged the award under the second of the invoked grounds, Art 190(2)(d) IPRG, relating to the right to be heard.

2.268 The general principle that non-compliance with pre-arbitral *Schiedsgutachten* affects jurisdiction of the arbitral tribunal was confirmed in a judgment of 7 July 2014.[433] In this case the *Bundesgericht* addressed the enforceability of a requirement to submit the dispute to a dispute adjudication board under clause 20 FIDIC.[434] On the facts of the case the parties opted for an ad hoc dispute board rather than a standing panel. When the dispute arose the Contractor notified its Employer of its intention to refer the dispute to the board in accordance with the contract. The parties were engaged in constituting the panel for several months. No dispute board procedure was successfully initiated and the Contractor submitted its claims straight to ICC arbitration.

2.269 The defendant challenged the arbitral jurisdiction by raising the point that the contractual dispute board procedure had not been complied with. The tribunal issued a partial award, finding that it had jurisdiction to hear the case. The arbitrators considered that submission of a dispute to the dispute board was not a precondition to initiating arbitration proceedings. The tribunal drew this conclusion from the permissive language of clause 20.4.[435] The tribunal also relied on the fact that the clause did not provide for a time-limit to constitute a dispute board, which implied the optional character of this step. The defendant challenged the partial award before the *Bundesgericht*.

2.270 In line with previous rulings, the court assumed that, in principle, non-compliance with a dispute board procedure affects the tribunal's competence to hear a case. The court disagreed with the arbitrators' finding that the word 'may' in clause 20.4 FIDIC implied the optional nature of the dispute board's procedure. It was pointed out that in clause 20.2 the word 'shall' is used[436] and clause 20.4 did not alter the mandatory nature of this step. The *Bundesgeright* also rejected the arbitrators' conclusion that lack of a time-limit for constitution of the dispute board implied that this ADR step was optional. On the facts of the case, however, the court held that non-compliance with the dispute board procedure was not fatal for the tribunal's jurisdiction. Referring to the rationale of the dispute board procedure, the court concluded that the board's decision would not put an end to the dispute, considering that the positions of the parties appeared irreconcilable. The court pointed out that the Employer was not cooperative in appointing the board, dragging the process out for 15 months beyond the date of the Contractor's referral. It was held that in such circumstances the Contractor could not be penalised for having commenced arbitration without first submitting the dispute to the board procedure.[437]

[433] BGer4A_124/2014, available at: www.swissarbitrationdecisions.com/sites/default/files/7%20juillet%202014%204A%20124%202014.pdf.

[434] See 1.45ff for the content, and 5.40ff for the enforceability of the clause.

[435] The main argument concerned the use of the word 'may' instead of 'shall'.

[436] 'Disputes shall be adjudicated by a DAB in accordance with Sub-Clause 20.4.'

[437] Importantly, the Bundesgericht also clarified that the law applicable to the interpretation of the arbitration agreement pursuant to Art 178 IPRG will also apply to the interpretation of any pre-arbitral procedures.

Jurisdictional classifications of non-compliance with expert determination have been criticised in the literature. Some authors consider compliance with pre-arbitral ADR as a matter irrelevant to arbitral jurisdiction, but having a bearing on arbitrators' ability to adjudicate on the merits of the case. Under this interpretation a tribunal confronted with a premature claim should dismiss it as inadmissible, or stay the proceedings. If the expert determination procedure is no longer possible to fulfill, the tribunal should definitely dismiss the claim.[438] This view assumes that arbitral jurisdiction is derived solely from an arbitration clause. Restrictions as to admissibility contained in contracts modifying arbitral procedure or the claim's substantive grounds (*materiellrechtliche Vorgabe*) do not affect the arbitrators' competence to hear a case.[439] An intermediate view assumes that although non-compliance with pre-arbitral ADR is an infringement of an arbitration clause, it does not justify annulment of the award under Article 190(2)(b) IPRG.[440] 2.271

Finally, it has been observed that Swiss law does not give an answer to the problem arising when a party has exhausted the requisite expert determination procedure, but an arbitral tribunal failed to take the expert's decision into account.[441] In such a situation it cannot be said that the tribunal lacked jurisdiction *rationae temporis* because the requisite procedure has been exhausted. It seems that by failing to take into account the expert's decision the tribunal is guilty of adjudicating on a matter outside its competence. It could be allowed that in such cases the tribunal lacks jurisdiction *ratione materiae*, while possessing jurisdiction *ratione temporis*, since the party bringing the claim duly went through the prescribed ADR steps. 2.272

Summary

Switzerland has still very little published jurisprudence to date on the matter of multi-tiered dispute resolution clauses.[442] The law on the enforceability of ADR emerging from the few rulings given cannot be considered as settled. As far as clauses providing for consensual ADR are concerned, the tendency is to reject their binding force in litigation. Swiss procedural law prescribes extensive pre-action conciliation duties. Where such conciliation duties do not apply and the parties 2.273

[438] M Schott, M Courvoisier in H Honsell, N Vogt, A Schnyder, S Berti (eds), *Basler Kommentar Internationales Privatrecht*, 3rd edn (Helbing Lichtenhahn Verlag, 2013) p 1917, para 54 ad Art 186 IPRG with reference to multi-tiered dispute resolution clause contained in FIDIC Forms of Contract.

[439] *ibid.* See also W Wegner, in S Berti (ed), *International Arbitration in Switzerland. An Introduction and a Commentary on Articles 176–194 of the Swiss Private International Law Statute* (Kluwer Law, International 2000) pp 467–468, para 20 ad Art 186 IPRG.

[440] M Schöll, Das Schiedsgutachten im Schwietzer Recht, n 416 above, 27ff.

[441] M Liatowitsch, J Menz, in *International Arbitration in Switzerland. A Handbook for Practitioners*, n 378 above, 324.

[442] This difficulty has been acknowledged by practitioners, see U Feller, M Frey, in *Multi-Tiered Dispute Resolution Clauses*, n 353 above 202.

enter into mediation agreements, such agreements are considered purely voluntary. By contrast to statutory conciliation, purely voluntary mediation clauses are of no procedural consequence. They may, however, be considered as substantive contracts, with contractual remedies for breach being theoretically available to the parties if the agreed procedure is not adhered to.

2.274 Expert determination is expressly provided for in the Swiss procedural code. ZPO does not prescribe, however, any sanctions for breach of expert determination clauses. A number of views concerning the nature of *Schiedsgutachten* clauses have been upheld in Swiss jurisprudence. According to the prevailing view, failure to submit the matter to an expert excludes adjudicating bodies from competence to decide on this matter.

2.275 The status of multi-tiered dispute resolution clauses is commonly analysed in the context of arbitral proceedings. Predominantly cases heard by the *Bundesgericht* concern the enforceability of the parties' ADR commitments in conjunction with arbitration agreements. The main interpretation assumes that failure to exhaust pre-arbitral tiers of the dispute resolution process results in tribunals lacking jurisdiction until the prescribed steps are complied with. Consequently, if a tribunal proceeds to hear the merits of the case notwithstanding the party's jurisdictional objections, a subsequent award can be annulled by the court under Article 190(2)(b) IPRG. In determining whether to annul the award on this basis the court has to establish if pre-arbitral ADR is prescribed in a sufficiently precise manner. Jurisdictional classification of non-compliance with ADR clauses has been adopted uniformly for both mediation and expert determination clauses.

2.276 Commentators criticising the jurisdictional classification of pre-arbitral ADR focus on the distinction between the jurisdiction of the tribunal and the admissibility of the claim. According to this view, failure to adhere to a sequence of ADR steps preceding arbitration affects the latter. In consequence, the tribunal receiving a premature claim should dismiss it as inadmissible or stay the proceedings, rather than refuse jurisdiction to hear the case. According to scholarly opinion enforcement by way of a stay most adequately reflects the intentions of parties to multi-tiered arbitration clauses.

2.277 Finally, an important feature of Swiss law on the enforceability of multi-tiered dispute resolution clauses is the search for pragmatic solutions rather than analysis of the underlying theoretical framework. The enforceability of clauses providing for pre-arbitral ADR is assessed on a case-by-case basis with a variety of solutions being considered. This pluralism in interpretation, so characteristic of Swiss jurisprudence, has left the law as to the enforceability of ADR as yet uncrystallised.[443]

[443] *ibid*; M Scherer, M Dawidowicz, *Switzerland. Arbitration Guide*, n 353 above, 5.

3

Comparative Conclusions

SUMMARY

This chapter contains a critical review of the presented material. Two broad areas of comparison are identified. The first focuses on the main characteristics of the analysed ADR clauses—their procedural or substantive nature, the scope of the duty they create, and how different legal systems prescribe the necessary elements for their validity. The second area of comparison concerns the means of enforcing ADR clauses. This section compares the availability of respective remedial actions in the described jurisdictions. Here the analysis is two-fold and comprises the scope of contractual liability of the claimant and the effects of a breach on prematurely initiated proceedings.

The main points will be:

(i) In continental systems of law great relevance is attached to ascertaining the legal nature of ADR clauses (3.1ff). The decision on this matter determines the effects of a given clause—whether they are purely procedural or also substantive. The tendency is to assign a procedural qualification to mediation clauses and a substantive qualification to expert determination clauses, the latter being largely an institution of substantive law. English law has no such discussion, as it treats ADR clauses as it would any other terms of a contract (3.7).

(ii) All systems of law similarly recognise the duty to undergo an agreed ADR process. As far as consensual methods are concerned—the mere initiation of a mediation process is sufficient to discharge the duty, actual participation in the negotiations not being required (3.22ff). The scope of the duty to fulfil the agreed process is easier to ascertain in the case of expert determination. It entails submitting the dispute to an expert in accordance with the contract (3.38).

(iii) In all analysed systems of law the courts underline that multi-tiered clauses should be drafted with sufficient precision (3.42ff). This involves express provisions regarding the mandatory, not just optional, nature of pre-trial ADR, as well as setting the time-limit for amicable negotiations after which the parties may proceed to the next tier of the dispute resolution mechanism.

(iv) The means of enforcement of multi-tiered dispute resolution clauses vary largely across the analysed jurisdictions (3.53ff). Contractual remedies are most easily available in England where dispute resolution clauses are treated just like other terms of the contract. This includes equitable remedies such as injunctive relief aimed at restraining the proceedings initiated in violation of an ADR clause. Moreover, litigants who choose English law as the law applicable to a multi-tiered clause benefit from a developed legal framework for expert determination and time-bar clauses. In those areas English law offers greater predictability, as compared to continental European jurisdictions.

(v) All analysed systems of law recognise the difficulty in quantifying damages for non-compliance with ADR clauses (3.64ff). The problem lies in relation to the extent of the loss arising from a party's failure to attempt an agreed ADR process. Liquidated damages prescribed in a contract are generally permitted, with the exception of England, where such clauses will not be upheld if the sum is punitive (3.73–3.75). This again raises the problematic issues of quantification.

(vi) As far as procedural effects of non-compliance with mediation clauses are concerned, the notion of inadmissibility of the proceedings prevails in Germany and France, despite different theoretical reasoning (3.83–3.87). In Germany the effects of mediation and expert determination differ, breach of the latter resulting in dismissal of the claim. In Switzerland the jurisdictional theory gained the greatest significance in the case of both mediation and expert determination clauses (3.92–3.93). This is especially relevant in the context of arbitration analysed further in Chapter four. Unlike in continental jurisdictions, under English law the procedural effectiveness of ADR clauses is at the discretion of the court (a stay being a discretionary remedy, (3.89)).

(vii) In all of the analysed legal systems the courts examined compliance with pre-trial ADR commitments not ex officio, but upon a plea raised by the defendant in the early stage of the proceedings (3.94–3.95). Raising a plea too late may preclude the court from ruling on the matter.

CONTENTS

Key Characteristics of Multi-tiered Dispute Resolution Clauses

Legal Nature of ADR Clauses

The analysis of the legal nature of ADR clauses is not a purely theoretical exercise. The decision as to the procedural or substantive nature of particular ADR methods may determine the consequences of non-compliance with the relevant clauses.[1] Amongst the analysed jurisdictions, continental European systems of law display a strong reliance on the relationship between the legal nature of a clause and its enforceability. Those legal systems follow a consistent trend demarcating consensual and quasi-adjudicative ADR. By contrast, English law treats both mediation and expert determination clauses uniformly. A comparison of those approaches will be presented below. 3.1

Legal Nature of Mediation Causes

As indicated, the available means for enforcement of mediation clauses may depend on whether such clauses are considered to be of a procedural or substantive nature. In Germany and France it is the procedural consequences of breach 3.2

[1] Particular sanctions are dealt with in the second part of this chapter (see 3.53ff below).

of mediation clauses that are at the centre of the court's attention. Substantive elements of mediation clauses, if analysed at all, are treated as a secondary issue.

3.3 In France, entering into a valid mediation clause excludes admissibility (*recevabilité*) of the claim until mediation is attempted by the parties in accordance with the contract. A plea of non-compliance with a mediation clause is classified as a *fin de non-recevoir*—an objection as to admissibility—classified as a procedural defence under the French Civil Procedure Code.[2] The consequences of filing the claim in court in breach of a mediation clause are different to those attached to a plea of non-compliance with an arbitration clause. The latter belongs to the category of procedural exceptions (*exceptions de procédure*). Importantly, however, both types of clause fall under a broad category of procedural defences.

3.4 Examination of substantive elements of mediation clauses has been undertaken predominantly in literature, rather than by the courts adjudicating on the enforceability of mediation clauses. The authors observe that mediation clauses give rise to an obligation of means (*obligation de moyens*), which compel the parties to exercise diligence and act in good faith in attempting pre-trial mediation. This is contrasted with the obligation to achieve a specified result (*obligation de résultat*), frequently considered inoperative due to the voluntary nature of the process.[3] The differentiation of substantive elements in mediation clauses does not, however, translate into the availability of contractual remedies for breach of the relevant contractual provision.

3.5 Similar observations can be made with respect to German jurisprudence. Some authors acknowledge substantive elements in ADR clauses providing for consensual ADR. This doctrinal debate is not, however, reflected in court judgments enforcing mediation or conciliation clauses. German judges invariably emphasise the procedural consequences of violating a duty to attempt mediation under the contract. In consequence, mediation clauses are analysed in line with other agreements relating to dispute resolution.[4]

3.6 By contrast, the substantive nature of mediation clauses has been recognised by the judiciary under Swiss law. The *Kassationsgericht Zürich* in the case of

[2] *Poiré v Tripier*, pourvoi n°00-19423, 00-19424, Bulletin civil 2003 MIXTE N° 1 p 1, on which 2.185ff. The categories of defences under the French Civil Procedure Code are described in 2.170–2.179.

[3] L Cadiet, J Normand, S Mekki, *Théorie générale du process* (Presses Universitaires de France, 2010) 469; C Jarrosson, 'Les clauses de renégociation, de conciliation et de mediation' in *Les principales clauses de contrats conclus entre professionnels* (Presses Universitaires d'Aix-Marseille, 1990) 141; C Jarrosson, 'Note—Cour de cassation (Ch commerciale) 28 novembre 1995 618–19; C Jarrosson, 'Les modes alternatifs de règlement des conflicts' (1997) 2 *Revue Internationale de Droit Comparé* 328, 337. See also 2.198–2.199.

[4] B Hess, *Rechtsgrundlagen der Mediation* in F Haft, K von Schliefen (eds), *Handbuch Mediation*, 2nd edn (CH Beck, 2009) 1062ff and the literature cited. The discussion on the legal nature of mediation clauses reflects a similar debate relating to jurisdiction and arbitration agreements (see 2.93–2.96 for details).

15 March 1999[5] held that the mediation clause in question was of a purely substantive nature. In consequence, it could only be enforced by way of contractual remedies. On the facts of the case, however, the court found no grounds for an award of damages or an order for specific performance. The court made clear that breach of a mediation clause is of no consequence for the prematurely initiated proceedings. The case is an unusual decision among continental jurisdictions, where the court subjected the enforceability of mediation clauses entirely to contract law rules. It must be noted that subsequent Swiss courts accepted the procedural consequences of mediation clauses in the arbitration context.[6]

This debate, so characteristic of continental jurisdictions, can be contrasted with the approach adopted in England. English law does not recognise a separate category of procedural contracts and the courts do not distinguish between procedural and substantive consequences of dispute resolution clauses. Instead, such clauses are treated equally to other contractual terms. They are subjected to the same rules concerning their interpretation and the available remedies for breach.[7] In addition to contractual means of enforcement, the court may award a stay of the proceedings for breach of a mediation clause. Importantly, however, the court will award the stay only if satisfied that the clause in question constitutes a valid contractual term. In order to bring the premature proceedings to a halt, the court will apply contractual principles to determine whether a binding obligation to mediate has arisen between the parties. 3.7

Treating dispute resolution clauses in line with other contractual terms caused initial reluctance by English courts to enforce clauses providing for consensual ADR. Mediation and negotiation clauses have been equated with 'agreements to agree', ie too uncertain to have binding force.[8] As a result, consensual ADR remained unenforceable until the pivotal decision in the *Cable & Wireless v IBM* case made in 2002.[9] By contrast, the German *Bundesgerichtshof* confirmed the enforceability of conciliation clauses as early as in 1983.[10] This discrepancy may be attributable to the existence of a well-established and comprehensive legal framework governing procedural contracts under German law. The German doctrine of *pacta de non petendo* allowed quick recognition of the emerging type of clauses providing for pre-trial conciliation. English law, lacking similar tools, acknowledged the enforceable nature of mediation clauses only after a policy shift towards popularisation of ADR following the Woolf reforms and the Civil Procedure Rules 1998. 3.8

[5] 15 März 1999—Kassationsgericht Zürich, (2002) 20 *ASA Bulletin* 373, on which see 2.230ff.

[6] On which, see 2.238ff.

[7] Arbitration clauses are examined in line with other agreements in English contract law, see eg, *Chitty on Contracts*, 32nd edn (Sweet & Maxwell, 2015) vol II, paras 32-001ff.

[8] On this aspect see 2.4–2.11.

[9] *Cable & Wireless PLC v IBM United Kingdom Ltd* [2002] EWHC 2059 (Comm), [2002] CLC 1319 (Com Ct).

[10] BGH NJW 1984, 669. The court based its findings on an even earlier case of the Celle Regional Court, OLG Celle NJW 1971, 288.

Legal Nature of Expert Determination Clauses

3.9 Several trends can be observed in relation to the character of expert determination clauses under the analysed jurisdictions. First, the most comprehensive legal framework governing expert determination has been developed in England. Secondly, the legal nature of expert determination and mediation clauses diverges under those jurisdictions that distinguish between procedural and substantive elements of dispute resolution clauses. Finally, the jurisprudence of continental jurisdictions tends to define expert determination in light of its normative source. An important factor for this assessment is the character of the expert's decision and its contractually binding force.

3.10 English legal practice has traditionally benefited from a comprehensive normative framework for expert determination, governing inter alia the binding force of the expert's decision, grounds for challenge of the decision before the court and the enforceability of expert determination clauses. Currently expert determination is treated as a fully-fledged ADR method[11] and is recommended by the courts as one of the main alternatives to court litigation.[12] English law defines the legal nature of expert determination clauses in a way similar to mediation or arbitration agreements. Expert determination clauses are considered to be contractual terms no different to other provisions of the contract. The binding force of clauses providing for this expert determination was recognised earlier than was the case with mediation.[13] This is owing to the non-consensual character of the process and the precise nature of the obligations it entails, which are independent of the cooperation between the parties.

3.11 The legal nature of expert determination clauses is less clear-cut under continental jurisdictions. Under the majority of analysed systems expert determination is not expressly provided for in statute, and thus inevitably lacks a defined normative framework. Legal foundations of this ADR method are frequently derived from substantive provisions of the law of obligations. This is the case under French and German law where expert determination (*expertise-arbitrage, Schiedsgutachten*) is inferred from determination of the performance by a third person.[14]

3.12 Accordingly, German discussion on the legal nature of expert determination clauses is influenced by the normative source of this ADR technique located in §§ 317–319 of the German Civil Code. Unlike mediation, expert determination is regarded as an institution of substantive law whereby the parties contractually commit to be bound by an opinion of a third party. An alternative

[11] J Kendall, C Freedman, J Farrell, *Expert Determination*, 5th edn (Sweet & Maxwell, 2015) para 1.1.11. The authors point out that expert determination alongside mediation is an 'other dispute resolution procedure' referred to in s 9, Arbitration Act 1996 (*ibid*, para 1.5.2.).

[12] *Yorkshire Electricity Distribution plc v Telewest Ltd* [2006] EWCA Civ 1418 at [47].

[13] *Channel Tunnel Group Ltd v Balfour Beatty Construction Ltd* [1993] AC 334 (HL).

[14] §§ 317–319, German Civil Code; Art 1592, French Civil Code, respectively.

stance, emphasising the quasi-judicial character of the expert's mandate, is not widely shared, and expert determination is rarely classified as one of procedural contracts.[15] The substantive nature of *Schiedsgutachten* is reflected in the way expert determination clauses are enforced by German courts.[16]

A similar discussion can be identified under French law where the normative source of *expertise-arbitrage* determines the classification of this ADR method as substantive.[17] Expert determination has no express legal grounds but is subjected to analogous application of Article 1592 of the Civil Code governing the setting of a contractual price by a third person. Unlike in Germany, however, the character of this method does not translate into the court's reaction to breach of an expert determination clause. In France failure to adhere to an expert determination clause has the same consequences as breach of a mediation clause. Non-compliance with both types of clauses gives rise to the same procedural defence classified as a *fin de non-recevoir* and leads to the rejection of the claim as inadmissible.[18] **3.13**

Unlike other continental systems, Swiss law contains provisions expressly regulating expert determination. They are contained in a procedural, not substantive act: Article 189 the Swiss Civil Procedure Code. Under this provision the function of an expert is prescribed narrowly as that of an evaluator of a relevant factual issue. It is, however, widely accepted that the scope of the expert's mandate under Article 189 of the Swiss Civil Procedure Code may involve determination of both factual and legal matters.[19] Consequently, Swiss law creates a framework for treating expert determination as a fully-fledged ADR technique in a way akin to English law. **3.14**

As under other continental systems, also Swiss jurisprudence treats the normative foundations of expert determination as the decisive factor in the debate on the legal nature of this ADR method. Notwithstanding the divergence of proposed solutions, commentators emphasise the procedural consequences of non-compliance with expert determination clauses.[20] Location of the legal framework **3.15**

15 See 2.128 for details.

16 BGH NJW-RR 1988, 1405 on which 2.130ff below.

17 *Prozessverträge.* See discussion in 2.207ff.

18 W Habscheid, 'L'expertise Arbitrage' in P Sanders (ed), *International Arbitration. Liber Amicorum for Martin Domke* (Martinus Nijhoff, 1967) 108, 116 and C Jarrosson, 'Observations on *Poire v. Tripier*' (2003) 3 *Arbitration International* 363, 367. See 2.212–2.213.

19 A Dolge, in K Spühler, L Tenchio, D Infanger (eds), *Basler Kommentar. Schweizerische Zivilprozessordnung*, 2nd edn (Helbing Lichtenhahn Verlag, 2013) p 982, para 12 ad art 189 ZPO.

20 D Hochstrasser, S Fuchs in H Honsell, N Vogt, A Schnyder, S Berti (eds), *Basler Kommentar. Internationales Privatrecht*, 3rd edn (Helbing Lichtenhahn Verlag, 2013) p 1690, para 298 ad Einleitung zum Zwölftes Kapitel (the matters left for an expert to determine are excluded from the court's cognition until the process is exhausted and the decision submitted); A Dolge, in K Spühler, L Tenchio, D Infanger (eds), *Basler Kommentar. Schweizerische Zivilprozessordnung*, 2nd edn (Helbing Lichtenhahn Verlag, 2013) p 988, para 39 ad Art 189 ZPO (jurisdiction of the adjudicative body is excluded until the expert procedure is complied with); M Schott, M Courvoisier in H Honsell, N Vogt, A Schnyder, S Berti (eds), *Basler Kommentar Internationales Privatrecht*, 3rd edn (Helbing Lichtenhahn Verlag, 2013) p 1917, para 54 ad art 186 IPRG (inadmissibility of the proceedings until compliance with the agreed expert determination process).

for expert determination in the Civil Procedure Code, as well as the consequences attached to non-compliance with its provisions, demonstrate the procedural attributes of this ADR method.

3.16 Swiss law prescribes the grounds under which the expert's decision can be challenged in court in a significantly more comprehensive manner than in other continental jurisdictions. Under Article 189(3)(a)–(c) of the Swiss Civil Procedure Code the expert's decision is not binding if: (i) it concerned matters relating to the legal relationship which were outside the parties' free disposal; (ii) there were grounds to recuse an expert; (iii) a decision was not given in an impartial manner; or (iv) the decision is manifestly wrong. Under German law the express basis for challenge of the decision, as prescribed by § 319 of the German Civil Code, contains only the last of those grounds. French regulation, Article 1592 of the French Civil Code, does not provide for any explicit basis upon which the parties may challenge the determination. It is, however, recognised that a decision which is manifestly incorrect, biased or issued under duress would not be binding.[21]

3.17 The largest body of cases governing grounds for challenge of an expert's decision exists under English law.[22] Particular attention must be devoted to its underlying premise that the courts cannot assume the role of an appellate body to review an expert's findings. In consequence, the court rarely interferes with the merits of the expert's decision but focuses on matters such as whether the expert acted in an impartial manner within the scope of his/her mandate under the contract.

3.18 Each of the analysed legal systems addresses the issue of procedural safeguards that must be observed in the expert determination process. The discussion focuses on the expert's impartiality, considered a core principle of the expert determination procedure. The wider question of procedural fairness in expert determination remains, however, unclear. Particular uncertainty in this matter is characteristic of those legal systems which do not expressly provide for expert determination. Issues such as the right to be heard and the expert's ability to give decisions in the absence of the parties remain unresolved. English law, under which it has been clarified that expert determination does not enjoy the same standard of procedural fairness as arbitration, provides some guidance in this matter.[23] It remains unclear, however, how the requirement of due process under Article 6 of the European Convention on Human Rights affects the expert determination procedure.

[21] Cour d'appel de Paris (1re Chambre civile) 30 juin 1995, (1996) 3 *Revue de l'Arbitrage* 500; W Habscheid, 'L'expertise Arbitrage', n 8 above, 104. Further on the grounds to challenge the expert's decision under continental jurisdictions, see 2.257 (Switzerland) 2.117 (Germany) and 2.209 (France).

[22] For an outline see 2.58.

[23] Comprehensively on this aspect J Kendall, C Freedman, J Farrell, *Expert Determination*, n 11 above, paras 14.13–14.15.

This problem of procedural safeguards in the expert determination procedure becomes particularly pertinent given the rapidly changing landscape for this ADR method. Initially, expert determination was utilised by the parties to obtain a decision on a narrow technical issue relevant under the contract. Modern expert determination is treated as a fully-fledged ADR method whereby an expert is empowered to decide on entire claims, determining facts and applying law. Although the decision issued in such a process is typically fully reviewable in subsequent proceedings, it may become final and binding if neither party issues a timely challenge. In such a case the expert's decision remains the only determination of the dispute, without enjoying the similar degree of court supervision, procedural safeguards, and detailed procedural framework, as arbitration awards. This dilemma is especially pressing in those jurisdictions which did not develop a comprehensive legal framework for expert determination and derive its foundations from related institutions. Such an approach, despite its obvious shortcomings, appeared sufficient in relation to the traditional form of expert determination. It is, however, inadequate, if applied to expert determination in its expanded form, where an expert decides on claims and not merely on narrow factual issues.[24] In consequence, integrating expert determination into escalation mechanisms may be a source of uncertainty, especially acute in continental jurisdictions. 3.19

In summary, the analysis of the legal nature of expert determination clauses concentrates on the interpretation of basic features of this ADR method under the legal system involved. Continental jurisdictions rely heavily on the normative sources of expert determination in determining the procedural or substantive nature of clauses providing for this dispute resolution technique. The legal framework for expert determination is often incomplete under those legal systems and does not reflect the nature of expert determination as an ADR technique. By contrast, English law has developed a comprehensive body of case law governing expert determination, under which clauses providing for this ADR method are treated just as other terms of the contract. It is uncertain, however, to what extent the right to fair trial under Article 6 of the European Convention on Human Rights interplays with expert determination as a final and binding dispute resolution method. 3.20

Scope of the Duty to Follow the Agreed ADR Process

The analysis of the scope of the duty created by various ADR clauses is crucial for the enforceability of tiered dispute resolution mechanisms. Defining the actions that are considered to exhaust a particular ADR step is a necessary step in 3.21

[24] J-F Poudret, S Besson, *Comparative Law of International Arbitration*, 2nd edn (Sweet & Maxwell 2007) para 17.

establishing breach of a given clause. It also provides clarity as to when the parties may proceed to the next tier of the dispute resolution mechanism. The diverging approaches to the scope of the duty arising under different types of ADR clause demonstrate the evolving position of European judiciary regarding the enforceability of multi-tiered clauses. Below the main approaches will be compared and contrasted.

Consensual ADR Methods

3.22 The scope of the duty arising under a particular clause is the main distinguishing feature of consensual and quasi-adjudicative ADR methods. It is the first group that judges found more problematic. The main difficulty in delineating the minimum standard of compliance with consensual ADR clauses is associated with the cooperative nature of the process. Two competing approaches can be identified in judicial responses to this dilemma.

3.23 The first model emphasises the voluntary nature of consensual ADR. Under this approach committing to mediation or negotiations before the dispute has arisen does not change this general quality of the process. In consequence, the parties are not bound by a clause providing for consensual ADR, which is considered an expression of intention, rather than a mandatory step. This approach is based on an assumption that by initiating the court proceedings the party is making it clear that it is not interested in reaching a settlement but seeks final adjudication of the dispute. In such circumstances referring the parties to mediation is considered futile.

3.24 This model has been adopted in Switzerland with reference to mediation clauses in litigation. Swiss law distinguishes between conciliation and mediation. Pre-trial conciliation attempt is a statutory duty, required in a majority of cases. As such it enforced by the courts. Mediation clauses can be contracted for wherever the statute does not require conciliation. Consequently, mediation is perceived as purely optional and the courts are reluctant to assume any consequences of breach of the parties' contractual commitment to mediate.[25]

3.25 In France the consensual nature of mediation has been initially considered as preventing the enforceability of mediation clauses.[26] The joint chambers of the

[25] P Ruggle, in K Spühler, L Tenchio, D Infanger (eds), *Basler Kommentar. Schweizerische Zivilprozessordnung*, 2nd edn (Helbing Lichtenhahn Verlag, 2013) p 1080, para 8 ad art 213 ZPO; C Kupman, C Bauer in K Hopt, F Steffek, *Mediation: Rechtstatsachen, Rechtsvergleich, Regelungen*, 866; I Meier, in N Alexander (ed), *Global Trends in Mediation* (Otto Schmidt, 2010) 355, 385. See also 2.228. The case of Kassationsgericht Zürich of 15 March 1999 (15 März 1999—Kassationsgericht Zürich, (2002) 20 *ASA Bulletin* 373) where mediation clauses have been considered as having purely substantive consequences is to an extent an exception to this rule. Characteristically, however, the court did not award any sanction for breach of the clause in question. Enforceability of mediation clauses is accepted in arbitration (see 2.240ff).

[26] Cour de cassation (1re Ch civ) 23 janvier 2001, RTD *civ* 2001, 359, (2001) 4 *Revue de l'Arbitrage* 751; Cour de cassation (1re Ch civ) 6 mars 2001, (2001) 4 *Revue de l'Arbitrage* 751.

Cour de cassation in *Poiré v Tripier*[27] have taken a different stand, however, and conclusively clarified that ADR clauses should be given effect by the courts. Similarly, English courts were traditionally reluctant to enforce an obligation requiring the parties to undergo amicable dispute resolution process before filing the claim in court. Such a stipulation was regarded as an 'agreement to agree', too uncertain to have any binding force. This interpretation, unfavourable to mediation clauses, continued until the Woolf Reforms and the Civil Procedure Rules. Following the breakthrough in the English court's approach to ADR the enforceability of mediation clauses was established in the *Cable & Wireless v IBM* case.[28]

In contrast to the other three legal systems, German law did not regard the cooperative nature of conciliation as an obstacle to enforcing conciliation clauses. In consequence, the binding nature of the parties' commitment to undergo a consensual ADR process has been established in Germany earlier than in all other jurisdictions.[29] It has to be borne in mind, however, that early relevant German case law predominantly considered clauses contained in the rules governing the conduct of the members of certain professions.[30] They were not contractual provisions concluded by the parties with equal bargaining power, hence the court could impose conciliation duties more readily disregarding the cooperative nature of the processes in question. **3.26**

An alternative model assumes that, despite the voluntary nature of the process, contracting in advance for consensual ADR is a source of binding obligations for the parties. Under this approach, referring the parties to mediation furthers observance of contractual promise and is not considered necessarily futile. The rationale behind this model focuses on the value of giving the parties a mere opportunity to resolve the dispute amicably. Despite the initially antagonistic position manifested by the claimant who initiated court proceedings, referral to mediation provides institutional framework for exploring the possibility of settlement for both parties. This approach has been consistently presented in Germany and currently prevails also in England and France. **3.27**

It is widely accepted that the mandatory, not permissive, language of mediation clauses is critical to their enforceability.[31] If the wording of a particular clause is decisive enough, the reinforcement of contractual duty is demanded by the **3.28**

[27] Cour de cassation (Ch mixte), 14 février 2003, *Bulletin civil*, 2003 Mixte, n° 1, p 1.

[28] *Cable & Wireless PLC v IBM United Kingdom Ltd* [2002] CLC 1319 (Com Ct).

[29] Fundamental rules governing the enforceability of conciliation clauses have been laid down in the decision of OLG Celle of 31 July 1970 (OLG Celle NJW 1971, 288) and the decision of the Bundesgerichtshof of 23 November 1983 (BGH NJW 1984, 669).

[30] eg veterinary practitioners (BGH NJW 1984, 669) or tax advisors (BGH NJW 1999, 647; Brandenburgisches OLG ANWBL 1998, 281).

[31] Note however instances where French and German judges enforced ADR provisions notwithstanding the permissive language of relevant clauses (*Séribo v Hainan Yangpu Xindadao Industrial Co Ltd* Cour de cassation (1ere civ), N° de pourvoi: 11-10347, available at: www.legifrance.gouv.fr and *LG Münster* of 21 December 2000 LG Münster DStRE 2001, 614, on which see 2.107, 2.147 and 2.151).

pacta sunt servanda principle, irrespective of the parties' de facto attitude to settlement negotiations. By requiring the claimant to exhaust the agreed ADR process the courts recognise that the parties' readiness to compromise may fluctuate. By imposing a sanction for breach of contractual ADR commitments the court or arbitral tribunal does not compel the parties to negotiate but enforces a contractual promise whose objective was to create a framework for exploring settlement options. Referring the parties to ADR in accordance with the contract is not based on an unrealistic assumption that settlement will be reached in any event. Whether or not the parties de facto negotiate is not a concern of the court when enforcing mediation clauses. Rather, the enforceability of consensual ADR compels the parties to attempt to negotiate, which in turn increases the chances of reaching the settlement. As summarised by a German judge in relation to a conciliation clause in the rules of the tax advisors' chamber:

> On the one hand, mediation under the rules of tax advisors' chambers (hereafter BO) is not compulsory. On the other hand, BO do not expect anything more than giving the chamber an opportunity to mediate and to express its view.[32]

3.29 Enforcing clauses providing for consensual ADR requires establishing the minimum standard of compliance with contractual duties they have created. The court faced with the breach must have certainty as to what actions the parties should undertake in order to exhaust the ADR process in accordance with the contract. A related problem concerns the question whether mediation clauses should be enforced in any event, or whether there are circumstances justifying disregarding a pre-trial mediation requirement.

3.30 Those legal systems under which mediation clauses are enforceable present a similar approach to the scope of the duty created by the parties' commitment to mediate. The courts do not expect the parties to actually engage in negotiations, which are inherently voluntary. The parties discharge their contractual duty by

[32] LG Münster DStRE 2001, 614. 'Zum einen sei ein Vermittlungsverfahren nach der Berufsordnung der Steuerberater nicht zwingend. Zum anderen verlange die Berufsordnung nicht mehr, als dass der Steuerberaterkammer Gelegenheit zur Vermittlung und Stellungnahme gegeben werde.' A similar summary was given by Giles J in an Australian case of the Supreme Court of New South Wales in *Hooper Bailie Associates Ltd v Natcon Group Pty Ltd* (1992) 28 NSWLR 194. The judge held [at 206]: 'Conciliation or mediation is essentially consensual and the opponents of enforceability contend that it is futile to seek to enforce something which requires the co-operation and consent of a party when co-operation and consent cannot be enforced; equally, they say that there can be no loss to the other party if for want of co-operation and consent the consensual process would have led to no result. The proponents of enforceability contend that this misconceives the objectives of alternative dispute resolution, saying that the most fundamental resistance to compromise can wane and turn to co-operation and consent if the dispute is removed from the adversarial procedures of the courts and exposed to procedures designed to promote compromise, in particular where a skilled conciliator or mediator is interposed between the parties. What is enforced is not co-operation and consent but participation in a process from which co-operation and consent might come. The distinction is evident in the opening words of the chapter dealing with mediation made compulsory by law in Rogers and McEwen (op cit para. 5.1): "Although parties to a dispute may ultimately refuse to settle in mediation, they are not always free to decline participation"'.

merely attempting mediation. Notwithstanding this principle, the analysed cases rarely clarify what exactly amounts to a mediation attempt.[33]

One of the few examples where such indications were given is the decision in the *Cable & Wireless* case by Colman J in the High Court.[34] The judge held that the fulfilment of the contractual duty arising under a tiered mediation clause obliges the party raising the claim to institute the mediation process. The minimum the parties are required do is to select the mediator in accordance with the contract and to present the case to him. **3.31**

A similar solution has been adopted in Germany. In an award of LG Münster of 12 December 2000[35] it has been concluded that the duty to attempt mediation before a relevant body of the tax advisors' chamber means taking such actions that are necessary to make the mandate of that body possible to perform. The court held that in practice such actions imply at least the filing of an appropriate motion with a competent chamber by a party raising the claim. Under French law the scope of the duty to attempt mediation has been examined in the context of substantive elements identifiable in ADR clauses. French commentators distinguish obligations to achieve a result (*obligations de resultat*) and obligations to employ means (*obligation de moyens*), reflected in the content of mediation agreements. It has been suggested that an obligation to achieve a result should be understood as the duty to initiate mediation in accordance with applicable norms.[36] Finally, the rules of various centres administering an ADR process contain express provisions defining the scope of the duty to undergo mediation.[37] **3.32**

It must be emphasised that neither the duty to further the contractually selected dispute resolution process, existing under German law (*Verfahrensförderungspflicht*),[38] nor the duty to act in good faith (*bonne foi*) in performing an ADR clause, required **3.33**

[33] cf the standard of compliance with mediation clauses under the ICC cases reported by J Carter, 'Issues Arising from Integrated Dispute Resolution Clauses' in AJ van den Berg (ed), *New Horizons in International Commercial Arbitration and Beyond. ICCA Congress Series 2004* (Kluwer International, 2005) 446, 462ff. See also Article 7(2) of the ICC Mediation Rules 2014, which clarifies that each party, by agreeing to refer a dispute to the Rules, agrees to participate in the Proceedings at least until receipt of the Mediator's note under this provision.

[34] [2002] CLC 1319 (Com Ct).

[35] LG Münster DStRE 2001, 614.

[36] L Cadiet, J Normand, S Mekki, *Théorie générale du procès*, n 3 above, 469; C Jarrosson, 'Note—Cour de cassation (Chambre Mixte), 14 février 2003' 410; C Jarrosson, 'La sanction du non-respect d'une clause instituant un préliminaire obligatoire de conciliation ou de mediation': Note—Cour de cassation (2e Ch civ) 6 juillet 2000; Cour de cassation (1re civ) 23 janvier et 6 février 2001' (2001) 4 *Revue de l'arbitrage* 752, 754.

[37] See eg Art 18, WIPO Mediation Rules under which mediation can be terminated by either party no later than after the conclusion of the first session. See also N Alexander, *International and Comparative Mediation Legal Perspectives* (Wolters Kluwer, 2009) 227, fn 48. On this topic also R Jacobs, 'Should Mediation Trigger Arbitration in Multi-Step Alternative Dispute Resolution Clauses?' (2004) 14 *American Review of International Arbitration* 164, 179, with reference to American practice: '[Mediation] is voluntary in participation but not attendance'.

[38] This duty has been established with respect to arbitration, see OLG Frankfurt a.M., 07.11.1997—24 U 248–95, NJW-RR 11/1998, 778. See also 2.157.

by French Civil Code,[39] expands the scope of the duty created by mediation clauses beyond the mere attempt to mediate. These duties are not interpreted as constituting an obligation to actually engage in negotiations. The scope of the duty to mediate is perceived similarly under English law, which lacks equivalent principles.[40] The courts require merely the commencement of the process by the party raising the claim. In conclusion, those systems under which the contractual duty to mediate is enforceable resolve the tension between the voluntary nature of consensual ADR and the *pacta sunt servanda* principle similarly.

3.34 A further issue concerns the question whether a mediation attempt is required in all circumstances, or whether there are any exceptions to the enforceability of mediation clauses. The analysed legal systems approach this problem slightly differently. Under English law stay of the proceedings as a result of breach of a mediation clause depends on the court's discretion. In consequence, a mediation attempt will not always be required. As explained by Colman J in *Cable & Wireless*,[41] if referring the parties to mediation would be a 'completely hopeless exercise', the court can refuse to penalise breach of a mediation clause. This exception is, however, interpreted narrowly.[42] The practice of English courts has established that it is not an obstacle to refer the parties to mediation even though one party is opposed to it.[43]

3.35 Similarly, under French law the likelihood of mediation being successful has been treated as a relevant factor for the enforceability of mediation clauses. Several court decisions take the stance that the sanction for breach of the parties' pre-trial

[39] Art 1134, French Civil Code. See also M van Der Haegen, 'Les Procédures de Conciliation et de Médiation Organisées par les principaux instituts d'arbitrage et de médiation en Europe' (1996) 2 *Revue de Droit des Affaires Internationales* 255, 260 (non-compliance with a mediation clause does not give rise to the claim for the order for specific performance but facilitates the proof that the party did not act in good faith performing the contract). For a comparative analysis of the requirement of good faith in mediation see N Alexander, *International and Comparative Mediation,* n 37 above, 227ff.

[40] On clauses expressly obliging the parties to act in good faith in ADR clauses governed by English law see D Jones, 'Various Non-Binding ADR Processes' in AJ van den Berg (ed), *New Horizons in International Commercial Arbitration and Beyond. ICCA Congress Series 2004* (Kluwer International, 2005) 368, 375.

[41] [2002] CLC 1319 (Com Ct) at 1328.

[42] On the court's discretion to enforce consensual ADR, see K Mackie, 'The Future of ADR Clauses after Cable & Wireless v. IBM' (2003) 19 *Arbitration International* 345, 348. cf 'futility exception' discussed in American jurisprudence J File, 'United States: Multi-Step Dispute Resolution Clauses' (2007) 7 *IBA Legal Practice Division Mediation Committee Newsletter* 33, 34.

[43] *Shirayama Shokusan Co Ltd v Danovo Ltd (No 1)* [2004] BLR 207, where Blackburne J held: 'In *Cable and Wireless plc v IBM United Kingdom Ltd* [2002] 2 All ER (Comm) 1041, Colman J observed that the making of ADR orders was commonplace (at any rate in the Commercial Court) even when one party objects to such an order and that, occasionally, such an order has been made even in the face of objections from both sides' (at para [19]). See also on this topic N Andrews, *Andrews on Civil Processes. vol II: Arbitration & Mediation* (Intersentia, 2013) paras 1.96–1.98.

ADR commitments depends on whether or not referring the parties to mediation would be entirely futile.[44]

3.36 By contrast, the German judiciary treated a futility argument as insufficient grounds to refuse enforcement of mediation clauses.[45] The reason for this rigorous stand may lie, once again, in the nature of the clauses analysed by German judges when the court's approach to ADR initially developed. As mentioned, the majority of court decisions in this period were concerned with conciliation clauses contained in the rules of institutional structures such as veterinary practitioners' bodies, tax advisors' chambers or housing cooperatives. Participation in such bodies implied the acceptance of the rules governing their structures. These included mandatory conciliation under the auspices of the relevant internal organisations. By acceding to such structures the participants accepted the competence of the relevant bodies to mediate in the dispute between them before it was brought to court. The court's readiness to enforce the dispute resolution mechanism can be greater in disputes between the members of a professional organisation than in the case of commercial partners. The decisions formed on this basis set out the foundation for the later treatment of consensual ADR in its modern, purely contractual and commercial, version.

3.37 By contrast, ADR clauses analysed in the precedent decisions of English courts concerned mediation contained predominantly in commercial contracts. ADR clauses concluded bilaterally and by equal parties could be subjected to a more flexible interpretation which took into account the parties' fluctuating attitude to an ADR process in the context of the commercial purpose of the relevant clause. Consequently, the voluntary nature of mediation is more emphasised in England than is the case under German law. Importantly, however, it is accepted under both legal systems that the plea of non-compliance with a consensual ADR clause will be disregarded if brought in bad faith or in order to delay hearing of the case.

Quasi-adjudicative ADR Methods

3.38 The scope of the duty to undergo an agreed ADR process is easier to define for quasi-adjudicative methods. Expert determination and dispute board procedures do not engage voluntary participation and a party wishing to proceed to final adjudication cannot unilaterally frustrate them. Quasi-adjudicative ADR techniques are capable of producing their end result—a final decision—regardless of the parties' attitudes. This feature of expert determination reduces ambiguity as

[44] See Cour de Cassation (1ère Chambre Civile), 4 janvier 1961, Bulletin civile N° 6, 6–7; Conseil d'Etat, 9 decembre 1991, N° 84308, Snoy, (1991) *Recueil Lebon* 423, on which see E Gaillard, J Edelstein, 'Mediation in France' in T Carbonneau, J Jaeggi, S Partridge (eds), *Handbook on International Arbitration and ADR* (JurisNet, 2006) 248.

[45] BGH NJW 1984, 669; OLG Celle NJW 1971, 288.

to the moment at which the relevant procedure should be considered exhausted.[46] Expert determination and dispute board clauses are, therefore, enforceable without reservations regarding the nature of the duty to undergo the agreed process, so long as such clauses are permitted under the legal system concerned, and the dispute has arisen when it was possible to fulfil the prescribed procedure.[47]

Necessary Elements of Enforceable Multi-tiered Dispute Resolution Clauses

3.39 The analysis of multi-tiered clauses in different jurisdictions provokes the discussion as to the necessary elements of their components. The starting point of the remarks concerning this matter is the enforceability of ADR clauses in litigation. Nevertheless, defining the necessary elements of enforceable escalation mechanisms under a particular legal system is equally valid in the arbitration context in cases where that system is applied to a multi-tiered clause.

Mandatory Character of Pre-adjudicative ADR

3.40 It is emphasised in the literature that drafters of multi-tiered clauses should avoid permissive language and make the mandatory character of pre-adjudicative ADR unambiguous.[48] Judges of both common law and continental jurisdictions confirm this observation.[49] In particular, lack of clear wording prescribing the obligatory nature of ADR commitments impairs the enforceability of clauses providing for

[46] This is subject to an important caveat: if the availability of the next tier of the dispute resolution process is conditioned upon taking necessary steps in the prescribed period of time, uncertainty may arise as to the date from which this period should be calculated. An example of a badly drafted clause in this respect can be observed in the Swiss case *Transporten Handelsmaatschappij 'Vekoma' BV v Maran Coal Corporation* Bundesgericht, I. Zivilabteilung, 17 August 1995 (1996) 14 *ASA Bulletin* 673. The case concerned arbitration procedure and is further described in 2.241ff and 4.18.

[47] The procedure may be impossible to fulfil if an expert is a person having a permanent role under the contract (eg the Engineer in construction contracts), and their mandate has come to an end, or if the dispute board's appointment has terminated and the dispute has arisen after those events. The FIDIC Conditions of Contract allow for submission of the dispute straight to arbitration if the dispute board's mandate has terminated. It must be observed that even without such a stipulation in the contract, the referral of the parties to the expert determination procedure should depend on whether the procedure is possible to fulfil. See also M Schott, M Courvoisier, in H Honsell, N Vogt, A Schnyder, S Berti (eds), *Basler Kommentar Internationales Privatrecht*, 3rd edn (Helbing Lichtenhahn Verlag, 2013) p 1919, para 60 ad Art 186 IPRG, who submit that in such a case the claim should be definitely dismissed.

[48] J Carter, 'Issues Arising from Integrated Dispute Resolution Clauses', n 33 above, 454–55; M Pryles, 'Multi-Tiered Dispute Resolution Clauses' (2001) 18 *Journal of International Arbitration* 159, 165; C Debatista, 'Drafting Enforceable Arbitration Clauses' (2005) 21 *Arbitration International* 233, 235.

[49] See eg LG Münster, 21.12.2000—12 O 439/00, DStRE 11/2001, 614.; *Cable & Wireless v IBM* [2002] CLC 1319 (Com Ct); *Poiré v Tripier*, Cour de cassation (Ch mixte), 14 février 2003, *Bulletin civil*, 2003 Mixte, n° 1, p 1.

consensual ADR methods. The court may interpret imprecise language as giving the parties an option, rather than prescribing a duty, to undergo the selected ADR process. The risk of courts adopting such an approach is particularly high under English law, traditionally reluctant to enforce vaguely drafted mediation and negotiation clauses.[50] Imprecise wording leaving scope for ambiguity as to the obligatory character of ADR may also hinder the enforceability of expert determination clauses.[51]

In summary, the language of a multi-tiered clause should clearly indicate the compulsory nature of the prescribed step. Clauses providing that the parties shall endeavour to resolve the dispute in good faith through mutual negotiations are unlikely to be enforced, unless the parties clearly prescribe the duty to undertake an attempt to resolve the dispute amicably, and include objective criteria indicating what is required to exhaust this negotiation phase. Equally, expert determination clauses should be drafted in a manner that is unambiguous as to the mandatory nature of the duty to submit the dispute to an expert before proceeding to the next stage of the dispute resolution mechanism.[52] **3.41**

Mediation Clauses as Elements of Enforceable Multi-tiered Dispute Resolution Mechanisms

Maintaining precision as to when an ADR step can be regarded as exhausted is critical for the enforceability of multi-step clauses containing mediation or negotiations. A helpful illustration of this requirement has been provided in the Swiss decision in *Vekoma v Maran*.[53] In this case the *Bundesgericht* annulled an arbitral award on grounds that the tribunal lacked jurisdiction. The multi-tiered clause in question required exhaustion of the pre-arbitral negotiation phase and contained a time-limit within which arbitration could be commenced after the parties' failure to resolve the dispute amicably. The parties had not specified, however, **3.42**

[50] See 2.4ff.

[51] An arbitration case—ICC Award No 10256, reported by D Jiménez-Figueres, 'Multi-Tiered Dispute Resolution Clauses in ICC Arbitration' (2003) 14 *ICC International Court of Arbitration Bulletin* 82, 87—provides a useful illustration of the impact which poor drafting of a particular tier has on the entire escalation mechanism. On the facts of the case the parties concluded a multi-step dispute resolution clause providing for negotiations and expert determination tiers before the final adjudication in the ICC court. The claimant initiated arbitration, bypassing the preceding ADR processes. The tribunal refused to enforce the first tier of the escalation mechanism, concluding that the negotiation clause lacked any binding force and was merely an expression of the parties' general intention to resolve disputes amicably. In addition, the tribunal did not enforce the subsequent expert determination either. The reason for denying the binding force of the quasi-adjudicative tier was the permissive language of an expert determination clause, as the clause provided that after the failure of negotiations the parties 'may' refer the dispute to an expert. According to the tribunal the language of the clause was insufficiently imperative to be enforceable. See also the Swiss decision: Tribunal fédéral, Ière Cour de droit civil, 4A_46/2011, Arrêt du 16 mai 2011, (2011) 29 *ASA Bulletin* 643 (summarised at 2.265–2.267).

[52] J Kendall, C Freedman, J Farrell, *Expert Determination*, n 11 above, para 7.4.2.

[53] *Transporten Handelsmaatschappij 'Vekoma' BV v Maran Coal Corporation* Bundesgericht, I. Zivilabteilung, 17 August 1995, (1996) 14 *ASA Bulletin* 673 (see 2.241ff for the summary).

when the negotiation phase was to be considered completed. The arbitral tribunal and the court reached different conclusions as to when the time-limit to commence arbitration started to run. In consequence, the court concluded that the tribunal had wrongly acquired jurisdiction, and annulled the entire award on this basis.

3.43 The commentators agree that the parties could have improved clarity by prescribing a time-period during which an attempt to resolve the dispute amicably should take place.[54] By such a stipulation the parties would agree to proceed to the next tier of the dispute resolution procedure after expiry of the prescribed time or within the specified period. By providing for a time period for negotiations the parties would eliminate uncertainty concerning the moment from which the time-limit to commence arbitration started running. The more precise the parties' formulation, the less scope there would be for diverging interpretations by different adjudicative bodies.

3.44 Other than prescribing a time-limit for carrying out consensual ADR, the parties may specify the right to unilaterally terminate mediation proceedings.[55] An example of such a formulation is contained in Article 8(1)(b) of the ICC Mediation Rules (2014)[56] and Article 3(b) of the Mediation Procedure of the International Institute for Conflict Prevention & Resolution.[57] A right to unilaterally terminate the process is also prescribed in Article 11(d) of the Model Law on International Commercial Conciliation. The Model Law also contains the provisions permitting the conciliator to terminate the process by his declaration, after consultation with the parties to confirm that further efforts at conciliation are no longer justified.[58] Furthermore, drafting enforceable mediation clauses requires prescribing the procedure for selecting the mediator. Such a procedure may be included in a clause itself or be provided under the rules of the centre administering the mediation process.

3.45 Detailed and precise provisions concerning the mediation procedure are key to the enforceability of tiered ADR mechanisms. Laconic and imprecise clauses are unlikely to be enforced.[59] By contracting for mediation under the auspices of one of the institutionalised mediation providers the parties may achieve a comprehensive arrangement of the mediation process and secure the enforceability

[54] See literature cited in 2.249.

[55] J Carter, 'Issues Arising from Integrated Dispute Resolution Clauses', n 33 above, 467.

[56] Under this provision termination may take place after the party has received the Mediator's note in accordance with Article 7(2) of the Rules. The Mediator's note informs the parties of the manner in which the mediation shall be conducted. Importantly, Article 7(2) of the ICC Mediation Rules 2014 clarifies that each party, by agreeing to refer a dispute to the Rules, agrees to participate in the Proceedings at least until receipt of such note from the Mediator.

[57] Under this provision each party may withdraw from mediation at any time after attending the first session, by written notice to the mediator and the other party or parties.

[58] Article 11(b).

[59] S Leonard, K Dharmananda, 'Peace Talks before War: the Enforcement of Clauses for Dispute Resolution Before Arbitration' (2006) 23 *Journal of International Arbitration* 301, 313.

their dispute resolution mechanism. Opting for tailor-made procedures instead does not render multi-tiered clauses automatically unenforceable, but shifts the burden of prescribing exhaustive ADR procedures onto the parties.[60] Such clauses are prone to interpretative difficulties and, if used in a transnational context, expose the parties to risks connected with diverging standards of preciseness developed under different jurisdictions.[61] In particular, the standard for preciseness of clauses providing for consensual ADR is set at a high level in England. In *Wah (Aka Alan Tang) and Another v Grant Thornton International Ltd and Others*[62] the court failed to find enforceable an obligation in a tailor-made multi-tiered clause despite it being exceptionally long and detailed. It must be noted, however, that this stringent interpretation has been abandoned in favour of a more relaxed stance by Teare J in *Emirates Trading Agency LLC v Prime Mineral Exports Private Ltd.*[63]

This approach can be contrasted with the position under continental European systems, where mediation clauses are enforceable irrespective of whether they refer to the rules of the recognised mediation centres or not.[64] The courts recognise the requirement of preciseness of mediation clauses, although it is not as strongly emphasised as it in England. In *Poiré v Tripier*[65] the French *Cour de cassation* held that comprehensive and clear drafting is necessary to enforce mediation clauses. The Swiss *Bundesgerichtshof* adopted a similar approach in its award of 6 June 2007 in which it refused to enforce a contractual conciliation procedure due to insufficiently precise wording of the clause.[66] Equally, the German judiciary takes the stance that mediation procedure must be clearly defined and unambiguous as to the scope of the pre-trial ADR steps.[67] Importantly, the question of unambiguous formulation of the ADR commitments is often considered from the perspective of the consequences which imprecise clauses can have on the access to court. 3.46

60 See remarks of Colman J in *Cable & Wireless v IBM* [2002] CLC 1319 (Com Ct) at 1327: '[C]ontractual references to ADR which did not include provision for an identifiable procedure would not necessarily fail to be enforceable by reason of uncertainty. An important consideration would be whether the obligation to mediate was expressed in unqualified and mandatory terms'. See also K Mackie, D Miles, W Marsh, T Allen, *The ADR Practice Guide* (Tottel Publishing, 2009) 153–155; C Debatista, 'Drafting Enforceable Arbitration Clauses', n 48 above, 236ff.

61 See also *Holloway v Chancery Mead Ltd* [2007] EWHC 2495 (TCC). Critically on this feature of English law N Andrews, *Andrews on Civil Processes. vol II*, n 43 above, paras 1.35 and 1.46. The author submits that in the absence of detailed provisions in the parties' agreement the courts should supply an implied term to regulate the essence of a mediation process.

62 *Wah (Aka Alan Tang) and Another v Grant Thornton International Ltd and Others* [2012] EWHC 3198 (Ch).

63 *Emirates Trading Agency LLC v Prime Mineral Exports Private Ltd* [2014] EWHC 2104 (Comm).

64 For a comparison of *essentialia negotii* of mediation clauses in different jurisdictions see N Alexander, *International Comparative Mediation: Legal Perspectives*, n 37 above, 191ff.

65 Cour de cassation (ch mixte), 14 février 2003, pourvoi n° 00-19423; 00-19424, Bulletin civil 2003 MIXTE N° 1 p. 1.

66 BGer 4A_18/2007, (2008) 26 *ASA Bulletin* 87 (on which 2.236–2.237).

67 OLG Celle NJW 1971, 288; BGH NJW 1977, 2263.

Expert Determination Clauses as Elements of Enforceable Multi-tiered Dispute Resolution Mechanisms

3.47 Like mediation, expert determination clauses require careful drafting when utilised as elements of multi-tiered mechanisms.[68] The need for precise delineation of the expert's mandate is vital to avoid ambiguity as to which issues are to be submitted for the expert's decision. Lack of clarity in this matter may lead to annulment of the expert's decision and may compromise the finality of the subsequent judgment or arbitral award.

3.48 A further essential element of expert determination clauses is the indication as to the effect of the expert's decision. As described above,[69] this ADR method occurs in three main forms: binding, semi-binding and non-binding expert determination. Semi-binding expert determination is an option commonly contracted for in multi-tiered clauses. In this form an expert's findings are fully reviewable in the subsequent tiers of the dispute resolution process.

3.49 Expert determination clauses may contain a clear statement that an expert is not an arbitrator. The jurisprudence of each of the analysed jurisdictions devotes a lot of attention to delineation of those two dispute resolution methods,[70] and so do the international arbitration authors.[71] Lack of clarity as to the expert's function may adversely affect the enforceability of multi-tiered clauses in those jurisdictions where expert determination does not benefit from a developed legal framework. For instance in France, where expert determination is derived from a related institution of contract law, the issue of whether a clause provides for expert determination or arbitration has generated a number of controversies.[72]

3.50 Enforceable expert determination clauses must specify how an expert is to be appointed.[73] As with mediation clauses, the procedure for appointment may be defined in a clause itself or derive from the rules of a centre administering the process. In addition, an expert may hold a permanent role under the contract. It must be emphasised that statutory provisions regulating the appointment of arbitrators in the absence of the parties' nomination do not apply to experts. In consequence, if the parties agree to appoint an expert jointly after the dispute has arisen, lack of

[68] J Jenkins, *Construction Law Arbitration*, 2nd edn (Wolters Kluwer, 2014) 63–65; J Carter, 'Issues Arising from Integrated Dispute Resolution Clauses', n 33 above, 456.

[69] 2.56–2.57.

[70] See 2.119–2.120 and 2.206.

[71] See G Born, *International Commercial Arbitration*, 2nd edn (Kluwer Law International, 2014) 281–82 and the literature cited.

[72] Cour de cassation (2e civ), 7 novembre 1974 (1975) 4 *Revue de l'arbitrage* 302; Cour de cassation (1re civ), 26 octobre 1976 (1977) 4 *Revue de l'arbitrage* 306. cf Cour d'appel de paris (1re civ), 14 mars 2002 (2002) 3 *Revue de l'arbitrage* 772; Cour d'appel de Paris (1re civ), 7 février 2002 (2005) 4 *Revue de l'arbitrage* 1056.

[73] J Kendall, C Freedman, J Farrell, *Expert Determination*, n 11 above, para 7.7.

cooperation by the other party cannot be rectified by the legal norms concerning the court's appointment of an arbitrator in default of the party. In such a case, if the parties do not provide for an alternative route, an expert determination clause may be considered unenforceable.[74] The parties may also include a provision that in default of cooperation by one of the parties, the other party will have a right to appoint an expert unilaterally.[75] Finally, the parties may decide that a body empowered to appoint an expert will be an arbitration centre administering the agreed expert determination procedure.

Typically, expert determination clauses contain provisions requiring an expert to act impartially. According to the analysis presented above, the duty to act independently of each of the parties is inherent to expert determination under all of the jurisdictions analysed in this study.[76] The requirement to act impartially becomes problematic in those cases where a person acting as an expert performs other duties under the contract. In particular, controversies arose around the function of the Engineer under the FIDIC Conditions, who, being appointed and remunerated by an Employer, was regarded as affected by biased. The Engineer under clause 20 FIDIC acts as an expert in the first tier of the dispute resolution mechanism. Concerns as to impartiality of the Engineer led to the introduction of dispute boards acting as an appellate panel for the Engineer's determinations.[77] **3.51**

It must be emphasised that the lack of a developed normative framework governing expert determination in many jurisdictions places the burden of specifying many aspects of this ADR method on the parties' contractual arrangements. The parties should at least decide on the scope of the matters to be submitted for expert determination, the procedure for appointment of an expert, and the consequences of the expert's decision. An expert determination clause may, however, contain more detailed provisions. Comprehensive contractual arrangements clarify the expert determination procedure, provide for a time-bar for notification of the dispute to an expert, include a time limit for the expert's decision or specify the consequences of expert's inactivity. Providing for extensive contractual provisions relating to expert determination may reduce uncertainty connected with different approaches to this ADR method in different jurisdictions and supplement their rudimentary normative framework. **3.52**

[74] See eg under Swiss law: Jugement du Tribunal de Première Instance de Gèneve, 12ème Chambre, JTPI/9028/2004, 5 juillet 2004, (2006) 24 *ASA Bulletin* 779. cf the position under English law under which J Kendall, C Freedman, J Farrell, *Expert Determination*, n 11 above, para 7.7.3 submit that the party raising the claim should in such a situation apply to court.

[75] Such a contractual arrangement is permitted under English law. See *Harben Style v Rhodes Trust, Thomas Cook v Rhodes Trust* [1995] 1 EGLR 118.

[76] 2.58 (England), 2.209 (France), 2.126 (Germany) and 2.257 (Switzerland).

[77] J Jenkins, *Construction Law Arbitration*, n 68 above, 58. See also 1.46 on the old version of FIDIC.

Means of Enforcing Multi-tiered Dispute Resolution Clauses

3.53 Each of the analysed jurisdictions has developed a diverging set of remedies available to the parties enforcing multi-tiered clauses. Such differences have been envisaged by the drafters of the UNCITRAL Model Law on International Commercial Conciliation in relation to consensual ADR. Article 13 of this act contains only a general directive addressed to courts or arbitral tribunals confronted with a plea of non-compliance with a conciliation clause. Under this provision the adjudicative body is supposed to 'give effect' to the parties' contractual commitment. It does not specify how breach of conciliation clauses is to be remedied or what its consequences are for the prematurely brought proceedings.[78]

3.54 Chapter two examined legal devices available for the parties to multi-tiered clauses in various jurisdictions. Each of the legal systems analysed in the present study recognises certain procedural and substantive consequences of breach of ADR clauses. This distinction is emphasised in continental jurisdictions, where it serves as a fundamental frame of reference for establishing the legal consequences of dispute resolution clauses. In general, continental systems are reluctant to attribute substantive consequences to breach of contractual dispute resolution mechanisms. Instead, the focus is on the procedural implications of multi-tiered clauses. By contrast, English law treats ADR clauses as equal to other terms of the contract. As such they are subjected to contract law rules. This approach does not, however, exclude sanctions for breach of ADR clauses, which continental systems would classify as procedural (such as stay of the proceedings). Drawing on the analysis of the means by which the parties may enforce contractual ADR mechanisms in the analysed jurisdictions, certain comparative conclusions will be proposed below.

Contractual Remedies

3.55 As indicated, the contractual implications of breach of ADR clauses are not a primary concern of judges in continental jurisdictions. In this respect the stance taken by *Kassationsgericht Zürich* is an exception.[79] In this case the court considered breach of mediation clauses to give rise to purely substantive consequences. In France and Germany the courts emphasise the procedural nature of ADR clauses,[80] limiting the availability of contractual remedies. This is not the case in

[78] See also 1.84–1.86.

[79] 15 März 1999—Kassationsgericht Zürich, (2002) 20 *ASA Bulletin* 373.

[80] In Germany it is the case with respect to mediation clauses.

England where ADR clauses are treated as contractual terms governed by the rules of contract law.

Specific Performance

Regardless of the theoretical framework adopted, specific performance is considered to be an inadequate remedy for breach of consensual ADR clauses in all of the analysed jurisdictions. The difficulty lies in defining the scope of the duty to be enforced, as well as in the voluntary nature of mediation or negotiations. **3.56**

A broad discussion relating to specific performance of ADR clauses took place in France. Specific performance, as a remedy for non-compliance with contractual dispute resolution mechanisms, has been analysed first in relation to arbitration clauses. This remedy is employed in cases where one party acts in contravention to an arbitration clause by refusing to cooperate in selecting an arbitrator. In this context specific performance is understood as the right to request the court to nominate an arbitrator in default of the other party. Because the court has no statutory ground for a similar competence in relation to mediation clauses, this remedy has been rejected in cases involving consensual ADR.[81] Lack of a statutory basis for the court's support of the ADR process equally affects quasi-adjudicative ADR. **3.57**

Furthermore, specific performance as a remedy for breach of mediation clauses has been considered inadequate under Article 1184 of the French Civil Code regulating the situation where one of the two parties does not carry out his undertaking. This is due to the unenforceable character of the commitments arising under consensual ADR methods.[82] As an alternative to specific performance the commentators suggested an award of a penalty remedy (*astreinte*)[83] but the judiciary has not adopted this solution. It has also been observed that, although it is not possible to compel the parties to perform their consensual ADR commitments, breach of mediation clauses facilitates proof of lack of good faith in fulfilling contractual obligations under Article 1134 of the French Civil Code.[84] **3.58**

Similarly, German judges reject an order for specific performance as a remedy for breach of ADR clauses, emphasising the procedural consequences of contracting for pre-trial ADR. The standpoint according to which one party may demand an order compelling the other party to take part in the agreed ADR process is a minority view.[85] An obstacle in awarding such a remedy concerns the **3.59**

[81] X Lagarde, 'L'efficacité des clauses de conciliation ou de mediation' (2000) 3 *Revue de l'arbitrage* 377, 396–97.

[82] C Jarrosson, 'Observations on *Poiré v Tripier*', n 18 above, 364.

[83] C Jarrosson, 'La sanction du non-respect d'une clause instituant un préliminaire obligatoire de conciliation ou de mediation', n 36 above, 755.

[84] M van Der Haegen, 'Les Procédures de Conciliation et de Médiation', n 39 above, 260.

[85] H Eidenmüller, *Vertrags- und Verfahrensrecht der Wirtschaftsmediation* (Schmidt, 2001) 23.

nature of the duty involved. Notably, even in the Swiss judgment where the court asserted the purely substantive nature of mediation clauses, such remedy was not awarded.[86]

3.60 Under continental jurisdictions the difficulty in ascertaining the scope of the duty created by consensual ADR methods precludes specific performance. In principle, however, it does not affect procedural remedies for breach of mediation clauses. This can be contrasted with the pre-*Cable & Wireless* position under English law. Under this line of English case law the voluntary nature of settlement negotiations was considered an obstacle to the enforceability of consensual ADR clauses in any way. They were considered to be 'agreements to agree' and denied the binding force due to the uncertainty of the duties involved.

3.61 This characteristic discrepancy between the continental approach and the traditional stance of English courts is a result of the fundamental difference in theoretical assumptions developed in both legal traditions. English law does not distinguish a separate category of contracts for dispute resolution, to which continental judges attribute a special status. For the latter, the analysis of the nature and content of ADR clauses is not limited to contract law rules. Jurisdictions such as France or Germany distinguish between substantive and procedural consequences of dispute resolution clauses, putting an emphasis on the latter. The focus on the procedural consequences of premature filing of the claim in contravention of the selected ADR process does not require the courts to interpret the duties enforced in line with contract law rules.

3.62 English law, subjecting dispute resolution clauses to the rules of contract law applicable to all other terms of the contract, inevitably encountered difficulties in ascertaining contractual consideration in agreements providing for consensual ADR. The change of the attitude to ADR, supported by legislative efforts to promote out-of-court dispute resolution, brought reformulation of the definition of the duties created by ADR clauses. In *Cable & Wireless*[87] Colman J explained that the rationale for sanctioning mediation clauses does not lie in compelling the parties to reach a settlement but in giving them an opportunity to do so.

3.63 Although English law confirmed the enforceable nature of ADR clauses, it does not permit an order for specific performance to enforce the duties arising from them. Under English law an order for specific performance is an equitable remedy awarded in exceptional circumstances.

Damages

3.64 An award of damages is one of the main remedies for breach of contract under each of the analysed jurisdictions. Notwithstanding this status, it is not always

[86] 15 März 1999—Kassationsgericht Zürich, (2002) 20 *ASA Bulletin* 37.
[87] [2002] CLC 1319 (Com Ct).

available in relation to breach of ADR clauses. The complication surrounding awarding damages for breach of an ADR clause is two-fold. First, the difficulty concerns the quantification of the loss arising from the party's non-compliance with mediation or expert determination procedures. Secondly, the mere availability of a claim in damages is questioned in those jurisdictions which emphasise procedural consequences of ADR clauses.

As far as the first issue is concerned, the judiciary invariably emphasises the difficulty in quantifying the sum of compensation for breach of an ADR clause. This is because the amount of loss arising from the party's failure to exhaust the ADR procedure is uncertain, which renders the assessment of damages unworkable. A party raising a claim in damages cannot assert that, if the parties had attempted mediation, the settlement would have been reached and certain loss would have been avoided. **3.65**

A difficulty also surrounds raising a claim in damages for breach of an expert determination clause. First, it is difficult to prove that had the claimant exhausted an expert determination procedure in accordance with the contract, a party would have secured a more favourable result in appropriate time. Secondly, it is also difficult to quantify the loss arising from a delay in referring a dispute to an expert, as it is not possible to predict when and with what outcome the case would have been decided, had the party acted in accordance with a tiered dispute resolution clause. Equally, if the referral to an expert is no longer possible the party cannot claim damages on the basis that the expert's decision would be more favourable to it than the decision reached by the court.[88] **3.66**

As indicated, further difficulty surrounds the mere availability of claims for damages under some jurisdictions. Uncertainty in this area is particularly acute under continental legal systems. In France, Germany and Switzerland contractual remedies for breach of ADR clauses were analysed in the context of the dichotomy between substantive and procedural elements of contracts for dispute resolution. The clearest statement of principle has been delivered by the Swiss judiciary in the judgment of *Kassationsgericht Zürich* of 15 March 1999,[89] where the court held that mediation clauses should be classified as substantive contracts. The duty arising under such agreements entails refraining from initiating court proceedings until the agreed procedure is complied. In line with this interpretation the court used the term 'non-aggression treaty' (*Nichtangriffspakt*) to describe the nature of ADR clauses. The court held that mediation clauses do give rise to purely contractual consequences but it did not award damages due to difficulties in ascertaining the extent of loss resulting from breach. Although this view has not been shared in **3.67**

[88] See *Sunrock Aircraft Corp v SAS* [2007] Lloyd's Rep 612.
[89] 5 März 1999—Kassationsgericht Zürich, (2002) 20 *ASA Bulletin* 373.

subsequent cases, the judgment is considered one of the most important rulings on the enforceability of ADR clauses expressed under Swiss law.[90]

3.68 Classification of ADR clauses as contracts giving rise to negative duties resonates with the German concept of *pactum de non petendo*. However, in contrast to the interpretation presented by the *Kassationsgericht Zürich*, the German judiciary does not associate substantive consequences with breach of ADR clauses. Violation of *pactum de non petendo* excludes actionability of the claim, which leads to inadmissibility of the proceedings.[91] Although the discussion on substantive elements of dispute resolution clauses takes place in German scholarship, it has never been reflected in case law.[92] In consequence, German courts invariably emphasise the procedural consequences of contracting for ADR.

3.69 French judges have reached a similar conclusion. The courts analysed the consequences of violation of ADR clauses almost exclusively in the context of procedural means of defence.[93] French literature undertook a broader discussion on the nature of ADR clauses. The authors identify substantive components in mediation clauses by analysing the duties they create with reference to the distinction between obligations of the result and means. The first type of duty (*obligation de résultat*) is completed by the mere initiation of the mediation process. The second (*obligation de moyens*) is realised by approaching the process in good faith and displaying a constructive attitude towards the agreed dispute resolution method.[94] Identification of substantive elements in ADR clauses does not directly translate into the availability of contractual remedies, however. Damages for breach of ADR clauses are treated as unavailable[95] or available only in theory,[96] the main obstacle being the difficulty in ascertaining the loss.

3.70 More extensive conceptual grounds for awarding damages for breach of ADR clauses have been developed in England.[97] Under English law dispute resolution clauses are treated as any other terms of the contract whose breach enables the parties to claim contractual remedies. Notwithstanding this principle, damages

[90] See C Boog, 'How to Deal with Multi-Tiered Dispute Resolution Clauses—Note—June 2007—Swiss Federal Supreme Court' (2008) 26 *ASA Bulletin* 103, 107, fn 10; A Jolles, 'Consequences of Multi-Tier Arbitration Clauses: Issues of Enforcement' (2006) 72 *Arbitration* 329, 329; J-F Poudret, S Besson, *Comparative Law of International*, n 24 above, para 13. On this case see also 2.230ff above.

[91] See 2.101ff.

[92] On this aspect also 2.93–2.96. See also F Fabian, 'The Enforceability of Mediation Clauses—the Approach of English and German Courts and ICC Arbitral Tribunals' (2005) 5 *SchiedsVZ* 250, 253.

[93] See 2.182ff for details. An alternative stand adopted by one chamber of Cour de cassation suggested that mediation clauses are devoid of any binding force (Cour de cassation (1re Ch civ) 23 janvier 2001, RTD civ 2001, 359; see 2.180).

[94] C Jarrosson, 'Les clauses de renégociation, de conciliation et de mediation', n 3 above, para 25ff; C Jarrosson, 'Note—Cour de cassation (Ch commerciale) 28 novembre 1995—Peyrin et autres v. société Polyclinique des Fleurs' 618–19; C Jarrosson, 'Les modes alternatifs de règlement des conflicts', n 3 above, 337. See also 2.198ff.

[95] X Lagarde, 'L'efficacité des clauses de conciliation ou de médiation', n 81 above, 398.

[96] C Jarrosson, 'La sanction du non- respect d'une clause instituant un préliminaire obligatoire de conciliation ou de mediation', n 36 above, 755.

[97] See 2.33–2.37 and 2.68–2.70.

are not considered the most adequate remedy for breach of dispute resolution clauses. According to the English judiciary such clauses should be enforced primarily by way of injunction rather than monetary compensation.[98] Damages may be taken into account as a means of secondary enforcement of dispute resolution clauses, so long as the extent of loss is ascertainable and the sum of compensation workable.[99] Although the English judiciary treats such claims with caution, damages have been permitted for breach of arbitration or jurisdiction clauses.[100] In these cases the amount of compensation reflected the sum awarded by a non-contractual forum. It remains unclear how damages would be ascertained in cases involving breach of an ADR clause.[101] It can be argued that the costs incurred by the defendant in the prematurely initiated proceedings can constitute the sum of compensation for breach of an ADR clause.

Importantly, availability of damages under English law does not exclude procedural sanctions for breach of an ADR clause. The relevant remedy is stay of the proceedings.[102] English law does not treat damages and stay of the proceedings as mutually exclusive.[103] The existence of certain procedural consequences of breach of ADR clauses does not determine the scope and availability of contractual remedies. **3.71**

Liquidated Damages

To avoid the difficulties in ascertaining the extent of loss generated by breach of ADR commitments, the parties may insert a liquidated damages clause into their multi-step dispute resolution mechanism. This solution is in principle admissible under all analysed jurisdictions. In particular, Swiss jurisprudence regards liquidated damages as a means of removing the uncertainty connected with judicial treatment of ADR clauses.[104] **3.72**

The difficulties with providing for liquidated damages in multi-tiered clauses arise under the English penalty doctrine, as summarised in *Dunlop Pneumatic Tyre Co Ltd v New Garage & Motor Co Ltd*.[105] English law prevents the parties from **3.73**

98 *OT Africa Line Ltd v Magic Sportswear Corp (The Kribi)* [2005] 2 Lloyd's Rep 170 (CA) 33; *Donohue v Armco Inc* [2002] 1 Lloyd's Rep 425 (HL); D Joseph, *Jurisdiction and Arbitration Agreements and their Enforcement*, 2nd edn (Sweet & Maxwell, 2010) paras 12.30ff; R Fentiman, *International Commercial Litigation*, 2nd edn (OUP, 2015) para 16.42.

99 *Randell, Saunders & Co Ltd v Thompson* (1876) 1 QBD 748, 752 (Blackburn J). See also R Fentiman, *International Commercial Litigation*, n 98 above, 2.248ff.

100 *CMA CGM SA v Hyundai MIPO Dockyard Co Ltd* [2009] 1 Lloyd's Rep 213 (Com Ct); *Donohue v Armco Inc* [2002] 1 Lloyd's Rep 425 (HL); *Ellerman Lines Ltd v Read* [1928] 2 KB 144 (CA).

101 See *Sunrock Aircraft Corp v SAS* [2007] Lloyd's Rep 612 in relation to expert determination clauses. See also comments in D Joseph, *Jurisdiction and Arbitration Agreements and their Enforcement*, n 98 above, p 492 para 14.15 and J Bailey *Construction Law* (Informa Law, 2011) para 23.39.

102 *Cable & Wireless v IBM* [2002] CLC 1319 (Com Ct).

103 *Mantovani v Carapelli SpA* [1980] 1 Lloyd's Rep 375 (CA).

104 D Brown-Berset, 'La médiation commerciale: le géant s'éveille' (2002) 2 *Revue de Droit Suisse* 319, 369; M Liatowitsch, J Menz, in E Geisinger, N Voser (eds), *International Arbitration in Switzerland. A Handbook for Practitioners*, 2nd edn (Wolters Kluwer, 2013) 327, fn 83.

105 *Dunlop Pneumatic Tyre Co Ltd v New Garage & Motor Co Ltd* [1914] UKHL 1.

contracting for a punitive, non-compensatory sum stipulated *in terrorem* of the offending party. Under the penalty doctrine the amount of liquidated damages must be quantified with the view to compensation and must reflect a genuine pre-estimate of loss. It will be held to be a penalty if the sum stipulated for is extravagant and unconscionable as compared with the greatest loss that could conceivably be proved to have followed from the breach. Furthermore, as held by Lord Watson in *Lord Elphinstone v Monkland Iron and Coal Co*,[106] there is a presumption that a provision is a penalty when 'a single lump sum is made payable by way of compensation, on the occurrence of one or more or all of several events, some of which may occasion serious and others but trifling damage'.

3.74 Taking these rules into account, the difficulties in ascertaining the level of damages likely to be suffered as a consequence of breach of ADR clauses may pose an obstacle in stipulating enforceable liquidated damages in multi-tiered dispute resolution mechanisms. Lord Dunedin's statement in *Dunlop Pneumatic Tyre* may, however, be of guidance in this context:

> It is no obstacle to the sum stipulated being a genuine pre-estimate of damage, that the consequences of the breach are such as to make precise pre-estimation almost an impossibility. On the contrary, that is just the situation when it is probable that pre-estimated damage was the true bargain between the parties.[107]

3.75 It remains to be seen if the courts will be sensitive to the difficulties faced by the parties to multi-tiered dispute resolution mechanisms when trying to make a prediction of the losses likely to result from breach of an ADR clause.

Dismissal of the Claim

3.76 Non-compliance with pre-adjudicative ADR may result in dismissal of the claim on the merits. Although this sanction does not necessarily reflect the court's reliance on the rules of contractual liability, it takes the form of a ruling *in meriti*. For this reason dismissal of the claim will be classified together with other substantive means of enforcement of ADR clauses.

3.77 Dismissal of the claim as unfounded has been treated as a primary sanction for breach of an expert determination clause by the German judiciary. According to the established line of court decisions, the court confronted with a premature claim raised without submitting the relevant issue to an expert is empowered to dismiss the claim on the merits as temporarily unfounded (*zur Zeit unbegründet*).[108] The principle has been approved in literature.[109]

[106] *Lord Elphinstone v Monkland Iron and Coal Co* (1886) HL 1886.

[107] With reference to *Castaneda and Others v Clydebank Engineering and Shipbuilding Co Ltd*, [1905] AC 6 (HL) 19 November 1904 (Lord Halsbury) and *Webster v Bosanquet* [1912] AC 394 (Lord Mersey).

[108] See eg BGH NJW-RR 1988, 1405. 983 BGH (2006) 4 *SchiedsVZ* 217, on which see 2.130–2.132.

[109] J Münch, in *Münchener Kommentar zur Zivilprozessordnung*, 4th edn (Beck, 2013) p 31, para 60 ad vor §§ 1025ff. ZPO; P Hartmann, in A Baumbach, W Lauterbach, J Albers, P Hartmann (eds), *Zivilprozessordnung*, 74th edn (CH Beck 2016), p 2737, para 17 ad Grundz § 1025; V Rieble, in

3.78 German law is the only system amongst the analysed jurisdictions where the effects of quasi-adjudicative and consensual ADR clauses differ. The latter are treated in line with procedural contracts and the courts focus on the impact of non-compliance with consensual ADR clauses on the prematurely initiated proceedings. By contrast, expert determination is treated as a purely substantive institution rooted in the law of obligations; hence the substantive sanction for non-compliance with clauses providing for this method.

3.79 For the sake of completeness an isolated position taken by *OLG Düsseldorf* has to be reported as relevant in the context of substantive sanctions for breach of ADR clauses. In a judgment of 30 November 1973[110] the court adopted the same sanction for breach of consensual ADR as in the case of expert determination clauses. It was held that failure to undergo conciliation in accordance with the agreed procedure results in dismissal of the claim as unfounded. This approach has not been shared by later judges, who distinguished between dismissal of an action as unfounded for breach of expert determination clauses, and rejection of an action as inadmissible as a consequence of non-compliance with conciliation clauses. The former takes the form of an award on the merits; the latter is a procedural order.

3.80 Dismissal of the claim as unfounded as one of the consequences of breach of multi-tiered clauses has been considered in Switzerland in the judgment of the *Kassationsgericht Zürich* of 15 March 1999.[111] This sanction was rejected, as the court refused to regard contractual ADR commitments as conditions of the claim. Dismissal of the action on the merits has also been considered inadequate by Swiss commentators.[112] In summary, dismissal of the claim as a sanction for breach of ADR clauses has been adopted exclusively under German law with respect to expert determination clauses.

Injunctive Relief

3.81 An injunction is an institution of English law aimed at securing compliance with the contract. English courts can grant an injunctive relief restraining foreign[113] proceedings brought in breach of an arbitration or jurisdiction clause.[114]

J. von Staudingers Kommentar zum Bürgerlichen Gesetzbuch mit Einführungsgesetz und Nebengesetzen (Sellier—de Gruyter 2015) pp 184, para 42 ad 317 BGB; G Wagner, *Prozessverträge–Privatautonomie im Verfahrensrecht* 655ff; G Wagner, 'Alternative Streitbeilegung und Verjährung' (2001) 3 NJW 182, 183.

110 OLG Düsseldorf ZfgG 1975, 228.

111 15 März 1999—Kassationsgericht Zürich, (2002) 20 *ASA Bulletin* 373.

112 A Jolles, 'Consequences of Multi-Tier Arbitration Clauses', n 90 above, 336.

113 When domestic proceedings are brought in breach of an arbitration clause the proper remedy is a stay (on which see 2.20–2.23 and 2.59–2.60), not injunction. See M Mustill and S Boyd, *Commercial Arbitration. 2001 Companion Volume to the Second Edition* 267.

114 The principal cases are: *Société Nationale Industrielle Aerospatiale v Lee Kui JAK* [1987] AC 871 (PC); *Airbus Industrie GIE v Patel* [1999] 1 AC 119 (HL); *Donohue v Armco* [2002] 1 Lloyd's Rep 425 (HL); *Turner v Grovit* [2002] 1 WLR 107 (HL); *Turner v Grovit* [2004] ECR I-3565 (ECJ); *OT Africa Line Ltd v Magic Sportswear Corp* [2005] 2 Lloyd's Rep 170 (CA).

The availability of an injunction as a tool sanctioning breach of ADR clauses has been confirmed by Colman J in *Cable & Wireless v IBM*.[115] It is based on the assumption that ADR clauses constitute enforceable rights and duties, similar in quality to those arising under other terms of the contract. Injunctive relief is considered to be a remedy more adequate than damages for breach of a contract containing a dispute resolution clause.[116] Injunctive relief is characteristic of English law and is described elsewhere in the study.[117] It is not available under continental jurisdictions.[118]

Procedural Consequences

3.82 Consequences of breach of ADR clauses for the prematurely initiated proceedings are at the centre of discussion on the enforceability of multi-step dispute resolution mechanisms. Each of the analysed legal systems has established that failure to exhaust pre-adjudication procedures may have certain procedural implications.[119] Three models can be identified. According to the first, an adjudicative body faced with a prematurely initiated claim declares inadmissibility of the claim and closes the proceedings without giving an award on the merits. Under the second model, non-compliance with the agreed ADR process results in a stay of the proceedings, granted to enable the offending party to discharge its contractual bargain. The third model assumes lack of jurisdiction of the adjudicative body until the agreed ADR process is complied with in accordance with the contract. Under all three models any procedural sanction for breach of an ADR clause is awarded upon a plea of the defendant, rather than ex officio.

Inadmissibility of the Proceedings

3.83 Declaration of inadmissibility (*irrecevabilité*, *Unzulässigkeit*) due to an obstacle to adjudicating on the merits of the case typically results in conclusion of the proceedings.[120] Declaration of inadmissibility as a procedural consequence

[115] [2002] CLC 1319 (Com Ct).

[116] *OT Africa Line Ltd v Magic Sportswear Corp (The Kribi)* [2005] 2 Lloyd's Rep 170.

[117] 2.24–2.32.

[118] Note, however, § 1004 of the German Civil Code and the availability of a prohibitory injunction against interference with ownership under this provision (for comparative remarks see M Whincup, *Contract Law and Practice*, 5th edn (Kluwer Law International, 2006) 380, para 13.66). This relief is not applicable in the present context.

[119] With the exception of Switzerland, with respect to mediation clauses (no procedural sanction, see 2.228 for details), and Germany, with respect to expert determination clauses (only substantive sanction, see 2.130–2.134 for details).

[120] In arbitration stay of the proceedings and a declaration of inadmissibility are not mutually exclusive. The proceedings can be stayed on grounds that the claim is temporarily inadmissible. (see 4.95–4.97 on the enforceability of multi-tiered clauses in arbitration). The present chapter focuses on court proceedings.

of breach of ADR clauses has been adopted under French and German law.[121] However, both systems reach this conclusion through different reasoning.

Under German law a declaration of inadmissibility reflects the lack of a certain property of the claim, which constitutes an obstacle to adjudicating on the merits of the case. This necessary quality is defined as 'actionability' (*Klagbarkeit*) understood as the ability to have the claim adjudicated in court. The parties may temporarily exclude actionability of the claim by entering into a *pactum de non petendo*—an agreement not to sue. Raising a claim in respect of which the parties have entered into a *pactum de non petendo* results in the claim being dismissed by the court via a procedural order declaring the proceedings inadmissible. The German judiciary classified ADR clauses as agreements not to sue. As a result of these agreements the claim cannot be heard *in meriti* until the prescribed dispute resolution procedures are complied with.[122] **3.84**

As indicated, French law adopts a similar result of non-compliance with contractual ADR commitments. According to the prevailing line of French case law breach of an ADR clause leads to inadmissibility of the claim.[123] The reasoning behind this conclusion refers to the classification of means of defence under the French Civil Procedure Code. Breach of an ADR clause is considered as giving rise to a plea of inadmissibility—*fin de non-recevoir.* Successful pleading of this procedural defence requires the court to conclude the proceedings as inadmissible without examining the merits of the case. **3.85**

Declaration of inadmissibility as a consequence of breach of ADR clauses has been contemplated in Swiss jurisprudence. It has been, however, considered an inadequate solution to govern the enforceability of ADR clauses in litigation. According to scholarly opinion and court decisions (whose prevalence is described in the literature as 'overwhelming')[124] mediation clauses are valid but not enforceable in the proceedings. Breach of an ADR clause is of no consequence for the prematurely initiated action and the parties may start litigation at any time notwithstanding their commitments under a tiered dispute resolution clause.[125] Swiss judges supported this conclusion by observation that the Swiss Civil Procedure Code does not regulate the procedural consequences of breach of ADR duties which the parties assumed voluntarily.[126] By contrast, where the duty to mediate results from **3.86**

[121] The remarks relating to German law will concern the position as to the enforceability of clauses providing for consensual ADR, as breach of expert determination clauses does not carry the same procedural consequences (see n 119 above). French law does not differentiate between expert determination and mediation clauses in this context.

[122] BGH NJW 1984, 669. See further 2.97ff.

[123] *Poiré v Tripier* Cour de cassation (Ch mixte), 14 février 2003, pourvoi n° 00-19423, 00-19424, Bulletin civil 2003 MIXTE N° 1 p 1; on which 2.185ff.

[124] I Meier, in N Alexander (ed), *Global Trends in Mediation,* n 25 above, 355.

[125] Breach of an ADR clause may, however, theoretically result in the party being liable in damages (*ibid.* See also 2.230ff).

[126] See 2.228 for details.

a statutory provision, it is treated as a necessary condition of the proceedings. Inadmissibility of the claim has been acknowledged as one of the possible consequences of breach of ADR clauses in arbitral proceedings.[127] This solution is not, however, reflected in Swiss cases relating to litigation.

3.87 Importantly, the lack of specific sanctions for breach of ADR clauses in the civil procedure codes of Germany or France has not hindered the enforceability of ADR clauses in those jurisdictions. German courts subjected ADR clauses to the theoretical framework of *pacta de non petendo*. French judges extended the category of *fins de non-recevoir* to accommodate dispute resolution clauses and accepted that the source of this defence may be contractual.[128] In this way the judiciary of those countries devised the sanction for non-compliance with ADR clauses without the need for legislative intervention.

Stay of the Proceedings

3.88 Stay of the proceedings is an alternative procedural response to breach of an ADR clause. As opposed to a declaration of inadmissibility, which typically entails conclusion of the prematurely initiated proceedings,[129] a stay means that the proceedings are halted and can be resumed in appropriate circumstances. Stay of the proceedings as a sanction for breach of a multi-tiered clause is aimed at creating an opportunity for the parties to fulfil their ADR commitments and return to the court for final adjudication, should they fail to resolve the dispute amicably.

3.89 Stay of the proceedings is a consequence of breach of an ADR clause under English law.[130] This procedural sanction mirrors the one for breach of an arbitration clause, as prescribed by section 9 of the Arbitration Act 1996. This parallelism is, however, subject to an important caveat. Stay of the proceedings under section 9 of the Arbitration Act 1996 is obligatory, while the stay for breach of an ADR clause depends on the court's discretion.

3.90 Stay of proceedings is a flexible tool to manage prematurely commenced proceedings and, as such, it has been contemplated in continental jurisdictions. In Germany it was suggested that it would be more practical if the court required the parties to fulfil contractual ADR by staying the proceedings rather than by closing

[127] BGer 4A_18/2007, (2008) 26 *ASA Bulletin* 87; Obergericht Thurgau, 23 April 2001 (2003) 21 *ASA Bulletin* 418.

[128] On this last aspect Cour de cassation (Ch mixte), 14 fevrier 2003, Bulletin civil, 2003 Mixte, n° 1, p 1, rejecting the view expressed earlier by Cour de cassation (2e civ), 10 février 1988, Bulletin, II, no 41, p 22.

[129] See n 120 above.

[130] *Channel Tunnel Group Ltd v Balfour Beatty Construction Ltd* [1993] AC 334 (HL) with respect to expert determination and *Cable & Wireless v IBM* [2002] CLC 1319 (Com Ct) with respect to mediation clauses. Unlike under other legal systems, English courts adopted stay of the proceedings as a consequence of non-compliance with an expert determination clause long before than they applied this sanction to breach of mediation clauses. The *Channel Tunnel* case was decided on 21 January 1993 and *Cable & Wireless* almost a decade later, on 11 October 2002.

the case and declaring the claim temporarily inadmissible.[131] It has been argued that the stay allows the court to quickly resume the suspended process in cases where the parties do not resolve the dispute via ADR. By contrast, a declaration of inadmissibility means conclusion of the proceedings and, should ADR prove unsuccessful, the claim must be filed again in court. This means more time and cost spent on instantiating the proceedings from scratch. Despite the clear advantage of the stay in this context, German courts have never adopted this solution due to the lack of precise legislative grounds.[132]

A similar discussion took place under French law. Conceptually, stay of the proceedings as a result of breach of the contractually agreed dispute resolution process could be inferred from the implied plea of the parties.[133] Despite the considerable practical value of this solution, many authors considered it as having no grounding in the provisions of the French Civil Procedure Code.[134] Equally, the judiciary rejected the stay as a sanction for non-compliance with contractual ADR. *De lege ferenda* some authors suggest that stay of the proceedings should become a codified sanction for breach of ADR clauses.[135] 3.91

Refusal of Jurisdiction

The third model of enforcement of ADR clauses involves refusal of jurisdiction by the adjudicative body until the agreed procedures are complied with. In all of the analysed continental systems this solution has been rejected with respect to litigation, on the assumption that the parties cannot oust the court's jurisdiction by contracting for ADR.[136] Similarly, English courts when imposing sanctions 3.92

[131] G Walter, 'Dogmatik der unterschiedlichen Verfahren zur Streitbeilegung' (1990) 103 *ZZP* 141, 162–64. See also F Friedrich, *Die Konsensvereinbarung im Zivilrecht. Ein Beitrag zu Verhandlungs-, Schlichtungs- und Mediationsvereinbarung für ein alternatives konsensuales Streitbeilegungsverfahren* (Nomos Universitätsschriften Recht, 2003) 185.

[132] This is notwithstanding the commentators suggestions to infer the stay from the provisions of the German Civil Procedure Code. G Walter, 'Dogmatik der unterschiedlichen Verfahren zur Streitbeilegung', n 131 above, 162–64 in reference to §§ 251, 251a ZPO.

[133] X Lagarde, 'L'efficacité des clauses de conciliation ou de mediation', n 81 above, 377ff. On the stay of the proceedings if conciliation duty arises under the statute, see G Virassamy, 'Les collèges et les comissions dans le règlement des litiges contractuels' in *Etudes offertes à Jacques Ghestin: Le contrat au début du XXIe siècle* (LGDJ, 2001) 959, para 8.

[134] S Guinchard, C Chainais, F Ferrand, *Procédure cvile. Droit interne et droit de l'Union européenne*, 30th edn (Dalloz, 2010) para 330; S Guinchard, *Droit et practique de la procédure civile* (Dalloz, 2004) para 193.15; C Jarrosson, 'Observations on *Poiré v Tripier*', n 18 above, 364; C Jarrosson, 'La sanction du non-respect d'une clause instituant un préliminaire obligatoire de conciliation ou de mediation', n 36 above, 762.

[135] C Jarrosson, 'La sanction du non- respect d'une clause instituant un préliminaire obligatoire de conciliation ou de mediation', n 36 above, 763.

[136] See J Münch, in *Münchener Kommentar zur Zivilprozessordnung*, 4th edn (Beck, 2013) p. 31, para 60 ad vor §§ 1025ff. ZPO; P Hartmann, in A Baumbach, W Lauterbach, J Albers, P Hartmann (eds), *Zivilprozessordnung*, 74th edn, (CH Beck, 2016), p 2737, para 17 ad Grundz § 1025; V Rieble, in *J. von Staudingers Kommentar zum Bürgerlichen Gesetzbuch mit Einführungsgesetz und Nebengesetzen* (Sellier–de Gruyter 2015) pp 184, para 42 ad 317 BGB for the German position;

for non-compliance with ADR clauses do not refuse jurisdiction but enforce the contractual bargain by stay of the proceedings.

3.93 Refusal of jurisdiction is often considered as a remedy for breach of ADR clauses in arbitration. This is owing to the fact that the nature of arbitral authority is contractual and can be made subject to conditions by the parties. By contrast, the inherent jurisdiction of the courts cannot be entirely removed or be contingent on compliance with contractual duties. Refusal of jurisdiction as a consequence of breach of multi-step dispute arbitration clauses is a topic of a separate chapter in the present study.[137]

Plea of Non-compliance with an ADR Clause

3.94 Under each of the presented legal frameworks the court does not enforce ADR clauses on its own motion, but upon a plea by the defendant. Lack of the requisite plea is considered to be a waiver of rights arising under an ADR clause. As far as the timing of the plea is concerned, in England and Germany the courts adopt rules analogous to those governing arbitration clauses. It is emphasised that the plea must be raised at an early stage of the proceedings, and should precede the defence on the merits.

3.95 This issue is more complex under French law, where a plea of non-compliance with an ADR clause and a plea of non-compliance with an arbitration clause belong to different categories of procedural defence and are governed by different provisions of the French Civil Procedure Code. Breach of an ADR clause is classified as giving rise to *fin de non-recevoir*, which under Article 123 of the French Civil Procedure Code can be submitted at any stage of the proceedings. This rule has been, however, modified by the judiciary in relation to ADR clauses.[138] In *Poiré v Tripier*[139] the joint chambers of French *Cour de cassation* held that the timing of the plea of non-compliance with an ADR clause is restricted despite it being classified as a *fin de non-recevoir*. Breach of ADR commitments has to be invoked at the outset of the proceedings, before defending the case on the merits. Failure to raise the plea before filing the substantive defence amounts to waiver of the rights arising under an ADR clause.[140]

15 März 1999—Kassationsgericht Zürich, (2002) 20 *ASA Bulletin* 373 for the Swiss position; and Cour de cassation (ch. mixte.), 14 février 2003, pourvoi n°00-19423; 00-19424, Bulletin civil, 2003 MIXTE N° 1 p 1 for the French position, where the court refused to classify breach of an ADR clause as *exeption d'incompetence*.

[137] See 4.15ff.

[138] eg the party delaying raising the *fin de-non recevoir* defence may face financial sanctions, see Cour de cassation (2e civ) 1er juillet 1981, Gaz Pal 1981, 750, note Viatte; Cass 2e civ, 27 février 2003. *Procédures* Mai 2003, n°111, obs Perrot.

[139] Cour de cassation (Ch. mixte), 14 février 2003, *Bulletin civil*, 2003 Mixte, n° 1, p 1.

[140] See L Cadiet, J Normand, S Mekki, *Théorie générale du procès*, n 3 above, 467 on *mutuus dissensus* as reversing the effects of mediation clauses.

Summary

Each of the discussed legal orders contains specific mechanisms to enforce the obligation to carry out pre-trial ADR procedure. The set of available remedies is limited in Switzerland, where the dominant stance is that voluntary mediation commitments are unenforceable in litigation. In France the proceedings brought in breach of a multi-level dispute resolution clause are concluded as inadmissible. German judges adopt the same sanction in respect of consensual ADR, while breach of an expert determination clause is classified as a matter of substantive law. In England the main remedy for breach of both mediation and expert determination clauses is stay of the proceedings. Regardless of the adopted consequence, by enforcing ADR clauses the courts ensure that examination of the dispute *in meriti* will not take place before the exhaustion of the agreed procedure. **3.96**

In all of the legal systems considered, substantive elements of ADR clauses have been discussed. Conceptually only under English law are contractual remedies for breach of ADR commitments available to the parties. This is because English law treats clauses providing for out-of-court dispute resolution methods as ordinary provisions of the contract, subjecting them to contract law rules. Continental jurisdictions tend to attribute a special status to contracts for dispute resolution, focusing largely on their procedural consequences. The discussion on contractual remedies for breach of ADR clauses is dominated by the difficulty of ascertaining the loss arising from non-compliance with consensual ADR commitments. **3.97**

4

Enforceability of Multi-tiered Dispute Resolution Clauses in Arbitration

SUMMARY

This chapter examines the enforceability of ADR clauses within an arbitration framework. It identifies the challenges surrounding the enforceability of multi-tiered clauses that are specific to arbitration. Two main theoretical concepts governing this issue are recognised. They originate from a well-established distinction between jurisdiction of the arbitral tribunal and admissibility of a claim. It is explained how the two theories have been applied in the awards of domestic courts and arbitral tribunals dealing with the enforceability of multi-tiered arbitration clauses in arbitration. The bulk of this chapter is devoted to a critical assessment of the jurisdiction theory. The admissibility theory is favoured and its ramifications explained.

The main points will be:

(i) Arbitral jurisdiction rests on a valid arbitration clause. It does not depend on whether the pre-arbitral ADR process has been exhausted in accordance with the contract (4.56).

(ii) The jurisdiction theory must be rejected for the following reasons. First, it creates the potential for negative jurisdiction conflict. Both adjudicative bodies may legitimately refuse to hear the case: an arbitral tribunal due to the violation of an ADR clause, and a court due to an arbitration agreement in the contract. This may be treated as prohibiting access to court and may result in the invalidation of the entire clause in certain jurisdictions (4.51). Secondly, the jurisdiction theory unbalances the position of both parties. It allows the claimant to render the whole arbitration clause inoperative by his failure to adhere to the ADR process agreed in the contract. Such an interpretation hardly corresponds with the intentions of the parties to arbitration clauses (4.47). Thirdly, certain policy considerations must be raised. Jurisdictional decisions of the arbitrators can be reviewed by the court in challenge or enforcement proceedings concerning the arbitral award. In such cases the court would be entitled to revise the arbitrators' findings on the subject of whether or not the ADR procedures were performed in compliance with the contract and, on this basis, declare the award void or unenforceable. This unnecessarily widens the scope of the court supervision of arbitration and undermines the notion of the finality of an arbitration award (4.54).

(iii) The admissibility theory does not raise the problems described above. According to this interpretation, non-compliance with a multi-tiered clause results in the arbitral tribunal's ruling the claim inadmissible pending the fulfilment of pre-arbitral ADR. The tribunal retains jurisdiction; hence a negative jurisdiction conflict does not arise. The arbitrators' determinations as to admissibility of the claims are final and cannot be reviewed in the post-award phase of arbitration. The admissibility theory ensures that the effect of the arbitral process is not compromised on grounds remote from the substance of the award and that an arbitral clause is enforced in accordance with the parties' intentions (4.57ff).

(iv) In the light of the admissibility theory ADR clauses are not treated as 'conditions' of an arbitration clause. As a consequence, they should be considered as severable from both the main contract and the arbitration clause (4.77ff).

(v) The admissibility theory gives the tribunal flexibility in choosing the form of an appropriate order. The ruling of inadmissibility may result in either conclusion of the proceedings or a stay, as can be observed in the existing arbitral awards (4.95–4.97).

CONTENTS

Enforceability in Court and Arbitration Contrasted

In order to ascertain the consequences of non-compliance with contractual ADR procedures the arbitral tribunal has to rely on the provisions of applicable law.[1] Consequently, a number of issues concerning the enforceability of multi-tiered clauses in litigation must be resolved to ascertain the effects of ADR clauses in arbitration proceedings.[2] The issues common to both court and arbitration are those that arise under domestic law, regardless of which adjudicative body applies it. They include inter alia: **4.1**

(i) assessment of the character of consensual ADR in terms of whether it is compulsory or optional;
(ii) the binding force of clauses requiring informal negotiations before proceeding to further steps of the dispute resolution procedure;
(iii) the scope of the duty to undergo the agreed ADR process;
(iv) the moment at which the duty to exhaust contractual ADR is satisfied;
(v) the validity of expert determination clauses providing that the expert's decision is to be binding upon the parties and can be enforced like a contract;
(vi) grounds on which the expert's decision can be challenged in the subsequent dispute resolution process;
(vii) the validity of a contractual time-bar;
(viii) whether ADR commitments can be enforced ex officio or only upon the plea of a party claiming non-compliance with an ADR clause; preclusion of such plea.

Apart from issues that concern courts and arbitral tribunals equally, the enforceability of multi-tiered clauses in arbitration raises additional questions resulting form the specifics of the arbitration context.[3] The fundamental distinctive feature of arbitration lies in the origin of the arbitrators' mandate to decide the dispute. **4.2**

[1] Reliance on national law is common in the literature dealing with the enforceability of ADR clauses in arbitration. See G Born, *International Commercial Arbitration*, 2nd edn (Kluwer Law International, 2014) 918ff; M Pryles, 'Multi-Tiered Dispute Resolution Clauses' (2001) 18 *Journal of International Arbitration* 159; B Cremades, 'Multi-Tiered Dispute Resolution Clauses' (CPR Institute for Dispute Resolution, 2004) 1ff; F Fabian, 'The Enforceability of Mediation Clauses—the Approach of English and German Courts and ICC Arbitral Tribunals' (2005) 5 *SchiedsVZ* 250; A Jolles, 'Consequences of Multi-Tier Arbitration Clauses: Issues of Enforcement' (2006) 72 *Arbitration* 329; C Boog, 'How to Deal with Multi-Tiered Dispute Resolution Clauses—Note—June 2007—Swiss Federal Supreme Court' (2008) 26 *ASA Bulletin* 103ff; S Leonard, K Dharmananda, 'Peace Talks Before War: The Enforcement of Clauses for Dispute Resolution before Arbitration' (2006) 23 *Journal of International Arbitration* 301. On the relevance of national laws see also 1.87–1.90.

[2] W Craig, W Park, J Paulsson, *International Chamber of Commerce Arbitration*, 3rd edn (Oceana Publications, 2000) para 28.02. The authors classify ADR clauses as 'preconditions to arbitration' governed by national law.

[3] It must be recalled that the enforceability of ADR clauses has not been harmonised on an international level. ADR clauses are not covered by the provisions of the New York Convention on the Recognition and Enforcement of Foreign Arbitral Awards 1958, and the effects of mediation clauses are not specified in Directive 2008/52/EC of the European Parliament and of the Council of 21 May 2008 on certain aspects of mediation in civil and commercial matters (on this aspect, see 1.87–1.90).

By contrast with that of judges, arbitrators' authority is of a contractual nature and derives from an arbitration clause.

4.3 The different sources of court and arbitral jurisdictions have implications for the effects of non-compliance with ADR clauses. Because arbitral jurisdiction stems from contract, it is sometimes considered that by agreeing to undergo a sequence of steps preceding arbitration, the parties make the effectiveness of an arbitration clause conditional. In this view, the competence of the tribunal to hear the case is not triggered until the fulfilment of the agreed pre-arbitral steps. Consequently, the enforceability of multi-tiered clauses in arbitration raises the question whether non-compliance with contractual ADR procedures affects the jurisdiction of an arbitral tribunal. A view advocating a positive answer to this question is referred to as the 'jurisdiction theory' in the present work.

4.4 The question whether the exhaustion of pre-arbitral procedures has a bearing on the jurisdiction of the tribunal determines the extent of the supervision exercised by the state court over arbitration. The interpretation that non-compliance with ADR commitments affects jurisdiction makes the arbitrators' findings in this matter reviewable by the court: the court may annul the award or refuse to enforce it in circumstances where the arbitrators proceed to hear the case despite the defendant's raising the plea of non-exhaustion of pre-arbitral ADR by the claimant. The possibility of recourse to the state court on grounds of improper acquisition of jurisdiction is, therefore, one of the key controversies relating to the enforceability of multi-tiered dispute resolution clauses in arbitration.

4.5 The grounds for a state court to review an arbitral award depend on the law applied by that court. In most of the normative models based on the UNCITRAL Model Law or the New York Convention, the grounds for annulment or refusal of enforcement of the arbitration award encompass the lack of jurisdiction of the tribunal.[4] A wrong assessment of jurisdictional objections raised by the parties, resulting in an improper acquisition of jurisdiction by the tribunal, may, therefore, lead to the setting aside of the award in the arbitral seat, or serve as grounds for refusal to enforce it in the country where the assets of a losing party are located.

4.6 Classifying compliance with pre-arbitral ADR commitments as determining the jurisdiction of the tribunal also has a bearing on the duty of the arbitrators to render an enforceable arbitral award.[5] In addition, making an award without taking into account the party's violation of the agreed ADR process may result in

[4] For the legal systems based on the UNCITRAL Model Law on International Commercial Arbitration the relevant provisions include Article 34(2)(a)(i) and (iii), on the grounds for challenge, and Article 36(1)(a)(i) and (iii), on the grounds for denial of recognition or enforcement of an arbitral award. In the New York Convention the jurisdictional grounds for refusal of enforcement of an award are set forth in Article V(1)(a). The New York Convention does not contain provisions regarding the challenge of an award (cf Article IX.1 of the European Convention on International Commercial Arbitration signed in Geneva on 21 April 1961 which outlines the reasons for challenge of an award which may serve as grounds for denial of recognition or enforcement of an award under this act).

[5] G Horvath, 'Duty of the Tribunal to Render an Enforceable Award' (2001) 18 *Journal of International Arbitration* 135. See also H-L Yu, P Molife, 'The impact of national law elements on international commercial arbitration' (2001) 1 *International Arbitration Law Review* 17, 18.

annulment or non-recognition of the award based on the arbitral tribunal's failure to conduct proceedings in accordance with the procedure agreed by the parties.[6]

Escalation dispute resolution mechanisms as part of an international arbitration framework are particularly exposed to difficulties emerging from the multiplicity of applicable legal systems. Article 16 of the UNCITRAL Model Law on International Commercial Arbitration establishes the competence of the arbitral tribunal to rule on its own jurisdiction (*Kompetenz-Kompetenz*) but leaves open the question of the law applicable to jurisdictional matters.[7] As observed in the literature, it is not clear whether the law applicable to an arbitration clause would also be applicable to pre-arbitral ADR commitments.[8] **4.7**

It must be noted that the legal systems that are of relevance to this enquiry entail, first, the procedural law of the arbitral seat. The law of the seat is applicable, inter alia, to the arbitral procedure (in the absence of the parties' agreement), the form of an arbitral award, its rectification and grounds for challenge.[9] Secondly, non-compliance with ADR clauses may be governed by the substantive law of the contract. This law is of particular relevance to the validity and effects of any contractual time-bar integrated into the ADR mechanism.[10] Thirdly, the law applicable to an arbitration clause may govern the entirety of the multi-step dispute resolution clause if it is assumed that ADR clauses are contractual conditions of arbitration clauses and as such constitute parts of an arbitration agreement. Finally, the effects of ADR clauses may be prescribed by the parties themselves in the contract or be included in another document of a contractual nature, such as the rules of a selected arbitration centre. **4.8**

The issue of law applicable to an ADR clause has been addressed by Moore-Bick LJ in *Sulamérica Cia Nacional De Seguros SA and others v Enesa Engenharia SA and others.*[11] In this case the judge envisaged the possibility of applying two different legal systems to an arbitration and mediation clause.[12] By contrast, the Swiss *Bundesgericht* came to the conclusion that the law applicable to an arbitration **4.9**

[6] See Art 34(2)(a)(iv), UNCITRAL Model Law on International Commercial Arbitration (grounds for challenge) and Art V(1)(d), New York Convention 1958 (grounds for refusal to recognise or enforce the award).

[7] For a commentary see P Binder, *International Commercial Arbitration in UNCITRAL Model Law Jurisdictions*, 3rd edn (Sweet & Maxwell, 2009) para 4-011.

[8] N Alexander, *International Comparative Mediation: Legal Perspectives* (Wolters Kluwer, 2009) 181 ('Where ADR is condition precedent to arbitration questions may arise as to the classification of an MDR clause. One issue relates to whether the mediation part of the clause forms part of the arbitration clause for purposes of interpretation under an arbitration statute or alternatively whether it can be treated separately under mediation regulations').

[9] The relevance of the seat is comprehensively described in G Born, *International Commercial Arbitration*, n 1 above, 2051ff.

[10] Contractual time limits may extinguish the claim (bar to the claim) or the right to have the claims heard in arbitration (bar to remedy). For further scrutiny of the two types of time-bar see 2.72ff.

[11] *Sulamérica Cia Nacional De Seguros SA and others v Enesa Engenharia SA and others* [2012] EWCA Civ 638; [2012] 1 Lloyd's Rep 671.

[12] 'I agree that it would be unusual (though not, I think, impossible) for different parts of a composite clause to be governed by different proper laws' (*ibid* at [28]).

agreement in accordance with Article 178 IPRG will also apply to the interpretation of any pre-arbitral procedures.[13]

4.10 In the above cases primary consideration was given to whether the law governing the effects of an ADR clause should be the same as the law applicable to an arbitration clause. An additional difficulty lies in the complex structure of multi-tiered mechanisms. As shown in the comparative part of the study, ADR clauses constituting integrated dispute resolution systems are not a homogenous group. It is not uncommon for a multi-tiered clause to contain distinct components of a different, procedural or substantive, character, with consequent impact upon analysis of the conflict of laws involved.

4.11 The problems relating to the lack of a uniform law of ADR and the multiplicity of legal systems applicable in international arbitration is of particular relevance to arbitral jurisdiction. Potential complications can be illustrated by the following hypothetical situation. An arbitral tribunal seated in Switzerland gives an award, following the dismissal of the defendant's plea as to non-compliance by the claimant with the parties' ADR commitments. The defendant who raised the unsuccessful plea loses the case on the merits and the award against him is to be enforced in France. The defendant challenges the award in Switzerland on grounds that the dismissal of the defendant's plea was unfounded and the tribunal should have denied jurisdiction. If the Swiss court upholds the defendant's objection, the award will be annulled in Switzerland, where the jurisdiction theory has gained significant judicial support. The question arises whether an award that can be annulled in Switzerland should be enforced in France. French law rejects jurisdictional theory and a successful plea of non-compliance with an ADR clause would not be treated as depriving a tribunal of jurisdiction to hear a case.

4.12 International regulations do not deal with this problem. The New York Convention, to which both countries are signatories, provides that recognition and enforcement of an award may be refused if the award has been set aside by the courts of an arbitral seat.[14] The formal grounds for refusing enforcement in France will, therefore, arise only after the setting aside of the award in Switzerland. Before this happens, however, the French court faces no obstacles in recognising and enforcing the award. Consequently, inconsistency in dealing with breach of ADR clauses in French and Swiss law leads to an undesirable consequence, namely, the enforcement of an award which is later annulled.[15]

[13] Bundesgesetz über das Internationale Privatrecht (IPRG). Award of 7 July 2014, 4A_124/2014, available at: www.swissarbitrationdecisions.com/sites/default/files/7%20juillet%202014%204A%20124%202014.pdf.

[14] New York Convention on the Recognition and Enforcement of Foreign Arbitral Awards 1958, Art V(1)(e).

[15] The consequences of the enforcement of an award which is later annulled, as well as the exceptions to the rule that annulled awards are unenforceable, are beyond the scope of the present study. For commentary see W Craig, W Park, J Paulsson, *International Chamber of Commerce Arbitration*, n 2 above, para 28.04; J Paulsson, 'Enforcing Arbitral Awards Notwithstanding a Local Standard Annulment' (1998) 9 *ICC Bulletin* 14ff; W Park, 'National Law and Commercial Justice: Safeguarding Procedural Integrity in International Arbitration' (1989) 63 *Tulane Law Review* 647, 688.

In the reverse situation where the arbitral award has been made in France but has to be enforced in Switzerland the award will not be annulled in the seat (because French law does not follow jurisdiction theory). The enforcement may, however, be refused in Switzerland, if the party against whom the enforcement proceedings have been brought succeeds in putting forward the view that the arbitrators have incorrectly acquired jurisdiction. In consequence, the award will be deprived of any real effect in the country where it has to be enforced, without any possibility of the parties setting the award aside in the country of its origin. **4.13**

The above scenarios show the significance of determining whether or not contractual ADR commitments affect arbitral jurisdiction. Arbitrators faced with a plea of non-compliance with pre-arbitral ADR commitments should bear in mind the consequences of their ruling for the enforcement of, or challenging of, an award. In particular, they should be aware of the risks connected with divergent standards of assessment. The complication illustrated shows the merit of harmonisation of legal systems as to whether or not non-compliance with contractually agreed ADR procedure affects the jurisdiction of a tribunal to hear a case. If the court of the arbitral seat and the court of the award's enforcement would follow the same rule in this matter, the incompatibility between the decisions would be avoided, and a primary objective of arbitration—an enforceable arbitration award—would be better preserved. **4.14**

Jurisdiction and Admissibility

As explained above, the enforceability of multi-tiered clauses in arbitration is concerned with a fundamental question as to whether compliance with an agreed ADR procedure invokes arbitral jurisdiction. The answer to this problem has significant consequences for the stability and effectiveness of any arbitral award. Classifying ADR commitments as matters affecting jurisdiction implies that a party who unsuccessfully raised non-compliance with pre-arbitral ADR may yet seek annulment of the award, or oppose its enforcement, on grounds that the tribunal wrongfully acquired jurisdiction. **4.15**

Two interpretations must be distinguished in providing a solution to this fundamental problem. According to the first theory, failure to exhaust contractual ADR before filing the claim in arbitration negatively affects the jurisdiction of the arbitral tribunal (the jurisdiction theory). Under the second interpretation non-compliance with the agreed ADR process has no bearing on the jurisdiction of the tribunal but, instead, affects admissibility of the claim (the admissibility theory). **4.16**

The distinction between jurisdiction and admissibility is strongly grounded in arbitration literature. The corresponding dichotomy of interpretations regarding the effects of ADR clauses can also be observed in cases decided by national courts. The domestic jurisprudence will be recapitulated below, and supplemented with reference to the case law of the ICC International Court of Arbitration. In the final **4.17** section of the present chapter a critical evaluation of the jurisdiction theory will be presented and an alternative laid out.

Position of National Laws

4.18 Analysis of the legal systems selected leads to the conclusion that jurisdiction theory has found its strongest judicial support in Switzerland. The exemplary case, widely commented on in both the domestic and the international literature, is the Federal Supreme Court decision in *Vekoma v Maran*.[16] In this case the court set aside an arbitration award on grounds of lack of jurisdiction. The jurisdictional objection concerned non-fulfilment of the contractual ADR by the claimant in arbitral proceedings. The tribunal rejected the defendant's objection and proceeded to give an award. The defendant raised the claimant's non-compliance with ADR clauses again in the national court, this time as grounds for annulment of the award. The court assessed the plea of non-compliance with pre-arbitral ADR differently to the tribunal. It took the stance that the arbitrators had unduly dismissed the party's objections and should not have proceeded with deciding the case on the merits. The court concluded that the award had been made without the tribunal having jurisdiction and, therefore, must be set aside.[17]

4.19 Subsequent court decisions confirmed this interpretation.[18] Consequently, under Swiss law, violation of contractual ADR commitments constitutes grounds for setting an arbitral award aside due to lack of jurisdiction under Article 190(2)(b) IPRG.[19] The jurisdiction theory has also been supported by those authors who treat exhaustion of contractual alternative dispute resolution procedures as a necessary condition of jurisdiction *ratione temporis*.[20]

4.20 The jurisdiction theory, although strongly articulated by the judiciary, is only one of several interpretations identified by Swiss commentators. The alternatives reject the premise that compliance with ADR clauses instantiates the competence of an arbitral tribunal. On one view, failure to adhere to pre-arbitral ADR requirements results in a premature claim being inadmissible. Another interpretation rejecting the jurisdiction theory advocates that premature filing of the claim in contravention to the agreed ADR process should result in the tribunal staying the proceedings.[21] Finally, it has to be noted that under the Swiss legal system, unlike in

[16] *Transporten Handelsmaatschappij 'Vekoma' BV v Maran Coal Corporation* Bundesgericht, I. Zivilabteilung, 17 August 1995 (1996) 14 *ASA Bulletin* 673.

[17] On this case see also 2.241ff.

[18] See eg Bundesgericht, 7 July 2014, 4A_124/2014, available at: www.swissarbitrationdecisions.com/sites/default/files/7%20juillet%202014%204A%20124%202014.pdf.

[19] Tribunal fédéral, Ière Cour de droit civil, 4A_46/2011, Arrêt du 16 mai 2011, (2011) 3 *ASA Bulletin* 643 and Obergericht Zürich, 11 September 2001, ZR 2002 (101) No 21, 77–81.

[20] B Berger, F Kellerhals, *International and Domestic Arbitration in Switzerland*, 3rd edn (Stämpfli Publishers/Hart Publishing/ C.H. Beck/ Manz, 2015) paras 582-84.

[21] M Schott, M Courvoisier, in H Honsell, N Vogt, A Schnyder, S Berti (eds), *Basler Kommentar Internationales Privatrecht*, 3rd edn (Helbing Lichtenhahn Verlag, Basel 2013) 1919, para 60 ad Art 186 IPRG.

any other jurisdiction analysed in this study, the courts classify mediation agreements as giving rise to purely substantive consequences.[22] This view excludes any procedural effect of ADR clauses, and stands in contrast to the jurisdiction theory.

4.21 An interpretation that failure to comply with the pre-arbitral steps of a dispute resolution mechanism results in arbitrators forfeiting jurisdiction to hear the case has also been adopted under English law. The decision in *Wah (Aka Alan Tang) & Another v Grant Thornton International Ltd & Others*[23] concerned an application for challenge of an arbitral award based on jurisdictional grounds under section 67 of the Arbitration Act 1996. In this case the court determined that compliance with an ADR clause was a prerequisite to arbitral jurisdiction. The controversy as to the effects of pre-arbitral ADR arose before the arbitral tribunal after the claimant bypassed an agreed conciliation attempt and filed his claim directly in arbitration. The tribunal adopted the position that a pre-arbitral settlement attempt was not a necessary condition of commencement of arbitration. Consequently, the arbitrators dismissed the defendant's jurisdiction objections and proceeded to hear the case. The defendant challenged the subsequent award on grounds that the tribunal lacked jurisdiction due to the claimant's failure to exhaust the agreed pre-arbitral procedure.

4.22 The court refused to set the award aside, finding that the conciliation clause in the contract was insufficiently precise to have any binding force.[24] Although the application for challenge was unsuccessful, the *Wah* case shows that under English law the court is empowered to review the tribunal's decision concerning the exhaustion of the ADR commitments.[25] This scrutiny is part of the court's review of the tribunal's jurisdiction and may result in annulment of the award. The interpretation based on this premise is one of long standing under English law, and has featured in many court decisions regarding both consensual and quasi-adjudicative ADR.[26] Importantly, section 9(2) of the English Arbitration Act 1996 provides that, the court confronted with a claim filed in contravention of the tiered arbitration clause is empowered to stay the proceedings 'notwithstanding that the matter is to be referred to arbitration only after the exhaustion of other dispute resolution procedures'.

[22] Kassationsgericht Zürich, 15 März 1999, (2002) 2 *ASA Bulletin* 373. This stand has been criticised by the commentators, see A Jolles, 'Consequences of Multi-Tier Arbitration Clauses: Issues of Enforcement', n 1 above, 332 and literature cited.

[23] [2012] EWHC 3198 (Ch).

[24] On this aspect see 2.4ff.

[25] Note the different standard for preciseness of ADR clauses adopted in *Emirates Trading Agency LLC v Prime Mineral Exports Private Limited* [2014] EWHC 2104 (Comm). On this issue see 2.48–2.53.

[26] *National Boat Shows Ltd and another v Tameside Marine* [2001] WL 1560826, [2001] Arbitration Law Reports 43; 2001 (1): 527–42; *Itex Shipping Pte Ltd v China Ocean Shipping Co (The Jing Hong Hai)* [1989] 2 Lloyd's Rep 522; *Mid Glamorgan County Council v Land Authority for Wales* (1990) 49 BLR 61; 32 Con LR 50. In this last case the court expressly stated that an arbitration clause in the ICE Conditions of Contract for construction authorises the arbitrators to hear only those claims which were submitted to the contractual dispute resolution procedure. Similarly, *Secretary of State for Transport v Birse-Farr Joint Venture* (1993) 62 BLR 36; (1993) 9 *Construction Law Journal* 213.

4.23 The jurisdiction theory has not been supported under French law. In the leading decision in *Poiré v Tripier*,[27] a plea of non-compliance with an ADR clause has been classified as an objection as to inadmissibility (*fin de non-recevoir*). This category of procedural defence is distinct from procedural exceptions (*exceptions de procedure*) which include jurisdictional objections. Consequently, under French law non-compliance with the ADR procedure agreed in a contract affects the admissibility of the claim (*recevabilité*), not the jurisdiction of the court.

4.24 This interpretation has been implemented in arbitration.[28] An arbitral tribunal applying French law should conclude the proceedings due to inadmissibility of a claim. The tribunal's assessment as to a party's compliance with an ADR procedure is not reviewable in court in challenge or enforcement proceedings held in France.[29] Moreover, adherence to the agreed dispute resolution process is not reviewable on public policy grounds.[30] It follows that under French law compliance with escalation dispute resolution mechanisms does not constitute a necessary condition of arbitral jurisdiction. The arbitrators' decision is final and cannot be reviewed by the court in proceedings involving judicial scrutiny of the arbitration award.

4.25 A similar approach has been adopted in Germany with respect to consensual ADR clauses.[31] According to the jurisprudence of the *Bundesgerichtshof* non-compliance with a mediation clause results in rejection of the claim as inadmissible (*unzulässig*). By including a mediation clause in the contract the parties temporarily exclude actionability of the claim (*Klagbarkeit*), interpreted as an ability to bring a legal action before an adjudicative body (a court or an arbitral tribunal).[32] It follows that in the case of non-compliance with a consensual ADR process prescribed in a contract an arbitral tribunal applying German law should reject the claim as inadmissible, instead of refusing jurisdiction.[33] The arbitrators' decision to hear the case despite a party claiming non-compliance with the ADR process does not result in the case being decided without requisite jurisdiction. Even an unjustified dismissal of the party's plea cannot be grounds to challenge the award or refuse its enforcement.

4.26 The German judiciary deals differently with expert determination clauses than it does with consensual ADR commitments. Premature filing of a claim in contravention of an expert determination clause results in the claim being dismissed

[27] Cour de cassation (Ch mixte), 14 février 2003, Bulletin civil, 2003 Mixte, n° 1, p 1. The judgment is analysed at 2.185ff.

[28] On *fin de non-recevoir* in arbitration see 2.214–2.217.

[29] Cour d'appel de Paris (1re civ) 4 mars 2005, (2005) 1 *Revue de l'Arbitrage* 143. See also J-F Poudret, S Besson, *Comparative Law of International Arbitration*, 2nd edn (Sweet & Maxwell, 2007) para 13, fn 59(b).

[30] Cour d'appel de Paris, 19 octobre 2010, unpublished. The judgment was later changed by the *Cour de cassation* for other reasons, see also 2.215.

[31] See 2.97ff.

[32] See eg BGH, NJW 1984, 669.

[33] K-P Berger, 'Law and Practice of Escalation Clauses' (2006) 1 *Arbitration International* 1, 6.

as unfounded (*unbegründet*).[34] Despite this discrepancy, for quasi-adjudicative methods, like for mediation, the arbitrators' decision as to fulfilment of pre-arbitral ADR does not concern jurisdiction and is not a part of *Kompetenz-Kompetenz* enquiry. As a consequence, under German law non-compliance with pre-arbitral tiers of the dispute resolution process creates neither grounds for challenge of an arbitral award, nor a defence against its enforcement.

In summary, the jurisdiction theory has been rejected under French and German law. In those systems the admissibility theory has been supported (in Germany, however, only in relation to mediation clauses). The jurisdiction theory has been followed in Switzerland, where the effects of non-compliance with multi-tiered clauses are discussed predominantly in the arbitration context. English law has adopted the jurisdiction theory in a qualified form. A claimant's failure to exhaust the agreed ADR process will result in the arbitral tribunal declining to hear the case. Under the English Arbitration Act 1996, however, in such a case the court also lacks jurisdiction and is obliged to stay the proceedings brought before it in contravention of a multi-tiered arbitration clause. **4.27**

ICC International Court of Arbitration

The ICC International Court of Arbitration[35] has on a number of occasions treated compliance with pre-arbitral ADR as a matter affecting jurisdiction of the tribunal. In the awards published by this body[36] the arbitrators' assessment of whether the agreed settlement procedures were exhausted in accordance with a contract is a part of the *Kompetenz-Kompetenz* determination. An important line of ICC case law concerns the question as to whether clauses providing for informal negotiations, or other consensual ADR methods, are capable of creating binding obligations that compel the parties to attempt settlement. **4.28**

In its early decisions the ICC Court considered clauses providing for pre-arbitral conciliation to be unenforceable. In Case no 2138 of 1974[37] the Court contrasted the consensual nature of conciliation with the adjudicative character of arbitral proceedings. While the enforceability of arbitration clauses was unquestionable in ICC jurisprudence, the tribunal considered the cooperative nature of conciliation **4.29**

[34] See 2.131.

[35] Hereafter also the 'ICC Court'.

[36] The relative inaccessibility of the awards issued by the ICC Court of International Arbitration has been pointed out by one of its arbitrators, R Knutson, 'Recent Treatment of Construction Awards by the ICC International Court of Arbitration', Paper given to a meeting of the Society of Construction Law, London, 3 February 2004, 1. Available at: www.international-arbitration-attorney.com/wp-content/uploads/arbitrationlawSCL_D45_Knutson_Mar04.pdf.

[37] L'affare no 2138 en 1974, JDI 1975, 934. French transcript with a commentary by Y Derrains available in S Jarvin, Y Derrains, *Collection of ICC Arbitral Awards. Recueil des sentences arbitrales de la CCI 1974–1985* vol 1 (Kluwer Law and Taxation Publishers, 1990) 242ff.

a sufficiently distinguishing feature to deny binding force to the clauses providing for this method of dispute resolution. As a result, the voluntary nature of the parties' participation in negotiating the terms of a settlement has been taken to render conciliation clauses unenforceable.

4.30 A similar conclusion was reached in Case no 4230 of 1975,[38] where the clause in question also provided for pre-arbitral conciliation. The claimant in arbitral proceedings failed to initiate a conciliation attempt, bypassing the process agreed in the contract. The defendant responded to the premature claim by raising a jurisdictional objection. The tribunal decided that the disputed clause had no binding force and rejected the defendant's objection, deciding that it had jurisdiction to hear the case.

4.31 The view that pre-arbitral consensual ADR is an option, not a duty, of the parties to multi-tiered clauses has been adopted in the later cases of the ICC International Court of Arbitration. In Case no 8073 of 1995[39] the tribunal took the position that the enforceability of a conciliation agreement depends on a clear statement as to the obligatory nature of a conciliation attempt. In the absence of express wording to this effect the clause is void of binding force.

4.32 Similarly, in Case no 8845 of 1996[40] the imprecise wording of a clause providing for pre-arbitral negotiations was treated by the ICC Court as a non-binding formulation of a general intention to resolve the dispute amicably, rather than a contractual duty. The tribunal held that parties are not obliged to engage in negotiations if it is clear from the beginning that the process will be of no effect. Consequently, a request for arbitration filed without an initial settlement attempt was considered effective and the tribunal established its jurisdiction.

4.33 In Cases no 5872[41] and 10256[42] the ICC Court once again held that pre-arbitral escalation mechanisms had no binding force. In both cases the tribunal was considering a three-tiered clause providing for pre-arbitral negotiations followed by mediation. It was held that the wording of the clause stating that the parties 'may' initiate mediation in case of failed negotiations did not create binding obligations. Because mediation was not considered an obligatory pre-condition of arbitration, the claimant's failure to initiate a settlement process had no implications for the tribunal's jurisdiction.

4.34 Under the aegis of the ICC judiciary, inserting a time-limit into a multi-tiered dispute resolution mechanism comprising consensual ADR methods increases the

[38] DI, 1975, 934–938. Cited by B Cremades, 'Multi-Tiered Dispute Resolution Clauses', n 1 above, 14.

[39] Available at: www.iccdrl.com.

[40] ICC Case No 8445 1996, (2001) XXVI Yearbook 167; English transcript available in: J-J Arnaldez, Y Derrains, D Hascher, *Collection of ICC Arbitral Awards. Recueil des sentences arbitrales de la CCI 2001–2007* (Wolters Kluwer, 2009) 53.

[41] ICC Case No 5872, cited by D Jiménez-Figueres, 'Multi-Tiered Dispute Resolution Clauses: Introduction and Commentary' (2003) 1 *ICC International Court of Arbitration Bulletin* 71.

[42] ICC Case No 10256, cited by Jiménez Figueres, *ibid* 87.

chance of it being enforced by a tribunal. In Cases no 8462[43] and 9977[44] the parties agreed the time-period for potential settlement negotiations after which arbitral proceedings could be initiated. Setting out a defined framework for the parties' attempt to resolve the dispute amicably clarified the mandatory character of the consensual ADR process and removed a previous ambiguity as to when the parties might progress to the next tier of the dispute resolution ladder. The ICC judiciary also underline the need for clarification of the activities parties must undertake to fulfil their ADR commitments. In this context the Court emphasises the relevance of precise formulation of even the most technical matters, such as which members of the management of the participating entities are required to take part in the ADR procedure in order to satisfy contractual requirements.[45]

A number of the published ICC Court of International Arbitration decisions in which the tribunal concluded it had no jurisdiction to hear the case concerned the FIDIC Conditions of Contracts for Construction. In Cases no 6276 and 6277 of 1990,[46] decided under the FIDIC Old Red Book, the claimant failed to submit the dispute to the Engineer before commencing arbitration. The tribunal held that the clause in question left no doubt as to the obligatory character of pre-arbitral steps. Failure to exhaust the expert determination procedure resulted in the tribunal's refusal to hear the case due to lack of jurisdiction.[47] **4.35**

Similarly, Case no 6535 of 1992[48] concerned compliance with a dispute resolution mechanism contained in clause 67 of the FIDIC Conditions. The dispute arose as to what amounted to a valid submission of the dispute to the Engineer. The clause provided that the party putting forward its claim to the Engineer must specify **4.36**

[43] ICC Case No 8462 Final Award of June 22, 1999 cited by A Jolles, 'Consequences of Multi-Tier Arbitration Clauses', n 1 above, 334.

[44] ICC Case No 9977, cited by D Jiménez-Figueres, 'Multi-Tiered Dispute Resolution Clauses', n 41 above, 84.

[45] In the ICC Case No 9977 the tribunal analysed the clause providing for negotiations between 'senior management representatives of the parties who will attempt to reach an amicable settlement within fourteen calendar days after submission'. The parties held several meetings between the managers. The tribunal, confronted with the question as to whether the contractual procedure has been satisfied in accordance with the contract, shared the defendant's view in principle, but dismissed the plea as precluded and held that the defendant's objections concerning strict compliance with the clause should have been raised *during* negotiations and not *after their conclusion.*

[46] ICC Case No 6276 and 6277, cited by D Jiménez-Figueres, 'Multi-Tiered Dispute Resolution Clauses', n 41 above, 76.

[47] Interestingly, on the facts of the case the defendant failed to nominate the Engineer to perform the function of an expert under the contract. The parties have not contracted for an alternative nomination procedure in case of the defendant's default in this respect. Despite the contractual ADR procedure being impossible to perform by the claimant, the tribunal denied jurisdiction on the grounds of non-compliance with pre-arbitral dispute resolution tiers.

[48] ICC Case No 6535 of 1992, (1993) 120 *Journal de Droit International* 1024. French transcript with a commentary by D Hascher available in J-J Arnaldez, Y Derains, D Hascher, *Collection of ICC Arbitral Awards. Recueil des sentences arbitrales de la CCI 1991–1995* (Kluwer Law International, 1997) 495ff. See also C Seppälä, 'International Construction Contract Disputes: Commentary on ICC Awards Dealing with the FIDIC International Conditions of Contract' (1998) 2 *ICC Bulletin* 34.

that the submission is made in accordance with the relevant clause. The tribunal adopted a rigorous interpretation according to which only strict compliance with the clause satisfied the agreed pre-arbitral procedure. Failure to invoke the relevant provision of the contract resulted in the submission breaching the necessary formalities. Because the claimant had failed to exhaust the ADR procedure in accordance with the contract, the tribunal held that it had no jurisdiction to decide upon any of the 216 claims raised by the claimant.[49]

4.37 Summing up, the judiciary of the ICC International Court of Arbitration examines, in a way similar to national courts, the circumstances in which multi-tiered dispute resolution clauses are the source of binding obligations. Early ICC decisions rejected the enforceability of clauses providing for consensual ADR due to their ambiguous formulation. More recently the enforceability of multi-tiered mechanisms has been made contingent on the precise wording of the relevant provisions. Inserting a time-period after which the parties are allowed to proceed to the next step of the dispute resolution ladder is the most common way of ensuring the enforceability of commitments to mediate or negotiate. Importantly, owing to the detailed and precise formulation of the clause, the obligatory character of the expert determination procedure contained in the FIDIC Conditions of Contract for Construction has never been questioned by the ICC Court.

4.38 Regardless of a fluctuating position in respect of the binding character of clauses providing for different ADR methods, the ICC Court has consistently analysed the effects of multi-tiered clauses as part of its *Kompetenz-Kompetenz* enquiry.[50] By this token, the published body of ICC decisions can be considered as strictly following the jurisdiction theory. The ICC Court's stand in this matter has stimulated both approving[51] and disapproving[52] comments in the arbitration literature. An extensive appraisal of the jurisdiction theory along with presentation of an alternative interpretation will be developed in the following section of this study.

Critical Evaluation of the Jurisdiction Theory

4.39 Rejection of the jurisdiction theory by some legal systems and a number of commentators must be approved. The jurisdiction theory presumes that the fulfilment of ADR clauses is a precondition to arbitration. Under this theory the

[49] A similarly rigorous stance has been taken in the ICC Case No 6238, cited by C Seppälä, 'International Construction Contract Disputes', n 48 above, 34.

[50] It has to be pointed out that the ICC court did not clarify which law had been applied to the assessment of the effects of ADR clauses.

[51] B Cremades, 'Multi-Tiered Dispute Resolution Clauses', n 1 above, 6ff; C Seppälä, 'International Construction Contract Disputes', n 48 above, 34–35.

[52] A Jolles, 'Consequences of Multi-Tier Arbitration Clauses', n 1 above, 335; À López de Argumedo Piñeiro, 'Multi-Step Dispute Resolution Clauses' in M Fernández-Ballesteros, D Arias (eds), *Liber Amicorum Bernardo Cremades* (La Ley, 2010) 736.

arbitral tribunal specified in an arbitration clause has no jurisdiction until the relevant ADR steps are exhausted. As will be shown below, adopting this interpretation leads to a number of undesirable consequences.

Under the jurisdiction theory a party bringing a claim may unilaterally decide whether or not the arbitral tribunal will be a competent forum under the contract. According to the fundamental assumption of this interpretation, the parties make the competence of the tribunal contingent on fulfilment of the agreed pre-arbitral ADR procedures. It is thus up to the claimant whether he submits the claim to the sequence of dispute resolution methods prescribed in the contract, and triggers jurisdiction of the arbitral tribunal. Classifying contractual ADR commitments as a condition of an arbitration clause implies that such a clause is entirely dependent on the intention of any party bringing the claim. **4.40**

Furthermore, the claimant's failure to exhaust the agreed procedures leaves the defendant with a dilemma whether to make an issue of this circumstance and, by this means, eliminate jurisdiction of the tribunal, or whether to continue the proceedings without enforcing the agreed ADR commitments. The latter solution conflicts with the mandatory character of the pre-arbitral steps. The former deprives the defendant of the advantage of having the claims against him finally adjudicated on and may generate uncertainty as to which forum is competent to decide the dispute. **4.41**

Importantly, despite the large number of judicial decisions supporting jurisdiction theory, the consequences of its application have not been clarified in many legal systems. The question arises: does an arbitral tribunal's refusal to hear a case result in revival of the state court's jurisdiction? It may be reasoned that, since ADR clauses have not been satisfied and their fulfilment constitutes a condition of the arbitration clause, the arbitration clause has not become effective. Lack of an effective arbitration clause implies the state court's jurisdiction to hear the case. **4.42**

In order to clarify this dilemma, two variants of the jurisdiction theory should be distinguished. Under the first, non-compliance with pre-arbitral ADR extinguishes the positive effect of an arbitration clause. The positive effect referred to is to establish the jurisdiction of an arbitral tribunal over a case.[53] Non-compliance with pre-arbitral ADR bars this positive effect by excluding the arbitral tribunal from competence to hear the case. Failure to satisfy contractual procedure does not, however, alter the negative effect of an arbitration clause understood as removal of the normal authority of courts. The jurisdiction of the court remains barred despite arbitral jurisdiction being contingent on the fulfilment of the ADR procedures. This first variant will be referred to as the 'qualified jurisdiction theory'. It has been adopted in England under section 9(2) of the Arbitration Act 1996, which expressly provides that the court shall stay proceedings brought in **4.43**

[53] Generally on the meaning of a positive and negative effect of an arbitration clause see A. Steingruber, *Consent in International Arbitration* (OUP, 2012) para 5.68ff.

breach of an arbitration clause notwithstanding that the matter is to be referred to arbitration only after the exhaustion of other dispute resolution procedures. It can thus be concluded that under English law failure to undergo the agreed ADR process does not alter the negative effect of an arbitration clause, as the authority of the courts remains excluded despite arbitral jurisdiction not having been activated.[54]

4.44 The second variant of the jurisdiction theory assumes that non-compliance with pre-arbitral ADR prohibits both the positive and negative effect of an arbitration clause (the 'full jurisdiction theory'). Under this interpretation an arbitration clause is entirely conditional upon fulfilment of ADR. Until the agreed procedures are complied with an arbitration clause is of no effect; hence, potentially, there is no obstacle to the state court accepting jurisdiction.

4.45 Adopting the full jurisdiction theory gives rise to a series of objectionable consequences. Under this interpretation the defendant confronted with a premature claim may pursue two alternative options each of which possesses significant drawbacks. He may proceed with the defence on the merits without seeking a sanction against the claimant for non-compliance with pre-arbitral ADR. This solution would leave the ADR duties unenforced but arbitral jurisdiction would remain untouched. Alternatively, the defendant may decide to object to the claimant's breach of an ADR clause and, in this way, oblige the tribunal to deny jurisdiction. This solution ensures enforcement of ADR commitments but it deprives the defendant of the advantage of having claims against him heard and decided by the selected contractual forum. In addition, under the full jurisdiction theory the tribunal's denial of jurisdiction would potentially activate the default competence of the courts.

4.46 Such a solution leads to results barely corresponding with the intentions of the parties to multi-tiered clauses. First, as argued in the literature, under the New York Convention a valid arbitration clause excludes the jurisdiction of the courts regardless of whether or not the contractual dispute resolution mechanism provides for pre-arbitral ADR.[55] The full jurisdiction theory would stand in contravention of this act.

4.47 Secondly, under the full jurisdiction theory a claimant's failure to exhaust pre-arbitral ADR prevents an arbitration clause from taking effect and renders the whole dispute resolution mechanism futile. The question whether or not to raise the plea of non-compliance with pre-arbitral ADR becomes, for the defendant, a decision as to which forum will be competent to hear the case. This manifestly

[54] R Merkin, L Flannery, *Arbitration Law* (LLP, 2004) para 8.5, point out that by staying the proceedings under s 9(2), Arbitration Act 1996 an English court does not refer the parties to arbitration, which in such circumstances would be premature. The authors contrast this solution with the one adopted under the UNCITRAL Model Law and the New York Convention.

[55] C Bühring-Uhle, *Arbitration and Mediation in International Business*, 2nd edn (Kluwer Law International, 2006) 339.

contravenes the intention of the parties opting for an out-of-court dispute resolution. As a result of the full jurisdiction theory, an arbitration clause becomes an option playing into the hands of the party raising the claim. If the efficacy of an arbitration clause is at the discretion of the claimant, the rights of the other party under an arbitration clause are illusory.

Thirdly, the question arises: is the court faced with an action on the merits empowered to impose a sanction for non-compliance with ADR clauses? Considering that under the jurisdiction theory ADR procedures are classified as necessary conditions of arbitration, and not litigation, the answer to this question must be in the negative. This renders the entire contractual dispute resolution mechanism ineffective by the unilateral act of a party refusing to adhere to the agreed dispute resolution framework. **4.48**

It must be emphasised that, in principle, there should be no theoretical obstacles to conditional arbitration clauses. The intention to create such obligations must be, however, clearly expressed in the relevant clause.[56] Providing for compulsory pre-arbitral ADR procedures is not the stipulation of such an intention. By agreeing on a sequence of ADR steps preceding final adjudication, the parties do not intend to make the effectiveness of an arbitration clause optional or conditional upon the will of a party bringing a claim. Quite the contrary, multi-tiered clauses commonly contain express provisions unambiguously stipulating the obligatory character of the prescribed procedures.[57] **4.49**

The difficulties described above are limited under the qualified jurisdiction theory. According to this theory, non-compliance with ADR clauses bars the positive effect of an arbitration clause, preventing the arbitrators from acquiring jurisdiction. It does not alter the negative effect of an arbitration clause to exclude a dispute from the jurisdiction of state courts. On this interpretation, a party failing to undergo the sequence of pre-arbitral ADR steps would not have its claims heard by an arbitral tribunal due to lack of jurisdiction, and, at the same time, it would not have an option to submit the dispute to the court. An arbitral clause in place, although conditional, would be considered as removing the state courts' normal authority to resolve disputes. **4.50**

The qualified jurisdiction theory does not distort the intention of the parties to have their claims heard in arbitration after the fulfilment of the prescribed ADR procedures. It is not, however, free from consequences that may be considered objectionable, or even prohibitive for the implementation of this approach in certain jurisdictions. This is because the qualified jurisdiction theory results in a **4.51**

[56] See 4.67–4.76 below on the exclusion of arbitral jurisdiction based on clear wording of the contract.

[57] As emphasised by A Jolles, 'Consequences of Multi-Tier Arbitration Clauses', n 1 above, 335: 'It is hard to imagine that parties made their agreement to exclude state courts in favour of arbitration contingent on compliance with pre-arbitral negotiation and/or conciliation, in the sense that, if one party had known that the other would not engage in the agreed pre-arbitral steps, it would have preferred to submit the dispute to litigation rather than to arbitration.'

negative jurisdictional conflict. Before the pre-arbitral ADR procedures are complied with, neither the tribunal, nor the court possesses jurisdiction. In consequence, there is no competent forum to hear the case. Such a solution may be treated as unduly restricting access to court in those jurisdictions where this enquiry plays a vital role in the court's assessment of the validity of multi-tiered clauses.[58]

4.52 The incompleteness of a domestic normative framework is a further obstacle to adoption of the qualified jurisdiction theory. In those jurisdictions which lack the rules providing for such an approach, there may be no sufficient grounds to infer that ADR commitments alter only the positive effect of an arbitration clause, and leave its negative effect untouched. Treating ADR clauses as conditions of arbitration implies that the effectiveness of the entire arbitration clause is temporarily suspended. Until such conditions are fulfilled, an arbitration clause is of no effect—whether positive or negative.

4.53 Amongst the systems herein analysed only English law expressly adopts the qualified jurisdiction theory. As already indicated, the provision establishing this interpretation is contained in section 9(2) of the Arbitration Act 1996, which empowers the state court to stay the proceedings 'notwithstanding that the matter is to be referred to arbitration only after the exhaustion of other dispute resolution procedures'. The ramifications of the qualified jurisdiction theory under English law can be summarised as follows. First, under English law an arbitral tribunal confronted with a premature claim brought in breach of the agreed ADR process is obliged to stay the proceedings, which is equivalent to denial of jurisdiction to hear the case. Secondly, if the tribunal does proceed to hear the case notwithstanding the defendant's plea of non-compliance with pre-arbitral ADR, the state court is allowed to review the arbitral award on grounds of lack of jurisdiction. Thirdly, if the tribunal accepts the plea and denies jurisdiction, the default competence of the state court is not revived, and the court confronted with a claim brought in breach of a multi-tiered clause is obliged to stay the proceedings. It must be noted that other systems analysed in this study lack such a crystallised framework for settling the effects of ADR clauses in arbitration.

4.54 Adopting the jurisdiction theory, even in its qualified form, does not eliminate a significant problem connected with treating ADR clauses as conditions of arbitration. Under both variants of the jurisdiction theory, the arbitrators' decision as to the claimant's compliance with pre-arbitral procedures is not final and can be reviewed by the court exercising its supervisory powers over arbitral jurisdiction. The tribunal's assessment regarding the fulfilment of a contractual dispute resolution procedure is of consequence for the future of the entire arbitral award. It may be argued that this is too far-reaching an impact of the claimant's failure

[58] See 2.137–2.144.

to exhaust pre-arbitral ADR. As such, it results in unnecessary expansion of the court's supervisory powers over arbitration.[59]

A further argument against any variant of the jurisdiction theory concentrates on its fundamental assumption that ADR clauses constitute conditions precedent to arbitration. First, it can be argued that an obligation under a contract does not constitute a future uncertain event and hence, cannot be a condition in a juridical sense. Secondly, realisation of a condition whose substance is to undergo the agreed ADR process would remain entirely within the power of one party. Such a condition can be classified as potestative, and considered unenforceable in certain jurisdictions.[60] **4.55**

As a result of the above drawbacks the jurisdiction theory should be rejected. Fulfilment of agreed ADR commitments does not constitute a condition of arbitral jurisdiction. Competence of an arbitral tribunal is contingent solely on an arbitration agreement, and exhaustion of ADR procedures has no bearing on its effectiveness. Despite being integrated into a dispute resolution mechanism, ADR clauses are not components of an arbitration clause in a juridical sense, even as part of a single progressive system of which the last tier encompasses arbitration. An arbitration clause is legally effective in a positive and negative way from the time of its valid conclusion, notwithstanding the claimant's duty to fulfil the agreed ADR procedure before submitting the claim in arbitration. **4.56**

Rejecting the jurisdiction theory does not imply that the tribunal confronted with a premature claim must proceed to hear the case on the merits without enforcing the obligations under an ADR clause. In this study it is submitted that, instead of denying jurisdiction, the tribunal should enforce an ADR clause by declaring inadmissibility of the claim. This interpretation relies on a well-established distinction between the two domains: jurisdiction of the tribunal; and admissibility of the claim brought before it.[61] Non-compliance with contractual ADR **4.57**

[59] This criticism has been raised, most notably, by Jan Paulsson on the basis of the *Vekoma v Maran* case (*Transporten Handelsmaatschappij 'Vekoma' BV v Maran Coal Corporation* Bundesgericht, I. Zivilabteilung, 17 August 1995 (1996) 14 *ASA Bulletin* 673) in which the Swiss court annulled an arbitral award on jurisdictional grounds because it found that the tribunal's decision as to fulfilment of the ADR steps was incorrect and the prescribed procedures had not been not exhausted in accordance with the contract: J Paulsson, 'Jurisdiction and Admissibility' in G Aksen, K-H Böckstiegel, M Mustill, PM Patocchi, AM Whitesell (eds), *Liber Amicorum in honour of Robert Briner* (ICC Publishing, 2005) 601, 602. For the facts of the case see 2.241ff. Paulsson's theory is further referenced below in 4.59.

[60] eg in France a condition under which the existence or performance of the contractual duty depends on the will of one of the contractors (*condition potestative*) renders the obligation void under the express provisions of the Civil Code to this effect (Article 1174). The classification of an ADR clause as *condition potestative* has led to unenforceability of multi-tiered clauses in early French jurisprudence (C Jarrosson, 'La sanction du non-respect d'une clause instituant un préliminaire obligatoire de conciliation ou de mediation: Note—Cour de cassation (2e Ch. civ.) 6 juillet 2000; Cour de cassation (1re civ.) 23 janvier et 6 février 2001' (2001) 4 *Revue de l'arbitrage* 752, 757. See also 2.180).

[61] J Paulsson, 'Jurisdiction and Admissibility', n 59 above, 601ff; M Waibel, *Investment Arbitration: Jurisdiction and Admissibility*, University of Cambridge Faculty of Law Research Paper No 9/2014, available at: ssrn.com/abstract=2391789 and dx.doi.org/10.2139/ssrn.2391789; Z Douglas, *International Law of Investment Claims* (CUP, 2009) paras 272ff; I Laird, 'A Distinction without a Difference?

commitments excludes admissibility of a claim until the agreed processes are exhausted. The arbitrators confronted with a premature claim should accept jurisdiction and within their authority declare the claim temporarily inadmissible. The relevant decision may take the form of either a stay, or conclusion of the proceedings without deciding the merits of the claim.[62]

4.58 The finality of the arbitrators' decision on whether or not the ADR procedures were complied with in accordance with a contract is an important feature of the proposed approach.[63] The arbitrator's findings regarding admissibility of the claim are not reviewable by the court in proceedings concerning annulment or enforcement of an arbitration award. Under the admissibility theory, compliance with ADR clauses is not a part of the arbitrators' *Kompetenz-Kompetenz* determination. This solution accords with Article 13 of the UNCITRAL Model Law on International Commercial Conciliation, which states that the arbitrators should give effect to the parties' stipulation prescribing exhaustion of conciliation before final adjudication.[64] As has been pointed out in the literature, in order to give effect to the contractual dispute resolution mechanism, the tribunal must first assert jurisdiction and only then impose a sanction for breach of ADR clauses.[65]

4.59 Although the distinction between jurisdiction and admissibility is currently associated with investment, rather than commercial arbitration,[66] it is applicable in both. Importantly, one of the main theorists of this distinction, Jan Paulsson, treats a frequently invoked Swiss case on the enforceability of multi-tiered clauses, *Vekoma v Maran*, as a starting point in his account of the admissibility theory.[67]

An Examination of the Concepts of Admissibility and Jurisdiction in *Salini v. Jordan* and *Methanex v. USA*' in T Weiler (ed), *International Investment Law and Arbitration: Leading Cases from the ICSID, NAFTA, Bilateral Treaties and Customary International Law* (Cameron May, 2005) 201ff; W Park, 'The Nature of Arbitral Authority: A Comment on Lesotho Highlands' (2005) 21 *Arbitration International* 483; W Park, *Arbitration of International Business Disputes. Studies in Law and Practice* (OUP, 2006) 71ff; G Zeiler, 'Jurisdiction, Competence and Admissibility of Claims in ICSID Arbitration Proceedings' in C Binder, U Kriebaum, A Reinisch, S Wittich (eds), *International Investment Law for the 21st Century: Essays in Honour of Christoph Schreuer* (OUP, 2009) 76ff. See also a discussion on ICSID arbitration awards relevant in the present context in G Born, *International Commercial Arbitration*, n 1 above, 936, fn 1583 and the comments in T Arntz, *Eskalationsklauseln. Recht und Praxis mehrstufiger Streiterledigungsklauseln* (Carl Heymanns Verlag, 2013) 119 on *Lauder v Czech Republic* (final award of 3 September 2001, available at: www.italaw.com/sites/default/files/case-documents/ita0451.pdf).

[62] Stay of the proceedings as a result of inadmissibility of the claim was ordered eg in *SGS Société Générale de Surveillance SA v Republic of the Philippines*, Case No ARB/02/6 (Decision of the Tribunal on Objections to Jurisdiction), available at: arbitration.org/sites/default/files/awards/arbr-2007-232-1.pdf.

[63] This aspect is particularly emphasised by J Paulsson, 'Jurisdiction and Admissibility', n 59 above, 601.

[64] On this provision see 1.84–1.86.

[65] A Jolles, 'Consequences of Multi-Tier Arbitration Clauses', n 1 above, 335. The author points out that the jurisdiction theory would contravene Art 13, Model Law.

[66] See n 60 above.

[67] *Transporten Handelsmaatschappij 'Vekoma' BV v Maran Coal Corporation* Bundesgericht, I. Zivilabteilung, 17 August 1995, (1996) 14 *ASA Bulletin* 673. The case is a key decision presenting the jurisdiction theory. See 2.241ff and 4.18.

In this case the Swiss Federal Supreme Court annulled an arbitration award on jurisdictional grounds based on the claimant's non-compliance with pre-arbitral ADR procedures in accordance with the contract. The author criticised this interpretation as having too far-reaching consequences for an arbitral award. In his view non-compliance with pre-arbitral dispute resolution procedures excludes admissibility of a claim without affecting the jurisdiction of the tribunal. Similarly, William Park voices his criticism of *Vekoma v Maran* in the context of admissibility as contrasted with jurisdiction of the tribunal.[68] It is symptomatic that the distinction between admissibility and jurisdiction is illustrated by those authors with reference to a commercial arbitration case which arose on the basis of a multi-tiered clause contained in a standard construction contract.

Application of the admissibility theory to the effects of non-compliance with pre-arbitral tiers of dispute resolution is based on an assumption that ADR clauses are not a part of an arbitration agreement. They have no bearing on the validity and effectiveness of an arbitration clause; hence, their fulfilment does not affect jurisdiction of the tribunal. The arbitrators' decision to impose a sanction for the claimant's infringement of the agreed ADR route takes the form of an order declaring the claim inadmissible. Adopting this solution removes the undesirable consequences of the full jurisdiction theory: uncertainty as to the competent forum, and potential revival of court jurisdiction. Such an approach also eliminates the drawbacks of the qualified jurisdiction theory—a negative jurisdictional conflict. The arbitrators make a respective order applying a sanction for breach of an ADR clause having established their authority. Consequently, the decision as to admissibility of claims is not a part of their *Kompetenz-Kompetenz* determination. As such, the arbitrators' findings whether the ADR procedures were complied with in accordance with the contract are final and cannot be reviewed by the court. The rationale behind this interpretation is clear: it furthers the notion of stability of arbitral awards and promotes limited court supervision over the arbitral process. **4.60**

The admissibility theory, as an effect of non-compliance with ADR clauses in arbitration, resonates with the equivalent sanction adopted in litigation by courts in certain jurisdictions. This correlation is manifest under, eg, French law, where the fulfilment of contractual ADR affects the admissibility of the claim (*recevabilité*), as contrasted with procedural bars such as lack of jurisdiction of the adjudicating body.[69] It can be argued that admissibility as an attribute of a claim denotes a different meaning in the context of litigation than it does in the context of arbitration.[70] It must be observed, however, that analysis of ADR clauses in both **4.61**

[68] W Park, 'The Nature of Arbitral Authority' 490–91.

[69] On the French notion of objections as to admissibility (*fin de non-recevoir*) in arbitration, see 2.214–2.217.

[70] cf B Berger, F Kellerhals, *International and Domestic Arbitration in Switzerland*, n 20 above, para 1163 ('Most conditions of admissibility and pleas of lack of admissibility are indeed the same in arbitration as in state court litigation').

arbitration and litigation allows a uniform classification of their effects in a general sense as influencing the properties of the claim, and not the competence of the adjudicative body. Consequently, the proposed interpretation is capable of serving as a frame of reference for establishing sanctions for non-compliance with ADR clauses in litigation, commercial arbitration and investment arbitration. Although the structure and sources of jurisdiction vary in those distinct adjudicative systems, in the present context the admissibility theory translates into all three frameworks.

4.62 Surprisingly, the contrast between admissibility and jurisdiction is not frequently referred to in the literature on the enforceability of multi-tiered clauses in arbitration. This is notwithstanding this distinction being expressly applied by Jan Paulsson and William Park to the *Vekoma v Maran* case, concerning the sanctions for non-compliance with a multi-tiered dispute resolution clause in a construction contract.[71] The confusion of dogma in this context is further increased by those authors who disregard this distinction, and use the term 'inadmissibility' to describe the jurisdiction theory. This tendency can be observed amongst some Swiss authors who treat jurisdiction *ratione temporis* as a condition of admissibility and conclude that contractual ADR commitments affect the temporal scope of an arbitration agreement, thereby excluding the jurisdiction of a tribunal until the agreed procedures are complied with.[72]

4.63 This characteristic merging of both spheres can also be seen in certain awards of the ICC Court of Arbitration. For example, in Case No 12739 of 2004 the tribunal reasoned that the arbitration was inadmissible until the end of pre-arbitral conciliation and concluded that, as a result, it had no jurisdiction to hear the case.[73] It must be assumed that the jurisprudence treating matters relating to jurisdiction of the tribunal as a part of a broader category encompassing admissibility of arbitral proceedings attaches a different meaning to the term 'admissibility' to that adopted in international arbitration doctrine. For the latter, admissibility is a category relating to the qualification of a claim, not arbitral jurisdiction.[74]

[71] Admittedly the authors proceed to develop this distinction with reference to arbitration cases based on international law.

[72] B Berger, F Kellerhals, *International and Domestic Arbitration in Switzerland*, n 20 above, paras 582–583 ('Temporal scope of the arbitration agreement is a procedural issue thus a condition of admissibility', 'More frequently it [the issue of jurisdiction ratione temporis—E.K.] arises if a dispute resolution clause provided that access to arbitral justice shall not be admissible until prior conciliation or mediation proceedings have failed, and the claimant, in disregard of that clause, immediately initiates arbitration. In such a case the respondent may seek to challenge the arbitral award invoking lack of jurisdiction ratione temporis, based on PILS, Art 190(2)(b) or CCP, Art 393(b).') and para 1164.

[73] ICC Case No 12739 (2004), unpublished. The relevant fragment is cited by M Büchler, T Webster, *Handbook of ICC Arbitration*, 3rd edn (Sweet & Maxwell, 2014) para 5–14.

[74] See especially M Waibel, 'Investment Arbitration: Jurisdiction and Admissibility', n 61 above, 7–9 and 65–66.

The deficiencies of jurisdiction theory have also been pointed out in the American arbitration literature.[75] According to US jurisprudence, a fundamental disadvantage of the jurisdiction theory lies in the uncertainty as to which adjudicative body—a court or an arbitral tribunal—has authority to hear the case until pre-arbitral ADR clauses are complied with. This uncertainty is a consequence of jurisdiction theory's underlying assumption that exhaustion of the agreed pre-arbitral ADR steps 'triggers' an arbitration clause, which otherwise remains ineffective. It has been recognised that such an interpretation facilitates the bypassing of an arbitration agreement and renders the entire dispute resolution mechanism ineffective.[76] **4.64**

As an alternative to the jurisdiction theory the concept of procedural arbitrability—as a correlate of substantive arbitrability—has been developed.[77] Substantive arbitrability concerns matters such as the validity of an arbitration clause or whether adjudicating on the claim is within the authority of the arbitrators. Accordingly, procedural arbitrability relates to matters such as whether certain ADR commitments apply to the dispute in question, whether they have been fulfilled, whether the parties have waived their rights under the ADR clauses or whether unjustified violation of ADR duties constitutes a bar to deciding the claim on its merits.[78] **4.65**

Adopting procedural arbitrability theory in establishing the effects of ADR clauses has important consequences for the stability of an arbitral award. The tribunal's findings concerning substantive arbitrability are subject to review by the court's supervisory powers. By contrast, the arbitrators' decisions as to procedural arbitrability are final and the tribunal's failure in this respect cannot serve as grounds to challenge an award or as a defence against its enforcement.[79] The consequences of identifying procedural arbitrability as governing the enforceability of multi-tiered clauses are in this respect similar to those following from rejection of the jurisdiction theory in favour of the admissibility theory. **4.66**

[75] T Stipanowich, 'Of "Procedural Arbitrability": the Effect of Noncompliance with Contract Claims Procedures' (1989) 4 *South Carolina Law Review* 847; G Born, *International Commercial Arbitration*, n 1 above, 937; R Jacobs, 'Should Mediation Trigger Arbitration in Multi-Step Alternative Dispute Resolution Clauses?' (2004) 14 *American Review of International Arbitration* 164ff; J File, 'United States: multi-step dispute resolution clauses' (2007) 7 *IBA Legal Practice Division Mediation Committee Newsletter* 33, 34ff. The authors critically assess the United States Court of Appeals for the First Circuit decision in *Him Portland, Llc v Devito Builders, Inc*, 317 F 3d 41; 2003 US App LEXIS 659 which follows the jurisdiction theory.

[76] See especially J File, 'United States: multi-step dispute resolution clauses', n 75 above, 35.

[77] On the distinction between procedural and substantive arbitrability see the Supreme Court decision in *John Wiley & Sons, Inc v David Livingston*, 376 US 543 (1964); 1964 US LEXIS 2250.

[78] On this theory see T Stipanowich, 'Of "Procedural Arbitrability"', n 75 above, 847ff, R Jacobs, 'Should Mediation Trigger Arbitration', n 75 above 165ff, J File, 'United States: multi-step dispute resolution clauses', n 75 above, 35, fn 27.

[79] *ibid*. Procedural arbitrability as the sole domain of arbitrators includes also contractual time-bar see R Jacobs, 'Should Mediation Trigger Arbitration', n 75 above, 167 and the authorities cited.

Explicit Exclusion of Arbitral Jurisdiction

4.67 Certain commentators rejecting the jurisdiction theory acknowledge that the parties may expressly make jurisdiction of an arbitral tribunal conditional upon fulfilment of certain actions related to a contractual dispute resolution mechanism.[80] This view conforms with the assumption that explicit determination of the effects of ADR clauses in an agreement is permitted by parties' freedom of contract. An approach according to which parties may expressly provide for the jurisdictional consequences of breach of their pre-arbitral ADR commitments is correct. The relevant stipulation, however, must be unambiguous and leave no scope for uncertainty as to the point at which an arbitration clause becomes effective.

4.68 An example of a contractual provision whereby the parties make jurisdiction of an arbitral tribunal conditional upon fulfilment of a prescribed procedure is contained in sub-clause 20.4 of the FIDIC Conditions of Contract for Construction. It provides that a party dissatisfied with the decision of a dispute board is obliged to notify the other party of its dissatisfaction and of its intention to commence arbitration. The notice has to be given within 28 days of receiving the decision and must state that it is given under the relevant clause. Failure to issue the notice has two consequences expressly provided in sub-clause 20.4. First, the clause sets forth that neither party shall be entitled to commence arbitration of a dispute unless a notice of dissatisfaction has been given in accordance with it. Failure to issue an appropriate notice in the prescribed time excludes the jurisdiction of the tribunal to hear the claim. Secondly, lack of the notice of dissatisfaction results in the dispute board's decision becoming final and binding. Consequently, non-compliance with the prescribed procedure not only excludes the competence of the tribunal to review the board's findings, but also renders the board's decision contractually binding on the parties.[81]

4.69 A contractual time-bar is a characteristic feature of the mechanism described above. In sub-clause 20.4 the parties expressly stipulate that upon the agreed period lapsing, a decision becomes final and not reviewable in arbitral proceedings. This can be interpreted as concluding an arbitration clause whose effectiveness depends on undertaking prescribed actions within an agreed time. As such it is an example of a 'bar to remedy' type of contractual time-bar.[82] A 'bar to remedy' clause provides that lapse of time prevents arbitral jurisdiction from coming into effect.

4.70 It follows that while the agreed time-period has not expired, an arbitral tribunal has jurisdiction to hear the case and the default authority of the court remains

[80] A Jolles, 'Consequences of Multi-Tier Arbitration Clauses', n 1 above, 335. The author does not expand this point, however.

[81] On sub-clause 20.4 FIDIC see also 5.46–5.49.

[82] On which see 2.74.

excluded. Conversely, lack of arbitral jurisdiction implies revival of the normal authority of the courts. Importantly, however, sub-clause 20.4 of the FIDIC Conditions provides that in such circumstances the dispute board's decision becomes final and binding on the parties. In consequence, since any failure to satisfy the time requirement implies that an arbitral tribunal will not be empowered to review the board's decision, equally, review by the state court will not be possible due to the final nature of the board's determination. Although hypothetically the court will have jurisdiction to hear the case, the only decision it will be empowered to make is to confirm the status quo between the parties as determined by the board's decision. The court faced with a claim of a party dissatisfied with the final and binding decision of the dispute board can only dismiss the claim and confirm the decision on grounds of its binding force under the contract.[83]

Although the parties agree that arbitral jurisdiction is conditional upon fulfilment of ADR, under stipulations such as sub-clause 20.4 FIDIC the complications connected with adopting the jurisdiction theory do not arise and the contractual dispute resolution mechanism serves its function without distorting the parties' intentions. Under the described mechanism the first effect of non-compliance with the agreed sequence of steps is procedural, and refers to the scope of the arbitrators' mandate. The tribunal is only authorised to conduct a full examination of a dispute, acting as a quasi-appellate body for the dispute board's decisions. Arbitral jurisdiction is, therefore, confined to revision of the board's determinations, which can only be triggered within a specified time. 4.71

The second consequence of non-compliance with the prescribed ADR sequence is finality of the decision. This effect is purely contractual, not least because the court's authority cannot be validly excluded. The theoretical possibility of bringing a claim in court exists, but review of the decision will not be possible due to the parties' agreement to this effect. This solution supplements the jurisdictional consequences of non-compliance with the multi-tier process. Importantly, it also removes uncertainty as to what the court's response should be when presented with a claim requesting review of the board's decision, filed in breach of the prescribed ADR process. 4.72

Conversely, a winning party who wants to enforce a decision that became final and binding as a result of the inactivity of the other party, who did not challenge it, should retain the advantage of arbitral jurisdiction. This solution has been adopted in the FIDIC Forms of Contract in sub-clause 20.7. This provision creates a specific ground for arbitral jurisdiction, namely, allowing one party to refer to the tribunal the other party's failure to comply with a dispute board's decision which has become final and binding. 4.73

[83] A similar situation arises when the court is faced with a claim in a matter previously settled by the parties.

4.74 The above framework conforms with the parties' intention to select an out-of-court dispute resolution system for any controversy under the contract. Admittedly, the court's default authority can potentially be activated by a losing party who, having lost an opportunity to challenge the dispute board's decision in arbitration, may request review in court. It does not change the fact, however, that the court in such circumstances can only give effect to the contract. The binding force of the dispute board's decision prevents the court from giving a judgment which would be different from the board's determination.

4.75 The above analysis gives rise to the following conclusion. A distinction should be made between situations where the agreed ADR has not been fulfilled and those where it has been but an arbitration clause did not come into effect because of the lapse of time. Only in the first group of situations does non-fulfilment of the agreed ADR process result in inadmissibility of the claim. In the second group, typically involving a contractual time-bar restricting arbitration, lack of jurisdiction should be accepted as the effect of non-compliance with contractual provisions.

4.76 In consequence, it is not justified to maintain that the admissibility theory governs the effects of non-compliance with clauses such as sub-clause 20.4 FIDIC, where the contractual limitation of time restricts access to arbitration (a 'bar to remedy' clause).[84] Contractual preclusion of this kind expressly refers to the jurisdiction of the adjudicative body.[85] In such cases the parties intended timely fulfilment of specified steps in the pre-arbitral procedure to be a condition of the jurisdiction of the tribunal. It must be emphasised that under FIDIC this effect has been supplemented by an additional provision implying that the absence of timely referral of the dispute to arbitration will result in the decision given at an earlier stage of the dispute resolution process becoming final. The absence of arbitral jurisdiction amounts to an inability to challenge the board's decision in any other process. Undoubtedly the consequence of the interpretation herein proposed is that compliance with contractual time-bar clauses in this context, as a matter relating to jurisdiction of an arbitral tribunal, can be reviewed by the state court in challenge and enforcement procedures regarding arbitral awards.

Consequences of Admissibility Theory

4.77 The finality of an arbitrators' decision as to admissibility of the claim is considered the main advantage of this theory as applied to the effects of ADR clauses. While this factor is of great practical relevance, further consequences of the admissibility theory, to which the literature has not devoted equal attention, will be analysed herein. First, applying the admissibility theory clarifies which adjudicative body is

[84] cf J Paulsson, 'Jurisdiction and Admissibility', n 59 above, 601.

[85] This model originates in English law. See 2.75 for details.

exclusively empowered to impose a sanction for non-compliance with an agreed ADR process. Secondly, the assumption that ADR clauses are not parts of an arbitration clause implies that they are separable from both a main contract and an arbitration agreement. Thirdly, rejecting the position that a tribunal's reaction to non-compliance with ADR should be denial of jurisdiction opens the ground up for discussion as to possible ways of declaring a claim inadmissible.

Competence to Adjudicate on Breach of an ADR Clause

4.78 It is not disputed that an arbitral tribunal is empowered to adjudicate on the consequences of breach of a pre-arbitral ADR process. Under the jurisdiction theory this assessment is part of the arbitrators' *Kompetenz-Kompetenz* determination, as illustrated by the ICC International Court of Arbitration cases analysed above.[86] In addition, the parties may expressly provide for the tribunal's jurisdiction to be contingent upon timely fulfilment of the prescribed sequence of steps, which empowers the tribunal to determine the enforceability of ADR clauses by means of their *Kompetenz-Kompetenz*.[87] Considering that the arbitrators' jurisdictional determinations are subject to national court supervision, under this approach multiple adjudicative bodies have authority to assess non-compliance with pre-arbitral ADR: an arbitral tribunal hearing the case; a national court of the arbitral seat when hearing an application for challenge of an award, and every national court in which recognition or enforcement of the award is sought.

4.79 By contrast, under the admissibility theory, the only adjudicative body empowered to apply a sanction for breach of ADR clauses is an arbitral tribunal confronted with a premature claim. This is because the admissibility theory is based on the premise that ADR clauses are not conditions of arbitral jurisdiction; instead, their fulfilment affects properties of the claim. As such, the decision in this matter is not a part of the *Kompetenz-Kompetenz* determination but relates to the claim itself.[88] The court's supervisory powers do not extend into this sphere, conceding instead to the principle of arbitral autonomy.[89]

Separability of ADR Clauses

4.80 Under the admissibility theory, ADR clauses comprising multi-tiered dispute resolution mechanisms are not parts of an arbitration clause. In particular, they

[86] See 4.28–4.38.

[87] As under sub-clause 20.4 FIDIC (on which see 1.50–1.51 and 5.46–5.49).

[88] cf G Born, *International Commercial Arbitration*, n 1 above, 937. The author classifies compliance with ADR commitments as a procedural requirement which does not relate to arbitral jurisdiction (in the absence of contrary intention of the parties). On a similar concept of procedural arbitrability, see 4.65–4.66.

[89] Modern arbitration systems recognise the rule that the scope of the court's intervention in the arbitral process must be strictly prescribed by law. For UNCITRAL-based jurisdictions the relevant provision includes Article 5 of the Model Law on International Commercial Arbitration stating: 'In matters governed by this Law, no court shall intervene except where so provided in this Law'.

cannot be classified as conditions of an arbitration clause; rather, they are independent from it. In consequence, the separability of ADR clauses is two-fold. Not only are they independent from arbitration clauses, but also they are separate from the main contract. The latter aspect derives from analogous application of the separability doctrine developed for arbitration and jurisdiction clauses.

4.81 The separability of an arbitration clause from the underlying contract implies that invalidity of an underlying agreement will not have an impact on that agreement's arbitration clause.[90] Under the separability doctrine, the arbitration agreement is autonomous and does not necessarily share the fate of the main contract. It follows that the arbitration agreement and the underlying agreement may have different qualities and requirements for their validity. Equally, they may be governed by different laws.[91]

4.82 This doctrine was first codified in Article 6(4) the Rules of the ICC Court of International Arbitration published in 1955.[92] It is currently common for this rule to be incorporated into the rules of major arbitration centres,[93] UNCITRAL Rules,[94] and UNCITRAL Model Law on International Commercial Arbitration.[95] In national laws the separability doctrine was first established in French and German law and is currently a fundamental principle of modern arbitration regimes.[96]

4.83 The separability doctrine has been extended to other types of dispute resolution agreements, including ADR clauses.[97] In many jurisdictions they are considered to be free-standing contracts, linked with the underlying agreement but independent

[90] G Born, *International Commercial Arbitration*, n 1 above, ch 3; J-F Poudret, S Besson, *Comparative Law of International Arbitration*, n 29 above, paras 162–182; E Gaillard, J Savage, *Fouchard, Gaillard, Goldman on International Commercial Arbitration* (Kluwer Law International, 1999) paras 388–451; J Lew, L Mistelis, S Kröll, *Comparative International Commercial Arbitration* (Kluwer Law International, 2003), paras 6-7–6-24; N Blackaby, C Partasides, A Redfern, M Hunter, *Redfern and Hunter on International Commercial Arbitration*, 6th edn (OUP, 2015) paras 2.101ff.

[91] See eg W Craig, W Park, J Paulsson, *International Chamber of Commerce Arbitration*, n 2 above, para 8.03.

[92] On the history of this article, Y Derains, E Schwartz, *A Guide to ICC Rules of Arbitration*, 2nd edn (Kluwer Law International, 2005) 112.

[93] Article 23.1, LCIA Arbitration Rules; Article 6(9), ICC Rules. For a commentary see P Turner, R Mohtashami, *A Guide to the LCIA Arbitration Rules* (OUP, 2009) paras 6.91–6.97; S Wade, P Clifford, J Clanchy, *A commentary on the LCIA Arbitration Rules 2014* (Sweet & Maxwell, 2015) paras 23-001ff; M Büchler, T Webster, *Handbook of ICC Arbitration*, n 73 above, paras 6-121ff; Y Derains, E Schwartz, *A Guide to ICC Rules of Arbitration*, n 91 above, 111–14.

[94] Art 21(2).

[95] Art 16(1). See also P Binder, *International Commercial Arbitration and Conciliation in UNCITRAL Model Law Jurisdictions*, n 7 above, para 4-009.

[96] See G Born, *International Commercial Arbitration*, n 1 above, 362ff for an overview. Commentators observe that the separability doctrine is commonly confused with the *Kompetenz-Kopmetenz* principle, see L Craig, W Park, J Paulsson, *International Chamber of Commerce Arbitration*, n 2 above, para 28.07; G Born, *International Commercial Arbitration*, n 1 above, 351; R Merkin, L Flannery *Arbitration Law*, n 54 above, para 9.7.

[97] See on mediation agreements N Alexander, *International and Comparative Mediation*, n 8 above, 188ff.

of it, to the effect that when the underlying contract is considered invalid or even non-existent, they do not automatically share its status. The separability of ADR clauses has been adopted, inter alia, under English law,[98] where the doctrine is also applied to the adjudication provisions contained within contracts covered by the statutory adjudication scheme under the Housing Grants, Construction and Regeneration Act 1996.[99] Similarly, the French *Cour de cassation* held that a mediation clause retains its binding force even if a dispute concerns the validity of the contract as a result of its separability (*séparabilité*).[100] The principle that a mediation clause does not share the fate of the main contract has also been recognised in Germany where the doctrine of separability (*Selbstständigkeit*), formulated for arbitration clauses, has been applied *per analogiam* to ADR clauses.[101]

The second aspect of separability of ADR clauses relates to their autonomous status with respect to arbitration clauses. As a concept resulting from the use of the admissibility theory to determine the consequences of breach of ADR clauses, the distinctness of arbitration clauses from ADR clauses can be considered a more novel and controversial approach than when that same autonomy is confined to the relationship with the underlying contract and stems from the well-established rules developed for arbitration clauses. As explained, taking ADR clauses as separate from arbitration clauses is a result of rejecting the classification of ADR steps as conditions of an arbitration clause. **4.84**

The autonomous legal status of ADR clauses is manifest under Article II(1) of the New York Convention—the provision that governs the enforceability of an arbitration clause. An argument raised against the enforceability, under this enactment, of ADR clauses as parts of arbitration clauses is that such clauses are not agreements **4.85**

> in writing under which the parties undertake to submit to arbitration all or any differences which have arisen or which may arise between them in respect of a defined legal relationship, whether contractual or not, concerning a subject matter capable of settlement by arbitration.[102]

[98] R Giles, 'Severability of Dispute Resolution Caluses in Contracts' (1994) 10 *Building and Construction Law* 393. See also *Sulamérica Cia Nacional De Seguros SA and others v Enesa Engenharia SA and others* [2012] EWCA Civ 638; [2012] 1 Lloyd's Rep 671 with reference to mediation agreements. For expert determination clauses see discussion in J Kendall, C Freedman, J Farrell, *Expert Determination*, 5th edn (Sweet & Maxwell, 2015) para 7.2.6.

[99] In *A&D Maintenance & Construction Ltd v Pagehurst Construction Services Ltd* (2000) 16 *Construction Law Journal* 199 the TCC court held that any disputes arising out of the contract must still be referred to adjudication in spite of the termination of the contract.

[100] Cass Civ 1ère, 08.04.1998, No 08-18009; Cass civ 2ème, 06.07.2000, No 98-17827, (2001) 4 *Revue de l'Arbitrage* 749.

[101] BGH NJW 1977, 2263; OLG Rostock 2006 3 U 37/06 18.09.2006; P Hartmann, in A Baumbach, W Lauterbach, J Albers, P Hartman (eds), *Zivilprozessordnung mit Gerichtsverfassungesetz und anderen Nebengesetzen*, 74th edn (CH Beck, 2016) p 2745, para 18 ad § 1029 ZPO and 2768, para 2 ad 1040 ZPO. See also § 139 BGB with the commentary by J. Ellenberger, in O Palandt, *Bürgerliches Gesetzbuch*, 75th edn (CH Beck, 2016) pp 156ff, paras 1ff ad § 139 BGB.

[102] M Pryles, 'Multi-Tiered Dispute Resolution Clauses', n 1 above, 161–62.

4.86 Multi-tiered clauses provide for a series of dispute resolution methods distinct from arbitration, the latter being considered as a last resort in case the resolution of a dispute is not achieved at earlier stages of the escalation process. Considering ADR clauses as parts of an arbitration clause would render arbitration clauses unenforceable under the New York Convention because such arbitration clauses would be outside the definition of its Article II.[103]

4.87 An additional argument, raised in the ADR literature, against treating ADR and arbitration clauses as a combined whole is related to the previous one. It rests on the premise that such an approach implies that the non-enforceability of one tier of the dispute resolution process would collapse the entire dispute resolution mechanism, rendering it unenforceable.[104] In this context the significance of treating ADR clauses as conditions the fulfilment of which instantiates the effects of an arbitration clause is particularly apparent. The reason to criticise this approach is that, if instead one accepts the autonomy of each tier of the dispute resolution procedure, the effectiveness of arbitration clauses is preserved.

4.88 An Australian decision of the Supreme Court of New South Wales in *Elizabeth Bay Developments Pty v Boral Building Services Pty Ltd*[105] may serve as an illustration of the negative consequences of treating multi-tiered clauses as an interrelated whole, instead of as independent contractual provisions. In this case the court analysed a tiered dispute resolution clause contained in a joint venture contract concluded between two parties. The contract contained a mediation clause requiring administration of the dispute through the Australian Commercial Disputes Centre (ACDC), followed by arbitration in accordance with the Arbitration Rules of the ACDC. The clause referred to a mediation appointment agreement which contained a stipulation committing the parties to 'attempt in good faith to negotiate towards achieving settlement of the dispute'. The relationship between the parties fell apart when Boral withdrew its participation in the project. In view of Boral's infringement of its contractual duties Elisabeth Bay terminated the contract and filed its claim for damages directly in court.

4.89 Although the claimant's action stood in contravention of both the mediation and the arbitration clause, the defendant confined his defence to claiming a breach of the first step of the dispute resolution process, namely the mediation procedure. The defendant treated the tiered dispute resolution clause as an integrated unit, assuming that the later tier of a dispute resolution mechanism (arbitration) has

[103] *ibid.* The author submits that the enforceability of an arbitration clause under the New York Convention would be possible after pre-arbitral procedures have been complied with. It must be recalled that the enforceability of arbitration clauses, notwithstanding pre-arbitral ADR commitments, has been guaranteed under English law in s 9(2), Arbitration Act 1996, see 4.53.

[104] N Alexander, *International and Comparative Mediation*, n 8 above, 190. The author makes the reservation, however, that separate treatment of each tier of the dispute resolution mechanism may not entirely reflect the intentions of the parties.

[105] *Elizabeth Bay Developments Pty v Boral Building Services Pty Ltd* (1995) 36 NSWLR 709.

not been activated yet. Confronted with such a plea, Giles J analysed the mediation clause in question and held that it was too uncertain to have a binding force.[106] On this ground the court asserted jurisdiction, which left an arbitration clause contained in the contract unenforced.

The decision in *Elizabeth Bay* illustrates the consequences of the assumption that under multi-tiered clauses an obligation to arbitrate only arises once the mediation process had been completed. Under this approach the unenforceability of one procedure may result in the unenforceability of another, invalidating even the provisions concerning final adjudication before the selected contractual forum.[107] The separability doctrine, applied to each tier of the dispute resolution process, avoids this unwelcome consequence. **4.90**

It follows that unenforceability of one tier of the dispute resolution mechanism should not alter the enforceability of another. In particular, it should not affect the effectiveness of an arbitration clause. Such an approach accords better with the intentions of parties contracting for an out-of-court dispute resolution process. The parties' error in formulating enforceable ADR duties should not collapse an arbitration clause which would otherwise be valid and enforceable. This conclusion is particularly relevant in the cross-border context in which multi-tiered mechanisms feature frequently, and where the degree of uncertainty as to the necessary requirements of enforceable ADR is considerable. As has been shown, the courts in different countries apply different measures to the minimum content of enforceable ADR commitments. In addition, standards in this respect may fluctuate even within one jurisdiction.[108] **4.91**

An often cited Swiss Federal Supreme Court decision in *Vekoma v Maran*[109] is another illustration of the negative consequences associated with treating particular clauses of a multi-tiered mechanism as inseparable and interrelated. The case attracted criticism due to the court's resort to the jurisdiction theory in determining the consequences of non-compliance with pre-arbitral ADR.[110] In this context various authors draw attention to the disadvantages related to the unenforceability of one tier of the dispute resolution ladder being spread over the entire clause.[111] **4.92**

[106] The judge concentrated on the passage compelling the parties to 'attempt in good faith to negotiate towards achieving settlement of the dispute'. While not bound to do so, Giles J followed in this respect the House of Lords' decision in *Walford v Miles* [1992] 2 AC 128 (HL) on which see 2.6.

[107] M Pryles, 'Multi-Tiered Dispute Resolution Clauses', n 1 above, 166. The author, however, remarks that it is not clear what the court's decision would have been if the claimant had raised breach of an arbitration clause as well as, or instead of, a mediation clause.

[108] This is of particular significance for negotiation clauses, whose enforceability generated a lot of controversy especially under the common-law systems. For the evolution of English position in this respect see the summary in 2.4–2.8.

[109] Bundesgericht, I. Zivilabteilung, 17 August 1995, (1996) 14 *ASA Bulletin* 673.

[110] See 2.249.

[111] J Carter, 'Issues Arising from Integrated Dispute Resolution Clauses' in AJ van den Berg (ed), *New Horizons in International Commercial Arbitration and Beyond. ICCA Congress Series 2004* (Kluwer International, 2005) 454 ('[P]arties may find themselves free to ignore all steps other than the final and

4.93 The separability of ADR clauses from arbitration clauses is of particular significance for the integrated mechanisms comprising expert determination. Because expert determination is in the spectrum of the legislator's interest to an extent much less than mediation, there is a considerable risk of such contractual provisions being of no effect in those jurisdictions which lack a developed legal framework for quasi adjudicative ADR.[112] Inevitably in such circumstances any invalidity of a pre-arbitral tier of a dispute resolution process would strip an arbitration clause of effect and render the entire clause a nullity. It must be also observed that in practice an expert's role is frequently performed by a person with a permanent function under the contract (eg an Engineer or an Architect in construction contracts) whose mandate expires after the contract's completion. In such situations ADR procedure before an expert may no longer be possible but it is difficult to assert that this invalidates the arbitration clause contained in the contract.[113]

4.94 The final consideration is the observation that ADR clauses may be governed by a different legal system to that governing an arbitration clause or the underlying contract.[114] Such a situation has been the subject of analysis in an English case *Sulamérica Cia Nacional De Seguros SA and others v Enesa Engenharia SA and others*.[115] In this case Lord Justice Moore-Bick notably contended that '[t]he fact that the mediation agreement in condition 11, and any mediation pursuant thereto, are governed by Brazilian law does not necessarily mean that any subsequent arbitration must be similarly so governed'.[116] The availability of different sets of rules governing respectively ADR and arbitration opens up the possibility of the parties 'insulating' ADR, and being free to choose a predictable legal system

binding one, defeating the purpose of the integrated clause and potentially even polluting it so that a final arbitration step is not available'.); T Varady, 'The Courtesy Trap Arbitration "if no amicable settlement can be reached"' (1997) 14(4) *Journal of International Arbitration* 5, 6 ('[A]ny formulation—even if it is just meant to be a gesture—becomes a possible stepping stone of various procedural gambits. The question arises from when and until when is the arbitration agreement actually operative, if resort to arbitration is contingent upon failure of settlement?'); P Friedland, 'The Swiss Supreme Court Sets Aside an ICC Award' (1996) 13(1) *Journal of International Arbitration* 111, 116 ('[A]n arbitration clause that refers to the parties' "agreement" that no settlement can be achieved is difficult to apply and potentially "pathological"').

[112] eg according to some commentators such stipulations would be invalid under Polish law as, in the absence of a normative framework governing expert determination, an expert may be perceived as usurping the mandate of a judge. (W Popiołek, 'Opinia prawna w sprawie charakteru postępowania w sprawie roszczeń wykonawcy oraz skutków niedochowania procedury zgłaszania roszczeń w świetle Warunków Kontraktowych FIDIC' (WPiA UŚ, 2007) 1ff).

[113] It must be noted that the FIDIC Conditions contain express provisions concerning the effectiveness of an arbitration clause after termination of the dispute board's mandate. In such a case the dispute board procedure is no longer required as a necessary step preceding arbitration (sub-clause 20.7).

[114] On different sets of legal rules applied in international mediation procedure, see H Eidenmüller, 'A Legal Framework for National and International Mediation Proceedings' (2002) *Journal of International Dispute Resolution* 14, 16 (Beilage 7 zu Heft 46/2002).

[115] [2012] EWCA Civ 638.

[116] *ibid* at [60].

to govern enforceability of pre-arbitral steps. This benefit has been a feature of arbitration clauses[117] and can be equally useful to ADR.

Stay of Arbitral Proceedings

It has been suggested in the arbitration literature that the preferred procedural reaction to non-compliance with ADR clauses is a stay of any prematurely initiated proceedings.[118] Stay of proceedings as a sanction for breach of an ADR (or arbitration) clause has been adopted under English law.[119] Importantly, a stay of proceedings in the present context does not have to imply denial of jurisdiction to hear the case.[120] **4.95**

Stay of proceedings is considered to be a solution well suited to arbitration. By ordering a stay the arbitrators halt the proceedings without renouncing their mandate.[121] By contrast, termination of the proceedings without deciding the merits of the case may be seen as bringing the arbitrators' mandate to an end. In such a case the tribunal would have to be re-nominated, should the ADR procedures be satisfied. The main advantages of this solution are, therefore, certainty as to the expiry of the arbitrators' mandate, and savings of time and money in constituting any subsequent tribunal, if the required ADR procedures are attempted but bring no result. Stay is thus perceived as a more adaptable solution than conclusion of the proceedings. **4.96**

In addition to the arguments raised in the literature, it must be observed that stay of proceedings understood as exercise of competence, not denial of it, is a solution removing a negative jurisdiction conflict associated with the jurisdiction **4.97**

[117] G Born, *International Commercial Arbitration*, n 1 above, 464–65: 'By applying a law different from that governing the parties' underlying contract, national courts and arbitral tribunals have insulated international arbitration agreements against challenges to their validity and legality based on (often idiosyncratic or discriminatory) local law. By providing the foundation for this result, the separability presumption has contributed significantly to the efficacy of international arbitration agreements and the arbitral process'.

[118] See especially the Swiss authors M Liatowitsch, J Menz, in E Geisinger, N Voser (eds), *Inernational Arbitration in Switzerland. A Handbook for Practitioners*, 2nd edn (Wolters Kluwer, 2013) 327; D Brown-Berset, 'La médiation commerciale: le géant s'éveille' (2002) 2 *Revue de Droit Suisse* 319, 373; N Voser, 'Sanktion bei Nichterfüllung einer Schlichtungsklausel. Note—Kassationsgericht Zürich, 15 März 1999' (2002) 20 *ASA Bulletin* 376, 378ff; A Jolles, 'Consequences of Multi-Tier Arbitration Clauses', n 1 above, 336–37; C Boog, 'How to Deal with Multi-Tiered Dispute Resolution Clauses', n 1 above, 109; J-F Poudret, S Besson, *Comparative Law of International Arbitration*, n 30 above, para 13. *De lege ferenda* this solution is suggested in French law: C Jarrosson, 'La sanction du non-respect d'une clause instituant un préliminaire obligatoire de conciliation ou de mediation', n 61 above, 763; X Lagarde, 'L'efficacité des clauses de conciliation ou de mediation' (2000) 3 *Revue de l'arbitrage* 377ff. See also À López de Argumedo Piñeiro, 'Multi-Step Dispute Resolution Clauses', n 53 above, 743.

[119] See 2.20–2.23 and 2.59–2.67. On stay of arbitral proceedings see J Bailey, *Construction Law* (Informa Law, 2011) 1167–68.

[120] See especially A Jolles, 'Consequences of Multi-Tier Arbitration Clauses', n 1 above, 335–37 with reference to Article 13 of the UNCITRAL Model Law on International Commercial Conciliation.

[121] See eg the Swiss Bundesgericht judgment of 20 September 2016 (4A_524/2016, available at: www.polyreg.ch/bgeunpub/Jahr_2016/Entscheide_4A_2016/4A.524_2016.html, where the court ruled that the arbitral proceedings did not have to begin afresh after being stayed for pre-arbitral conciliation.

theory.[122] It has to be also recalled that stay of proceedings is not incompatible with the admissibility theory. Although in case of inadmissibility of the claim arbitrators more frequently choose to conclude the proceedings, a stay has sometimes been applied in cases where determination as to inadmissibility of the claim was at issue in investment arbitration.[123] Importantly, however, stay of proceedings pending the fulfilment of the agreed ADR process is not a solution prescribed in the rules of major arbitration centres or provided for in legal frameworks governing arbitration in national jurisdictions. Lack of legal grounds for such an order may be an obstacle to this solution being adopted by those arbitrators who follow a more formalistic approach in terms of arbitral procedure.[124]

Summary

4.98 The most important conclusion of the present chapter is that non-compliance with pre-arbitral ADR has no bearing on jurisdiction of the arbitral body but rather affects admissibility of the claim. Accepting the jurisdiction theory leads to a number of unacceptable results. First, it may create a negative jurisdictional conflict whereby neither the court, nor an arbitral tribunal is empowered to hear the case. Secondly, it gives the party raising the claim a power to render the entire dispute resolution mechanism inoperative, by means of mere refusal to adhere to the contractual framework. Thirdly, treating ADR clauses as conditions of arbitral jurisdiction excessively expands the scope of the matters that fall under the judicial supervision of an arbitral process and so compromises the principle of finality of arbitral awards.

4.99 An alternative to the jurisdiction theory is an approach according to which non-compliance with pre-arbitral dispute resolution procedures affects the admissibility of the claim. This approach assumes that preconditions to hearing the case on the merits are distinct from those relating to the competence of an arbitral tribunal, with the latter resting solely upon an arbitration clause. A decision as to inadmissibility of a claim may conclude the proceedings or take the form of a stay. In the event of failure to resolve the dispute amicably, the party raising the claim may file it anew or request the proceedings to be resumed by the tribunal. The main consequences of the admissibility theory are, first, finality of the arbitrator's

[122] On which, see 4.31.

[123] *SGS Société Générale de Surveillance SA v Republic of the Philippines*, Case N° ARB/02/6 (Decision of the Tribunal on Objections to Jurisdiction), available at: arbitration.org/sites/default/files/awards/arbr-2007-232-1.pdf.

[124] In the ICC Case no 12739 of 2004 (unpublished) the tribunal confronted with a claim raised in breach of pre-arbitral ADR refused to stay the proceedings because such an order was not prescribed in the ICC Rues or an arbitration clause. The relevant fragment of the award is cited in M Büchler, T Webster, *Handbook of ICC Arbitration*, n 73 above, para 5-14.

findings in respect of the parties' compliance with pre-arbitral ADR, and secondly, separability of the individual tiers of the dispute resolution mechanism from each other as well as from the underlying contract.

The parties may expressly base arbitral jurisdiction upon fulfilment of contractually prescribed procedures. Frequently such contractual terms include a time-bar restricting the parties' access to arbitration. The practice of utilising this mechanism in the worldwide model forms of contracts shows that a bar to arbitration is usually connected with finality of the decision obtained in the quasi-adjudicative ADR process. In such stipulations the authority of the tribunal is legitimately limited to full review of decisions resulting from earlier tiers of the escalation process. Failure to challenge it in the prescribed time renders it final. A court faced with a claim by a party dissatisfied with a final and binding decision can only confirm its binding status under the contract. **4.100**

5

Typology of Multi-tiered Dispute Resolution Clauses

SUMMARY

Drawing on the analysis presented in this work, this chapter contains a classification of multi-step dispute resolution clauses based on three criteria:

(i) the type of clause (5.1ff);
(ii) the function of a clause (5.10ff);
(iii) the consequences of non-compliance with the agreed process (5.15ff).

The most important typology is that based on the effect of non-compliance with the agreed process. This typology is further illustrated by a flow chart (p 213). The concluding section of the work contains an application of the presented solutions to one of the most commonly used multi-tiered arbitration clauses, contained in the FIDIC Forms of Contract for Construction (5.40ff).

CONTENTS

Type of ADR

5.1 The nature of the relevant ADR method ties in with the matter of its enforceability. The main premises of the present work are, first, the need for deconstruction of any integrated mechanisms and, secondly, the distinction between consensual and quasi-adjudicative components. As will be shown, examining multi-tiered clauses in terms of each stage (deconstruction) and with regard to the type of the ADR method involved (distinction between consensual and quasi-adjudicative) is the key to understanding the consequences of non-compliance with contractual dispute resolution mechanisms in various jurisdictions.

Clauses Comprising Consensual ADR Methods

5.2 Distinguishing between the clauses providing for consensual techniques and those comprising quasi-adjudicative ADR methods takes into account the differing scope of the duties which such contractual provisions create. The distinction is also clearly reflected in those jurisdictions under which the two types of clause are each subjected to a different regime governing their enforceability. The most prominent example is under German law, where breach of a mediation clause results in the claim being rejected as inadmissible through a procedural order. By contrast, failure to submit the dispute to an expert renders the claim unfounded, which requires the court to make a judgment on the merits.

5.3 The distinction between quasi-adjudicative and consensual ADR had even greater repercussions in English law. For a considerable period of time the main line in English case law was to treat consensual ADR as 'agreements to agree', and so as too uncertain to have any binding force. Expert determination clauses did not raise any such controversy, being considered enforceable owing to the precise nature of the duty they create. Consequently, the enforceability of expert determination clauses was established long before the courts confirmed the binding nature of obligations arising out of mediation clauses. Although the two methods are now equated, in terms of the consequences of non-compliance, the enforceability of mediation clauses continues to be perceived as a more problematic issue than the enforceability of expert determination.[1] Such a distinction is unique to English law and has not been taken up in continental systems, where mediation is the leading ADR technique and the enforceability of mediation clauses is more established than is the case with any other ADR method.

5.4 Consensual ADR methods are not a uniform group. It is uncertain whether contractual provisions requiring the parties to undergo informal negotiations can be governed by the same regime that governs the enforceability of mediation agreements.

[1] P Hibberd, P Newman, *ADR and Adjudication in Construction Disputes* (Blackwell, 1999) 148–49.

Negotiation clauses are commonly provided for as the first tier of a dispute resolution mechanism, frequently preceding more formalised ADR steps such as mediation.[2] They are enforceable as long as they are expressed in a precise and unequivocal manner, enabling courts, or arbitral tribunals, to establish the scope of the duty they create.[3] Typically, express provisions as to the mandatory character of this step, together with a time-frame designed as a period within which the negotiations are to take place, provide sufficient grounds for accepting the binding and enforceable nature of such obligations.[4] If that is the case, the duty of the party raising the claim is to initiate the negotiation process and refrain from proceeding to the next rungs of the dispute resolution ladder until the agreed period has elapsed.

Mediation clauses within escalation mechanisms are, despite the consensual nature of this ADR, enforceable in the majority of the legal systems selected herein for analysis.[5] The stance taken by the Swiss judiciary, which rejects any procedural consequences of mediation agreements in litigation, is an exception. Importantly, under Swiss law contracting for mediation is frequently not necessary. The Swiss Civil Procedure Code demands compulsory conciliation in the majority of cases. Obedience to this aspect of the Code is a compulsory condition of litigation. Conversely, the Swiss judiciary accepts the binding nature of mediation clauses in arbitration proceedings where the statutory duty to attempt conciliation does not apply. 5.5

National legal systems tend to institutionalise mediation. They widely accept the binding force of provisions prescribing mediation as a necessary condition of filing any claim in court or arbitration. This is notwithstanding the fact that the international standards governing mediation are in their formative stages. By contrast with arbitration, matters relating to mediation are not unified at an international level. 5.6

Clauses Comprising Quasi-adjudicative ADR Methods

Multi-tiered clauses comprising quasi-adjudicative methods are commonplace in the construction industry.[6] They feature in the standard forms of contracts which provide a basis for major infrastructure projects all over the world. Their 5.7

[2] See 1.12–1.17 above.

[3] J Carter, 'Issues Arising from Integrated Dispute Resolution Clauses' in AJ van den Berg (ed), *New Horizons in International Commercial Arbitration and Beyond. ICCA Congress Series 2004* (Kluwer International, 2005) 447.

[4] See especially C Boog, 'How to Deal with Multi-Tiered Dispute Resolution Clauses—Note—June 2007—Swiss Federal Supreme Court' (2008) 26 *ASA Bulletin* 103, 105–6. See also 2.48–2.53.

[5] *Cable & Wireless PLC v IBM United Kingdom Ltd* [2002] EWHC 2059 (Comm), [2002] CLC 1319 (Com Ct); Cour de cassation (ch mixte), 14 février 2003, pourvoi n° 00-19423; 00-19424, Bulletin civil 2003 MIXTE N° 1 p. 1 (*Poiré v Tripier*); BGH NJW 669, 1984; 15 März 1999—Kassationsgericht Zürich, (2002) 20 *ASA Bulletin* 373.

[6] See 1.45ff for an overview.

widespread popularity does not, however, translate into top-down juridical frameworks for quasi-adjudicative clauses. While mediation increasingly becomes the focus of attention amongst legislators throughout Europe, expert determination and other quasi-adjudicative ADR methods remain the domain of practice rather than statutory legal solutions. With the exception of England, where expert determination has been the subject of a comprehensive body of case law, European legal systems lack a normative background within which to regulate expert determination as a form of ADR. Instead, positions are derived from related contract law mechanisms (France, Germany). Such mechanisms are not concerned with dispute resolution as such; rather, they are devices which are grounded in the law of obligations and regulate the specification of performance by a third party.[7] The lack of a comprehensive normative framework in many systems of law is therefore the most considerable risk connected with the use of this class of multi-tiered dispute resolution clauses.

5.8 Expansion of multi-tiered clauses based on the expert determination paradigm extends beyond construction contracts, where this method has traditionally been used. Expert determination became a commonplace in a variety of fields, where obtaining a preliminary decision issued by a competent neutral third party is an effective means of keeping the parties' dispute out of court.[8] But it is the expert's mandate that undergoes the most characteristic transformation. From an evaluator of a narrow factual question, the expert evolved into a decision-maker who determines entire claims and is empowered to interpret the contract and apply law.[9] In this form expert decision is typically fully reviewable in the further stages of the dispute resolution process. Importantly, dispute boards, as a relatively recent derivative of expert determination, were devised pursuant to this modern approach. By contrast, the more traditional determinations of an expert acting as an evaluator were typically binding on both the court and the parties, who could only challenge it in exceptional circumstances.

5.9 It must be stressed that the changing nature of expert determination has not prompted the requisite legislative response. With the exception of England, where the normative framework is comprehensive, the enforceability of expert determination within multi-tiered clauses reflects the search for pragmatic solutions rather than any doctrinal analysis of legal premises. The absence of a normative structure, in conjunction with the widening function of an expert, may considerably hinder the enforceability of multi-tiered clauses with quasi-adjudicative ADR components.

[7] See 2.207ff for French and 2.116ff for German solutions.

[8] On the wide use of expert determination in business and industry see J Kendall, C Freedman, J Farrell, *Expert Determination*, 5th edn (Sweet & Maxwell, 2015) paras 4.1ff.

[9] See clause 20.1 FIDIC under which the Engineer is empowered to preliminarily determine contractors' claims under the contract. On this term see 5.40–5.42 below.

Function of the Clause

The purpose of an ADR method may influence the enforceability of a multi-tiered clause. The second typology of dispute resolution mechanisms is based on the function of ADR techniques within multi-tiered dispute resolution clauses. A distinction must be drawn between escalation clauses aimed at facilitating settlement and those whose function is to provide a preliminary determination of a dispute, binding on the parties in a contractually prescribed manner. The relevance of this distinction is reflected in judicial decisions as to whether a clause, although formally binding, may be disregarded and the party's plea of non-compliance dismissed. As will be shown, this distinction is largely related to the previous one concerned with the class of ADR methods involved. **5.10**

Methods Aimed at Facilitating Settlement

Multi-tiered clauses composed of ADR methods facilitating settlement involve consensual techniques. These include, inter alia, negotiations, mediation, conciliation, early neutral evaluation and mini-trial. The rationale for sanctioning compliance with this type of clause lies in creating a framework for the parties' settlement negotiations. An argument against their enforceability concentrates on the cooperative nature of consensual ADR. According to this argument, premature filing of the claim in court or arbitration in contravention of the agreed process is indicative of an antagonistic approach of the party raising a claim. This, in turn, is likely to render any attempts at amicable resolution futile. Enforcing an ADR clause would in such circumstances be a waste of time.[10] **5.11**

The legal systems selected for analysis respond variously to this dilemma. The apparent uselessness of mediation is a defence commonly raised by claimants confronted with the defendant's plea of breach of contractual ADR clauses. It is also a matter that has been treated inconsistently within different jurisdictions. Although the answer to the question whether referring the parties to mediation will be futile depends largely on the circumstances, certain tendencies can be observed. The most inflexible stand on this matter emerges from the German judiciary which dictates rigid compliance with conciliation provisions regardless of the claimant's arguments that the negotiations will be of no effect.[11] At the other end of the spectrum is Swiss law with its position that mediation clauses are unenforceable due to the consensual nature of the process. English law can be classified as taking a '*via media*'. The English courts' acknowledgement of the theoretical utility of **5.12**

[10] W Craig, W Park, J Paulsson, *International Chamber of Commerce Arbitration*, 3rd edn (Oceana Publications, 2000) 105–6.

[11] See 2.150–2.151.

contractual ADR does not guarantee enforceability. In the leading case on multi-tiered mediation clauses, Colman J held that breach of the relevant clause can be enforced so long as referring the parties to mediation will not be obviously futile.[12]

Methods Fulfilling other Functions

5.13 Methods performing functions other than amicable resolution are quasi-adjudicative ADR: namely, expert determination and dispute boards. The characteristic feature of such methods is their leading to a material result—a binding decision issued by a single neutral person or a panel of experts. Quasi-adjudicative ADR techniques do not depend on voluntary participation by the other party. Once launched, the parties retain only limited control over the agreed process, which cannot be unilaterally frustrated by the party opposing the claim. The function of such contractual provisions extends beyond facilitating settlement by the parties, or keeping their dispute out of court.[13] The reason for contracting for quasi-adjudicative ADR lies in obtaining a decision that is binding on contractually prescribed terms. Such a decision plays an important role in the subsequent dispute resolution process, should the parties seek final adjudication by court or arbitral tribunal. Among other functions, it forms an important part of evidence and an expert is commonly heard as a key witness if the case reaches arbitration or litigation.[14] Moreover, expert determination or dispute board clauses may involve rules governing the contemporaneous keeping of records which document events at the time of, or very close to the time of, the claim, and contain restrictions on the admissibility of particular types of evidence.[15]

5.14 The defence stating that the prescribed procedure would be of no effect does not apply to quasi-adjudicative ADR. Unlike consensual methods, expert or dispute board determination is capable of achieving the requisite result in any event, regardless of the attitudes of the parties. By the same token, an argument that reference to ADR may cause unnecessary delay fails for quasi-adjudicative ADR. Referring the parties to the agreed process may facilitate the subsequent arbitral or

[12] *Cable & Wireless PLC v IBM United Kingdom Ltd* [2002] EWHC 2059 (Comm), [2002] CLC 1319 (Com Ct) at 1327.

[13] The persuasive role of dispute boards is considerable. According to statistical data a vast majority of controversies is finally decided at this stage and does not go to arbitration (see 1.41 for reference).

[14] H Brown, A Marriott, *ADR Principles and Practice*, 3rd edn (Sweet & Maxwell, 2011) para 7-026. See also sub-clause 20.6 FIDIC ('Nothing shall disqualify the Engineer from being called as a witness and giving evidence before the arbitrators on any matter whatsoever relevant to the dispute … Any decision of the DB shall be admissible in evidence in the arbitration.').

[15] See eg sub-clause 20.1 FIDIC, under which the Contractor is obliged to keep such contemporary records as may be necessary to substantiate any claim under the contract. In *Attorney General for the Falklands Islands v Gordon Forbes Construction (Falklands) Ltd* (2003) 6 BLR 280, Sanders J held that under a corresponding provision, clause 53 of the FIDIC 'Old Red Book', it is not possible to avoid the contractual requirement of keeping contemporary records by submitting witness statements at some point after the event.

court proceedings. Typically, a dispute that has undergone quasi-adjudicative procedure is clearly defined in terms of the controversial points between the parties, and the case material contains important factual information gathered close to the time when the claim arose. In addition, the scope of the duty created by expert determination clauses is clear, and hence, easier to enforce than in the case of consensual ADR. Clauses providing for quasi-adjudicative ADR require submission of the dispute to an expert (or a panel of experts), which is within the gift of the party raising the claim and requires no cooperation with its opponent.

Consequences of Non-compliance

The third typology is based on the consequences of non-compliance with particular tiers of multi-step clauses. Given the focus of the present study, this is the typology that most powerfully rears its head in comparative analysis of the enforceability of multi-tiered dispute resolution clauses in litigation and arbitration. The latter, offering greater complexity in questions of enforceability, will be taken as a starting point. In addition, arbitration provides the framework for a fundamental distinction between clauses containing and not containing a time-bar to the pursuit of claims. The matters concerning litigation, if applicable, will be examined at the end of each section. **5.15**

Clauses Without a Time-bar

Clauses without a time-limit on performance of ADR steps typically imply that the agreed dispute resolution process can be initiated at any time. This type of ADR mechanism was central to analysis of the legal systems described in this study. ADR clauses without a time-bar dominate the literature concerned with enforceability of multi-tiered dispute resolution mechanisms. **5.16**

Breach, by premature filing of the claim in arbitration, of an ADR clause without a time-bar can have two types of consequences. First, an arbitral tribunal may consider that it lacks jurisdiction to hear the case until the agreed procedures are complied with (jurisdiction theory). This stance has been evaluated, and found wanting, in the present study.[16] Secondly, an arbitral tribunal may declare the claim inadmissible (admissibility theory).[17] **5.17**

Jurisdictional disqualification for non-compliance with pre-arbitral ADR is a solution adopted in Swiss law. The jurisdiction theory has also been adopted in English law, where ADR commitments are treated as a necessary condition of arbitration and premature filing of a claim leads to stay of the proceedings. In both **5.18**

[16] See 4.39ff.
[17] On which 4.57ff.

England and Switzerland the state court controls an arbitral tribunal's findings as to the tribunal's jurisdiction. Accepting the jurisdiction theory extends the scope of judicial supervision of arbitration to matters concerned with monitoring compliance with pre-arbitral ADR.

5.19 The jurisdiction theory occurs in two variants: it can be either full, or qualified. According to the full jurisdiction theory, non-compliance with pre-arbitral ADR excludes both the positive and negative effects of an arbitration clause. Exclusion of the positive effect means that the tribunal is incompetent to hear the case until the agreed procedures are complied with. Exclusion of the negative effect implies that the normal authority of the courts is retained. Full jurisdiction theory rests on the assumption that fulfilment of ADR commitments is a condition of an arbitration clause, and until this condition if fulfilled its effects are suspended.

5.20 Under the qualified jurisdiction theory, non-compliance with pre-arbitral ADR excludes only the positive effect of an arbitration clause, leaving its negative effect unaffected. The continuing negative effect removes the competence of the courts. Exclusion of a positive effect implies that jurisdiction of an arbitral tribunal cannot be established either. Such a solution has been adopted under section 9(2) of the English Arbitration Act 1996 under which the court must refuse to hear the case if the parties concluded a valid arbitration clause, notwithstanding that arbitration can only be commenced after fulfilment of the various ADR steps agreed in the contract.

5.21 Admissibility theory allows an alternative to depriving the tribunal of jurisdiction to hear the case. It rests on the assumption that an arbitration clause, despite being integrated into a sequence of ADR steps preceding final adjudication, retains its independent binding force. It is effective in both the positive and negative senses, notwithstanding the parties' commitment to undergo a given ADR procedure before filing the claim in arbitration. The tribunal, having asserted jurisdiction in accordance with a valid arbitration clause, is empowered to impose a sanction for any breach of the parties' ADR commitments by declaring the claim inadmissible until the agreed process is complied with.

5.22 Admissibility theory avoids the flaws of jurisdiction theory. First, jurisdiction theory implies that the party bringing a claim by unilateral act decides which forum will be competent to hear the case, ie whether arbitral jurisdiction is established or not. Full jurisdiction theory creates uncertainty as to which adjudicative body is competent to hear the case if a party has failed to fulfil ADR and the tribunal has been denied jurisdiction. The qualified jurisdiction theory resolves this dilemma by stating that neither the court nor the arbitral tribunal is competent to hear the case, thereby leading to a negative jurisdictional conflict. Finally, the jurisdiction theory in its full and qualified versions unduly extends the scope of judicial supervision to matters which should be left to the arbitrators to decide. Classifying compliance with ADR as a jurisdictional issue means that the fate of the entire arbitral award may depend on the court's account of whether an alternative dispute resolution route was duly pursued.

Under admissibility theory the arbitrators' decision as to the claimant's compliance with pre-arbitral ADR is final and cannot be reviewed by the court. As a result, the controversy whether amicable solutions were duly pursued or not cannot serve as a ground to challenge the otherwise final award. **5.23**

The jurisdiction theory, as an interpretation based on the premise that jurisdiction can be conditional, is not applicable in litigation. Also the admissibility theory, understood as described above, does not directly translate into court proceedings. Although admissibility of the claim in arbitration is different to admissibility in litigation, certain authors dealing with ADR in arbitration refer to domestic concepts of admissibility rooted in court proceedings.[18] Most prominently, non-compliance with ADR clauses in litigation has been treated as a matter affecting admissibility in France and Germany (*irrecevabilité, Unzulässigkeit*). **5.24**

Clauses Containing a Time-bar

The second category of multi-tiered mechanisms entails clauses containing a time-bar restricting the dispute resolution process. This group is not homogenous. Taking guidance from English law, where limitation of time by contract is a well-established institution of arbitration law, the following two categories of clauses must be distinguished: clauses constituting a bar to the claim itself, and those establishing a bar to pursuit of any remedy in arbitration.[19] **5.25**

Clauses Prescribing a Bar to the Claim

Clauses providing for a bar to the claim after expiry of an agreed period are common in multi-tiered dispute resolution mechanisms in construction contracts. They prescribe a duty to notify the claim to the Engineer (or a person performing a similar function) in a timely manner, otherwise the claim is extinguished. Such mechanism is contained, for example, in clause 61.3 of the NEC3 English model contract for construction, as well as in clause 20.1 of the internationally applied FIDIC Forms of Contract. Clause 61.3 NEC3 stipulates that 'if the Contractor does not notify a compensation event within eight weeks of becoming aware of the **5.26**

[18] B Berger, F Kellerhals, *International and Domestic Arbitration in Switzerland*, 3rd edn (Stämpfli Publishers/Hart Publishing/ C.H. Beck/ Manz, 2015) para 1163 ('Most conditions of admissibility and pleas of lack of admissibility are indeed the same in arbitration as in state court litigation'). See also G Born, *International Commercial Arbitration*, 2nd edn (Kluwer Law International, 2014) 930, fn 1564; M Pryles, 'Multi-Tiered Dispute Resolution Clauses' (2001) 18 *Journal of International Arbitration* 159; F Fabian, 'The Enforceability of Mediation Clauses—the Approach of English and German Courts and ICC Arbitral Tribunals' (2005) 5 *SchiedsVZ* 250; A Jolles, 'Consequences of Multi-Tier Arbitration Clauses: Issues of Enforcement' (2006) 72 *Arbitration* 329; C Boog, 'How to Deal with Multi-Tiered Dispute Resolution Clauses', n 4 above, 103ff; B Cremades, 'Multi-Tiered Dispute Resolution Clauses' (CPR Institute for Dispute Resolution, 2004) 1ff.

[19] R Merkin, L Flannery, *Arbitration Law* (LLP, 2004) paras 13.18–13.27. M Mustill and S Boyd, *Commercial Arbitration*, 2nd edn (Butterworths, 1989) 202–4. On this topic see also 2.72ff.

event, he is not entitled to a change in the Price, the Completion Date or a Key Date.' Clause 20.1 FIDIC contains a similar mechanism, under which

> if the Contractor fails to give notice of a claim within such period of 28 days, the Time for Completion shall not be extended, the Contractor shall not be entitled to additional payment, and the Employer shall be discharged from all liability in connection with the claim.

5.27 The consequences of non-compliance with expert determination clauses containing a time-bar to the claim can be two-fold. They depend on whether the time-period for submission of the dispute to an expert is still running or has elapsed.

Before the Lapse of the Prescribed Time

5.28 In this type of situation the time-period for notification and submission of the claim is still running and exhaustion of the agreed ADR process is possible. Non-compliance with the expert determination procedure bears the same consequence as in the case of clauses not containing the time-bar. Consequently, premature filing of the claim in court or arbitration will be dealt with in accordance with the accepted approach of applicable law. In arbitration the tribunal may follow the jurisdiction or admissibility theory. In litigation the matter will be governed by the domestic rules applicable to breach of expert determination clauses.

After the Lapse of the Prescribed Time

5.29 The second type of situation involves cases where the time-period for notification and submission of the dispute has elapsed. Here the consequences of filing the claim in court or arbitration without first exhausting the expert's procedure is a matter concerning the operation of time-bar clauses under applicable law. This type of situation does not engage the enforceability of ADR clauses per se; instead, it concerns the effects of the limitation of time by contract under the relevant jurisdiction. If limitation of time by contract is permissible under the applicable law, lapse of the prescribed period results in the claim being extinguished. In such a case the arbitral tribunal can only dismiss the claim on the merits, as the entitlement sought is time-barred. The court would analyse this matter in the same way, by examining the enforceability of a time-bar provision under applicable law.

Clauses Prescribing a Bar to the Remedy

5.30 The second type of contractual time-bar can only be found in arbitration agreements, as it restricts the right to have the claims heard in arbitration.[20] Here expiry of the prescribed time-limit only prevents the claim from being heard in arbitration, instead of extinguishing it entirely. If the clause bars the claimant's right to go to arbitration, he remains entitled to pursue his claim in court proceedings.

[20] Consequently, this type of time-bar does not relate to litigation. See 5.39 below.

Conversely, pursuing the claim in arbitration despite the expiry of the time-limit will result in the tribunal refusing jurisdiction to hear the case.

An example of a clause restricting a party's right to pursue a remedy in arbitration is contained in 20.4 FIDIC. The time-limit introduced by this clause is connected with serving a notice of dissatisfaction with the dispute board's decision. It provides that neither party shall be entitled to commence arbitration of a dispute unless a notice of dissatisfaction has been given within 28 days after receiving the decision. The clause further stipulates that if no notice of dissatisfaction has been given by either party within 28 days after it received the decision, the decision becomes final and binding upon both parties. **5.31**

As with the 'bar to the claim' type of clause, two situations must be distinguished. The first is the situation where the contractual time-period has not begun or is still running. Here the prescribed ADR procedure has yet to be exhausted in accordance with the contract and the claimant can undertake the agreed steps. The second situation is when the contractual time-limit has expired, the claimant failed to fulfil the necessary steps preceding arbitration, but he files the claim in arbitration notwithstanding the time-bar. **5.32**

Before the Lapse of the Prescribed Time

Before the expiry of the contractual time-bar the ADR procedure is able to be carried out in accordance with the contract and the time-limit to bring a claim in arbitration can still be observed. Taking clause 20.4 FIDIC as an example, this group of situations encompasses commencing arbitration without first obtaining the dispute board's decision (when the time-period for notice of dissatisfaction has not started running) or before the notice of dissatisfaction has been given (when the time-period is still open). In this group of situations the effects of the time-bar have not yet materialised; therefore, premature filing of the claim in arbitration should be treated as a normal breach of an ADR clause. Consequently, two general routes are possible: the arbitrators may consider the breach as having consequences for either the jurisdiction of the tribunal, or the admissibility of the claim. **5.33**

A secondary issue is what the state court's reaction should be if the claimant brings an action in court in contravention of the agreed ADR process and an arbitration clause. As previously, the answer to this question depends on which of the possible interpretations one adopts: the jurisdiction theory (in its qualified or full version); or the admissibility theory. Under the full jurisdiction theory the court would not be empowered to refuse to hear the case. This is because in this interpretation an arbitration clause is seen as conditional upon fulfilment of the agreed ADR steps. Until the contractual process is exhausted, an arbitration clause is of no effect in both positive and negative senses; therefore, the default authority of the courts is retained. Under the qualified jurisdiction theory the court would refuse to hear the case due to the existence of an arbitration clause, notwithstanding its positive **5.34** effects being activated only upon exhaustion of the contractual ADR process (as under section 9(2) of the English Arbitration Act 1996). Consequently, until the fulfilment of ADR, neither court, nor arbitral tribunal would be empowered to hear the case. Under the admissibility theory the court would refuse to hear the case in favour of arbitration due to a valid free-standing arbitration clause. The tribunal would acquire jurisdiction; hence, the negative jurisdictional conflict would not arise, and it would declare the claim temporarily inadmissible.

After the Lapse of the Prescribed Time

5.35 The second category of cases entails situations where the prescribed time restricting the parties' right to pursue claims in arbitration has expired. The tribunal confronted with a claim should in such circumstances deny jurisdiction. In this group of situations it is the time-bar provision that is being enforced, not an ADR clause itself. Looking at sub-clause 20.4 FIDIC, this situation would arise if a party, having obtained the dispute board's decision on a contentious matter, fails to give notice of dissatisfaction in a timely manner but challenges the decision in arbitration regardless of the expiry of the time-limit for doing so.

5.36 It must be underlined that in the above circumstances the jurisdictional consequences of the party's default are a result of the clear wording of a time-bar clause to this effect. The tribunal lacks jurisdiction not because an ADR clause is enforced, but due to the contractual time-bar restricting its competence. This situation must be distinguished from the jurisdiction theory governing the effects of ADR clauses without a time-bar. Here lack of jurisdiction on the part of the tribunal to entertain the claim after the expiry of contractual time-limit does not imply the undesirable effects connected with the jurisdiction theory, set out earlier in this work.[21]

5.37 After lapse of the contractual period the right to pursue the claim in arbitration is barred, but the claim itself remains valid and can be enforced in court. However, in a typical multi-tiered clause containing a time-bar, losing the right arbitrate is supplemented by provisions establishing the finality of the decision obtained at the earlier stage of the escalation ladder. In sub-clause 20.4 FIDIC the parties' failure to take steps aimed at challenging the dispute board's decision within the prescribed 28-day period results in it becoming final and binding. The tribunal's denial of jurisdiction in such circumstances does not open a possibility for the party to have the decision reviewed by the court.

5.38 In sum, this type of clause ascribes exclusive competence to hear challenges to dispute boards' decisions to the arbitral tribunal. A full review of the dispute can only be entertained in arbitration. This right is, however, limited in time. Failure to challenge the decision precludes any further jurisdiction of the arbitral tribunal and renders the decision final. In such circumstances even if the claimant initiates

[21] See 4.39ff.

court proceedings, he will not obtain a full review of the dispute. According to the contract the parties agreed to be bound by the dispute board's decision, and the court can only confirm its binding force.

Owing to a different source of jurisdiction, a 'bar to remedy' type of clause is not applicable to litigation. Parties cannot contractually oust the jurisdiction of the courts or limit their jurisdiction in time. The extent of such clauses in arbitration rests on the premise that once the right to pursue a claim in arbitration becomes time-barred the default authority of the courts automatically revives. Because litigation plays the role of a default adjudicative system, access to which must be guaranteed, the right to assert the claim in litigation cannot be barred. **5.39**

Consequences of Non-compliance with Various Tiers of Clause 20 of the FIDIC Conditions of Contract for Construction

The first tier of the dispute resolution mechanism provided for in clause 20 of the FIDIC Conditions involves first, the party's notification of a claim and secondly, determination of it by an Engineer: **5.40**

> 20.1: If the Contractor considers himself to be entitled to any extension of the Time for Completion and/or any additional payment, under any Clause of these Conditions or otherwise in connection with the Contract, the Contractor shall give notice to the Engineer, describing the event or circumstance giving rise to the claim. The notice shall be given as soon as practicable, and not later than 28 days after the Contractor became aware, or should have become aware, of the event or circumstance …
>
> If the Contractor fails to give notice of a claim within such period of 28 days, the Time for Completion shall not be extended, the Contractor shall not be entitled to additional payment, and the Employer shall be discharged from all liability in connection with the claim …
>
> The Engineer shall proceed in accordance with Sub-Clause 3.5 [Determinations] to agree or determine
>
> (i) the extension (if any) of the Time for Completion (before or after its expiry) in accordance with Sub-Clause 8.4 [Extension of Time for Completion], and/or
> (ii) the additional payment (if any) to which the Contractor is entitled under the Contract.

Failure to notify of an entitlement within the prescribed time extinguishes the claim. Commencing arbitration would, in such circumstances, result in dismissal of the action due to the claim having extinguished. If the time to notify the claim has not expired yet, bringing a premature claim in arbitration would result in the tribunal ether denying jurisdiction, or declaring the claim inadmissible. **5.41**

5.42 If the claimant initiated litigation in contravention of the entire dispute resolution mechanism, the court, applying either the qualified jurisdiction theory or the admissibility theory, could refuse to hear the case due to an arbitration clause in the contract. Under the full jurisdiction theory the consequences of a premature claim in court are uncertain. There seem to be no grounds for the court to refuse to hear the case, if an arbitration clause is to be fully conditional upon exhaustion of ADR steps.

5.43 The second tier of the dispute resolution mechanism is triggered by a party dissatisfied with the decision of the Engineer. It requires that party to submit the dispute to the dispute board:

> 20.2: Disputes shall be referred to a DB for decision in accordance with Sub-Clause 20.4 [Obtaining Dispute Board's Decision] …
>
> 20.4: If a dispute (of any kind whatsoever) arises between the Parties in connection with, or arising out of, the Contract or the execution of the Works, including any dispute as to any certificate, determination, instruction, opinion or valuation of the Engineer, either Party may refer the dispute in writing to the DB for its decision, with copies to the other Party and the Engineer. Such reference shall state that it is given under this Sub-Clause …

5.44 Failure to submit the dispute to the dispute board has similar consequences to those connected with violation of the first tier before the Engineer. If a party initiates arbitration without obtaining the board's decision the tribunal could deny jurisdiction or declare the claim inadmissible.

5.45 If the party initiates court proceedings instead of submitting the dispute to the dispute board in accordance with the contract, the court could deny jurisdiction due to an arbitration clause being in place (under the qualified jurisdiction theory and admissibility theory). Alternatively, under the full jurisdiction theory, according to which the effects of an arbitration clause are not triggered until compliance with pre-arbitral ADR steps, the court would not be empowered to refuse to hear the case. In such circumstances, however, the claim should be dismissed and the final and binding nature of the Engineer's determination should be confirmed, as provided by the contract. This is because failure to challenge the Engineer's determination before the dispute board in accordance with clause 20 obligesthe parties to comply with the decision (sub-clause 3.5: 'Each Party shall give effect to each agreement or determination unless and until revised under Clause 20 [Claims, Disputes and Arbitration]').

5.46 The third tier of the escalation mechanism provided for in clause 20 FIDIC requires the party dissatisfied with the board's decision to notify the other party of its dissatisfaction and intention to commence arbitration:

> 20.4: If either Party is dissatisfied with the DB's decision, then either Party may, within 28 days after receiving the decision, give notice to the other Party of its dissatisfaction and intention to commence arbitration …
>
> Except as stated in Sub-Clause 20.7 [Failure to Comply with Dispute Board's Decision] and Sub-Clause 20.8 [Expiry of Dispute Board's Appointment], neither Party shall be

> entitled to commence arbitration of a dispute unless a notice of dissatisfaction has been given in accordance with this Sub-Clause …
>
> If the DB has given its decision as to a matter in dispute to both Parties, and no notice of dissatisfaction has been given by either Party within 28 days after it received the DB's decision, then the decision shall become final and binding upon both Parties.

The notice of dissatisfaction with the dispute board's decision must be given within the prescribed time; otherwise the party will lose its entitlement to have the dispute reviewed by the arbitral tribunal. Sub-clause 20.4 contains the second type of time-bar provision constituting a bar to the claim being heard in the contractual forum. The consequences of the expiry of the contractual time-limit are two-fold. First, the jurisdiction of the tribunal is eliminated. Secondly, the dispute board's decision becomes final and binding. **5.47**

Initiating arbitration without first giving a valid notice of dissatisfaction to the other party results in the tribunal's forfeiting jurisdiction, if the time-limit for serving such a notice has expired. Loss of arbitral jurisdiction revives the normal authority of the courts. However, if the dissatisfied party seeks to then challenge the board's determination in court, the court cannot review it. Instead, it should confirm the contractually binding nature of the board's determination. Conversely, the party satisfied with the decision, which became final and binding, can directly refer to arbitration the other party's failure to comply with its terms (sub-clause 20.7). **5.48**

If the time to serve a notice of dissatisfaction is still running, and a party initiates arbitral proceedings within this period, the tribunal should deny jurisdiction due to the clear contractual provision to this effect. Under the unambiguous wording of sub-clause 20.4 the right to have claims heard in arbitration arises only if a valid notice of dissatisfaction has been given. Bringing a claim in court while the time-period for notice is still running poses certain difficulties. Theoretically, forfeiture of a tribunal's jurisdiction triggers the authority of the courts. At the same time the decision is not yet final and binding and it will only become binding after the expiry of a 28-day period from its receipt. It seems justified for the court to refrain from reviewing the decision in this period due to the objective of clause 20, under which the parties selected arbitration as the forum empowered to hear challenges to dispute boards' determinations. In practice, however, the time in which the court could potentially review the decision is too short to for it to be a significant concern. **5.49**

The fourth tier of the dispute resolution procedure under clause 20 FIDIC involves a 'cooling off' period: **5.50**

> 20.5: Where notice of dissatisfaction has been given under Sub-Clause 20.4 above, both Parties shall attempt to settle the dispute amicably before the commencement of arbitration. However, unless both Parties agree otherwise, arbitration may be commenced on or after the fifty-sixth day after the day on which a notice of dissatisfaction and intention to commence arbitration was given, even if no attempt at amicable settlement has been made.

5.51 This stage of the dispute resolution process is designed to provide a framework for the parties to explore settlement options. It occurs after a party dissatisfied with the dispute board's decision has notified the other party of its dissatisfaction and its intention to commence arbitration. Sub-clause 20.5 provides the time-frame within which settlement negotiations can take place. Arbitration can only be commenced after expiry of the prescribed period, regardless of whether the parties in fact negotiate. Sub-clause 20.5 does not compel the parties to undertake friendly discussions aimed at reaching settlement, which could be seen as contrary to the consensual nature of the process and potentially unenforceable. By providing for a clear time-frame, sub-clause 20.5 leaves no ambiguity as to the moment at which the parties may proceed to the next tier of the dispute resolution mechanism.

5.52 Bypassing this tier and filing the claim in arbitration prematurely may result in either denial of jurisdiction by the tribunal, or inadmissibility of the claim. Alternatively, if the party files a claim in court while the time to undertake negotiations is still running, the court can refuse to hear the case due to an arbitration clause being the last tier of clause 20 FIDIC. This consequence would be adopted, first, under the admissibility theory, where arbitration clauses are separate from ADR clauses and effective from the time of their conclusion. Secondly, the court would refuse jurisdiction in favour of arbitration under the qualified jurisdiction theory, according to which the negative effect of an arbitration clause continues notwithstanding the party's duty to exhaust pre-arbitral ADR.

5.53 The fifth tier of the dispute resolution mechanism contained in clause 20 FIDIC involves arbitration:

> 20.6: Unless settled amicably, any dispute in respect of which the DB's decision (if any) has not become final and binding shall be finally settled by international arbitration. Unless otherwise agreed by both Parties:
>
> (a) arbitration proceedings shall be conducted as stated in the Particular Conditions,
> (b) if no arbitration proceedings are so stated, the dispute shall be finally settled by institutional arbitration under the Rules of Arbitration of the International Chamber of Commerce,
> (c) the dispute shall be settled by three arbitrators, and
> (d) the arbitration shall be conducted in the language for communications defined in Sub-Clause 1.4 [Law and Language].
>
> The arbitrators shall have full power to open up, review and revise any certificate, determination, instruction, opinion or valuation of the Engineer, and any decision of the DB, relevant to the dispute.

5.54 Failure to observe this step by initiating proceedings in court, instead of arbitration, engages the domestic rules governing the enforceability of arbitration clauses.[22]

[22] See also Art II(3), New York Convention 1958.

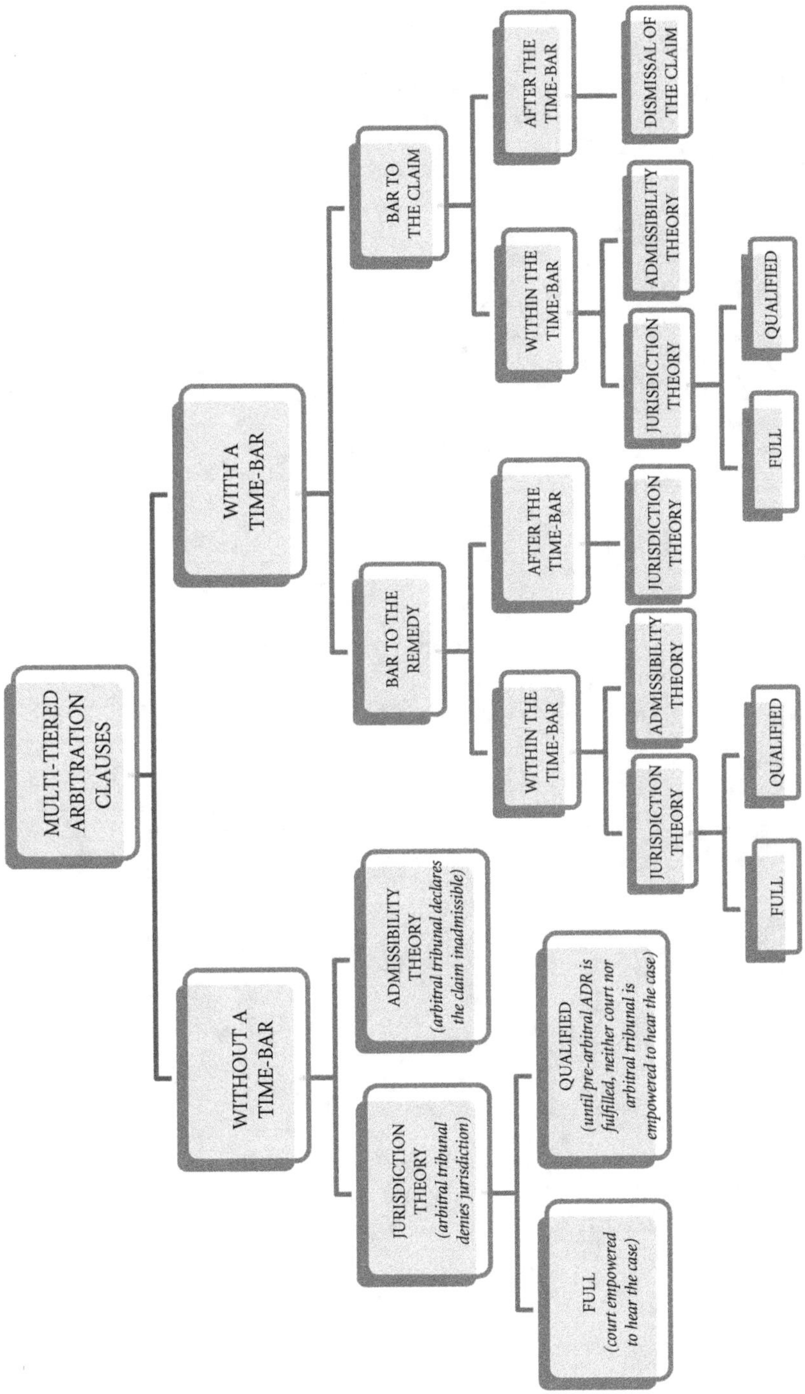
MULTI-TIERED ARBITRATION CLAUSES
WITH A TIME-BAR
WITHOUT A TIME-BAR
BAR TO THE CLAIM
BAR TO THE REMEDY
AFTER THE TIME-BAR
WITHIN THE TIME-BAR
DISMISSAL OF THE CLAIM
ADMISSIBILITY THEORY
JURISDICTION THEORY
QUALIFIED
FULL
AFTER THE TIME-BAR
JURISDICTION THEORY
WITHIN THE TIME-BAR
ADMISSIBILITY THEORY
JURISDICTION THEORY
QUALIFIED
FULL
ADMISSIBILITY THEORY (arbitral tribunal declares the claim inadmissible)
JURISDICTION THEORY (arbitral tribunal denies jurisdiction)
QUALIFIED (until pre-arbitral ADR is fulfilled, neither court nor arbitral tribunal is empowered to hear the case)
FULL (court empowered to hear the case)

6

Drafting Enforceable Multi-tiered Dispute Resolution Clauses

SUMMARY

This final chapter contains conclusions relating to drafting enforceable multi-tiered dispute resolution mechanisms. Insufficient standardisation and institutionalisation of ADR creates significant challenges in this regard.[1] The factors that should be taken into account include the requirements relevant under an applicable legal system in relation to each ADR tier. The parties should also carefully draft the provisions affecting the multi-level mechanism as a whole, focusing particular attention to the transition between particular levels of the dispute resolution ladder. The following aspects are emphasised:

(i) precise wording of a clause leaving no scope for ambiguity as to a mandatory character of each tier (6.1);
(ii) detailed provisions exhaustively regulating each ADR clause comprising the escalation mechanism (6.2ff);
(iii) a time-frame for each of the selected ADR processes (6.6–6.7);
(iv) clear provisions relating to the scope and effects of the decisions reached in quasi-adjudicative ADR (6.8–6.9);
(v) consequences of non-compliance with each ADR tier (6.11);
(vi) requirements under the local law such as a waiver of a limitation plea and availability of interim measures during the ADR phase of the dispute resolution process (6.12–6.13).

CONTENTS

[1] J Carter, 'Issues Arising from Integrated Dispute Resolution Clauses' in AJ van den Berg (ed), *New Horizons in International Commercial Arbitration and Beyond. ICCA Congress Series 2004* (Kluwer International, 2005) 446, 447.

Mandatory Language

6.1 An ADR clause must be mandatory if it is to be legally enforceable or valid.[2] If the wording of an ADR provision is vague it leaves scope to conclude that the clause is merely an invitation to participate in a process, rather than an enforceable obligation. Imprecise clauses are likely to be ignored by the party bringing the claim, and considered unenforceable by the court or arbitral tribunal. In addition, if ADR is integrated into an arbitration framework, flawed formulation of an ADR tier may pollute the entire arbitration clause, rendering arbitration unavailable.[3] To mitigate the risk of unenforceability of the agreed mechanism each component of a multi-tiered clause should provide that the dispute *shall* or *will* be referred to the agreed process. Permissive formulation saying that the dispute *may* be referred to a selected ADR procedure should be avoided, as it creates scope for ambiguity as to the parties' intentions.

Detailed Content

6.2 Precise description of the processes comprising a multi-tiered mechanism is fundamental to the enforceability of escalation clauses.[4] The content of the relevant provisions will differ for consensual and quasi-adjudicative ADR components.

Mediation and Negotiations Clauses

6.3 Contracting for consensual ADR may involve particular risks associated with a strict approach to the enforceability of such clauses adopted in certain jurisdictions.

[2] T Varady, 'The Courtesy Trap Arbitration "If No Amicable Settlement Can Be Reached"' (1997) 14(4) *Journal of International Arbitration* 5ff; J Carter, 'Issues Arising from Integrated Dispute Resolution Clauses', n 1 above, 454–55. See also *Sulamerica Cia Nacional De Seguros SA and others v Enesa Engenharia SA and others* [2012] EWCA Civ 638.

[3] Under the jurisdiction theory (see eg Swiss decision in *Vekoma v Maran* Bundesgericht, I. Zivilabteilung, 17 August 1995, (1996) 14 *ASA Bulletin* 673), criticised in this work (4.39ff).

[4] K Mackie, D Miles, W Marsh, T Allen, *The ADR Practice Guide* (Tottel Publishing, 2009) 153ff; J Kendall, C Freedman, J Farrell, *Expert Determination*, 5th edn (Sweet & Maxwell, 2015) paras 7.3.1ff; J Jenkins, *Construction Law Arbitration*, 2nd edn (Wolters Kluwer, 2014) 63–64.

In some legal traditions consensual ADR is treated as inherently voluntary and unenforceable,[5] in others a very high standard of preciseness of the relevant clauses is adopted.[6] English courts in particular are reluctant to imply terms into incomplete clauses.[7] In order to address this risk the parties to multi-tiered clauses should include detailed provisions as to the mediation or negotiation process required or select a recognised ADR provider offering a set of detailed rules governing the conduct of mediation.

The following factors should be considered when drafting mediation or negotiation agreements: **6.4**

(i) The clause must clearly prescribe the agreed process. The selection of the particular process after the dispute has arisen cannot be left to subsequent agreement by the parties.

(ii) If a mediation clause is agreed, the procedure for an appointment of a mediator must be spelled out. The parties may provide for a tailor-made procedure, in which case the clause should specify the consequences of lack of cooperation by the other party in the appointment. Alternatively, an ADR organisation can be used to nominate or appoint a mediator. The identity or discipline of the neutral person can be specified.

(iii) The clause should contain detailed provisions defining the scope of the duty to attempt mediation or negotiations. The clause should make clear when the parties will be considered as having fulfilled the duty to mediate (eg by presenting mediator with the case and participating in the first session). When delineating the minimum standard of compliance, the parties should avoid too onerous obligations, which could be regarded as violating the voluntary nature of the process, and therefore considered unenforceable.

(iv) The clause should specify which representatives of the parties are to take part in mediation or negotiations for the agreed step to be considered exhausted.

(v) The clause should contain details regarding the conduct of the ADR procedure. In particular it should provide for a detailed timetable for compliance with specific stages of the process (eg appointment of a mediator, exchange of case summaries etc).

(vi) To avoid ambiguity, the clause should stipulate that submission to the court or arbitral tribunal is not permitted during the conduct of mediation or negotiations.

[5] See 2.228 on Swiss law, where clauses providing for consensual ADR methods are unenforceable in litigation.

[6] See 2.40ff on the English discussion.

[7] *Holloway v Chancery Mead Ltd* [2007] EWHC 2495 (TCC).

(vii) The clause should stipulate how the costs of the ADR process will be apportioned. The clause should also include a provision dealing with the situation where one party refuses to pay the fee due.

(viii) The clause should specify the law applicable to the escalation mechanism.[8]

Expert Determination and Dispute Board Clauses

6.5 Precise formulation of expert determination and dispute board provisions is central to the effectiveness of tiered dispute resolution mechanisms. In England expert determination clauses are an established concept of contract law; hence certain basic terms will be implied by the courts (eg a term that an expert must act fairly or a term that the parties are required to cooperate in enabling the expert determination to be performed). In other systems, expert determination does not benefit from a broad legal framework and the effectiveness of the agreed mechanism relies solely on the provisions of the clause in question. In any case expert determination clauses should exhaustively set out the agreed process in detail. The following elements of expert determination and dispute board clauses should be taken into account:

(i) The clause should clarify that an expert (dispute board) is not an arbitrator (arbitration tribunal). The clause may contain a provision that the expert (dispute board members) should be independent.

(ii) The clause should set out the issue to be determined by an expert (dispute board). Particular care is needed when the contract provides that only certain types of claims must be submitted for expert determination. Ambiguity in this respect may lead to satellite disputes about whether expert determination is the correct procedure for the referral, and prevent the operation of the tiered mechanism.

(iii) The clause should specify the effect of the decision (see also Section 4 below).

(iv) The clause should contain a procedure for appointment of an expert (members of a dispute board) and their requisite qualifications. The appointment may be by agreement or by a professional body. In case of the former, the clause should contain provisions dealing with the other party's refusal to

[8] Failure to address this issue may lead to uncertainty. See the judgment of the Swiss *Bundesgericht* of 7 July 2014, (BGer4A_124/2014, available at: www.swissarbitrationdecisions.com/sites/default/files/7%20juillet%202014%204A%20124%202014.pdf) where it was decided that, in the absence of the parties' agreement to the contrary, law applicable to the arbitration clause governs the entire escalation mechanism. Cf the English decision in *Sulamerica Cia Nacional De Seguros SA and others v Enesa Engenharia SA and others* [2012] EWCA Civ 638 (CA) where it was held that in such circumstances the mediation and arbitration clause can be governed by different legal systems. On this aspect see 4.94 above.

cooperate and agree to the terms of appointment.[9] In case of the latter, the clause should not contain a requirement that an application to the appointing authority must be made jointly by the parties. In order to avoid the risk of one party obstructing the reference, the clause should set out in detail the terms of engagement and state that the parties agree to be bound by the decisions under such terms.

(i) The clause should set out the required qualifications of an expert (members of the dispute board).

(ii) The clause should specify whether the expert (dispute board) is empowered to award interest or costs.

(iii) The clause should specify whether the expert (members of a dispute board) will be barred from acting as witnesses in subsequent arbitral or court proceedings.

(iv) If no standard rules are adopted, the clause should set out the procedure for reference. This includes whether the parties have a right to make representations or submissions, and if yes, time limits by which the representations or submissions are to be made and other directions relating to the conduct of the procedure. The clause should also specify whether the parties can reverse their positions, and the consequences of raising precluded points. Alternatively, the parties may empower the expert (dispute board) to adopt an appropriate procedure. In such a case the expert (dispute board) will be able to vary the procedure in the way he thinks fit. If the parties require the expert (dispute board) to provide reasons for the decision, they should include a provision to this effect.

(v) The clause should clarify the extent of expert's (dispute board's) powers to ascertain or investigate the facts and law relating to the claim.

(vi) To avoid ambiguity, the clause should stipulate that submission to the court or arbitral tribunal is not permitted during the reference.

(vii) If the parties wish to restrict the reference to an expert (dispute board) to a specified time, they should contain time-bar provisions in their multi-tiered dispute resolution clause. In that case the clause should clearly specify the consequences of the lapse of the agreed time period.[10]

(viii) The clause should set out how remuneration of the expert (dispute board members) will be paid. The clause should also include a provision dealing with the situation where one party refuses to pay the fee due.

(xiii) In case of dispute boards, the clause should specify whether the panel is a standing body formed when the contract is entered into, or whether it will only be appointed once the dispute has arisen.

(xiv) To avoid ambiguity the clause should specify law applicable to the escalation mechanism.[11]

[9] The courts have no power to appoint experts.
[10] On the two types of consequences of time-bar provisions see 2.72ff, 5.25ff, 5.41 and 5.48.
[11] See text to n 8 above.

Time-scale for Each ADR Step

6.6 Providing for a time-scale for compliance with a given ADR step is relevant for both consensual and quasi-adjudicative ADR components of multi-tiered clauses. As far as mediation and negotiation clauses are concerned, including a time-period for settlement negotiations gives certainty as to when the relevant step can be considered exhausted, if the settlement attempt proves unsuccessful. The time-limit must be drafted with caution. First, it must clearly identify the starting point of the running of the agreed period. Ambiguity as to when the period commences may result in the court and the tribunal reaching different conclusions as to when the ADR phase should have been considered as exhausted. This may be fatal for a subsequent arbitral award.[12] Secondly, the parties should carefully select the length of the negotiation window. Providing for too long a period may lead to the unenforceability of the clause on grounds that the reference to ADR in accordance with the contract will unduly delay the proceedings.

6.7 Providing for a time-scale for the reference is also desirable in expert determination clauses. The parties should specify two issues. First, the clause should make clear whether the expert's (board's) failure to make the determination within the time-scale provided entitles the party to proceed to the next step of the dispute resolution mechanism. Secondly, the clause should make clear whether the determination made after the prescribed time-limit is binding on the parties. Such a stipulation would remove ambiguity as to whether a decision issued out of time has been made in accordance with the contract.

Effects of the Decision

6.8 Prescribing the effects of the outcome achieved in the agreed ADR process is relevant for clauses providing for quasi-adjudicative ADR (expert determination and dispute boards). These methods result in a neutral person (panel) issuing a decision whose binding force should be carefully identified in a multi-tiered clause.

6.9 The parties wishing to be bound by expert determination which is not reviewable in the subsequent dispute resolution process should include wording to the effect that the decision is final and binding. In this context 'final' means that the decision is not subject to review, and 'binding', that the parties are obliged to comply with the decision.[13]

[12] Under the jurisdiction theory (*Vekoma v Maran* Bundesgericht, I. Zivilabteilung, 17 August 1995, (1996) 14 *ASA Bulletin* 673), criticised in this work (4.39ff).

[13] *cf* in the context of finality of an arbitral award Gloster J's decision in *Shell Egypt West Manzala GmbH v Dana Gas Egypt Ltd* [2009] EWHC 2097 (Comm), on which *Andrews on Civil Processes. vol II: Arbitration & Mediation* (Intersentia, 2013) paras 3.39 and 18.97.

Semi-binding expert determination clauses are more challenging and require exhaustive drafting. In this model the parties agree to be bound by the decision unless and until it is finally reviewed in arbitration or litigation. The permissible scope for review must be precisely delineated and free from ambiguity. The parties should consider the following factors: 6.10

(i) The clause should clearly stipulate that the expert's (dispute board's) decision is binding unless reviewed in court or arbitration, or affected by an agreed settlement of the dispute.
(ii) The clause should contain a provision to the effect that the expert's (dispute board's) decision can be challenged by a dissatisfied party within a specified time. After the lapse of the prescribed time the decision shall become final and binding on the parties. Such a stipulation ensures that the party who disagrees with the decision cannot have it reviewed after a lapse of the prescribed time for challenge.
(iii) If arbitration is prescribed as the last tier of the dispute resolution mechanism, the clause should provide that non-compliance with the expert's (dispute board's) decision can be referred directly to arbitration without having to exhaust the multi-tiered process. This ensures that the party in whose favour the decision has been granted can benefit from an arbitration clause. The clause should also provide that a party who disagrees with the decision, loses the entitlement to have it reviewed in arbitration after a lapse of the prescribed time for challenge (see point (ii) above).
(iv) The parties may include a time-bar preventing reference to an expert after a specified time-period. The effect of the time-bar in such circumstances is extinguishment of a contractual right. If the parties desire to achieve this effect, the stipulation must be unambiguous as to there being no other means of establishing the right which is time-barred and, consequently, extinguished. The drafters should consider the risk of unenforceability of such time-bar provisions in those civil law jurisdictions which prohibit altering the statutory limitation periods by contract or provide that the statutory time-limits cannot be waived in advance.[14]

Consequences of Non-compliance

The parties may describe the consequences of failure to comply with the agreed ADR procedure.[15] The available options include: 6.11

(i) *Liquidated damages*. The parties to multi-tiered clauses may secure compliance with the agreed ADR step by providing for liquidated damages as a

[14] See eg Art 141(1), Swiss Code of Obligations; Art 119, Polish Civil Code.

[15] See general observations in C Boog, 'How to Deal with Multi-Tiered Dispute Resolution Clauses Clauses—Note—June 2007—Swiss Federal Supreme Court' (2008) 26 *ASA Bulletin* 103, 111;

sanction for premature filing of the claim. This stipulation poses difficulties in those legal systems which follow the penalty doctrine, according to which the clause is unenforceable unless it contains a proportionate estimation of loss.[16]

(ii) *Indemnity*. Providing for indemnity against any loss arising from a failure to comply with an ADR clause allows the parties to avoid difficulties associated with penalty clauses. However, as a promise to reimburse for any cost associated with the other party ignoring an ADR clause, it exposes the parties to uncertainty due to the unquantifiable extent of loss arising from such default.

(iii) *Specific procedural and substantive consequences*. The parties may include specific provisions determining the procedural consequences of non-compliance with prescribed ADR steps. The most common stipulation of this kind is a provision to the effect that, unless the relevant step is complied with in accordance with the clause, an arbitral tribunal will not have jurisdiction to hear the case. If the clause provides for such a consequence, it typically also envisages further substantive implications of the party's failure to adhere to the prescribed framework. These include an expert's decision obtained at an earlier stage of the process becoming final and binding. The parties will include such a provision if their intention is that expert determination is only reviewable in arbitration and can only be challenged within a specified time-period. This option is commonly utilised in multi-tiered clauses in construction contracts.[17]

Availability of Interim Measures

6.12 Prior to commencement of the escalation dispute resolution process it may be necessary for a party to seek interim relief. In many legal systems both the arbitral tribunal and the courts have concurrent jurisdiction to order interim measures. The duty to fulfil certain ADR steps prior to final adjudication should not preclude access to interim relief. In order to avoid ambiguity as to whether resort to interim measures is permissible before exhausting a contractual ADR procedure, the parties should include express provisions to that effect.

D Jiménez-Figueres, 'Multi-Tiered Dispute Resolution Clauses in ICC Arbitration' (2003) 14 *ICC International Court of Arbitration Bulletin* 82, 93–94.

[16] See 2.38 and 3.72–3.75 on the English position.
[17] See 4.67ff for details.

Waiver of a Limitation Plea

In some legal systems a statutory limitation period is neither stayed nor suspended by the commencement of an ADR procedure.[18] In consequence, it is possible for the claim to become time-barred during the conduct of an ADR procedure. In order to avoid this consequence the parties to multi-tiered clauses should include a provision obliging them to waive their right to rely on the statute of limitation for the duration of ADR. 6.13

Summary

Flawed drafting is the main enemy of multi-tiered dispute resolution clauses. As the uniform law of ADR is in its formative stages, the responsibility for the enforceability of the agreed dispute resolution mechanisms largely lies on the parties. Although precise and detailed drafting is required if multi-tiered provisions are to be effective, or even simply legally valid (see 2.4ff), commercial parties tend not to give this topic appropriate attention. The result is that dispute-resolution clauses are often left to be negotiated as the last aspect of the deal, or simply included as mechanical and unexamined 'boiler-plate'.[19] This creates uncertainty as to the enforceability of contractual dispute resolution mechanisms. The risk is greater if a tiered clause is likely to be scrutinised within two or more legal systems and by different adjudicative bodies. 6.14

The current approach to drafting multi-tiered dispute resolution mechanisms, characterised by neglect and lack of cooperation between transactional and contentious limbs of legal practices, is counterproductive. As remarked by Charles Debatista, 'These clauses are intended by commercial parties to assist them in resolving existing disputes, not to raise another dispute as to how to resolve those disputes.'[20] Without a change in the traditional attitude to drafting dispute resolution provisions, the effectiveness of proper conflict management will continue to be compromised. 6.15

[18] See 2.253–2.254 on Swiss law.

[19] Dispute resolution provisions are sometimes referred to as 'midnight clauses'. See A Redfern, M Hunter, N Blackaby, C Partasides, *Redfern and Hunter on International Arbitration*, 6th edn (OUP, 2015) para 2.04.

[20] C Debatista, 'Drafting Enforceable Arbitration Clauses' (2005) 21 *Arbitration International* 233, 240.

BIBLIOGRAPHY

Abrams, Pamela, Goriely, Tamara, Moorhead, Richard, *More Civil Justice? The Impact of the Woolf Reforms on Pre-Action Behaviour* (Law Society and Civil Justice Council, 2001).

Acker, Wendelin, Konopka, Silvia, 'Schiedsgutachten im Bau- und Anlagenbauvertrag: Grenzen und Möglichkeiten' (2003) 6 *SchiedsVZ* 256.

Alexander, Nadja (ed), *Global Trends in Mediation* (Kluwer Law International, 2006).

Alexander, Nadja, *International Comparative Mediation: Legal Perspectives* (Wolters Kluwer, 2009).

Allen, Tony, Mackie, Karl, Miles, David, Marsh, William, *The ADR Practice Guide* (Tottel Publishing, 2009).

—— *Mediation Law and Civil Practice* (Bloomsbury, 2013).

Andrews, Neil, 'The Duty to Consider Mediation: Salvaging Value from the European Mediation Directive' in N Trocker and A De Luca (eds), *La Mediazione Civile all Luce della Direttiva 2008/52/CE* (Firenze University Press, 2011).

—— *Andrews on Civil Processes. vol I* (Intersentia, 2013).

—— *Andrews on Civil Processes. vol II* (Intersentia, 2013).

—— *Contract Law* (CUP, 2011).

—— *English Civil Procedure. Fundamentals of the New Civil Justice System* (OUP, 2003).

—— *Modern Civil Process* (Mohr Siebeck, 2008).

—— 'A New Civil Procedural Code for England: Party-Control "Going, Going, Gone"' (2000) 19 *Civil Justice Quarterly* 19.

Arnaldez, Jean-Jacques, Derains, Yves, Hascher, Dominique, *Collection of ICC Arbitral Awards (Recueil des sentences arbitrales de la CCI) 2001–2007*, vol V (Wolters Kluwer, 2009).

Arnaldez, Jean-Jacques, Derains, Yves, Hascher, Dominique, *Collection of ICC Arbitral Awards (Recueil des sentences arbitrales de la CCI)* 1991–1995, vol 3 (Kluwer Law International, 1997).

Arntz, Thomas, *Eskalationklauseln. Recht und Praxis mehrstufiger Streiterledigungsklauseln* (Carl Heymanns Verlag, 2013).

Bailey, Julian, *Construction Law* (Informa Law, 2011).

Bamberger, Heintz, Roth, Herberth (eds), *Kommentar zur Bürgerlichen Gesetzbuch*, 3rd edn (CH Beck, 2012).

Baumbach, Adolf, Lauterbach, Wolfgang, Albers, Jan, Hartmann, Peter (eds), *Zivilprozessordnung mit FamFG, GVG und anderen Nebengesetzen*, 74th edn (CH Beck 2016).

Bean, David, *Injunctions*, 11th edn (Sweet & Maxwell, 2012).

Berger, Bernhard, Kellerhals, Franz, *International and Domestic Arbitration in Switzerland*, 3rd edn (Stämpfli Publishers/Hart Publishing/ C.H. Beck/ Manz, 2015).

Berger, Klaus Peter, *Private Dispute Resolution in International Business—Handbook*, vol II, 3rd edn (Wolters Kluwer, 2015).

—— 'Law and Practice of Escalation Clauses' (2006) 22 *Arbitration International* 1.

Berti, Stephen (ed), *International Arbitration in Switzerland. An Introduction and a Commentary on Articles 176–194 of the Swiss Private International Law Statute* (Kluwer Law International, 2000).

Berti, Stephen, *Introduction to Arbitration—Swiss and International Perspectives* (Helbing & Lichtenhahn, 1999).

Besson, Sébastien, Poudret, Jean-François, *Comparative Law of International Arbitration*, 2nd edn (Sweet & Maxwell, 2007).

Binder, Peter, *International Commercial Arbitration and Conciliation in UNCITRAL Model Law Jurisdictions*, 3rd edn (Sweet & Maxwell, 2010).

Böckstiegel, Karl-Heinz, Kröll, Stefan, Nacimiento, Patricia, *Arbitration in Germany* 2nd edn (Kluwer Law International, 2015).

Boog, Christopher, 'How to Deal with Multi-Tiered Dispute Resolution Clauses—Note—June 2007—Swiss Federal Supreme Court' (2008) 26 *ASA Bulletin* 103.

Born, Gary, *International Civil Litigation in United States Courts*, 3rd edn (Kluwer Law International, 1996).

—— *International Commercial Arbitration*, 2nd edn (Kluwer Law International, 2014).

Bösch, Peter, 'Der Nachbarstreit und dessen Beilegung, Mediation—ein neuer Weg' (1998) 94 *Schweizerische Juristen-Zeitung* 77.

de Bournonville, Philippe, *L'Arbitrage* (Larcier, 2000).

Boyd, Stewart, Mustill, Michael, *Commercial Arbitration*, 2nd edn (Butterworths, 1989).

—— *Commercial Arbitration. 2001 Companion Volume to the Second Edition* (Butterworths, 2001).

Brown, Henry, Marriott, Arthur, *ADR Principles and Practice*, 3rd edn (Sweet & Maxwell, 2011).

—— *ADR Principles and Practice*, 2nd edn (Sweet & Maxwell, 2009).

Brown-Berset, Dominique, 'La médiation commerciale: le géant s'éveille' (2002) 121 *Revue de Droit Suisse* 319.

Büchler, Michael, Webster, Thomas, *Handbook of ICC Arbitration*, 3rd edn (Sweet & Maxwell, 2014).

Bühring-Uhle, Christian, *Arbitration and Mediation in International Business*, 2nd edn (Kluwer Law International, 2006).

Bunni, Nael, *The FIDIC Forms of Contracts* (Blackwell Publishing, 2005).

Cadiet, Loïc, 'Panorama des modes alternatifs de règlement des conflits en droit français' (2011) 28 *Ritsumeikan Law Review* 147.

—— 'Conciliation in France: a Cross between Tradition and Modernity' in *The Recent Tendencies of Development in Civil Procedure Law—Between East and West* (Justitia, 2007).

Cadiet, Loïc, Normand, Jacques, Mekki Amrani, Soraya, *Théorie générale du procès* (Presses Universitaires de France, 2010).

Carbonneau, Thomas E, Jaeggi, Jeanette, Partridge, Sandra (eds), *Handbook on International Arbitration and ADR* (JurisNet, 2006).

Carter, James, 'Issues Arising from Integrated Dispute Resolution Clauses' in Albert Jan van den Berg (ed), *New Horizons in International Commercial Arbitration and Beyond. ICCA Congress Series 2004 Bejing12* (Kluwer International, 2005).

Chern, Cyril, *Chern on Dispute Boards*, 2nd edn (Wiley-Blackwell, 2011).

Chiarloni, Sergio, Gottwald, Peter, Zuckerman, Adrian (eds), *Civil Justice in Crisis. Comparative Perspectives of Civil Procedure* (OUP, 1999).
Chitty on Contracts, 32nd edn (Sweet & Maxwell, 2015).
Collins, Lawrence (ed), *Dicey, Morris, Collins on the Conflict of Laws*, vol I, 14th edn (Sweet & Maxwell, 2006).
Colman, Anthony, 'ADR: An Irreversible Tide' (2003) 19 *Arbitration International* 303.
Connerty, Anthony, 'The Role of ADR in the Resolution International Disputes' (1996) 12 *Arbitration International* 47.
Coulon, Jean-Marie, *Réflexions et propositions sur la procédure civile, Rapportau gardedes Sceaux* (Paris, Ministre de la Justice, 1997).
Craig, Laurence, Park, William, Paulsson, Jan, *International Chamber of Commerce Arbitration*, 3rd edn (Oceana Publications, 2000).
Cranston, Ross, Zuckerman, Adrian (ed), *Reform of Civil Procedure. Essays on 'Access to Justice'* (Clarendon Press, 1995).
Cranston, Ross, *How Law Works: The Machinery and Impact of Civil Justice* (OUP, 2006).
Cremades, Bernardo, 'Multi-tiered Dispute Resolution Clauses' (2003) 14 *ICC International Court of Arbitration Bulletin*, No 1 (CPR Institute for Dispute Resolution, 2004).
de Boisséson, Matthieu, de Juglart, Michel, Bellet, Pierre, *Le droit Français de l'arbitrage* (Gide, Loyrette, Nouel, 1983).
de López Argumedo Piñeiro, Alvaro, 'Multi-Step Dispute Resolution Clauses' in M Fernández-Ballesteros and David Arias (eds), *Liber Amicorum Bernardo Cremades* (La Ley, 2010).
Debatista, Charles, 'Drafting Enforceable Arbitration Clauses' (2005) 21 *Arbitration International* 233.
Delvolvé, Jean-Louis, Rouche, Jean, Pointon, Gerald, *French arbitration law and practice*, 2nd edn (Wolters Kluwer, 2009).
Demeyere, Luc, 'About Dispute Resolution and Conflict Management' (2003) 19 *Arbitration International* 313.
Derains, Yves, 'Expertise technique et référé arbitral' (1982) 3 *Revue de l'Arbitrage* 239.
Derains, Yves, Schwartz, Eric, *A Guide to ICC Rules of Arbitration*, 2nd edn (Kluwer Law International, 2005).
Dobbins, Robert, 'The Layered Dispute Resolution Clauses: from Boilerplate to Business Opportunity' (2005) 1 *Hastings Business Law Journal* 159.
Douglas, Zachary, *International Law of Investment Claims* (CUP, 2009).
Eidenmüller, Horst, 'A Legal Framework for National and International Mediation Proceedings' (2002) *Journal of International Dispute Resolution* 14, 16 (Beilage 7 Betriebs-Berater Heft 46/2002).
—— 'Vertrags- und verfahrensrechtliche Grundfragen der Mediation: Möglichkeiten und Grenzen privatautonomen Konfliktmanagements' in Breidenbach et al (eds), *Konsensuale Streibeilagung: akademisches Symposion zu Ehren von Peter F. Schlosser aus Anlass seines 65. Geburtstages* (Gieseking, 2001).
Einholzer, Heiner, *Die Streitbeilegungsabrede. Ein Beitrag zu altemativen Formen der Streitbeilegung, namentlich zur Mediation* (Universitätsverlag Freiburg, 1998).
Farrell, James, Freedman, Clive, Kendall, John, *Expert Determination*, 5th edn (Sweet & Maxwell, 2015).
Fentiman, Richard, *International Commercial Litigation*, 2nd edn (OUP, 2015).
File, Jason, 'United States: Multi-step dispute resolution clauses' (2007 July) *IBA Legal Practice Division Mediation Committee Newsletter* 33.

Fouchard, Philippe, Gaillard, Emmanuel, Goldman, Berthold, *Traité de l'arbitrage commercial international* (Litec, 1996).

Friedland, Paul, 'The Swiss Supreme Court Sets Aside an ICC Award' (1996) 13(1) *Journal of International Arbitration* 111.

Friedrich, Fabian, 'Schlichtungs- und Mediationsklauseln in Allgemeinen Geschäftsbedingungen' (2007) 1 *SchiedsVZ* 31.

—— 'The Enforceability of Mediation Clauses—the Approach of English and German Courts and ICC Arbitral Tribunals' (2005) 5 *SchiedsVZ* 250.

Furst, Stephen, Ramsey, Vivian (eds), *Keating on Construction Contracts*, 10th edn (Sweet & Maxwell, 2016).

Gaillard, Emmanuel, Savage, John (eds), *Fouchard, Gaillard, Goldman on International Commercial Arbitration* (Kluwer Law International, 1999) 25–29.

Gearing, Matthew, Gill, Judith, Sutton, David, *Russell on Arbitation*, 23rd edn (Sweet & Maxwell, 2007).

Gee, Steven, *Commercial Injunctions*, 6th edn (Sweet & Maxwell, 2016).

Geisinger, Elliott, Voser, Nathalie (eds), *International Arbitration in Switzerland. A Handbook for Practitioners*, 2nd edn (Wolters Kluwer, 2013).

Genn, Hazel, 'Understanding Civil Justice' (1997) 50 *Current Legal Problems* 155, 156.

Genton, Pierre, Schwab, Yves, 'The Role of the Engineer in Disputes Related More Specifically to Industrial Projects' (2000) 17(4) *Journal of International Arbitration* 1.

Ghestin, Jacques (ed), *Traité de droit civil* (Librairie Générale de Droit et de Jurisprudence, 1996).

Giles, Robert, 'Severability of Dispute Resolution Clauses in Contracts' (1994) 10 *Building and Construction Law* 393.

Gorchs-Gelzer, Béatrice, 'Regard critique sur l'ordonnance n° 2011-1540 transposant la directive médiation' (2012) 1/65 *Droit et procédures* 2.

Gould, Nicholas, 'NEC3: construction contract of the future?' (2008) 24 *Construction Law Journal* 286.

Greger, Reinhard, Stubbe, Christian, *Schiedsgutachten: aussergerichtliche Streitbeilegung durch Drittentscheidungen* (CH Beck, 2007).

Grenwood, Lucy, 'A Window of Opportunity? Building a Short Period of Time into Arbitral Rules in Order for Parties to Promote Settlement' (2011) 27 *Arbitration International* 199.

Guillaume-Hofnund, Michèle, *La Médiation* (Presses Universitaires de France, 2005).

Guinchard, Serge, Chainais, Cécile, Ferrand, Frédérique, *Procédure cvile. Droit interne et droit de l'Union européenne*, 30th edn (Dalloz, 2010).

Guinchard, Serge, *Droit et practique de la procédure civile* (Dalloz, 2004).

Guldener, Max, *Schweizerisches Zivilprozessrecht der Schweiz*, 3rd edn (Schulthess, 1979).

Habscheid, Edgar, 'Die aussergerichtliche Vermittlung (Mediation) als Rechtsverhältnis' (2001) 8 *Aktuelle Juristische Praxis* 938.

Habscheid, Walther, *Droit Judiciaire Privé Suisse*, 1st edn (Libraire de l'Université Georg et Cie SA, 1981).

—— 'L'Expertise-arbitrage' in Pieter Sanders (ed), *International Arbitration. Liber Amicorum for Martin Domke* (Martinus Nijhoff, 1967).

—— 'Das Scheidsgutachten. Ein Grenzgebiet zwischen materiallen Recht und Prozessrecht' in Hans Nipperdey (ed), *Das deutsche Privatrecht in der Mitte des 20. Jahrhunderts: Festschrift für Heinrich Lehmann zum 80. Geburtstag* (Tom II, W de Gruyte, 1956).

Hacke, Andreas, *Der ADR-Vertrag. Vertragsrecht und vertragliche Gestaltung der Mediation und anderer alternativer Konfliktlösungsverfahren* (Recht und Wirtschaft, 2011).

Haft, Fritjof, von Schlieffen, Katharina, *Handbuch Mediation. Verhandlungstechnik, Strategien, Einsatzgebiete*, 2nd edn (CH Beck, 2010).

Harbst, Ragnar, 'Adjudication on the Rise in Germany?' (2010) 26 *Construction Law Journal* 698.

Hartley, Trevor, 'Antisuit Injunctions in Support of Arbitration: West Tankers Still Afloat' (2015) 64 *International Comparative Law Quarterly* 965.

Hartmann, Peter, *Zivilprozessordnung*, 61st edn (CH Beck, 2003).

Héron, Jaques, *Droit judiciaire privé* (Montchrestien, 1991).

Hibberd, Peter, Newman, Paul, *ADR and Adjudication in Construction Disputes* (Blackwell Science, 1999).

Honsell, Heinrich, Vogt, Nedim, Schnyder, Anton, Berti, Stephen (eds), *Basler Kommentar Internationales Privatrecht*, 3rd edn (Helbing Lichtenhahn Verlag, 2013).

Hopt, Klaus, Steffek, Felix (eds), *Mediation. Principles and Regulation in Comparative Perspective* (OUP, 2013).

—— *Mediation: Rechtstatsachen, Rechtsvergleich, Regelungen* (Mohr Siebeck, 2008).

Horn, Norbert, 'Arbitration in International Financial Transactions' (2000) 16 *Arbitration International* 281.

Horvath, Günther, 'Duty of the Tribunal to Render an Enforceable Award' (2001) 18 *Journal of International Arbitration* 135.

Hrustanpasic, Dado, 'Time-Bars and the Prevention Principle: Using Fair Extensions of Time and Common-sense Causation' (2012) 28 *Construction Law Journal* 379.

Hughes, Will, Murdoch, John (eds), *Construction Contracts. Law and Management*, 4th edn (Taylor & Francis Group, 2008).

Hunter, Armin, 'Die Mediationsvereinbarung—Regelungsgegenstände und vertragrechtliche Qualifizierung' (2003) 5 *SchiedsVZ* 226.

—— *Das Internationale privat- und Verfahrensrecht der Wirtschaftsmediation* (Mohr Siebeck, 2005).

Ibara, Rochfelaire, *L'aménagement de la force majeure dans le contrat: essai de théorie générale sur les clauses de force majeure dans les contrats internes et internationaux de longue durée* (Thèse Droit. Université de Poitiers, 2012).

Jacobs, Rachel, 'Should Mediation Trigger Arbitration in Multi-Step Alternative Dispute Resolution Clauses?' (2004) 14 *American Review of International Arbitration* 161.

Jaeger, Axel-Volkmar, Hök, Götz-Sebastian, *FIDIC—A Guide for Practitioners* (Springer, 2009).

Jarrosson, Charles, 'Note—Cour de cassation (Ch. commerciale) 28 novembre 1995—*Peyrin et autres v. société Polyclinique des Fleurs*' (1996) 4 *Revue de l'Arbitrage* 614.

—— 'Les clauses de renégociation, de conciliation et de mediation' in *Les principales clauses de contrats conclus entre professionnels* (Presses Universitaires d'Aix-Marseille, 1990).

—— 'La sanction du non-respect d'une clause instituant un préliminaire obligatoire de conciliation ou de mediation: Note—Cour de cassation (2e Ch. civ.) 6 juillet 2000; Cour de cassation (1re Ch. civ.) 23 janvier et 6 février 2001' (2001) 4 *Revue de l'Arbitrage* 752.

—— 'Les modes alternatifs de règlement des conflits' (1997) 49 *Revue Internationale de droit comparé* 325.

—— 'Note—Cour de cassation (Chambre Mixte), 14 février 2003 et Cour d'appel de Paris (14e Ch. A.), 23 mai 2001' (2002) 2 *Revue de l'Arbitrage* 406.

—— 'Note—Cour d'appel de Paris (1re Chambre civile) 29 avril 2003' (2003) 4 *Revue de l'Arbitrage* 1299.

—— 'Observations on Poiré v Tripier' (2003) 19 *Arbitration International* 363.

—— *La notion d'arbitrage* (Bibliothequè de Droit Privé, Thome CXCVIII, 1987).

Jaynes, Gordon, 'Dispute Review Boards—Yes!' (1993) 10 *International Construction Law Review* 455.

Jenkins, Jane, *Construction Law Arbitration*, 2nd edn (Kluwer Law International, 2014).

Jiménez Figueres, Dyalá, 'Multi-Tiered Dispute Resolution Clauses in ICC Arbitration: Introduction and Commentary' (2003) 14 *ICC International Court of Arbitration Bulletin* 71.

—— 'Amicable Means to Resolve Disputes: How the ICC ADR Rules Work' (2004) 21 *Journal of International Arbitration* 91.

—— 'Multi-Tiered Dispute Resolution Clauses in ICC Arbitration' (2003) 14 *ICC International Court of Arbitration Bulletin* 82.

Jolles, Alexander, 'Consequences of Multi-Tier Arbitration Clauses: Issues of Enforcement' (2006) 72 *Arbitration* 329.

Jolowicz, JA, 'The Woolf Report and the Adversary System' (1996) 15 *Civil Justice Quarterly* 198.

Joly, André, *Procédure civile et voies d'exécution* (Sirey, 1969).

Jones, Douglas, 'Can Prevention be Cured by Time Bars?' (2009) 26 *International Construction Law Review* 57.

—— 'Expert Determination and Arbitration' (2001) 67 *Arbitration* 17.

—— 'Various Non-Binding (ADR) Processes' in Albert Jan van den Berg (ed), *New Horizons in International Commercial Arbitration and Beyond. ICCA Congress Series 2004 Bejing12* (Kluwer International, 2005).

Joseph, David, *Jurisdiction and Arbitration Agreements and their Enforcement*, 3rd edn (Sweet & Maxwell, 2015).

Karrer, Pierre, Kälin-Nauer, Claudia, 'Is there a *Favor Iurisdictionis Arbitri*?' (1996) 13 *Journal of International Arbitration* 31.

Kirchhoff, Lars, *Constructive Interventions. Paradigms, Process and Practice of International Mediation* (Wolters Kluwer, 2008).

Knutson, Robert, '*Recent Treatment of Construction Awards by the ICC International Court of Arbitration*' (A paper given to a meeting of a Society of Construction Law in London on 3 February 2004).

Kröll, Stefan, Lew, Julian, Mistelis, Loukas, *Comparative International Commercial Arbitration* (Kluwer Law International, 2003).

Krüger, Wolfgang (ed), *Münchener Kommentar zum Bürgerliches Gesetzbuch*, 7th edn (CH Beck, 2016).

Lachmann, Jens-Peter, *Handbuch für die Schiedsgerichtspraxis*, 3rd edn (Schmidt, 2008).

Lagarde, Xavier, 'Droit processuel et modes alternatifs de règlement des litiges' (2001) 3 *Revue de l'Arbitrage* 423.

—— 'L'efficacité des clauses de conciliation ou de mediation' (2000) 3 *Revue de l'arbitrage* 377.

Laird, Ian, 'A Distinction without a Difference? An Examination of the Concepts of Admissibility and Jurisdiction in Salini v. Jordan and Methanex v. USA' in Todd Weiler (ed), *International Investment Law and Arbitration: Leading Cases from the ICSID, NAFTA, Bilateral Treaties and Customary International Law* (Cameron May, 2005).

Latham, Michael, *Constructing the Team: Final Report of the Government/Industry Review of Procurement and Contractual Arrangements in the UK Construction Industry* (HMSO, 1994).

Leandro, Antonio, 'Towards a New Interface Between Brussels I and Arbitration?' (2015) 6 *Journal of International Dispute Settlement* 188.

Lee, Joel, 'ADR Clauses and Enforcement' (2003) *Lloyd's Maritime & Commercial Law Quarterly* 164.

Leimert, Corina, Sessler, Anke, 'The Role of Expert Determination in Mergers and Acquisitions under German Law' (2004) 20 *Arbitration International* 151.

Leonard, Sarah, Dharmananda, Kanaga, 'Peace Talks before War: the Enforcement of Clauses for Dispute Resolution before Arbitration' (2006) 23 *Journal of International Arbitration* 301.

Lindeperg, Michèle, *Médiation et conciliation de proximité* (Rapport presenté au nom de la section du cadre de vie, Conseil économique et social, 2001).

Lionnet, Klaus, *Handbuch der internationalen und nationalen Schiedsgerichtsbarkeit*, 3rd edn (Boorberg, 2005).

Lyons, James, 'Arbitration: The Slower, More Expensive Alternative?' (1985) Jan–Feb *American Lawyer* 107.

Mackie, Karl, 'The Future of ADR Clauses after Cable & Wireless v. IBM' (2003) 19 *Arbitration International* 345.

McGaw, Mark, 'Adjudicators, Experts and Keeping out of Court' (1992) 8 *Construction Law Journal* 332.

McGee, Andrew, *Limitation Periods*, 7th edn (Sweet & Maxwell, 2014).

Melnyk, Tanya, 'The Enforceability of Multi-Tiered Dispute Resolution Clauses: the English Law Position' (2002) 4 *International Arbitration Law Review* 113.

Merkin, Robert, Flannery, Louis, *Arbitration Law* (LLP, 2004).

Messerschmidt, Burkhard, Voit, Wolfgang (eds), *Privates Baurecht*, 2nd edn (CH Beck, 2012).

Moore, Christopher, *The Mediation Process: Practical Strategies for Resolving Conflict*, 3rd edn (Jossey-Bass, 2003).

Münchener Kommentar zur Zivilprozessordnung, (4th edn Beck, 2013).

Musielak, Hans-Joachim, Voit, Wolfgang (eds), *Zivilprozessordnung mit Gerichtsverfassungsgesetz*, 13th edn (Vahlen, 2016).

Olawatura, Okanunle, 'Managing Multi-Layered Dispute Resolution under the Arbitration Act 1966—Smashing Bricks of Intention' (2001) 4 *International Arbitration Law Review* 70.

Palandt, Otto, *Bürgerliches Gesetzbuch*, 75th edn (CH Beck, 2016).

Park, William, *Arbitration of International Business*, 2nd edn (OUP, 2012).

—— 'The Nature of Arbitral Authority: A Comment on Lesotho Highlands' (2005) 21 *Arbitration International* 483.

—— 'National Law and Commercial Justice: Safeguarding Procedural Integrity in International Arbitration' (1989) 63 *Tulane Law Review* 647.

—— 'Determining Arbitral Jurisdiction: Allocation of Tasks between Courts and Arbitrators' (1997) 8 *The American Review of International Arbitration* 133.

—— *Arbitration of International Business Disputes. Studies in Law and Practice*, 1st edn (OUP, 2006).

Paulsson, Jan, 'Enforcing Arbitral Awards Notwithstanding a Local Standard Annulment' (1998) 9 *ICC Bulletin* 14.

——'Jurisdiction and Admissibility' in Gerald Aksen (ed), *Global Reflections on International Law, Commerce and Dispute Resolution, Liber Amicorum in honour of Robert Briner* (ICC Publishing, 2005).

Philips, Gerald, 'Is creeping legalism infecting arbitration?' (2003) 58 *Dispute Resolution Journal* 37.

Poudret, Jean-François, Besson, Sébastien, *Comparative Law of International Arbitration*, 2nd edn (Sweet & Maxwell, 2007).

Pryles, Michael, 'Multi-Tiered Dispute Resolution Clauses' (2001) 18 *Journal of International Arbitration* 159.

—— 'Arbitrating Disputes in the Resource Industries' (2005) 21 *Arbitration International* 405.

Redfern, Alan, 'Experts and Arbitrators—an International Perspective' (2001) 4 *International Arbitration Law Review* 105.

Redfern, Alan, Hunter, Martin, Blacaby, Nigel, Constantine Partasides, *Redfern and Hunter on International Arbitration*, 6th edn (OUP, 2015).

Répertoire de procédure civile et commerciale (Dalloz, 1955).

Risse, Jörg, *Wirtschaftsmediation* (CH Beck, 2003).

Roquette, Andreas, Otto, Andreas, *Vertragsbuch Privates Baurecht*, 2nd edn (CH Beck, 2011).

Rosenberg, Leo, Schwab, Karl Heinz, Gottwald, Peter, *Zivilprozeßrecht*, 17th edn (CH Beck, 2010).

Rubino-Sammartano, Mauro, *International Arbitration Law and Practice*, 2nd edn (Kluwer Law International, 2001).

—— 'FIDIC's clause 20.1—a civil law view' (2009) 4 *Construction Law International* 14.

Sanders, Pieter, 'L'Arbitrage dans les Transactions Commerciales à Long Terme' (1975) 1 *Revue de l'Arbitrage* 83.

Sassier, Monique, *Arguments et propositions pour un statut de la Médiation Familiale en France: Rapport remis à Madame la Ministre déléguée à la famille, à l'enfance et aux personnes handicapées* (Ministère délégué à la famille, à l'enfance et aux personnes handicapées, 2001).

Scherer, Matthias, 'Case Law—Introduction to the Case Law Section' (2011) 29 *ASA Bulletin* 616.

Scherer, Matthias, Dawidowicz, Martin, *Arbitration Guide IBA Arbitration. Switzerland* (Lalive, 2012).

Schöll, Michael, 'Reflexions sur l'expertise-arbitrage en droite Suisse' (2006) 24 *ASA Bulletin* 621.

—— *Das Schiedsgutachten im Schweizer Recht—Grundriss und Praxisfragen* (Heymanns, 2007).

Schütz, Jürg, *Mediation und Schiedsgerichtsbarkeit in der Schweizerischen Zivilprozessordnung: eine Untersuchung zur Streitbehandlungslehre: Verfahrensvergleich und -auswahl anhand gesetzlich geregelter Alternativen zum staatlichen Zivilprozess—Mediation, Schiedsgerichtsbarkeit und deren Hybridisierung* (Stämpfli, 2009).

Schwab, Karl Heinz, Walter, Gerhard, *Schiedsgerichtsbarkeit*, 7th edn (CH Beck, 2005).

Seppälä, Christopher, 'The new FIDIC provision for a Dispute Adjudication Board' (1997) 8 *International Business Law Journal* 967.

——'The new FIDIC provision for a Dispute Adjudication Board' (1997) 14(4) *International Construction Law Review* 443.

——'International Construction Contract Disputes: Commentary on ICC Awards Dealing with the FIDIC International Conditions of Contract' (1998) 9 *ICC Bulletin* 34.

Seriki, Hakeem, *Injunctive Relief and International Arbitration* (Informa Law, 2015).

Sessler, Anke, Leimert, Corina, 'The Role of Expert Determination in Mergers and Acquisitions under German Law' (2004) 20 *Arbitration International* 151.

Solus, Henry, Perrot, Roger, *Droit judiciaire privé* (Sirey, 1969).

Spüchler, Karl, Tenchio, Luca, Infanger, Dominik (eds), *Basler Kommentar. Schweizerische Zivilprozessordnung*, 2nd edn (Helbing Lichtenhahn Verlag, 2013).

Stein/Jonas Kommentar zur Zivilprozessordnung, 23rd edn (Mohr Siebeck, 2014).

J. von Staudingers Kommentar zum Bürgerlichen Gesetzbuch mit Einführungsgesetz und Nebengesetzen (Sellier–de Gruyter, 2015).

Sternlight, Jean, 'Is Binding Arbitration a Form of ADR?: An Argument That the Term "ADR" Has Begun to Outlive its Usefulness' (2000) 1 *Journal of Dispute Resolution* 97.

Stipanowich, Thomas, 'ADR and the "Vanishing Trial": The Growth and Impact of "Alternative Dispute Resolution"' (2004) 1 *Journal of Empirical Legal Studies* 843.

—— 'Rethinking American Arbitration' (1988) 63 *Indiana Law Journal* 425.

Stubbe, Christian, 'DIS-Schiedsgutachtensordnung (DIS-SchGO) und DIS-Gutachtensordnung (DIS-GO)' (2010) 3 *SchiedsVZ* 130.

—— 'Kombination des Schiedsgutachtensverfahren mit anderen Verfahrenstypen' in Karl-Heinz Böckstiegel, Klaus Peter Berger, Jens Bredow (eds), *Schiedsgutachten versus Schiedsgerichtsbarkeit* (Heymans, 2007).

—— 'Schiedsgutachten als modernes ADR-Instrument' (2006) 3 *SchiedsVZ* 150.

Sundaram, Jae, 'Does the Judgment of the CJEU in *Gazprom* Bring about Clarity on the Grant of Anti-Suit Injunctions under the Brussels I Regulation?' (2015) 27 *Denning Law Journal* 303.

Tochtermann, Peter, 'Mediationsklauseln Teil I. Mediationklauseln in Allgemainen Geschäftsbedingungen' [2008] 2 *Zeitschrift für Konfliktmanagement* 57.

Tochtermann, Peter, *Die Unabhängigkeit und Unparteilichkeit des Mediators* (Mohr Siebeck, 2008).

Train, François-Xavier, 'Note—Cour d'appel de Paris (1re Ch. C), 4 mars 2004' (2005) 1 *Revue de l'Arbitrage* 151.

Tricot, Jean-Philippe, 'Chronique de droit des modes amiables de règlement des conflits' (2011) 1 *Revue de l'arbitrage* 207.

Turner, Peter, Mohtashami, Reza, *A Guide to the LCIA Arbitration Rules* (OUP, 2009).

Tweedale, Andrew, Tweedale, Karen, *Arbitration of Commercial Disputes* (OUP, 2007).

van den Berg, Albert Jan (ed), *New Horizons in International Commercial Arbitration and Beyond. ICCA Congress Series 2004 Bejing12* (Kluwer Law International, 2005).

van Der Haegen, Marc, 'Les Procédures de Conciliation et de Médiation Organisées par les principaux instituts d'arbitrage et de médiation en Europe' (1996) 2 *Revue de Droit des Affaires Internationales* 255.

van Ginkel, Eric, 'The UNCITRAL Model Law on International Commercial Conciliation. A Critical Appraisal' (2004) 21 *Journal of International Arbitration* 1.

Varady, Tibor, 'The Courtesy Trap Arbitration "if no amicable settlement can be reached"' (1997) 14(4) *Journal of International Arbitration* 5.

Virassamy, Georges, 'Les collèges et les comissions dans le règlement des litiges contractuels' in *Etudes offertes à Jacques Ghestin: Le contrat au début du XXIe siècle* (LGDJ, 2001).

Voser, Nathalie, 'Sanktion bei Nichterfüllung einer Schlichtungsklausel. Note—Kassationsgericht Zürich, 15 März 1999' (2002) 20 *ASA Bulletin* 376.

Wade, Shai, Clifford, Philip, Clanchy, James, *A commentary on the LCIA Arbitration Rules 2014* (Sweet & Maxwell, 2015).

Wagner, Gerhard, 'Alternative Streitbeilegung und Verjährung' (2001) 3 *Neue Juristische Wochenschrift* 182.

—— *Prozessverträge—Privatautonomie im Verfahrensrecht* (Mohr Siebeck, 1998).

Waibel, Michael, *Investment Arbitration: Jurisdiction and Admissibility* (University of Cambridge Faculty of Law Research Paper No 9/2014).

Walter, Gerhard, 'Dogmatik der unterschiedlichen Verfahren zur Streitbeilegung' (1990) 103 *Zeitschrift für Zivilprozessrecht (ZZP)* 141.

Walther, Fridolin, 'E-confidence in e-commerce durch Alternative Dispute Resolution' (2001) 7 *Aktuelle Juristische Praxis* 755.

Whincup, Michael, *Contract Law and Practice: The English System, with Scottish, Commonwealth, and Continental Comparisons*, 5th edn (Kluwer Law International, 2006).

Wortmann, Beda, 'Choice of Law by Arbitrators: the Applicable Conflict of Law System' (1998) 14 *Arbitration International* 97.

Yu, Hong-Lin, Molife, Peter, 'The impact of national law elements on international commercial arbitration' (2001) 4(1) *International Arbitration Law Review* 17.

Zander, Michael, 'The Government's Plans on Civil Justice' (1998) 61 *Modern Law Review* 383.

—— 'The Woolf Report: Forwards or Backwards for the New Lord Chancellor?' (1997) 16 *Civil Justice Quarterly* 208.

Zeiler, Gerold, 'Jurisdiction, Competence and Admissibility of Claims in ICSID Arbitration Proceedings' in Christina Binder, Ursula Kriebaum, August Reinisch, Stephan Wittich (eds), *International Investment Law for the 21st Century: Essays in Honour of Christoph Schreuer* (OUP, 2009).

Zuckerman, Adrian, Cranston, Ross (eds), *The Reform of Civil Procedure: Essays on 'Access to Justice'* (OUP, 1995).

—— 'The Woolf Report on Access to Justice' (1997) 2 *Zeitschrift für Zivilprozess International* 31.

INDEX

www.ingramcontent.com/pod-product-compliance
Lightning Source LLC
LaVergne TN
LVHW011851200926
848484LV00002B/436
9781509910410